D0502663

THE PEACE BROKERS

THE PEACE BROKERS

Mediators in the Arab-Israeli Conflict, 1948-1979

SAADIA TOUVAL

PRINCETON UNIVERSITY PRESS
PRINCETON, NEW JERSEY

Published by Princeton University Press, 41 William Street, Princeton, New Jersey
In the United Kingdom: Princeton University Press, Guildford, Surrey

Library of Congress Cataloging in Publication Data will be found on the last printed page of this book

Publication of this book has been aided by a grant from the Paul Mellon Fund of Princeton University Press

This book has been composed in Linotron Trump

Clothbound editions of Princeton University Press books are printed on acid-free paper, and binding materials are chosen for strength and durability

Printed in the United States of America by Princeton University Press, Princeton, New Jersey

All that we do is done with an eye
to something else.

ARISTOTLE, *Nicomachean Ethics*

Contents

Maps

Preface

It is not for lack of attempts to resolve it that the Arab-Israeli conflict has gone on for so long. For over sixty years, repeated efforts have been made to reconcile the incompatible claims to Palestine made by Arab and Jewish national movements, but to no avail. Since the establishment of the State of Israel in a part of Palestine in 1948, these attempts have focused on concluding a peace between Israel and the Arab states; and in the face of the obstacles to the conclusion of peace, efforts have occasionally been directed at more limited measures of reducing the conflict.

Almost all these attempts involved intermediaries. This book is about those among the intermediaries whose efforts to advance peace, whether successful or not, had a particularly important impact on the course of Arab-Israeli relations. The beginning of the peacemaking efforts coincided with the establishment of Israel. The day before Israel proclaimed its independence, the United Nations resolved to appoint a mediator. Count Folke Bernadotte of Sweden, who assumed the post, failed to resolve the conflict but did help to bring about a truce in the fighting. After Bernadotte was assassinated, Ralph Bunche, a UN official of American nationality, was appointed acting UN mediator. He is credited with bringing about the armistice agreements between Israel and the neighboring states in 1949. The UN Palestine Conciliation Commission, which engaged in intensive negotiations between 1949 and 1951, failed to accomplish anything. President Eisenhower's secret emissary Robert Anderson's attempt at mediation between Egypt and Israel, in 1955-1956, was also ineffective. After the 1967 war, peacemaking activity was intensified. UN Special Representative Gunnar Jarring failed in his efforts, and so did the African heads of state in 1971. U.S. Secretary of State William Rogers succeeded in mediating an agreement for an Egyptian-Israeli cease-fire and for the resumption of the Jarring negotiations in 1970, but his attempt to obtain an Egyptian-Israeli disengagement along the Suez Canal in 1971 was in vain. After the 1973 war, Henry Kissinger helped to bring about the Egyptian-Israeli and Syrian-Israeli disengagement agreements in 1974. He failed in his attempt to conclude the second Egyptian-Israeli disengagement in March 1975, but succeeded when he renewed his attempt a few months later. Crowning these endeavors was the American mediation under President Jimmy Carter's direction, which led to the Camp David accords in September 1978 and to the signing of the Egyptian-Israeli peace treaty on March 26, 1979.

In addition to these, there were numerous other attempts by governments, organizations, and private individuals, who in large ways and small sought to promote peace, reduce border strife, or resolve specific issues such as problems relating to water development projects, denial of navigation rights, exchange and treatment of prisoners, and property matters. A partial list of such intermediaries would include UN Secretary General Dag Hammarskjöld, the UN Truce Supervision Organization, the International Committee of the Red Cross, U.S. Special Ambassador Eric Johnston, President Tito of Yugoslavia, Dom Mintoff of Malta, King Hassan of Morocco, President Ceaucescu of Rumania, the American Quaker representative Elmore Jackson, British M.P. Maurice Orbach, and the French-Jewish painter and intellectual Marek Halter. It seems almost impossible to recount the endeavors of all the intermediaries, much less to examine them in detail. Here I shall cover only the major attempts by mediators to promote a settlement or to significantly reduce the intensity and scope of the conflict.

The book examines the work of the mediators from the perspective of international politics—the struggle for power between states—and from a peacemaking perspective—the effectiveness of the mediators' contributions to the resolution or reduction of the conflict. Both perspectives give rise to numerous questions. What interests prompted the mediators to undertake the role? What did they expect to gain from their intervention, besides the obvious satisfaction of helping the Arabs and Israelis to resolve their conflict peacefully? What effects did their interventions have for Arab-Israeli power relations? For regional and global power struggles? Should the conclusion of agreements and the reduction of tensions really be credited to the mediators, or would the agreements have been concluded irrespective of the mediators? How can one explain the success of some and the failure of others? What qualities and techniques on the part of mediators were conducive to success?

These are difficult questions to answer. Although conclusive and definitive judgments cannot be made, I have nevertheless attempted to provide some reasoned evaluations. To evaluate the work of the early mediators I have examined published diplomatic documents. For the study of later mediators I have relied mainly on secondary sources, and have used newspapers and autobiographies as well. I have also benefited from conversations with a number of Israeli participants in the negotiations. Unable to read Arabic, I have used only Western and Israeli sources. I have tried, however, to keep my biases within reasonable bounds.

In the preparation of this study I received invaluable help in different forms from many sources to whom I am indebted. My colleague, Asher Arian, until recently Dean of the Faculty of Social Sciences at Tel Aviv University, provided constant encouragement. Ziva Lahat, Director of the Social Sciences Library at Tel Aviv University, the late Ruth Kasparios, and the library staff were always ready to search for needed and occasionally obscure publications. Loyal and reliable help was furnished by my research assistants Sarah Carmi and Nohi Dankner, as well as by Yosef Lowenberg, Naftali Nesher, Zephania Shatsky, and Tal Zabari. Helpful comments and criticism were contributed by Nadav Safran who read several chapters and by I. William Zartman who read the entire manuscript, as well as by John C. Campbell and Arthur Lall who reviewed the manuscript on behalf of the publisher. Sanford G. Thatcher, Assistant Director of Princeton University Press lent encouragement, and helped expedite the publication of the book. The manuscript gained considerably from the editorial endeavors of Anita Safran and Connie Wilsack, in Tel Aviv, and Marilyn Campbell at Princeton University Press. Gaul Machlis drew the maps. Rose Langbart, Sylvia Weinberg, and Gila Ban typed and retyped with much care several drafts of the manuscript. The preparation of the study has been assisted over the years by financial grants from the Ford Foundation, through the Israel Foundation Trustees, from the Tel Aviv University Research Project on Peace, and from the Research Committee of the Faculty of Social Sciences. The John Foster Dulles Committee of the Princeton University Library and Professor John W. F. Dulles kindly granted permission to quote from the personal papers of John Foster Dulles deposited at the Princeton University Library. The editors of the *Jerusalem Journal of International Relations* allowed me to reproduce parts of my article "Biased Intermediaries" that appeared in the first issue of the *Journal.* I am grateful to them all.

March 1982

THE PEACE BROKERS

ONE

The Compleat Mediator

In addition to examining the work of the mediators, this book also seeks to evaluate some of the assertions that the theoretical literature on mediation makes. Case studies, whether discussing labor disputes or international peacemaking, usually seek to explain the success or failure of intermediaries' efforts and draw lessons from their experiences. Because of its preoccupation with the effectiveness of third-party intervention, the theoretical literature carries a distinct prescriptive strain. This chapter reviews these prescriptions, seeks to clarify the premises upon which they are based and to examine their logical consistency and mutual compatibility. I challenge the commonly held assumption that mediators, to be effective, must be impartial. I shall explain why they need not be impartial, and why mediators who are perceived as biased can perform their role effectively.

In subsequent chapters I shall have an opportunity to comment on the validity of some of the prominent and recurrent themes of writings about intermediaries in international conflicts, and to illustrate my suggested revisions on the question of impartiality, and see whether they were relevant to the outcomes of mediators' efforts.

Definitions and Functions

Before discussing the prescriptions for success, some definitions and clarifications of the roles and functions of mediators might be helpful.

An intermediary is a third party who intervenes diplomatically in an international conflict with the stated purpose of contributing toward its abatement or resolution, and whose intervention is accepted by the parties to the conflict. Intermediaries differ from other third parties in that they are restricted to diplomatic involvement and may not employ violence; their intervention is acceptable to both sides in the conflict.

Intermediaries are differentiated according to the roles they perform. A conventional distinction is among the performance of good offices, conciliation, and mediation, corresponding to the degree of involvement in the negotiations. (Arbitration, being a judicial procedure, is outside the scope of this discussion.) Intermediaries who confine their activities mainly to the technical aspects of helping the adversaries to communicate with each other, such as providing a meeting place or transmitting messages, are described as performing good offices. If they also try to modify the parties' images of each other and to influence them to make concessions by clarifying to each his opponent's views and the bargaining situation that both face, they are regarded as engaged in conciliation. Intermediaries who also make suggestions pertaining to the substance of the conflict, and seek to influence the parties to make concessions by exerting pressures and offering incentives, are called mediators. These distinctions are not universally applied in the literature. Moreover, the formal titles given to diplomatic initiatives may be misleading. For example, notwithstanding their formal titles, both the United Nations Palestine Conciliation Commission and Gunnar Jarring, entitled the UN Secretary-General's Special Representative, engaged in mediation. Nevertheless, the distinction between the three roles is useful for analytical purposes.

A successful mediator is one who is believed to have contributed to the abatement or resolution of a conflict, by helping to bring about an agreement between the adversaries to reduce or eliminate hostile behavior in their mutual relations. Successful mediation may also (but need not necessarily) resolve issues that were in dispute, change the images or attitudes of the adversary, or eliminate the basic sources of the conflict.

Mediation is the most versatile of intermediaries' roles, and may subsume the roles of good offices and conciliation. One of its major functions is to help the parties in conflict to communicate with each other. It is commonly assumed that by facilitating communications, intermediaries contribute to the reduction or resolution of conflict, because in some conflicts, at least, the differences stem from a misunderstanding of the other's true position, or even from mere lack of information, which hampers effective bargaining and negotiations. To be sure, in the contemporary world, where wide publicity is given to governmental positions and to internal political debates, even adversaries who do not communicate directly do not suffer from a dearth of information about each other. Yet information received through the mass media is often incomplete and inaccurate. Therefore, even in an environment permeated by the mass media, a mediator may perform an important communications function when the information he transmits is believed to be more reliable and more accurate than that of the media.

Furthermore, in view of the emotions generated by the conflict, messages passed directly between the parties or received through the mass media may be distorted or misperceived. Some authors believe that information passing through a mediator is less likely to be distorted because he can minimize the emotional disturbances that affect reception. Undistorted information is of course crucial for effective bargaining and negotiations. It enables each side to arrive more rapidly at correct evaluations of the adversary's position, his degree of commitment, his interests and his motives; and to identify the common interests that can serve as a basis for agreement.[1]

Mediators also seek to influence the parties to change their positions so as to make agreement between them possible. By employing reasoning and persuasion the mediator, like the conciliator, may attempt to influence the parties to change their perceptions of each other and of the environment, and to clarify the bargaining situation that they face. Mediators may actively help the parties withdraw from commitments by suggesting justifications and rationalizations, and by comparing the irrelevance or dysfunction of their commitments to the advantages of discarding them.[2]

The mediator's role differs from that of the conciliator by the means he has at his disposal in influencing the parties to alter their stand. Whereas the conciliator must confine himself to argumentation and reasoning, the mediator also bargains with the parties. His intervention transforms the situation from a bilateral bargaining relationship between two adversaries to a trilateral one. In seeking to influence the parties to make concessions, the mediator may apply pressures and offer incentives. He may restructure the situation in order to raise the costs of an uncompromising stand, and promise rewards in return for flexibility. His behavior is constrained by his desire to safeguard his role as intermediary; nevertheless, within certain limits, he can use his resources to bargain with the parties.

In order to help the parties to reach agreement the mediator may manipulate the issues under discussion. He may introduce new ideas or suggest the agenda and order of business. He may define the subject of the negotiations and separate the intractable issues from those on which agreement seems possible. He may suggest how to "fractionate" issues, and how to formulate balanced packages of mutually acceptable concessions and advantages. Furthermore, mediators usually make substantive proposals and recommend compromise formulas.

The mediator may also serve to protect the parties from risks they believe they are incurring by offering concessions. It has been pointed out that concessions are often inhibited by the "bargainers' dilemma." Each side worries that the adversary will interpret a desire for a settlement, or hints of possible concessions, as indications of weakness. Such an interpretation may lead the adversary to escalate his expectations and increase his pressure. A bargainer thus faces the dilemma of how to yield without appearing weak. In such situations mediators may help to justify and rationalize concessions; their intercession may also serve as a face-saving device. Experiments conducted by social-psychologists suggest that actors may be less inhibited in offering concessions through a mediator than directly to an adversary, perhaps believing that concessions offered through a mediator are less likely to be interpreted as a sign of weakness. Mediators may also compensate parties for the disadvantages that they incur because of the concessions they make. Finally, mediators can further protect the parties from some of the risks that their concessions entail by monitoring compliance with the agreements concluded between the adversaries, and by guaranteeing their observance.[3]

The Requisites for Success

What the literature has to say about the requisites for success can be divided into two main headings: 1) the circumstances of the mediator's intervention; 2) his attributes and qualities. (There is also much discussion in the literature of the tactics available to mediators, but this will not concern us here.) A systematic analysis will help clarify the premises upon which these requisites are predicated, and describe the relationship between them and the functions for which they are believed necessary.[4]

The Circumstances of Intervention

Three basic aspects of the circumstances have a bearing upon a mediator's success: the issue in conflict, the environment in which the mediator's intervention takes place, and its timing.

The issue. There is general agreement that the issue in conflict has an important bearing on the success of a mediator's efforts. There also seems to be wide consensus that the more importance the parties attach to an issue, the less likely it is that mediation will succeed. Presumably, if the conflict concerns interests that are believed to affect the state's ability to survive or its self-image and identity, intermediaries will be unlikely to succeed. Territorial issues, which are often seen as related to the survival or identity of the antagonists, would thus be especially difficult to settle.[5] This seems highly relevant to the failure of the many attempts to settle the Arab-Israeli conflict.

Issues are, of course, not static. They change with internal changes in the parties, in the environment, and with fluctuations in the course of the conflict. To some extent, the mediator's success may depend upon his skill in manipulating issues, fractionating them, or redefining them so as to make them appear less important to the parties concerned.[6]

The environment. Of particular relevance are the attitudes of other actors, who may assist the mediator by lending him diplomatic or other support, or hinder his efforts by encouraging uncompromising behavior by one or both sides to the conflict. They may, of course, behave neutrally. Mediation that takes place in the "gray areas" of the world, or among parties that are being courted by competing powers, is likely to encounter interference, and the chances for its success are smaller. Mediators are seldom passive in the face of the environment. They will usually seek to mobilize the support of other actors. Or they may attempt to insulate the conflict from interference by them.[7]

Timing. There seems to be wide agreement that the mediator's success depends to a significant extent on whether his intervention takes place at a propitious moment. But what is the propitious moment and how can it be recognized before it slips away? To say that the propitious moment is when flexibility is on the increase only raises further questions. In what situation is flexibility on the increase? Is it enough that one party be inclined toward greater flexibility, or is it necessary that both sides show flexibility? Several authors have suggested that flexibility is related to phases in the "life cycle" of conflicts, and that it is likely to be greater during the period of incipiency, when commitments are likely to be small and relatively easier to abandon than at later stages.[8] However, opinions as to why flexibility may recur at a later stage differ. Inis Claude raised the possibility that some disputes may "wither into insignificance" with the passage of time. What he seems to have in mind is that national priorities may change. Issues on which the parties were obdurate may lose their significance.[9] Others ascribe the reappearance of flexibility to the outcome of the test of strength that has taken place between the adversaries. However, there is no agreement on the kind of outcome most conducive to a settlement. According to one view, it is a deadlock or a stalemate. This is described as a situation of power parity, and of "high and still rising price of nonsettlement for all parties."[10] Frank Edmead disagrees with this view; by implication, so do F. S. Northedge and M. D. Donelan. They claim that the timing is propitious when *one* of the parties feels exhausted or suffers a defeat, requiring it to revise its expectations.[11] Yet, would not one side's flexibility encourage its adversary to stand firm, or even escalate its demands, thus making the mediator's task more difficult?

Edmead offers an additional reason why mediation early in the conflict, or after exhaustion has set in, stands a greater chance of success than mediation during an escalatory phase. He calls attention to the compensatory benefits that the mediator can offer in return for concessions, suggesting that these will cost the mediator relatively little early in the conflict, before the parties have invested much of their resources in support of their stands, or after one party has been exhausted, since even a small accretion of benefits or resources may then appear important to it.[12]

A mediator may passively bide his time, and then intervene at the appropriate moment. Alternatively, he may seek to influence the evolution of the conflict toward a situation when mediation would be appropriate. George Modelski writes that "a stalemate can always be induced by international action." Edmead suggests that the mediator may attempt to *create* a situation that is appropriate for mediation by discouraging or preventing a party from acquiring fresh resources necessary for the continued pursuit of the conflict, or encourage it to spend the resources available to it on other objectives. He may also act to reduce that party's expectations of success by manipulating other variables in the situation, such as threatening to offer fresh resources to the adversary.[13]

To be sure, the mediator's freedom of action to engage in such activities is constrained by the requirement that his intervention be acceptable to both parties. More will be said on this point. But it is indeed conceivable that, subject to such a constraint, a mediator may still have enough latitude to seek to create a situation in which his mediation will stand a chance of succeeding.

The Mediator's Qualities: Impartiality and Bias

Most students of the subject agree that the mediator's functions can be carried out effectively only if he is regarded as impartial by the parties to the conflict. Indeed several writers come close to claiming that impartiality is an indispensable quality for a mediator: it is a necessary condition for his acceptability by the parties to the conflict and for the effective performance of his functions.

Oran Young has claimed impartiality to be among the "basic qualities" of an intermediary, among the ". . . resources which come very close to being defining characteristics. . . ." Impartiality, according to Young, is only one of several requirements that "constitute a set of optimal conditions. . . . A high score in such areas as impartiality . . . would seem to be at the heart of successful intervention in many situations."[14] Elmore Jackson made a similar claim by stressing "that the parties in conflict [need to] have maximum confidence in the mediatory arrangements and personnel. . . . It would be difficult, if not impossible, for a single mediator who was distrusted by one of the parties, to carry out any useful function."[15] Northedge and Donelan assert that a "condition which needs to exist before mediation is even possible, to say nothing of its being effective, is that mediation and the proposed mediator should be acceptable to both parties." But, "mediation may be objected to if one or the other of the parties believes that any conceivable mediator would tend to be biased against itself and in favour of the other state."[16]

As is evident from these quotes, the term impartiality is usually employed to refer to the subjective perceptions of the parties in conflict. Some variations can be discerned, however. Jackson, rather than speaking of impartiality, specifies that the parties in conflict need to have *confidence* in the mediator. This implies a general positive attitude and disposition of the parties toward the intermediary. Other writers are less demanding, and only require the absence of bias. Young links the definition of impartiality specifically to the parties' perceptions of the intermediary's interests: ". . . the existence of a meaningful role for a third party will depend on the party's being perceived as an impartial participant (in the sense of having nothing to gain from aiding either protagonist and in the sense of being able to control any feelings of favoritism) in the eyes of the principal protagonists."[17]

To be effective the intermediary must carry some influence with the parties to the conflict. Implied in the requirement of impartiality is the assumption that it is this quality that is the principal source of his influence. The parties will trust the communications transmitted through the intermediary if they believe him to be impartial. They will be open to his suggestions only if they do not regard him as favoring the adversary.

The assumption, so widely held, that mediators must be impartial to be effective needs however to be revised. The mediators in the Arab-Israeli conflict were not perceived by the parties as impartial; moreover, there are additional examples in recent history that indicate that impartiality is neither an indispensable condition for the acceptability of mediators, nor for their success. Among the additional examples are the Anglo-American mediation between Italy and Yugoslavia over Trieste (1948-1954), and the Soviet mediation between India and Pakistan (1965-1966). I shall try to show why it is not necessary for mediators to be perceived as impartial.

A reevaluation of the theoretical requirement of impartiality raises some questions: How does the suspicion that the mediator is biased affect his performance as a channel of communications? When are mediators who are believed to favor the adversary acceptable? How can mediators persuade a party in a conflict to offer concessions if the party views the mediator as favoring its adversary, and consequently mistrusts the mediator's suggestions?

Regarding the intermediary's role as a communication channel, it has been asserted that emotions tend to distort communications between opponents in conflicts, and that communications through intermediaries are apt to be less affected by such distortions. Moreover, there is a presumption that impartial intermediaries will be less likely to distort information deliberately. Yet this presumption seems unjustified; even well-meaning and impartial intermediaries may sometimes manipulate the messages they are conveying. Carl Stevens, writing about mediation in labor disputes, has commented on this: "the mediator does not have a direct interest in eliminating bluff from negotiations. His objective is agreement. Elimination of bluff may be a means to this end. However, it might be that conniving in a bluff will be a means to this end."[18]

A mediator *may* strive to transmit all the information as accurately as possible; "alternatively the intermediary may go beyond this to select or even to manipulate the information he transmits to the original players in the interests of achieving an early settlement of the issues at stake."[19]

Even when a mediator strives to transmit the information accurately, there is a possibility, well nigh a likelihood, that the information received will become distorted. Robert Jervis's article, "Hypotheses on Misperception," lists some of the possibilities for distortion of direct communications between two actors.[20] As in the game of "telephone," the chances of misperceptions and distortions are increased once communications are transmitted through a third party. Communication between the adversaries is now a two-step process, and misperceptions can occur at either or both of the two steps. In the first step, the mediator may misperceive the information conveyed to him by the first party and transmit the distorted information to the other party. In the second step, the other party to the conflict may misperceive the information conveyed to him by the mediator.

Now let us remove the assumption that the mediator is regarded as impartial by the antagonists. The image each antagonist has of the mediator, his biases, his motives, and his interests, will influence the interpretation of the communications received from him. If the mediator is believed to favor the adversary, what he communicates will be interpreted in a manner that follows from this assumption. Indeed, in the evaluation of information it is often standard procedure to make allowance for assumed biases of the source of the information and the channel of transmittal. But such information can still be useful and may be taken into account when decisions are made. It follows then that even when one or both sides in a conflict regard the mediator as biased or as favoring the adversary, this need not detract from his ability to serve as a communications channel between the parties.

An answer to the second problem—the acceptability of

biased mediators—can be found in the context in which the acceptance takes place. The decision hinges not on whether the mediator is impartial, but on the evaluation of available alternatives. A third party may be accepted as a mediator not because both original parties to the conflict desire the third's involvement, but because they consider it the most preferable alternative. Northedge and Donelan claimed that "there is no such thing . . . as enforced mediation."[21] If "enforced" is understood in its literal meaning, then forced mediation may indeed not exist. But biased mediators can be the preferred alternative among even less acceptable choices, rather than the expression of free desire.

In order to answer the question of how mediators who are regarded as biased can be persuasive, we must first seek the source of their powers of persuasion. Theoretical explanations of the mediator's persuasive power make it contingent upon his impartiality. The information that he passes along, the logical reasoning he develops, and the suggestions and ideas he introduces, all persuade because their source is impartial. A bargaining version of this view explains the parties' acceptance of the mediator's suggestions as a choice that appears to them less costly than nonacceptance. The cost consists of "external disapproval";[22] the parties to the conflict are believed to be willing to accept a mediator's suggestion because they do not wish to provoke criticism. This explanation of the mediator's persuasive ability implies that he possesses bargaining power. It is important to note that this bargaining power *derives from the mediator's impartiality:* it is the rejection of impartial advice that generates disapproval and lends weight to criticism.

Another explanation of the mediator's influence, which is not contingent upon his being impartial, is based on the assumption that mediators, like all other actors in international politics, are motivated by some interests, whether humanitarian or materialistic or some combination of the two. Young mentions among possible self-interested motives the expectation of benefits to be derived from the performance of a mediator's role (such as enhanced status, influence, salary), and the avoidance of costs—damage to oneself that might ensue if the conflict between the protagonists were to continue.[23] The mediator whose interests are affected by the conflict and by its outcome has already shed a considerable amount of impartiality. But what if in addition he is partial to one of the adversaries?

When a third party intervenes in a two-sided conflict, the situation changes since there is now a three-sided relationship. Usually in triads the outcome of the contest and the division of spoils are affected by the formation of coalitions.[24] If the mediator is assumed to be impartial, then he may not join a coalition, and the only coalition possible is between the two antagonists.

If, however, the mediator is biased, he may participate in a coalition. Both the threat that he will join in a coalition with the adversary and the actual participation in a coalition provide the mediator with bargaining power. In view of the conflict between the two original antagonists, it is the mediator rather than his partner who is open to bids to defect from the coalition. Regardless of whether he only threatens to join a coalition or actually joins one, the mediator's position in a triad provides him with a considerable bargaining advantage. Yet the mediator does not possess full freedom of action. His conduct is constrained by his need to safeguard his continued acceptability to both sides. Moreover, the promotion of his own interests depends to some extent on the behavior of the parties to the conflict. By their behavior, and specifically by the concessions they grant, the parties are able to influence the satisfaction of the mediator's interests. This implied threat of withdrawing consent to the third party's playing a mediator's role is of course one of the most important bargaining assets of the parties vis-à-vis the mediator.

The parties are understandably concerned at what the

mediator might do, and desire to influence *his* behavior. Each will seek to prevent a coalition being formed against him. When the intermediary is perceived as biased, the party that considers itself as favored by the mediator will seek to maintain good relations and to prevent a rapprochement between him and the adversary. The party that views the mediator as favoring its antagonist will seek to reverse the relationship and win the mediator's sympathy, or at least try to sow discord between the mediator and its antagonist.

Viewing mediation as three-cornered bargaining calls also for an explanation of concessions. Should the granting of concessions be regarded as the outcome of bargaining between the adversaries, or as the outcome of bargaining between each of the parties and the mediator? The conventional view is that concessions are exchanged between the adversaries. The mediator helps the parties to arrive at a realistic understanding of the possibilities or to save face,[25] but the concrete bargaining is between the adversaries. Yet, if we view the mediator as an actor who seeks to promote his self-interest and bargains in the process with both parties, then it seems reasonable to see concessions as an outcome of bargaining between each party and the mediator. An exchange of concessions between each party and the mediator would then take place concurrently with the exchange of concessions between the adversaries. To the extent that a party to a conflict who offers a concession expects it to be reciprocated, the party would probably expect counterconcessions from *both* its adversary and the mediator. The mediator may help to save the face of the side granting a concession; yet, he is unlikely to be a mere passive cover-up, but rather a bargainer who trades concessions with the parties.

In conclusion, if we regard mediators as bargainers, they need not be impartial; indeed, being perceived as biased may sometimes be an asset, enhancing the mediator's bargaining power with both sides in a conflict.

Some Additional Qualities

Skill and personal qualities appear in many lists of the desired qualities of mediators. Two kinds of skills are relevant. One is an expertise about the conflict, the context within which it is waged, and the parties involved.[26] The other is experience in conflict resolution in general.[27] Useful personal qualities include tact, intelligence, persuasiveness, humility, and patience.[28]

There is some disagreement about the importance of personal qualities. Carl Stevens, an analyst of labor negotiations, is critical of the emphasis upon personal qualities. In his view, they are necessary but not sufficient.[29] Jean-Pierre Cot, on the other hand, claims that wisdom and experience are essential qualities for international conciliation. According to him "the institutional set-up that enables them to intervene is secondary."[30]

Skills and personal qualities can be useful for both conciliation and bargaining. They seem to be essential when the mediator's principal means of influence is reasoning. But are they equally important when he possesses additional means of influence? Does the possession of resources that enable the mediator, through pressures and incentives, to induce the parties to make concessions compensate for lack of skills or abrasive personalities?

Scholars have also discussed the relative advantages and disadvantages of the mediator being an international organization or a government.[31] Governments suffer from the disadvantage that their motives are always suspect. On the other hand, they often possess resources that endow them with influence. Therefore, they would seldom succeed by using the conciliator's methods, but may be more successful as bargainers. The more powerful the state, the more able it is to influence the parties to alter their positions. International organizations have at times been regarded as possessing both kinds of advantages in some measure, being both less suspect than governments and possessing resources enabling them to bargain.[32] But this seems an idealized description. In reality the opposite is often the case: they suffer from the disabilities of being both distrusted and weak. Representatives of international organizations are frequently suspected of promoting the interests of the nation of which they are citizens or of a particular coalition within the organization. And as their own resources are limited, they are seldom effective in influencing states through bargaining.

It has been observed that a single mediator is usually more effective than a commission or a group of states. In theory, the efforts of a group of states enjoys wider international support than the action of a single state. A group of states possesses the advantage of greater resources and potentially greater bargaining power than a single state. In practice, however, the complicated and cumbersome processes of consultation and decision-making that take place within groups tend to diminish their effectiveness considerably. Moreover, they are often incapable of coordinating their policies and mobilizing their resources in support of the mediation in which they are engaged. Single states, on the other hand, are capable of reacting more quickly and flexibly to changing diplomatic situations; this can affect the outcome of the mediator's efforts much more than potential but unusable power.[33]

There is a broad consensus that a mediator will stand a better chance of success if he is instructed by a general mandate, rather than by specific terms of reference. In some bargaining situations specific terms of reference may be an asset, as the commitment they represent defines the limits of the mediator's freedom of action. But taken as a whole the drawbacks of specific terms of reference tend to outweigh their advantages. They restrict the mediator's flexibility, become dated and irrelevant, or else raise problems of interpretation that complicate the intermediary's relations with one or both parties.[34]

The requirements for successful mediation discussed above do not amount to a theory. But they can serve as a framework for a comparative analysis of mediation attempts. Historical events can always be rationalized and explained, and this applies to the outcomes of mediation efforts in the Arab-Israeli conflict as well. My objective is not limited to explaining the success or failure of each mediation attempt; I will also try to evaluate current generalizations about the requisites for successful mediation.

United Nations Partition Plan, 1947

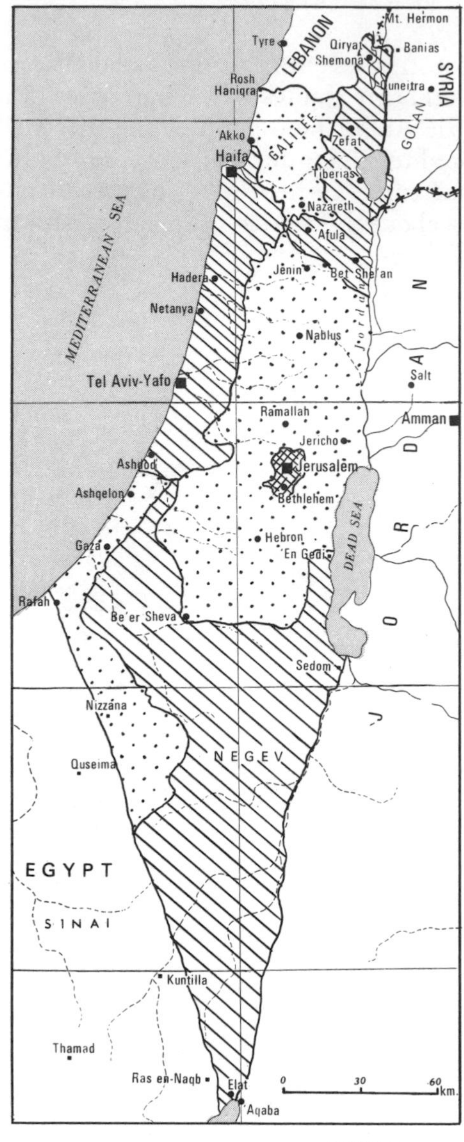

Jewish state

Arab state

International area of Jerusalem

International boundary

The Second Bernadotte Plan

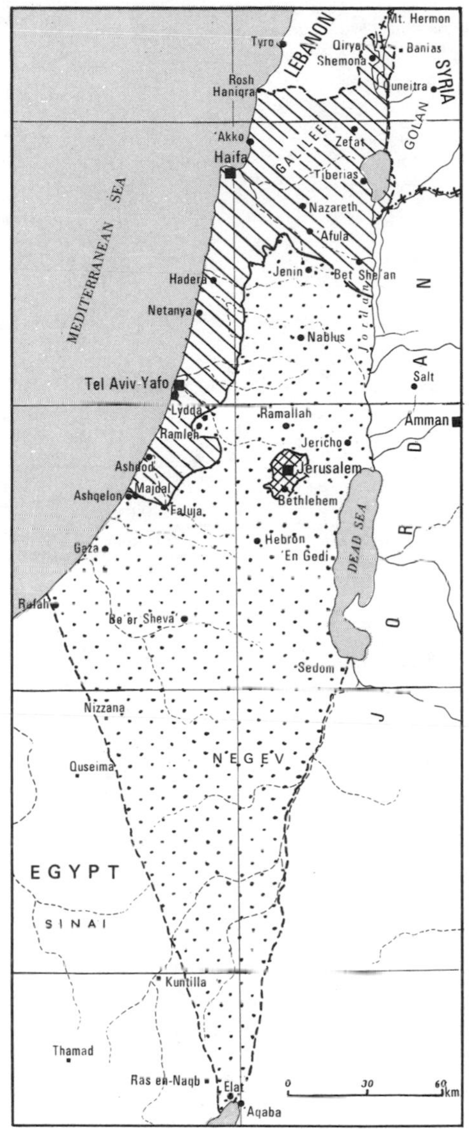

Jewish state

Arab territory

International area of Jerusalem

International boundary

Armistice Agreements, 1949

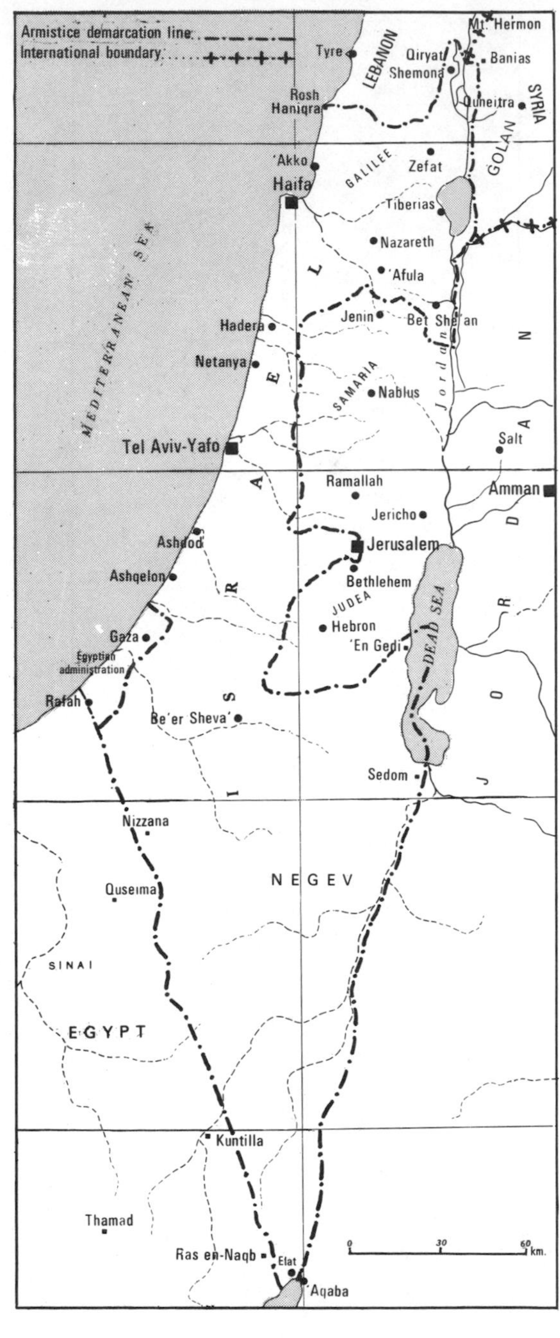

Cease-fire, Disengagement, and Peace Treaty Lines, 1967-1979

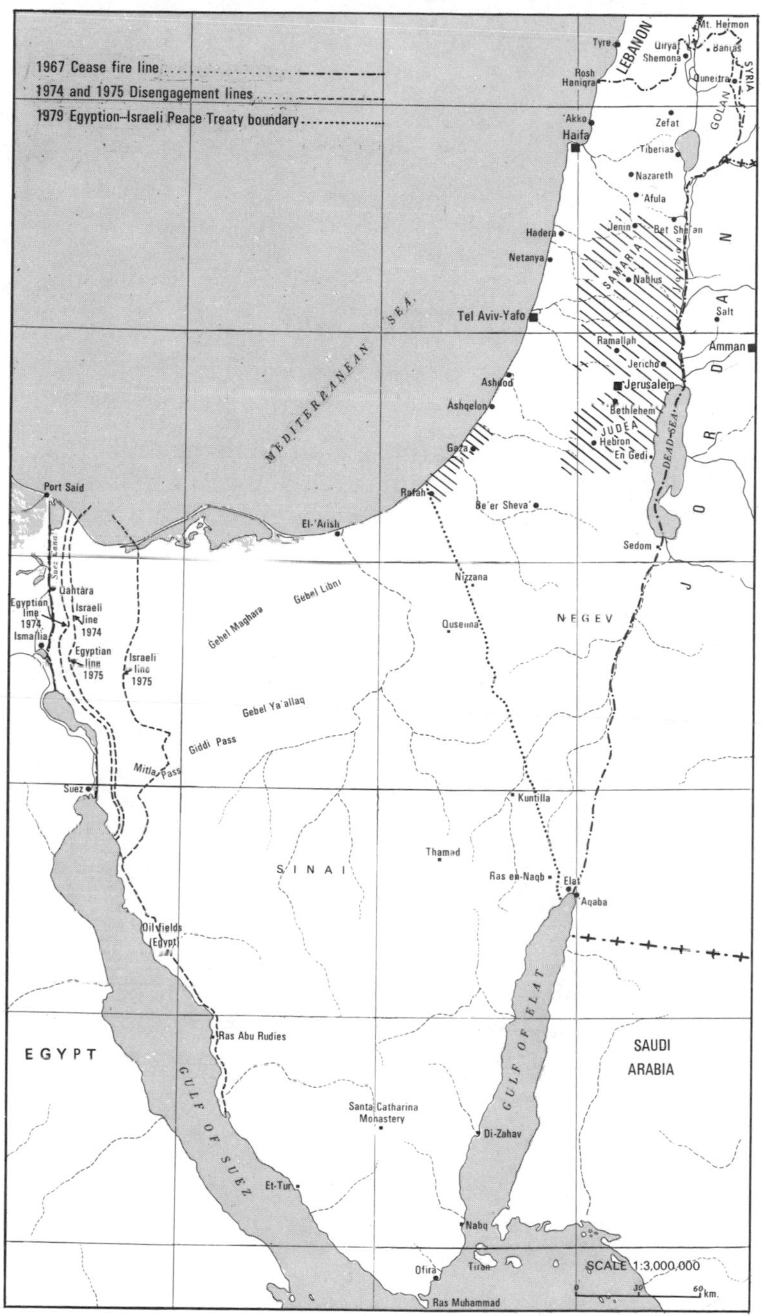

TWO

Bernadotte

The first major effort to find a solution to the Arab-Israeli conflict following the termination of the British mandate and the proclamation of Israel's independence was a UN initiative entrusted to Count Folke Bernadotte of Sweden. It ended in tragedy: Bernadotte was assassinated by Jewish extremists in Jerusalem on September 17, 1948. His mediation efforts also failed. Both his proposals for a comprehensive settlement were rejected by the parties concerned, and did not win the endorsement of the international community. His attempts to accomplish a more limited goal—the demilitarization of Jerusalem—also came to nothing. The only accomplishments to which Bernadotte contributed were the two periods of truce in June and in July 1948. But these are overshadowed by the diplomatic failures and by the tragic circumstances of his death.

To explain this failure, it is necessary to examine Bernadotte's diplomacy. In particular, I shall try to determine the extent to which he deserves credit for the truces and blame for the diplomatic debacle of his mission.

The Background

The origin of Bernadotte's mission lies in the disagreements over the deteriorating situation in Palestine that divided the international community in the spring of 1948.

The decision to appoint a mediator was taken on May 14, 1948, at the conclusion of a special session of the UN General Assembly, which had been convened on U.S. initiative. As it had become apparent that the implementation of the UN partition plan adopted on November 29, 1947 had run into serious difficulty because of Arab opposition and British noncooperation, the United States temporarily abandoned its support for partition and proposed instead that UN trusteeship or some other provisional regime be established in Palestine when the British mandate ended. This American initiative was opposed, however, by several Western governments and by the Soviet bloc, which continued to support the partition plan. In view of the doubts that a UN decision on a provisional regime could actually be implemented, and in an effort to win the necessary two-thirds of the vote in the General Assembly, the U.S. proposal was gradually modified. The discussions were held under the pressure of the May 14 deadline, when the British administration over Palestine was to come to an end. On May 13, a subcommittee of the First Committee of the General Assembly amended the American proposal in a manner that significantly altered its meaning. Instead of appointing a UN commissioner, it now proposed the appointment of a UN *mediator*. On the following day, in the very hours that the British administration was coming to an end and the Jewish community in Palestine was proclaiming its independent statehood in conformity with the 1947 UN decision, the General Assembly adopted the resolution appointing a mediator.[1]

The assembled states remained divided on the substance of policy. But they shared the desire to resolve the problem peacefully, and to limit the damage to the prestige and authority of the UN that would be caused by conflict over the implementation of the UN partition resolution. The appointment of the mediator reflected a procedural compromise on how to tackle the problem. It was accompanied by hopes, if not designs, for using the mediator to achieve contradictory desired outcomes. These divergences were reflected in the mediator's instructions, which represented a compromise: no mention was made of the partition resolution, either to uphold or invalidate it. The terms of reference empowered the mediator:

(a) To use his good offices with the local and community authorities in Palestine to:
- (i) Arrange for the operation of common services necessary to the safety and well-being of the population of Palestine;
- (ii) Assure the protection of the Holy Places, religious buildings and sites in Palestine;
- (iii) Promote a peaceful adjustment of the future situation of Palestine.[2]

The General Assembly entrusted the choice of mediator to a committee composed of the representatives of the Big Five (China, France, the Soviet Union, the United Kingdom, and the United States). There is some evidence that Bernadotte's candidacy was proposed by UN Secretary-General Trygve Lie.[3] In selecting him the great powers must have entertained some expectations about his attitudes. Bernadotte, a nephew of the king of Sweden and president of the Swedish Red Cross, was known for his humanitarian work during and after the Second World War. The Soviet Union probably hoped that being a Swede, he would perform his mission in a manner consistent with Sweden's neutrality between East and West. The Western powers probably felt confident that his personal dislike for Communism would assure that he would not permit the Soviet Union to exploit the situation.[4] There has been some speculation as to possible expectations concerning his attitudes to the Arab-Jewish conflict and the implementation of partition. Bernadotte had been credited with securing the release of thousands of prisoners, including Jews, from Nazi camps in the closing days of the Second World War.[5] This could have produced the expectation that he would sympathize with the establishment of a

Jewish state. Any such expectations were soon proved wrong.

Bernadotte's own motives in accepting the mediator's position seem to have been a blend of a sense of mission and personal ambition. Describing his thoughts on whether he should accept the task, Bernadotte relates that he was aware of the magnitude of the difficulty, but he nevertheless felt that if he were to refuse, he would probably reproach himself for the rest of his life for not having tried. He seems to have been concerned not only about the fate of the Arabs and Jews, but no less so about the international situation and the fear that "the Jewish-Arab conflict might become the spark which would ignite the world."[6]

The First Truce

The civil war between the Arabs and the Jews in Palestine began on the morrow of the UN partition resolution on November 29, 1947. On May 15, 1948, as the British mandate came to an end and the State of Israel was proclaimed, the regular armies of the neighboring Arab states crossed the border and intervened in the fighting, with the purpose of preventing the establishment of the Jewish state. On June 11, the fighting in Palestine halted, in compliance with a UN Security Council call for a four-week truce. As three previous Security Council resolutions had gone unheeded, this compliance requires some explanation.[7]

The May 29 resolution differed from previous ones in stating that defiance might require the council to consider action under chapter seven of the UN Charter. The implied threat of sanctions may have been one reason for the parties' agreement to the truce. But additional reasons must be considered, and of particular interest is the question of Bernadotte's contribution.

Due weight must be given to the military and political circumstances. From Israel's standpoint, a cease-fire was highly desirable. The invasion by Egypt, Jordan,[8] Syria, and Iraq had placed Israel in dire straits. Its most urgent task was to cope with the immediate emergency and stop the Arab advance. To do so, Israel had to transform its poorly equipped and clandestinely organized fighting forces into a cohesive and well-trained army, subject to civilian authority. With the end of the British mandate, immigrants began to flow into the country. Men and women of military age among them had to be formed into military units. As the weapons purchased before independence began to arrive, troops had to be instructed in their use. For all these reasons Israel's leaders, including the military command, were agreed that a cease-fire was desirable.[9] In addition to these military circumstances, political considerations made Israel favorably disposed toward a truce. Israel's attitude toward the United Nations was ambivalent at that time, as the hopes that the UN would take action to help implement its partition resolution gave way to disappointment at its impotence. Yet, on another level there persisted the view that defiance of the UN was both morally and politically wrong. Israel derived its legitimation in part from the United Nations resolutions. Thus, in purely political terms, Israel endeavored to make its policies conform as much as possible to relevant UN resolutions. This predisposition was reflected in the Proclamation of Independence, which made several references to the UN. Foreign Minister Moshe Sharett's[10] statement to the Provisional State Council (provisional legislature) on June 17, that Israel accepted the truce because it wished its foreign policy to be based upon "mutual agreement and understanding with the United Nations," seems an accurate reflection of Israel's attitudes at that time.[11]

As the Arab side was a coalition, the influence of the military situation upon Arab attitudes and decisions was more complex. By May 24, the advances of the Arab armies had been halted, and Israel had begun to counterattack. About this time, Arab leaders must have recognized that their expectation that the invasion by the Arab armies of Palestine would quickly put an end to the attempt to establish a Jewish state was not realized. The dreams of victory had not yet faded completely, but it had become quite clear that this would be a longer campaign than previously hoped. The exhausted Jordanian and Egyptian armies suffered from shortages of supplies and ammunition. Yet because of the expectations that the Arab governments had aroused among their peoples, and because none could afford to be accused of defeatism or lack of solidarity with the common Arab cause, attitudes toward the Security Council's call for a truce were conflicting. Coalition politics and the processes of intergovernmental decision-making made Arab acceptance of the cease-fire more difficult. The debates at the Arab League meetings on the issue were sometimes bitter. Jordan, supported by Egypt and Iraq, wanted a truce; while Syria, Lebanon, and Saudi Arabia opposed it.[12]

Arab attitudes too were influenced by diplomatic considerations. They had become unsympathetic toward the UN as a consequence of the partition resolution, but recurrent and persistent defiance of UN resolutions placed Arab governments in an uncomfortable position. Not only did the Arabs resist the efforts to implement the partition resolution, but they also defied repeated Security Council resolutions ordering a cease-fire. It was difficult to sustain this defiance indefinitely, especially in the light of the implied threat of sanctions. Their ultimate acceptance of the truce may, in some part, have been due to their desire to shed the image of being in conflict with the UN.[13]

This was the context within which Bernadotte's intervention took place. His negotiations were concerned mainly with how to allay Arab fears that the truce might enable Israel to improve its military position. The Arabs at first made their acceptance of the truce conditional upon the cessation of all Jewish immigration into Israel. This became the most sharply contested issue in the negotiations, since it could be interpreted by the parties as affecting their core values. The Zionist claim that Jews ought to have the right to immigrate into Palestine had been at the basis of the Arab-Jewish conflict since the early 1920s.

Bernadotte asked that the Security Council rule on this issue. But since this could have upset the carefully phrased compromise embodied in the May 29 resolution, the council authorized Bernadotte to provide his own interpretation of the resolution. The negotiations on this matter gave rise to some acrimonious exchanges between him and Sharett, in the course of which Bernadotte complained that he thought the foreign minister "had no confidence whatever" in him as mediator. Bernadotte finally settled the matter by imposing restrictions on the immigration of "fighting personnel" and "men of military age," thus going some way toward accommodating the Arab viewpoint; but he did not prohibit all immigration as the Arab states had demanded. His ruling was accepted by both parties, and the truce consequently came into effect on June 11.[14]

Thus, Bernadotte made some contribution to the attainment of the truce, but his contribution was probably not crucial. It is unlikely that had he not acted as he did, the fighting would have continued until a clear-cut military outcome was reached. The military and diplomatic circumstances in which the parties found themselves disposed them to accept a truce. Bernadotte himself recognized this. Explaining the parties' compliance he recorded in his diary that "both parties agreed eventually to a truce" because "they realized that from a military point of view they had reached a deadlock, in any case temporarily."[15]

The Security Council resolution helped the parties to make the necessary decisions. It was a goad and a face-saving device: both sides could claim that they had accepted the truce not out of weakness, but because of respect for the UN.

However, Bernadotte's contribution was not entirely negligible. His detailed interpretation of the general terms of the May 29 Security Council resolution had proved acceptable to both parties. Bernadotte's involvement also facilitated certain decisions, especially those of the Arabs. The appointment of a mediator nourished the Arab hope that the UN partition resolution could be reversed, and Bernadotte's explicit statements at his initial meetings with Arab leaders that he did not consider himself bound by the partition resolution encouraged them to cooperate with him.[16] His ruling on the truce terms further helped the Arabs to comply with the cease-fire by allaying their fear that Israel would take advantage of the truce to significantly strengthen its military power. His contribution was not crucial—it probably did not make the difference between truce and no truce—yet it was significant in obtaining timely compliance with the Security Council's decision.

The Debacle of the June 27 Suggestions

Bernadotte's next important step was to present the Arab states and Israel with suggestions for a settlement that he hoped might serve as a basis for further discussions. These were rejected by both sides. The episode had far-reaching consequences. It hindered Bernadotte's efforts to extend the four-week truce; on its expiration the war was resumed. Even more important was the effect of the suggestions upon the parties' attitudes toward him. His suggestions also seemed to the parties to carry "lessons," which inspired their policies in subsequent months.

The main points of these suggestions dated June 27 were:

(1) Palestine, as defined in the original mandate (i.e., according to the 1922 borders, comprising Transjordan), might form a Union of two members, one Arab and one Jewish. (In other words, the Arab part of Palestine would be joined with the realm of King Abdullah of Jordan).

(2) The organs of the Union should be entrusted with promoting common economic interests, operating common services, and coordinating foreign policy and defense; although subject to the provisions of

the Union each member would exercise full control over its own affairs, including its foreign relations.

(3) Immigration should be within the competence of each member for a period of two years. Thereafter, it would be conditional upon agreement of both members. Any disagreements would be submitted to the United Nations Economic and Social Council whose decision would be binding.

(4) Refugees should be entitled to return to their former places of residence.

(5) As a basis for boundary negotiations Bernadotte proposed amendments to the partition lines: (a) That the whole or part of the Negev be in Arab territory (the partition plan had allocated it to Israel); (b) that the Western Galilee be included in Jewish territory; (c) that Jerusalem be included in the Arab territory (and not given international status); and (d) that free ports be established at Haifa (to include the oil refineries and terminals) and at Lydda airport.[17]

Bernadotte had been criticized for this failure not only by the Arabs and the Israelis who found fault with the proposals, but also by his fellow UN officials who implicitly questioned his diplomatic tactics. Trygve Lie, the secretary-general, said that he should not have presented his suggestion in a formal manner without "the benefit of advance soundings with each party." He also recalled his own advice to Bernadotte "to avoid making any proposals to the Arabs and Israelis which had but a slim chance of acceptance." Pablo de Azcárate, a UN official involved in the Arab-Israeli negotiations between 1948 and 1952, criticized the preparation of the proposals as hasty and cursory.[18]

Bernadotte's proposals deviated from his own preferred tactic. His primary goal was to obtain an extension of the truce. He expected that the main obstacle to this would be the opposition of some of the Arab states. He did not believe a mere call for extension would suffice: it would be necessary to offer the Arabs incentives to enter into negotiations. He hoped to achieve this by submitting tentative and vaguely formulated proposals. In his own words:

> We were all agreed that these proposals should be drawn up in rather vague terms. Their purpose should be first and foremost to convince both parties of the desirability of prolonging the truce so as to make it possible to continue the discussions. If we put forward too precise proposals, the result might easily be an abrupt rejection. . . . But if we could gain time, if we could keep the discussions going, then there was reason to hope that the war-mongering elements on both sides would quiet down.[19]

But his proposals were not vague enough. They were vague in describing the division of powers in the Union he proposed. But they were specific in denying independent statehood to the Jews, and in its recommended territorial apportionment. These specifics doomed the proposals. While the abolition of sovereign statehood was unacceptable to the Jews, the existence of a Jewish entity and the territorial proposals were anathema to some of the Arab states.

It is difficult to explain how Bernadotte could have made such a tactical mistake. But the miscalculations and preconceptions that led to the formulation of his proposals can be reconstructed.

Bernadotte's main targets were the Arabs, since they were more reluctant to negotiate. But among the Arab states, the inducements he offered were of benefit mainly to Jordan: he suggested that it annex Jerusalem and the Arab part of Palestine, including the Negev. Bernadotte justified the incorporation of the Arab part of Palestine into Jordan in terms of the political circumstances as he perceived them. In his view, the Palestine Arabs had never developed "a specifically Palestinian nationalism." With their political and military collapse, "the demand for a separate Arab State in Palestine is consequently relatively weak," and "most Palestinian Arabs would be quite content to be incorporated in Transjordan." In view of the major role that Jordan's Arab Legion played in the fighting, and King Abdullah's special interest in becoming the custodian of Islam's holy places in Jerusalem, King Abdullah had "more at stake" in the conflict than any of the other Arab parties.[20] While much of this may have corresponded to reality, Bernadotte did not attach sufficient weight to one implication of his proposal: territory seized by Egypt in the course of the war would be transferred to Jordan, thus depriving Egypt of the fruits of its military achievements. He expected "that certain of the other Arab States, in particular Egypt, would not find the proposal particularly attractive,"[21] but apparently, did not attach much importance to it. Bernadotte may have hoped that Egypt and the other Arab states would find sufficient satisfaction in his refusal to consider the partition plan and the establishment of a sovereign Jewish state as a starting point for negotiations.

If the proposals per se did not sway the Arab coalition, he believed that the dynamics of the situation might still lead to their acceptance. He apparently envisaged a process where the inducements offered to Jordan, coupled with Britain's influence in Amman, would strengthen King Abdullah's inclination to accept the extension of the truce; and that the other Arab states would be unlikely to renew the fighting if Jordan refrained.[22] Britain and the United States indeed advised the Arabs to agree to extend the truce. Britain argued that the mediator's proposals offered an "opportunity for a solution on lines much more favorable to the Arab Governments than before." Britain also cautioned the Arab governments that a resumption of the fighting on Arab initiative would lead to Security Council action, which would make it difficult for Britain to resume arms deliveries, and furthermore that the Arab governments would be incurring the risk of "serious military reversals."[23]

Yet Bernadotte's expectations were proved wrong. He overrated British influence, and Jordan, while considering the proposals attractive, was unwilling to betray Arab solidarity by taking an independent course.

Bernadotte expected that Israel's reaction to his proposals would be unfavorable. But he must have misunderstood or underestimated the value that Israel attached to sovereign independent statehood. He thought that if the Arabs accepted his proposals, Israel could be prevailed upon to cooperate. He or his associates therefore advised Israel to delay its response until after the Arabs had replied.[24] Israel's view of Bernadotte's suggestions was, however, negative. After all, they denied Israel what it believed it had already attained—sovereign statehood. The suggestions were discussed at the cabinet meetings of June 30 and July 2. David Ben-Gurion's summary of these discussions reveals that there was unanimous opposition to the restrictions on Israel's sovereignty, to the imposition of limitations on immigration, and to the incorporation of Jerusalem in Arab territory. Opinion was divided about the suggested exchange of parts of the Negev for the Western Galilee, and on the establishment of *economic* links with Jordan. But even those who thought that Israel should consider some economic association with Jordan were unwilling to give up any sovereign rights, and were concerned about the strong British influence in that country.[25]

Bernadotte either did not foresee or did not care that his proposals would stimulate Israel's suspicions that he was a "British agent." Britain was known to favor the incorporation of the Negev in Arab territory and its annexation to Jordan. Since Britain had a defense treaty with Jordan, this would have enabled Britain to establish bases there. Israeli officials interpreted this as an indication that Bernadotte was working for Britain. Since they regarded Britain as hostile to Israel, they ceased to expect that Israel could gain by cooperating with Bernadotte.[26]

The resemblance of Bernadotte's proposals to ideas advocated by British officials in their discussions with their American counterparts, as evidenced in the published

American diplomatic documents, is indeed striking. In June these ideas were in flux, as the British were moving from advocacy of a federal link between Israel and Jordan to a preference for separate sovereignties. The United States essentially adhered to the 1947 plan and opposed any diminution of Israel's sovereignty. Territorial arrangements similar to those suggested by Bernadotte were also proposed by British officials, as was the possibility of incorporating Jerusalem in Jordan.[27]

It is unlikely that Bernadotte consciously sought to promote British designs. The similarity of his recommendations to British views can be explained without this. These ideas were circulating in British and American diplomatic circles, and reached Bernadotte through his contacts with British and U.S. officials. Bernadotte attached importance to these views for two reasons. First, Britain was the dominant power in the region, and therefore, for purely pragmatic reasons, its views and interests had to be accommodated as much as possible. For example, John Reedman, one of Bernadotte's senior advisors, when recommending the exchange of the Negev for the Western Galilee, said that this "modification would eliminate one of the main British objections to the whole partition plan and pave the way for a lasting settlement."[28] Secondly, Bernadotte was predisposed to accept British views because they were similar to his own: he shared their dislike of the 1947 partition plan. That Bernadotte already held this view when he assumed his post is evident from his diary. He believed that the partition plan had been a mistake, that the creation of a separate Jewish state was bound to lead to war, and that the creation of a unitary state "with far-reaching rights for the Jews," would have been preferable. Furthermore, Bernadotte entertained the idea of placing Jerusalem under Arab rule even before he arrived in the Middle East, as evidenced by his account of his conversation with French Foreign Minister Bidault on May 26, 1948.[29] All that can be established is that Bernadotte held such views from the outset of his mission.

The influences under which he formed them remain uncertain.

The Second Truce

After receiving the negative Arab and Israeli reponses to his proposals, Bernadotte again visited Amman, Cairo, and Tel Aviv in an effort to elicit an agreement to extend the truce. Israel agreed to an extension, but on July 8 the Arab governments rejected it.[30] Fighting was resumed on July 9. This time it lasted ten days, ending on July 18 as a result of the UN Security Council resolution of July 15, which ordered the parties to cease fire and threatened sanctions in the event of noncompliance. Unlike the resolution of May 29 that called upon the parties to observe a cease-fire for four weeks, the July 15 resolution stated that the truce should remain in force "until a peaceful adjustment of the future situation in Palestine is reached."[31]

The mediator's contribution to this second truce was unimportant. The truce was accepted because of the defeats that some of the Arab armies suffered in the fighting, and because the strong Security Council resolution enabled the Arab governments to comply without losing face. There was no problem in persuading Israel to accept, since Israel had agreed to extend the four-week truce. Moreover, despite Israel's military achievements in the ten days of fighting, it also needed the respite.

Bernadotte participated in the diplomatic effort to obtain an appropriate Security Council resolution. As soon as the war was resumed on July 9, he appealed to the United States to arrange a Security Council resolution. King Abdullah, who had been reluctant to resume fighting, encouraged him to send such an appeal. In his message, Bernadotte informed the U.S. secretary of state that "Arab officials" had privately intimated to him that a strong Security Council resolution threatening sanctions "would give them a way out without incurring risk of internal dissension. It would permit [the] Arabs to say in effect [that] we are unable to fight the world." Similar reports that Jordanian and Egyptian leaders would welcome such a Security Council resolution reached Washington and London from diplomatic representatives in the Middle East.[32]

A few days later, Bernadotte left for UN headquarters. He wanted to address the Security Council meeting and to make sure that the council's action met the exigencies of the situation. Bernadotte told the council emphatically that he was unable "to get a result" without its backing, and asked for a resolution ordering a cease-fire and threatening sanctions. According to Bernadotte, the truce had to be given first priority. In his view, "mediation, unless one finds itself in military distress, can make little headway during hostilities, since negotiations are influenced by the daily fortunes of battle."[33]

Thus, Bernadotte played some part in interpreting the formal diplomatic stance of the Arab governments to the members of the Security Council. But other diplomats performed similar functions. Moreover, this time, the principal actors at the Security Council were predisposed to adopt a strongly worded resolution. Once again it seems that although Bernadotte made some contribution to attaining this truce, this contribution was not crucial: the outcome would have been similar even if Bernadotte had not taken part in the process.

The "Bernadotte Plan"

Bernadotte's final act, shortly before he was assassinated, was to submit recommendations to the UN General Assembly that met in Paris in September 1948. The outline for a settlement contained in these recommendations differed in several important respects from his June proposals, signifying a new approach to the problem. In June, he had submitted his suggestions to the parties, and proposed that they serve as a basis for discussions with them. By September, he no longer believed that such negotiations would lead to an agreement. This time, he submitted his report to the UN and expressed the conviction that the proposal "if firmly approved and strongly backed by the General Assembly, would not be forcibly resisted by either side."[34] In other words, he proposed an imposed settlement. I shall examine how Bernadotte reached this conclusion.

Upon his return from Lake Success, Bernadotte met Arab and Israeli leaders and tried to discern changes in their attitudes, and to test his own ideas on how to go about promoting a settlement.

At his meetings with Arab leaders, Bernadotte attempted to persuade them that Israel's existence was a fact, that the UN would not renege on its support for the establishment of the Jewish state, and that they had no choice but to recognize this reality.[35] His impression was that Azzam Pasha, the secretary-general of the Arab League, whom he considered the most irreconcilable of the Arab leaders, now realized "deep down that the Arab world cannot any longer hope for a Palestine in which there will not be an independent Jewish State. He certainly did not admit it directly or in so many words." The Egyptian prime minister, Nokrashi Pasha, did, but told Bernadotte that the Arab states would never accept or recognize such a state. The leaders of Lebanon and Jordan expressed similar views. Although he saw that the Arab leaders were unyielding on the ultimate settlement, he was reassured about the preservation of the truce and concluded that the Arab states did not intend to resume the war.[36]

Israel did not wish to resume the war either. But it viewed the indefinite continuation of the truce as an economic and military burden, fraught with diplomatic disadvantages as well. The world was getting used to a status quo that forced Israel to maintain a large mobilized army and to stretch its resources to the limit. Israel remained a state whose sovereignty was restricted: the limitations on the admission of immigrants of military age and on the importation of arms were still in force. As the number of states extending diplomatic recognition to Israel stayed at less than twenty, some Israeli leaders believed that the indeterminate political-military situation deterred additional states from extending diplomatic recognition.[37]

Consequently, Israel wanted a resumption of the negotiations toward a political settlement. Bernadotte was increasingly regarded as an obstacle to this; no negotiations could be conducted without his involvement. But estimating that Bernadotte was, consciously or unconsciously, an instrument of British policy, Israel did not want him to submit any new proposals. On July 29, Sharett told Israel's provisional parliament that Israel did not accept his method of mediation, but that Israel would welcome a mediation directed at bringing the two parties into direct negotiations. A few days later Israel requested Bernadotte to transmit a proposal to the Arab states for the opening of direct negotiations. Although Bernadotte did not believe that such negotiations were feasible, he conveyed Israel's invitation, and brought back the Arab governments' negative reply.[38]

Bernadotte himself was at this stage unwilling to take new steps toward a settlement. His reluctance reflected the caution he had developed following the failure of his previous attempt. He found the Arab leaders divided on how to proceed. Azzam Pasha advised him on July 24 to "hasten slowly." In view of the political unrest in the Arab world following their failure to win the war, he asked Bernadotte not to force the issue but to wait until the agitation quieted down.[39] On the other hand, on August 1, the prime minister and foreign minister of Jordan expressed the hope that "the United Nations would reach [a] decision . . . before too long, so that the present trying situation would not have to continue much longer." Undoubtedly, they wanted Bernadotte's proposal for the annexation of the Arab part of Palestine to be confirmed and legitimized by the UN. Bernadotte recorded that "they were particularly anxious to discuss with me what was to be done with the Arab part of Palestine."[40] Two days later, he heard the Egyptian prime minister express opposition to the union of the Arab part of Palestine with Jordan. Nokrashi Pasha "considered that the wisest course would be to constitute the Arab part of Palestine a separate and independent state supported by the Arab League." He did not wish to imply recognition of Israel, since he added that "the Arabs would continue to regard Palestine as Arab territory and the Jews as rebels."[41]

There was little that Bernadotte could do to reconcile the opposing Israeli and Arab positions, or to harmonize inter-Arab differences. Having become wiser by the failure of his June 27 suggestion, he recognized the limits of his capabilities. That experience, as well as his visit to UN headquarters and the constant difficulties he encountered with maintaining the truce, taught him another important lesson: UN support was indispensable for success, and without it he would be able to accomplish nothing. And in view of the dominant American influence in the UN at that time, American backing was a prerequisite for UN support. To give teeth to his mission, he wanted the United States to contribute a large contingent of observers and legal experts to examine allegations of truce violations. For the demilitarization of Jerusalem he required a force of "6,000 well-armed and fully trained soldiers," he informed Secretary of State George Marshall. He was deeply disappointed that the United States was unwilling to supply him with the personnel he requested, and even threatened to resign.[42]

He concluded that he could not further his mediation effort until the United States and Britain agreed on a common policy. Bernadotte's views were conveyed to Secretary of State Marshall by Ralph Bunche on August 9. Marshall's summary of this conversation is interesting:

> As for long-range settlement, Bernadotte is not eager to offer suggestions until he is assured that U.S. and U.K. governments are in agreement on general lines of an equitable settlement. Bernadotte of course realizes that

> Jews on the one hand will make exorbitant demands and Arabs will refuse to countenance officially existence of Jewish State. Nevertheless, mediator is said to feel that if U.K. and U.S. are in agreement and if these governments can reach a general line in accord with his views (upon which he does not insist), chances are that both Jews and Arabs, although violently protesting, may quietly move along lines of eventual settlement.[43]

Bernadotte hoped that the United States and Britain would agree on a common policy in time for the UN General Assembly to take action during its next session, due to start in September. In the meantime, on August 12, he flew to Stockholm to attend the International Red Cross conference. While there, the U.S. tried to persuade him not to bring the matter to the forthcoming General Assembly. Temporarily Bernadotte seemed ready to follow this advice. But when he met Trygve Lie in Paris on September 1, he agreed with Lie that action by the General Assembly was desirable, if not urgent.[44]

What restored Bernadotte to his initial inclination to seek General Assembly action was the instability of the truce. The danger to the truce stemmed in part from incessant truce violations by all parties. But more serious was Israel's proclaimed unwillingness to accept the truce status quo indefinitely. Bernadotte's orders from Stockholm that the restrictions on immigration be tightened further reenforced this sentiment.[45] Bernadotte may have been stimulated to take an initiative also by Israel's open expressions of displeasure with the way he conducted his mission. An article published on August 27, in *Davar*, a newspaper assumed to reflect the opinions of the national leadership, proposed that Bernadotte's mission be terminated. Israel also reported its dissatisfaction with the mediator to the UN Secretariat. At the same time, Israel sent private messages to Arab leaders inviting them to enter into negotiation. That Bernadotte took offense at Israel's repeated attempts to dispense with his services is suggested by Bernadotte's notations in his diary.[46]

Upon returning from Stockholm and Paris Bernadotte held another round of conversations with Arab and Israeli leaders. He now gained the impression that the Arabs had resigned themselves to accepting partition. Yet the truce was in danger of collapse. His thinking now followed a similar logic as when he sought to extend the four-week truce in June: then he believed that the truce could be stabilized only by engaging the parties in discussions of a political settlement. Now, again, he linked the limited objective of stabilizing the truce with the far-reaching goal of a political settlement. But this time the settlement proposals were to be supported by Britain and the U.S., and endorsed by the UN. Strong UN action was thus to be expected to produce the combined result of stabilizing the cease-fire and reaching a final settlement of the problem.[47]

Bernadotte's report to the General Assembly was comprehensive. It contained a summary of his activities and negotiations regarding a political settlement, the truces, Jerusalem, and the refugees. Bernadotte undertook to acquaint the members of the UN "with certain of the conclusions on means of peaceful adjustment" that he had reached. It differed from his June 27 suggestions in a number of important respects: It stated that Israel existed, and no longer proposed a Union. There was no mention of restrictions on immigration. Jerusalem was to be placed under UN control. The proposal that the Arab part of Palestine be attached to Jordan was modified; Bernadotte now proposed that the decision be left to the Arab states, although he mentioned the existence of "compelling reasons" for the merger. It affirmed in stronger language the Arab refugees' right to return, and demanded compensation for those who did not wish to do so. One important territorial provision remained essentially unchanged: the Negev was to be included in Arab territory and the Galilee in Israel.

The procedure to be followed on the road to peace was totally different from the suggestions of June:

(1) The "conclusions" were addressed to the UN, whereas the June "suggestions" had been addressed to the parties involved.
(2) Bernadotte did not expect that a proposal based on these conclusions "would readily win the willing approval of both parties"; but he was convinced that the proposal "if firmly approved and strongly backed by the General Assembly, would not be forcibly resisted by either side." In other words, he proposed an imposed settlement.
(3) If a formal peace was unattainable, then the truce should be superseded by an armistice "which would involve either complete withdrawal and demobilization of armed forces or their wide separation by creation of broad demilitarized zones under United Nations supervision."
(4) He recommended the establishment of a conciliation commission which would supervise the observance of the settlement, and assist in the continuation of the conciliation process.[48]

In view of the absence of mention of any further role for the mediator, some observers have concluded that Bernadotte intended to terminate his own mission. Fred Khouri wrote that Bernadotte "felt he had exhausted his usefulness," and wanted the UN to appoint a conciliation commission to replace him. David Forsythe holds a similar view, claiming that Bernadotte felt "that personality conflicts had developed between himself and certain of those with whom he was dealing. He felt that in such situations, it was the mediator's job to be expendable."[49] In view of the suspicion with which he came to be regarded by Israel, this is indeed possible, but there is no evidence on the public record to confirm this interpretation.

Again, Bernadotte's recommendations were very close to British views, and to a slightly lesser extent to those of the United States. The process by which this parallel thinking developed is not clear. But there is evidence that Britain and the U.S. had indeed intended to influence his recommendations.

By the end of August, Anglo-American consultations had produced a wide measure of agreement on an Arab-Israeli settlement: Israel should be fully sovereign and independent; the Arab parts of Palestine should be incorporated in Jordan; and the boundaries proposed by the 1947 UN partition plan should be altered so as to eliminate their irregular hourglass shape and make Israel more compact. Accordingly, the Western Galilee was to be given to Israel and the Negev to Jordan; and finally, Jerusalem was to be internationalized, but without an Israeli corridor linking Israel to Jerusalem.[50]

However, Britain and the United States continued to disagree on tactics. They shared the idea that Arab-Israeli negotiations were unlikely to produce agreement. In view of this, Britain thought that the Security Council should endorse boundaries determined by the mediator; any breach of these boundaries would be considered a threat to peace requiring enforcement by the Security Council. The United States, however, consistently held that under the UN Charter, the Security Council could act to prevent a threat to peace, but was not authorized to enforce any political settlement. In addition, the State Department believed that a request for Security Council action would be inexpedient in view of the likelihood of a Soviet veto. Pervading the State Department's reluctance to submit the issue to the UN was the concern that this would involve much publicity, and thus project the Arab-Israeli conflict into the domestic political arena at the time of the forthcoming presidential election. Instead, Americans preferred Arab and Israeli acquiescence to be obtained by the United States and Britain exerting "extreme diplomatic pressure" on both sides. If this were to prove successful, then toward the end of the General Assembly's session it might be possible "to pass quickly" a resolution incorporating the mediator's suggestions in order to enable the parties to save face in acquiescing to this settlement.[51]

Bernadotte's views about the terms for a settlement were known to be similar to those agreed upon by Britain and the United States. Perhaps for this reason, the United States and Britain expected no difficulty in persuading Bernadotte to submit *their* plan as his own. As a British official observed, it was "important that from moment proposals became known they should carry as label 'Mediator—made in Sweden.' "[52]

Yet a hitch nearly developed as the mediator, unaware of the advice being prepared for him, readied his report to the General Assembly. When the State Department and the Foreign Office learned, around September 10, that the mediator's report was almost complete and ready to be sent to Paris, they each hastily dispatched an official to Rhodes to make sure that Bernadotte's proposals were in accord with the agreed Anglo-American plan. The two officials, Robert McClintock and Sir John Troutbeck, arrived in Rhodes on September 13.

According to McClintock's telegram to Washington they found that Bernadotte had already prepared the draft of his report. They were unable to review the whole of Bernadotte's report, and therefore concentrated their attention on his recommendations (the conclusion to Part 1 of the report). In view of the similarity of these recommendations to the agreed Anglo-American policy, their talks were "devoted more to the perfection of Bernadotte's first draft . . . than to matters of substance in which all three were in agreement."

This understates the impact of their mission. The two diplomats apparently played an important role in persuading Bernadotte to propose that Jerusalem be placed under UN, rather than Arab, control. Their talks also helped to set aside some other disagreements. Bernadotte drew Israel's southern boundary at the latitude of Faluja. In this, he had the support of the British representative. The American envoy believed that the boundary should be drawn further south, in the vicinity of the Gaza-Beersheba road. On Jerusalem there was disagreement about the nature of the UN role. Britain and the United States also continued to disagree about the role of the Security Council in imposing a settlement. However, this did not cause much difficulty at Rhodes since Bernadotte's recommendations stated that frontiers "should be established" by the UN, a phrase which reportedly came from the 1947 UN resolution and thus neutralized McClintock's objections.

As for tactics, Bernadotte was determined that the issue be dealt with by the forthcoming General Assembly. McClintock was unable to dissuade him from pursuing this course. Bernadotte's insistence on UN action stemmed from his belief that the Arabs would acquiesce in the existence of a Jewish state only if another UN resolution to this effect were adopted, and that Israel, under severe strain because of the extended truce, might use the UN's inaction as a pretext for taking matters into its own hands. McClintock seems to have been much impressed by Bernadotte. He ended his telegram by observing that Bernadotte, "who is sternly determined to advocate only a solution based on equal justice to both sides, feels that now is the optimum moment: that if not 'now' it is 'never,' and that the General Assembly must seize the opportunity."[53]

Bernadotte completed his report at Rhodes on September 16. On the following day he was murdered in Jerusalem by members of Lohamei Herut Israel (LEHI), an organization that had fought the British administration in Palestine, and refused to disband when Israel was established.[54] Bernadotte's assassination settled the question of whether the subject would be discussed by the General Assembly, and the item was duly inscribed on the agenda.

At the General Assembly, Bernadotte's recommendations engendered much diplomatic activity. Britain and the U.S. had agreed to work jointly for the approval of the report by the Assembly. As part of this effort, Secretary of State Marshall issued a public statement in Paris on September 21 saying that the U.S. considered Bernadotte's conclusions as offering "a generally fair basis for settlement of the Palestine question," and that the U.S. "strongly urges the parties and the General Assembly to accept them in their entirety as the best possible basis for bringing peace. . . ." Foreign Secretary Bevin performed his part by declaring in Parliament on the following day that "the recommendations of Count Bernadotte . . . have the wholehearted and unqualified support of His Majesty's Government."[55]

However, both Israel and the Arab coalition rejected the plan. So did the Soviet bloc. Israel's Foreign Minister Sharett declared in the provisional parliament that Israel regarded the partition resolution of November 29 as the only legal basis for a negotiated settlement, and would demand that the territorial allocations of that resolution be amended in Israel's favor.[56] British and American diplomats had hoped that the Arab states would not lobby actively to organize opposition to the recommendations, but in this they were disappointed. The Soviet bloc was also vehemently opposed to Bernadotte's plan, considering it an attempt to reestablish British control over parts of Palestine.

For a few weeks, the outcome hung in the balance. But as the U.S. presidential election campaign was in progress, and both President Truman and his rival Thomas Dewey competed for the support of Jewish voters, U.S. support for Bernadotte's plan began to weaken. The change in U.S. policy and the active opposition of Israel and its friends, the Arab states and their friends, and of the Soviet bloc, determined the outcome of the UN debate. After several draft resolutions had undergone repeated amendments and revisions, the General Assembly finally approved a resolution on December 11, 1948 that incorporated a few of Bernadotte's recommendations, but without any acknowledgment to him or to his report. The most important of these were the establishment of a Conciliation Commission and a revised version of the recommendation concerning the repatriation of Arab refugees. Britain's efforts notwithstanding, the resolution made no new apportionment of Palestine.[57]

The defeat of Bernadotte's recommendations at the General Assembly marked the final failure of his mission.

An Assessment

With the exception of his contributions in arranging the truces, Bernadotte accomplished none of the assignments included in his terms of reference: "(i) Arrange for the operation of the common services . . . (ii) Assure the protection of the Holy Places . . . (iii) Promote a peaceful adjustment of the future situation of Palestine." He also failed to attain the objectives that he had set for himself in the course of his mission: the extension of the first truce, the demilitarization of Jerusalem, and the return of Arab refugees.

The failure of Bernadotte's mission can be attributed to a multitude of factors, some of which were beyond his control or influence. Yet his own mistakes were significant. It is difficult to avoid the impression that had there been fewer of them, his mission might not have resulted in so total a failure. The mistakes were not only Bernadotte's but also those of his staff, on whom he placed great reliance. Bernadotte himself lacked several qualities that might have helped him. He was neither well-informed about the Arab-Jewish conflict nor about inter-Arab politics. He also lacked the personal charm, tact, and persuasive ability which can be so helpful to mediators.

His deficiencies should have been compensated for by the talents assembled on his staff, for among them were several experts on the Arab-Israeli conflict. His senior advisor was Ralph Bunche, who in 1947 served on the staff of the UN Special Committee on Palestine (UNSCOP), and after Bernadotte's death, succeeded him as Acting

Mediator, winning a reputation of a skillful mediator. It is not clear to what extent Bernadotte was the leader of a team, or to what extent he was influenced by his staff; but there is no doubt that the staff shared some responsibility for Bernadotte's mistakes.[58]

Bernadotte's assignment was colossally difficult—to reconcile the incompatible claims of Arab and Jewish nationalisms to the small and emotion-evoking territory named Palestine. Bernadotte could have tried to divide this broad problem into more limited issues that might have been more manageable, instead of twice proposing terms for a final and comprehensive settlement. His mistake was compounded by his seeking to accomplish the limited goals of extending and preserving the truces by linking them to the terms for a comprehensive settlement. By doing so he contributed to the Arab refusal to extend the first truce, and he stimulated Israel to break the second. (About this, more will be said in the next chapter.) Furthermore, he was unable to define clear priorities. Initially, a cease-fire was his first priority. But, by coming to view negotiations on his suggestions for a comprehensive settlement as a means to maintain the truce, a comprehensive settlement became a tactic, and a very inappropriate one indeed. Concurrently, he worked on more limited problems, such as the demilitarization of Jerusalem and the refugee problem, but this was not a gradualist approach to conflict resolution: these efforts were pursued unsystematically.

One of the main reasons for Bernadotte's failure was his lack of resources with which to influence the parties' positions. His status as UN Mediator carried only slight authority. The UN's inability to implement its resolutions on Palestine between November 1947 and May 1948 and its failure to prevent the invasion of Palestine by the armies of member states greatly weakened respect for the organization and its officials in the Middle East. His prominent status in Sweden as the king's nephew and as president of the Swedish Red Cross did not endow him with power to influence Arab and Israeli policies. He possessed no resources that could enable him to provide incentives or to threaten punishment. Even the international disapproval of the parties' behavior, which he occasionally used as a threat, was not under his control. The international context within which Bernadotte acted added to his difficulties. The Cold War inhibited cooperation between the Western powers and the Soviet Union. The Soviets distrusted him, which prevented the UN from providing him with more effective backing. His mission coincided with the Berlin blockade, which riveted the attention of the American and British leaders, and probably reduced their ability to handle the Arab-Israeli crisis effectively.

That he lacked resources and influence was not Bernadotte's fault. But that he was not aware of this weakness was his failing. Had he been aware of it, he might have perhaps tailored his goals to his capabilities. Instead, he greatly overestimated his influence. His naiveté is reflected in his initial belief that if the Arabs refused to accept the cease-fire and truce, then "within one week hundreds of bombers, provided by the United Nations, will attack Arab troops and capitals." He also entertained some fuzzy ideas about appealing to the people above the heads of their leaders, submitting his proposals to approval by plebiscite.[59] He was not sufficiently aware of the limitation on the UN power to arrange plebiscites, or the complexity of administering them. Nor did he appreciate that in a competition between a UN mediator and the political leadership of the communities involved, the mediator did not stand much chance of winning. His exaggerated self-confidence explains why he realized only belatedly, after the rejection of his June proposals, that without strong Anglo-American backing he could accomplish little.

His overconfidence is also reflected in the hasty and superficial manner in which he prepared his proposals. For thirty years Jews and Arabs had been unable to agree on a solution: Bernadotte expected that his frameworks for a comprehensive settlement, prepared in ten days in June, and perhaps at somewhat greater leisure during August and September, would solve the problem.

Bernadotte's proposals reflected a curious blend of realism and wishful thinking. His territorial proposals were essentially based on the military status quo. The Negev was in Arab hands, and the Western Galilee had been taken by Israel. The idea of legitimizing this situation by calling it an exchange seemed sensible. His proposal to place Jerusalem under Jordanian rule can also be said to have reflected the relative military advantage that Jordan held on that front when the first truce came into effect. Yet he displayed astonishing ingenuousness in proposing to abolish Israel's independence, and to ask Egypt to cede to Jordan the territory it had conquered in the war.

Another of Bernadotte's mistakes was to arouse Israeli suspicions to such an extent that it became very difficult for them to cooperate with him. He failed the crucial test that faces every mediator: how to induce both adversaries to cooperate with him by ensuring that the incentives offered to one side do not undermine his effectiveness with the other. The inducements he offered to the Arabs during the first month of his mission—his repeated assertion that he was not bound by the partition plan, his ruling on the immigration question, and finally his proposal that Israel's sovereign statehood be abolished, damned him in the eyes of the Israelis. Even more devastating was his apparent close connection with the British. Had he been merely suspected of bias, Israel would probably have tried to win him over. The consequent competition for his understanding and sympathy would have enhanced his influence with both sides. But he was suspected not merely of bias, but of being in the service of Israel's foes.

Lastly, some of Bernadotte's mistakes seem to have been due to misleading intelligence. His belief (in August and September) that the Arabs would acquiesce to partition, given a face-saving UN resolution, was obviously wrong.

He was not alone in erring; this misperception was rife among British and American diplomats at that time. His proposal to exchange the Negev for Galilee was also influenced by erroneous intelligence that Israel might accept such an arrangement.[60]

Though some of the intelligence that reached Bernadotte was faulty, his mistake was his uncritical acceptance of the opinions and views of others, and especially of the British. There may have been extenuating circumstances, related to the inherent quality of the mediating agency which he represented. He was a lone individual, who lacked the backing and firm, self-interested guidance of a government, so he grasped the anchor of the omnipresent and self-confident British officials. But essentially, his failure was his own—had he been more politically astute, he would not have stumbled into so many pitfalls in so short a time.

THREE

Ralph Bunche

Dr. Ralph Bunche, who became Acting Mediator after Bernadotte was assassinated, stands out among the intermediaries as highly successful and abundantly praised. He is credited with the conclusion of the armistice agreements between Israel and its four neighbors in 1949. In recognition of his work, he was awarded the Nobel Peace Prize in 1950. Trygve Lie, the UN Secretary-General, wrote that "It is obvious that there would not have been an armistice . . . without the skill and dedication of Ralph Bunche." James G. McDonald, the American ambassador to Israel, referred to him as "brilliant," and said that in achieving the armistice agreements Bunche "worked a miracle." Ben-Gurion, who was usually critical of the UN's role, praised him too, as did Walter Eytan, who described him as an "ideal" mediator.[1] Arabs are reported to have been more critical of him, and on occasions quite distrustful. However, one observer claims that Bunche carried "more personal influence in Arab circles than had been enjoyed by his predecessor."[2]

The success attributed to Bunche and the praise bestowed upon him contrast so much to the images formed of most other mediators and the criticism directed at them, that it arouses our curiosity. In fact, not all of Bunche's endeavors were crowned with success, but the armistice agreements he engineered outshone the failures of the initial phase of his mission. His first goal, to win UN endorsement for Bernadotte's recommendations, came to naught. His efforts to preserve the truce were also unsuccessful. So was his attempt to bring about Israel's withdrawal to the lines it held on the Egyptian front prior to the October fighting. The mention of his frustrations and failures does not belittle his achievements, but the record calls for an evaluation of his role. How much was he to blame for the failures? Did he really deserve the credit for the armistice agreement?

Bunche and the Bernadotte Plan

During his first two months in office, Bunche worked hard to get the Bernadotte plan endorsed by the UN General Assembly. He delivered two strong statements in its support to the General Assembly's First (Political) Committee, and was also much involved in behind-the-scenes diplomacy, trying to persuade Arab and Israeli delegates to moderate their opposition to the proposals. He also participated in Anglo-American consultations aimed at resolving differences between the two powers and presenting a mutually agreeable draft resolution to the General Assembly.[3]

Bunche's intensive and sustained activity on behalf of Bernadotte's plan requires an explanation. Theoretically, Bunche could have made a new start when he assumed the mediator's role by disengaging from Bernadotte's recommendations. He did not do so for several reasons: first, perhaps, out of a sense of loyalty to Bernadotte. In talks with Israeli officials, he even referred to Bernadotte's recommendations as his "sacred legacy."[4] Bunche was also deeply committed to the recommendations. He had been much involved in their drafting. He has described his role thus: "I had a very close hand in it. . . . Every word of the report was prepared by myself and my staff on the Island of Rhodes after full consultation with Count Bernadotte."[5] Moreover, he was concerned that if Bernadotte's plan were not endorsed by the Assembly, no resolution would be adopted on Palestine at all, and that without UN action the truce would break down.[6]

Bunche's efforts were to no avail. As we have seen, the combined opposition of Israel's friends, the Arab states and their supporters, and the Soviet bloc, prevented its adoption.

The Breakdown of the Truce and the Question of Israel's Withdrawal

While Bunche was devoting his energies to diplomatic activity in support of Bernadotte's plan, the uneasy truce broke down. Israel launched an offensive against Egyptian forces in the Negev (October 15-22), captured the northern Negev, including Beersheba, and encircled a sizeable Egyptian force at Faluja. Two weeks later, Israel moved against the irregular Arab forces in the central Galilee (October 28-31), and succeeded in capturing the entire Galilee, except for small stretches along the eastern border with Syria.

These offensives were prompted by the sense of military and political peril that had weighed upon Israeli leaders since July. The corridor linking Jerusalem to the coast was not yet secure, and the city could again fall under siege. The Egyptians were a mere thirty miles south of Tel Aviv. The Iraqi army was poised eight miles from the coast. The irregular Arab Liberation Army still held parts of the Galilee. The cease-fire was only a truce, and the need for continued preparedness stretched Israel's meager resources. The "lesson" that Israel drew from Bernadotte's recommendations was that the territorial proposals would tend to reflect existing front lines and military realities. Consequently, the inclination to launch an offensive, to "finish off" the war, or at least improve the prospects for a more favorable settlement, was very strong.[7]

Aware of Israel's restlessness, Bunche conveyed an informal warning to Israeli leaders that the great powers would not tolerate a renewal of fighting. The warning was coupled with an inducement—the information that the U.S. might accept some modification in favor of Israel of the Negev boundary proposed by Bernadotte. He also suggested to Trygve Lie that the Security Council reaffirm the truce.[8] But because of the strained relations between the West and the Soviet Union over the Berlin blockade, and over the West's bringing the Berlin issue to the Security Council, the moment was inopportune for placing the Palestine truce on the agenda. In any case it is doubtful whether even a reaffirmation of the truce by the Security Council would have changed Israel's determination to counter the military and political threats that it believed it faced.

As soon as the fighting started Bunche and his aides began efforts to terminate it. When these efforts proved to no avail, the Security Council was convened on October 19. At that meeting the council decided to endorse Bunche's call for a cease-fire. It also adopted a somewhat ambiguously worded request for the withdrawal of forces to previous positions.[9] The cease-fire came into effect on October 22. Bunche's contribution to this was threefold: not only did he urge the Security Council to act, but indirectly authored the council's decision, as the council adopted the suggestions he had made in his report on the situation. In addition it was his staff who made the technical arrangements for the cease-fire to come into effect.

The parties readily agreed to the cease-fire. Egypt's acceptance is very understandable—the military situation it faced was highly unfavorable, and potentially dangerous. Israel's compliance also stemmed from its assessment of the military-political situation. Its offensive had attained one of its main objectives: the Egyptian forces had been pushed out of the northern Negev. To continue the fighting in an effort to improve Israel's position south of Jerusalem would have entailed the military risk of drawing into renewed fighting the armies of additional Arab states. Moreover, Abba Eban, Israel's representative at the UN, had telegraphed from Paris where the UN was in session that failure to comply might reverse the favorable atmosphere that had prevailed during the Security Council session and bring about a stronger resolution.[10]

Once the cease-fire was restored, Bunche requested that Israel withdraw to the lines it held prior to October 14. Bunche's request was argued in terms of principle: the maintenance of the truce required not only that the cease-fire be observed, but also that the parties remain at the positions occupied by them when the truce came into effect.[11]

Israel refused however to withdraw. It pointed out the disadvantage in restoring lines that jeopardized the supply routes to Israeli-held areas in the Negev. Israel held that the withdrawal ought to be subject to negotiations, as the wording of the Security Council decision attested:

> . . . After the cease-fire, the following conditions might well be considered as the basis for further negotiations looking toward insurance that similar outbreaks will not again occur and that the truce will be fully observed in this area: (a) Withdrawal of both parties from any positions not occupied at the time of the outbreak, . . .[12]

But the principal reason behind Israel's refusal to withdraw was its belief that Bunche's and some of the council members' pressure for withdrawal was motivated by their wish to facilitate the implementation of Bernadotte's recommendations. Bernadotte's proposal to give the Negev to the Arabs corresponded to the front lines that had existed prior to the Israeli offensive, when Israel held only a small enclave in the northern Negev, cut off from the rest of Israel. Since Israel's offensive was aimed in large measure at preventing the implementation of Bernadotte's proposal, its unyielding position on this was hardly surprising.

On November 4, in view of Israel's noncompliance, the Security Council adopted a further resolution requesting withdrawal, this time unequivocally. The council's decision rested on an unstable majority. The principle espoused by Bunche—that no party be permitted to derive any advantage by resorting to the use of force—commanded much support. But the implicit link between the Israeli withdrawal and Bernadotte's recommendation that the Negev be allotted to the Arabs divided the delegations. At British insistence, the resolution hinted at sanctions. But to enable the major powers to keep close control over any possible future action on this issue by the acting mediator, it was decided to establish a committee, comprising the five permanent members of the council with the addition of Belgium and Columbia, "to give such advice as the acting mediator may require with regard to his responsibilities under this resolution."[13]

A New Approach: An Armistice

Faced with a deadlock and the prospect of head-on collision with Israel, Bunche displayed remarkable resourcefulness and initiated a new approach. He proposed the establishment of an armistice. The idea of an armistice as an arrangement that might stabilize the truce had previously been discussed by Bernadotte and his staff. As formulated in Bernadotte's final report, the armistice was expected "to involve either complete withdrawal and demobilization of armed forces or their wide separation by creation of broad demilitarized zones under United Nations supervision."[14] Now, the idea appeared to offer an additional advantage: an armistice could be an expedient for circumventing a crisis over Israel's withdrawal. It provided a framework within which Israel could be persuaded to withdraw, and the conditions necessary for the implementation of Bernadotte's proposals could be restored.

Bunche's contribution on this matter was all-important. He took the initiative, raised the proposal at the right moment, and persuaded the Security Council and the parties to accept it. He spoke about it initially at the Security Council meeting on October 28 that was convened to discuss Israel's withdrawal. Subsequently, he elaborated on his views at two closed meetings of the Security Council on November 9 and 10, and helped in drafting and negotiating the text of the resolution that was formally adopted by the Security Council on November 16.[15] The resolution said that the council:

(1) Decides that, in order to eliminate the threat to the peace in Palestine and to facilitate the transition from the present truce to permanent peace in Palestine, an armistice shall be established in all sectors of Palestine;

(2) Calls upon the parties directly involved in the conflict in Palestine, as a further provisional measure under Article 40 of the Charter, to seek agreement forthwith, by negotiations conducted either directly or through the Acting Mediator, with a view to the immediate establishment of the armistice, including:

(a) The delineation of permanent armistice demarcation lines beyond which the armed forces of the respective parties shall not move;

(b) Such withdrawal and reduction of their armed forces as will ensure the maintenance of the armistice during the transition to permanent peace in Palestine.[16]

In adopting this approach, Bunche did not abandon the pursuit of other objectives. He retained his commitment to the Bernadotte plan and continued to work for its endorsement by the Assembly. He also continued to press for Israel's withdrawal to the lines of October 14. Meanwhile, the armistice approach served its immediate purpose of averting the crisis over Israel's withdrawal. Even before the Security Council adopted its resolution calling for an armistice, Bunche drew up a plan for withdrawal, the separation of forces, and the establishment of a neutral zone between Egyptian and Israeli forces, and had it submitted to the parties on November 14. While Israel considered its reply, the Security Council passed the resolution calling for an armistice. The new resolution enabled Israel to evade the question of withdrawal by combining its reply to Bunche's specific withdrawal and separation of forces plan with the reply to the two Security Council resolutions calling for withdrawal and for the establishment of an armistice respectively.[17]

Bunche termed Israel's reply "statesmanlike";[18] the threat of crisis was averted. But the question of withdrawal remained a major issue, as Egypt made its acceptance of armistice negotiations conditional upon Israel's withdrawal. And Britain, still hopeful of salvaging the territorial arrangements of the Bernadotte plan, also continued to press for the withdrawal at the meetings of the Security Council's subcommittee.

The Armistice: Agreement in Principle

The conclusion of the armistice agreements involved two steps: bringing the parties to accept an armistice in principle, and detailed negotiation of the agreements.

It is difficult to assess Bunche's contribution to the first of these steps, because the circumstances in which each state found itself seem to have been sufficient reason for them to accept the principle of armistice. It was very difficult for Israel to endure the burdens of war indefinitely. An armistice could create a more stable and secure situation, which would enable Israel to demobilize some of its forces and reduce the defense burden. It would also have some diplomatic advantages. In giving the UN an alternative goal, it might help prevent endorsement of the Bernadotte plan in the General Assembly. Moreover, it offered the tactical advantage of extricating Israel from the predicament in which it found itself as a result of its refusal to withdraw to the lines of October 14. Armistice negotiations about agreed demarcation lines would circumvent the question of withdrawal and render the October 14 lines obsolete.

In early January, following Israel's second successful

offensive against Egyptian forces, there was some debate in Israel on whether it should enter into armistice talks, or press its advantage to force Egypt into peace negotiations. Yigal Allon, at that time the commander of the Egyptian front, opposed the armistice and advocated the continuation of military pressure until Egypt agreed to peace. But the government was faced with a British threat to intervene on Egypt's behalf and with American warnings to Israel not to risk a confrontation with Britain. In the government's view, this prevented Israel from pressing its advantage any further. Similar considerations deterred Israel from trying to improve its military position and bargaining prospects on the eastern front, where it faced the Jordanian and Iraqi armies. Under these circumstances, an armistice appeared attractive. It was hoped that it might serve as a prelude to peace.[19]

Egypt's decision to attend the Rhodes armistice talks has usually been explained by the military pressures to which it was subject. These were of crucial importance, but an overemphasis on the military pressures tends to obscure the underlying political considerations that influenced Egyptian policy. The military considerations were simple. As a consequence of the October fighting a considerable Egyptian force was encircled at Faluja. The Egyptian government and military were greatly concerned about the fate of these encircled forces, and sought ways to extricate them with minimal loss of face. Yet this predicament did not induce Egypt to enter into the armistice negotiations, to which it had agreed in principle. As a condition for entering into negotiations, Egypt demanded that Israel first comply with the Security Council's decision of November 4 and withdraw its forces in accordance with Bunche's request. On December 22 Israel launched another major offensive, routing the Egyptian forces and penetrating deep into Sinai. The Egyptian forces in the Gaza Strip were cut off and it seemed that this area too would soon fall to Israel. Under the pressure of another Security Council cease-fire resolution (December 29),

British threats, and American warnings, Israel withdrew from Sinai—but not before the Egyptian army had been incapacitated. Thus, it can be said that Egypt agreed to enter into negotiations under duress. Refusal or even delay would have brought on Egypt additional military disasters, with incalculable domestic political consequences.[20]

This was probably a sufficient reason for Egypt to drop its conditions and enter into immediate negotiations. But it obscures the highly important political background of this decision. For months Egypt and Jordan had been engaged in bitter competition for control of the Arab parts of Palestine. Bernadotte's proposals had intensified the rivalry and each side sought to rally support for its claim. A Palestinian congress, which met in Gaza under the auspices of Egypt and the Arab League, proclaimed on October 1, 1948, the establishment of an "All-Palestine Government." King Abdullah's response was to convene a rival Palestinian congress in Jericho on December 1. This congress called for the unification of Palestine and Transjordan and proclaimed Abdullah as King of All Palestine.[21]

The Arab coalition was falling apart, and Egypt and Jordan sought to reach separate agreements with Israel in the hope of protecting their gains. As early as October, Jordan explored the prospects of Israeli acquiescence to the annexation of the territory it held on the West Bank, and tried to find out Israel's intentions for Gaza, which both Jordan and Egypt coveted. Israel's response was noncommittal, and the talks continued, overlapping the Egyptian-Israeli negotiations at Rhodes. Dayan relates that at one meeting with King Abdullah, the king urged Israel "in the strongest possible terms not to give Gaza to Egypt. He himself [Abdullah] needed it as an outlet to the Mediterranean. He had no doubt that we could come to terms on this point. The essential thing was not to allow Gaza to go to the Egyptians. 'Take it yourselves,' he said, 'give it to the devil, but don't let Egypt have it!' "[22]

Egypt, notwithstanding its public pronouncements that negotiations with Israel were out of the question and while still insisting on Israeli withdrawal to the October 14 lines, approached Israel in an attempt to explore terms for a settlement. Specifically Egypt sought to find out whether Israel would accept Egyptian jurisdiction over the coastal strip south of Ashdod and the strip along the Egyptian-Palestinian border, which had been allocated to the Arab state in the 1947 UN partition resolution. Egypt also wanted Israel to withdraw from the areas in the south that had not been allocated to it in the partition plan. Ben-Gurion reports that the Israeli Cabinet discussed the matter on November 4, and authorized the foreign minister to continue the contacts. Israel was prepared to discuss Egyptian annexation of the desert strip along the international border, but rejected their annexation of the coastal strip.[23]

Lebanon also seemed eager to enter into negotiations, hoping to bring about the evacuation of a number of Lebanese villages that Israel occupied.

The most reluctant to negotiate was Syria, and it required strenuous efforts on the part of Bunche and American diplomats to obtain Syrian consent to armistice negotiations, but in this case too, acceptance can be explained by the political and strategic circumstances in which Syria found itself. After Egypt had concluded an armistice agreement, and Lebanon and Jordan were in the midst of negotiations, Syria risked having to face Israel alone. Finally, on March 21, Syria notified Bunche that, in principle, it was willing to accept the Security Council's call.[24]

Thus in the case of Egypt, Jordan, and Lebanon, Bunche did not have to overcome any basic reluctance to negotiate with Israel. All three were disposed to enter into negotiations with the purpose of seeking a political settlement; Bunche's task was to transform this willingness into formal armistice negotiations. He contributed to the convening of the armistice conferences mainly by his availability. Most important, he enabled the Arab states to save face by justifying their attendance as the response to the request of the UN Acting Mediator, rather than to Israeli pressure.

The Armistice Negotiations

There were four armistice agreements: Egypt-Israel, Lebanon-Israel, Jordan-Israel, and Syria-Israel. Bunche played an important role in concluding three of the agreements. Much of the negotiations between Jordan and Israel were conducted in direct talks without Bunche's presence—perhaps without his knowledge. In this case, his role was minor. In all other cases, his contribution was both procedural and substantive.

At the procedural level, we must include the banal, but crucial contribution of "good offices." Bunche convened the conferences, arranged for an agreed venue, and provided all the technical arrangements. Theoretically, any third party could have done this. Yet the fact that a UN mediator was available greatly expedited these arrangements and helped avert complications.

Bunche also received much praise as a skillful chairman. Bunche could influence the agenda and the atmosphere of the meetings; he apparently had great impact on both. His ability to melt the icy atmosphere that prevailed at the outset of the Egyptian-Israeli meeting was noted by Eytan, who observed that "if the delegations set the pace, Dr. Bunche set the tone."[25] This was no mean contribution: a tense conference can have positive results, but a relaxed atmosphere undoubtedly facilitates agreement. In fact, he chaired only two conferences, the Egyptian and the Jordanian; one of his deputies, Henri Vigier, chaired the Lebanese and Syrian conferences. Another important contribution that Bunche made as chairman was to help maintain secrecy. Even his reports to the Security Council were sparing of details.[26] The preservation of secrecy facilitated agreement in that it prevented domestic political repercussions that might have hampered the negotiations.

However, Bunche's most important impact as chairman was to keep the conference in session until agreement was reached. Bunche relates that at one point when the Rhodes negotiations seemed to be deadlocked, an Arab delegate proposed that the chairman call for an adjournment. Bunche refused. He observed that "in a sense the delegations there were trapped because once having brought them to the island the negotiations would continue until one or both of delegations themselves would take the responsibility for breaking them off."[27] Since neither side was prepared to take the responsibility for breaking off the negotiations, they continued until an armistice agreement was eventually concluded.

On the substantive level, the construction of the framework of the armistice agreements may be considered one of Bunche's major accomplishments. Someone had to design the pattern. The fact that Bunche proposed the framework lent it authority, and prevented much debate and disagreement. Bunche's intelligence, expert knowledge of the problems, and skill in draftsmanship were undoubtedly of value in this.

But Bunche's most important substantive contribution was in formulating compromise solutions to issues on which the parties disagreed. There were plenty of these—concerning principles, territorial delimitations, and demilitarization arrangements. It is striking that even on such important issues, governments were willing to accept Bunche's compromises. Before explaining how Bunche effected such changes, it might be instructive to list the most difficult issues on which the parties were divided.

The Egyptian negotiations began with a fundamental contradiction between the Egyptian and Israeli views about the principles that were to guide territorial apportionment. Egypt, seeking to retain as much of the Negev as possible, proposed that the Security Council resolution of November 4, calling for the withdrawal of forces that had advanced beyond the positions held on October 14, be implemented. Israel claimed that the situation that had existed prior to October 14, with Egypt interfering with supplies to the Israeli-held portions of the Negev, was unacceptable and inherently unstable. Bunche's compromise consisted of incorporating both principles in the armistice agreement. Article 4 of the agreement thus affirmed "the principle that no military or political advantage should be gained under the truce ordered by the Security Council is recognized. . . . It is also recognized that the basic purposes and spirit of the Armistice would not be served by the restoration of previously held military positions. . . ."[28] The fact that the resultant mixture was not a clear ruling was less important than that it was accepted by both parties. Another controversy arose about Israel allegedly reneging on a commitment to release the besieged Egyptian forces at Faluja by January 25. Bunche resolved this by proposing that Israel allow supplies into the besieged area.[29]

However, on at least one occasion Bunche's compromise proposals delayed agreement, rather than expediting it. Egypt demanded that Israel evacuate Beersheba. Bunche at first supported an Egyptian request that it be permitted to appoint a "civilian governor" for the town. After Israel had rejected this, Bunche proposed a compromise whereby Egypt would drop its demand for a governor, and Israel would withdraw its forces from the town and confine its presence to Beersheba's vicinity. Israel rejected this too. But since these proposals had originated with Bunche and been endorsed by the U.S., Egypt could not easily back down. Only after further diplomatic exchanges involving UN Secretary-General Trygve Lie, Washington, and Moscow did Bunche alter his position. This enabled the Egyptians to yield too, and the deadlock was resolved.[30]

In the Lebanese negotiations, Israel made its withdrawal from Lebanese border villages conditional upon the withdrawal of Syrian forces from Lebanon and from areas that were captured by Syria west of the old Syria-Palestine international border. Furthermore, Israel requested minor rectifications of the old Lebanon-Palestine border. The negotiations, held at a customs post on the Lebanon-Israel boundary, were chaired by one of Bunche's deputies, Henri Vigier. Bunche was at Rhodes presiding over the Jordan-Israel conference, but he nevertheless participated in working out a compromise. The compromise supported the withdrawal of Syrian forces from Lebanon, but did not admit a link between Syrian withdrawal from the area Syria occupied along the Syrian-Israeli border and the Lebanese negotiations. He proposed that at one sector the boundary be amended so as to place a road within Israeli control, but he did not accept Israel's other claims for border rectification.[31]

In the Syrian negotiations, the central issue was Israel's demand that the Syrian forces withdraw to the old international border, which would constitute the Armistice Demarcation Line. Syria, on the other hand, wished to retain the territory it had occupied during the war. This controversy was also referred to Bunche, who had already returned to Lake Success. Once again Bunche formulated an acceptable compromise: the Syrian forces were withdrawn to the border that became the Armistice Demarcation Line, but certain areas along the border were demilitarized.[32]

As already mentioned, Bunche's contribution to the Jordanian negotiations was more limited. The crucial negotiations did not take place at the Rhodes armistice conference, but were conducted secretly in Amman between King Abdullah and Israeli representatives. There were two major issues. One arose from Iraq's desire to withdraw its forces from Samaria, and Jordan's intention to take over the territory evacuated by Iraq. In return for acquiescence in the Jordanian takeover, Israel demanded a strip of territory approximately three miles wide, running the length of the Iraqi front, on the grounds that this was vital for the defense of its narrow "waist," and provided other important advantages. Israel threatened that unless Jordan agreed, its forces would move to take over the entire area that the Iraqis were about to evacuate. Implied in the threat was an attractive offer: Israeli acquiescence to Abdullah's annexation of the West Bank areas that were already under his control and of most of Samaria, which had hitherto been held by the Iraqi army. The second issue in the Jordanian negotiations concerned the triangular area north of Eilat. Jordan's Arab Legion had taken up positions in the area, and Jordan aimed at annexation here too. While the negotiations were in progress, Israeli forces moved into Eilat, and the Jordanians were compelled to retreat to the international border. King Abdullah appealed to Britain and the United States to help him counter the Israeli presence, but their intervention was ineffective. Jordan consequently accepted Israel's demand for the strip along the Iraqi front and for the incorporation of the southern Negev in Israel. The agreement was concluded on March 31. The terms of this agreement were incorporated into the framework of the armistice agreement that was signed at Rhodes on April 3.[33]

Although Bunche played no part in helping Jordan and Israel reach agreement on these issues, he nevertheless facilitated it. The pattern of armistice agreements that he had shaped provided a basis for the negotiations. Moreover, the conference that he chaired at Rhodes served to legitimize the agreement in the eyes of an Arab public, which acquiesced in the UN-sponsored armistice agreements but was critical of any other dealings with Israel.

An Evaluation

Like his predecessor, Bunche also represented the UN. His mission was hindered by some of the same handicaps—he faced the same problem and the same parties as Bernadotte's mission did. Yet he was more successful than Bernadotte.

We may start the search for an explanation of this contrast in Bunche's background and personality.[34] Bunche was a black American. He grew up in a disadvantaged environment, went to UCLA, and earned a Ph.D. from

Harvard. In the 1930s he was Professor of Government at Howard University. During the Second World War he worked for the Office of Strategic Services (OSS) in Washington, and subsequently served with the State Department. Upon his appointment as Acting Mediator, he had already completed eighteen months of intensive work on Palestine. His involvement began early in 1947, when he served as director of the Department of Trusteeship and Information from Non-Self-Governing Territories in the UN Secretariat, and Trygve Lie asked him to study possible solutions to the Palestine problem. In the spring of 1947 he was appointed to the staff of UNSCOP, the United Nations Special Committee on Palestine, which had recommended partition. After the partition plan was adopted by the General Assembly, Bunche became principal secretary of the UN's Palestine Commission, established to plan for the transfer of authority from the British government to the new states. When Bernadotte was appointed mediator, Trygve Lie sent Bunche to head Bernadotte's secretariat as his own "special representative."[35] Bunche was highly knowledgeable about the problem in all its many details, and became familiar with all the ideas and proposals to solve it. His position also brought him into close contact with many officials—Arab, Israeli, British, and American. In addition to his acquaintance with the political leaders, he also developed a wide network of contacts in the bureaucracies.

Bunche's personal attributes greatly facilitated his work. He was creative, articulate, and possessed remarkable drafting skill. He is said to have had charm and a sense of humor. His intelligence, his ability to circumvent difficult issues by vague formulations, and his personal charm combined to make him a gifted salesman of ideas and compromise formulae. In contrast to Bernadotte, he was a realist. He was usually able to gauge the limits of his influence and avoid confrontations he could not win. He was also able to recognize changes in the political and military environment and adjust his policies accordingly.

These attributes helped him in several ways. One important function in which he apparently excelled was the devising of compromises. In this task he drew on his intellectual abilities, as well as his political talents. It required an understanding of the issues and their implications, of the political constraints under which the leaders of the parties involved operated, and of the interests of the great powers. It also required drafting skill and tact. His contemporaries' praise, as well as the fact that a high proportion of his proposals were accepted, testify to Bunche's ingenuity and effectiveness. Probably the most complicated situation concerned the delimitation of the Egyptian-Israeli armistice line. Bunche had to consider here not only Egyptian and Israeli interests, but also Jordanian pretensions, British aspirations, and American predicaments; hence the protracted negotiations over the status of Beersheba. In the end, it was the frozen front line that determined the shape of the Armistice Demarcation Line. The losers received some consolation from Article XI, which perhaps gave them some measure of hope for the future in saying that no provision of the agreement "shall in any way prejudice the rights, claims and positions of either Party hereto in the ultimate peaceful settlement of the Palestine question."

A criticism that can be directed at Bunche's compromise formulae is that they were ambiguous; they covered up disagreements without resolving them. Bunche undoubtedly hoped that such issues would either be superseded by events and become irrelevant, or else be resolved peacefully in due course. This did not always happen. In some cases, most notably Bunche's compromise formulae concerning the demilitarized zone along the Syrian-Israeli line, the disagreements reemerged vehemently.[36]

It is not enough to draft a compromise; it is also necessary to persuade the parties to accept it. In this Bunche was almost always assisted by the energetic efforts of the U.S. diplomatic mission, acting under orders from Washington in close cooperation with Bunche. The intensity and extent of American involvement in the armistice negotiations is in striking contrast to the sporadic and hesitant intervention during Bernadotte's tenure as mediator. The new style of U.S. involvement was in part on its own initiative, but Bunche also stimulated this participation by his repeated requests that American diplomats intervene in one capital or another. In this he was reinforced by frequent appeals from the parties to the conflict, who also asked for American diplomatic intervention. Throughout the negotiations Bunche maintained constant communications with Washington, both through formal channels via the UN Secretariat and through informal direct channels to his former colleagues in the State Department. Yet communication channels alone cannot assure collaboration: this was the result of the respect in which Bunche was held. Washington was disposed to accept his judgment and advice, and to accede to his frequent requests for diplomatic intervention in support of the stance he took and the compromises he advanced. Washington's views carried greater influence in Middle Eastern capitals than the views of the UN Acting Mediator. But Bunche undoubtedly deserves credit for his ability to win and sustain the willing and effective cooperation of the American diplomatic machine.[37]

Bunche considered himself an international civil servant, but the governments that dealt with him attributed greater significance to his being an American with connections in Washington than to his UN status. His background endowed him with a measure of personal authority and influence that Bernadotte did not possess. Bunche's authority and influence amounted to bargaining power. When Bernadotte sought to induce changes in Arab or Israeli attitudes, he occasionally threatened that he would report matters to the UN—a threat that had little effect on the parties concerned. Bunche's displeasure had to be taken somewhat more seriously, since he had the power not merely to embarrass through public criticism, but also to stir up the Washington bureaucracy. This could produce American diplomatic intervention and affect U.S. attitudes and relationships with the government in question on other issues, too. Each of the principals in the conflict had subjects under discussion with the United States. Israel was interested in aid and in admission to the UN. Jordan wanted recognition, diplomatic relations, and also support of its candidacy for UN membership. Egypt desired aid, and a more benevolent attitude toward Egyptian efforts to revise its treaty relationship with Britain. Syria was interested in aid, and in assurances that the United States would not support King Abdullah's scheme for a "Greater Syria" under his rule. This is not to say that Bunche was considered all-powerful, but because of his connections in Washington, he was treated with greater respect than Bernadotte was.

Bunche's qualifications and his bargaining power help to explain his successes, but they cannot explain them entirely. We must also take into consideration his specific goals and the circumstances under which he worked to accomplish them.

As we have seen, all five states had come to view the armistice as an optimal solution. Israel accepted the armistice because it could not press its military advantage any further. Egypt, Jordan, Lebanon, and Syria acquiesced because it promised to protect them from further Israeli pressure. Thus, one can argue that it was the situation, or specifically the balance of forces, that enabled the conclusion of the armistice agreements. But the situation by itself did not create the armistice; it only made it possible. Bunche's contribution lay in recognizing the reality of the situation and in defining a limited goal that was commensurate with his restricted bargaining power. He no longer tried to establish a framework for a settlement of the entire conflict. An armistice would entail relatively little change in Egyptian and Jordanian policies. They had formerly agreed to a truce; now they were asked to accept an armistice. They had already negotiated with Israel secretly; now they were asked to accept negotiations publicly. The war had established front lines that were expected to be frozen under the truce. Now they were asked to reaffirm their acceptance of these provisional lines, pending a final settlement. All this required some adjustments in policies, but did not require any drastic or far-reaching revision; under the prevailing circumstances, this did not require too much pressure from the mediator. His bargaining power and his ability to exercise pressure were small, but sufficient to accomplish this limited goal.

Bunche's two major failures also call for an explanation. The fact that the UN General Assembly did not endorse Bernadotte's recommendation was Britain's failure, as well as Bunche's, but Bunche should not have set himself this objective. It was a double mistake: first, he obviously shared in Bernadotte's miscalculation in formulating the package; he considered that its endorsement by the General Assembly was a realistic goal and he believed that it would advance the settlement. He erred again in adhering to this goal after becoming Acting Mediator and not redefining his priorities upon assuming office.

It was unrealistic of Bunche to expect that the comprehensive settlement proposal submitted by Bernadotte could obtain a two-thirds majority in the General Assembly. He should have foreseen that the many parties affected—Israel, the Arab states, Britain, the U.S., the Soviet Union, and other actors—would all seek to influence the outcome of the General Assembly proceedings. In view of the forthcoming presidential election in the U.S., sustained American support could not be taken for granted. Moreover, he ought to have taken into account that the deliberations at the UN were likely to take many weeks, and that in the meantime the unstable truce in Palestine might collapse and undermine the political and military assumptions on which the recommendations were based. Bunche's involvement with the Bernadotte plan was a failure of judgment.

Bunche's attempt to force Israel's withdrawal to the

lines of October 14 was another miscalculation. He was apparently much impressed by the resolve that the great powers demonstrated in the Security Council resolution of July 15, threatening sanctions in the event of noncompliance with the cease-fire. Yet he overlooked the difference in the situation. It was easier to get great power backing for a cease-fire than for a withdrawal order of debatable merits. Only Britain supported it strongly. The Soviet Union withheld its backing (and may even have encouraged Israel), because it believed the withdrawal would facilitate Bernadotte's proposal to hand the Negev to the Arabs, and thus enable Britain to establish military bases there. The Western members of the Security Council recognized the instability inherent in the restoration of the October 14 lines.

This episode, though another failure of judgment on Bunche's part, can also be hailed as an example of his political talent and realism, for he quickly found a way to retreat without losing face. He set himself a new goal, the establishment of an armistice. It was a goal for which he could expect to obtain Security Council support, and which was a much more suitable way of stabilizing the situation in Palestine and ending the war.

In summary, Bunche's successes can be explained by the fortuitous coincidence of circumstances, his own astute political judgment and flexibility, and bargaining power. The absence of any of these ingredients would have spelled failure.

Compared to Bernadotte and to some of his successors, Bunche can be considered a successful mediator. It was not his fault that his accomplishments did not endure, and that the armistice agreements were not followed by peace, as he and others had hoped.

FOUR

The United Nations Conciliation Commission

Another intermediary, the United Nations Conciliation Commission for Palestine (PCC), was established by a General Assembly resolution on December 11, 1948. It conducted intensive negotiations through much of 1949, and continued its efforts, albeit less intensively, in 1950 and 1951. These endeavors ended in total failure; the Conciliation Commission was unable to accomplish any of the tasks assigned to it.

Several writers hold that the circumstances that prevailed when the Conciliation Commission was launched were particularly propitious for a settlement. U.S. participation in the commission was widely expected to endow it with sufficient influence to obtain concessions necessary for a settlement. The commission's subsequent failure, despite the allegedly auspicious circumstances, has stimulated inquiry. Some have attributed the commission's failure to insufficient American backing. Another view shifts the brunt of the blame to the commission's own tactics: convening conferences at which all interested Arab states were present, instead of engaging in conciliation between Israel and each Arab state separately; and accepting the Arab refusal to meet Israeli representatives in face-to-face negotiations. In fact, the reasons for the commission's failure are more complex, and deserve a thorough examination.

A Golden Opportunity?

Opinions vary on the exact time when the alleged opportunities for a settlement existed, as well as about the specific conditions that made these particular moments in history propitious for peace.

Fred Khouri claims that "the UN and the big powers allowed a golden opportunity to slip by" in the fall of 1948, after Bernadotte submitted his recommendations to the UN General Assembly. According to Khouri, much of the blame rests with the U.S. and Britain, who were then capable of exerting pressure on the parties, but failed "to agree on a 'firm and equitable decision' [as Bernadotte had recommended] and did not provide the strong backing required to implement even those decisions which were made."[1] Khouri believes that the circumstances allowed for a settlement to be thus imposed as long as: (1) The Cold War had not intruded into the Middle East; (2) Western prestige in the Middle East remained high; (3) Arab and Israeli positions had not yet "fully hardened," and incidents along the armistice demarcation lines had not produced tension and acute antipathy. Khouri holds that such conditions existed in 1948 and 1949, disappearing only by the second half of 1951.

Nadav Safran and David Forsythe claim that chances for a settlement disappeared shortly after the conclusion of the armistice agreements. To quote Forsythe:

> . . . flexibility and pragmatism were there in the Arabs' diplomacy, as indicated by negotiations under Bunche and under the CCP at Beirut prior to Lausanne. The flexibility existed at least until the armistice agreements were signed, reducing the threat of Israeli coercion, and until the weakness of Western prodding on the Arabs indicated the reduction of an outside stimulus to peacemaking.[2]

After the conclusion of the armistice agreements, only Jordan among the Arab states remained interested in peace, as is evidenced by the negotiations it conducted with Israel. Safran has attributed Jordan's willingness to make peace, although the armistice now protected it from military sanctions, to the rewards that it expected to receive: the consolidation of its territorial gains from the 1948 war, and the acquisition of an outlet to the Mediterranean through free-port rights in Haifa.[3]

Scholarly analyses as well as contemporary impressions by diplomats share the view that the main obstacle to peace—the Arab refusal to accept Israel's existence—could have been overcome in the early months of 1949. (Some would say even later.)[4] A certain ambiguity in statements emanating from the Arab side suggested some flexibility in their stand. Mark Ethridge, the U.S. representative on the commission, reported from Cairo on February 14 that the Egyptian foreign minister had informed the commission that Egypt "would not approve 'historical injustice in Palestine.' " This phrase was a code for the refusal to accept Israel's existence. Nevertheless, the same telegram also reported that the foreign minister expressed a preference for direct negotiations with Israel, but added that Egypt would have to wait and see whether Israel wanted peace, and whether it would abide by UN resolutions.[5] Flexibility was also seen in the shift of emphasis in diplomatic contacts, which now gave increased prominence to the issues of refugees and boundaries. In 1948, the Arabs had spoken mainly of the inadmissibility of partition. Such statements did not cease, but the Conciliation Commission, and American diplomats, interpreted the Arabs' focusing their claims on refugee and boundary issues as an indication that they were contemplating recognizing and making peace with Israel.[6]

Those who claim that the Arab position was flexible seem cognizant of the Arab governments' fears of domestic political reactions to a peace with Israel. However, Khouri, and to some extent Forsythe too, believe that this obstacle could have been overcome had the U.S. exerted sufficient pressure, which would have provided the Arabs with a face-saving excuse for making peace.[7] Some American diplomats, including Ethridge, held a similar view, claiming that Egypt, and perhaps other Arab governments, would have welcomed an imposed peace. Presumably, the terms would have been such as to enable the Arab governments to save face, and international pressure would have been such as to make it clear that the governments had no choice but to yield.[8]

Safran and Forsythe blame the commission at least in part for the failure to achieve peace in the first half of 1949. According to Safran, "the commission made the fatal mistake of assembling all the Arab delegations together as one party and thus put them in a position in which none of them would dare make any concession for fear of being accused by the others of being soft on Israel."[9] More generally, the commission's tactics served to shield the Arab governments from Israeli pressure, and to create conditions for inter-Arab rivalry to hinder diplomatic flexibility.

Rephrased in the concepts of timing discussed in Chapter 1, Safran claims that peace was within reach when one side maintained a military advantage and the other felt threatened. The intermediaries' intervention served to protect the weaker party and to create a stalemate under which attitudes remained uncompromising; peace therefore remained elusive. Khouri, on the other hand, does not regard an imbalance as propitious for peacemaking, and believes that peace could have been attained if that advantage had been eliminated. He claims that had the United States and the UN intervened more forcefully and exerted pressure on both sides (thus creating a *stalemate* in the military-political contest between Israel and the Arab states), peace could have been attained. Implicitly, Khouri and Safran disagree in their assessments of the situation. Safran considers intervention to have caused a stalemate that hindered a settlement, while Khouri thinks that the external intervention was not forceful enough to create a stalemate, and that it was Israel's advantage that hindered a settlement.

Further assessment of these views requires a detailed examination of American policies, the commission's tactics, and Arab and Israeli responses. A brief summary of the commission's activities will help place them in their proper context.

The Commission's Activities—A Summary Record[10]

The commission's terms of reference, defined by the General Assembly resolution of December 11, 1948 that established the commission, included specific instructions as well as some phrased in more general terms. The general mandate charged the commission to assume the functions assigned to Bernadotte as UN Mediator, to carry out specific functions assigned to it by the General Assembly or the Security Council, and "to assist the Governments and authorities concerned to achieve a final settlement of all questions outstanding between them." The specific instructions charged the commission to prepare and submit to the next General Assembly proposals for an international regime for Jerusalem, and "to facilitate the repatriation, resettlement and economic and social rehabilitation of the refugees and the payment of compensation."[11] The General Assembly appointed the United States, France, and Turkey to serve as the commission.

Although the December 11 resolution requested that the commission "begin its functions at once," it did not meet until January 17. Even then, Ethridge, the American representative, was still unavailable; he joined his colleagues, who had established their headquarters in Jerusalem, only on February 2. In the meanwhile, important developments had occurred in the Middle East: Israel had launched an offensive against the Egyptian forces in the Negev, and as a result Egypt was persuaded to enter into armistice negotiations; and on January 13, Bunche had opened the Egyptian-Israel armistice conference at Rhodes.

When the Conciliation Commission assembled in Jerusalem in early February, it decided not to involve itself in Bunche's armistice negotiations, since their success "might be jeopardized" if responsibility were transferred at such a delicate stage from Bunche to the commission. This decision marked not only the separation between the armistice negotiations and the search for a final settlement, but also the growth of dissension between the two peacemaking missions.

During February, the commission visited Israel, Jordan, Egypt, Saudi Arabia, Iraq, Syria, and Lebanon in order to establish contacts with political leaders and officials and hold preliminary discussions with them. In these discussions, the Arab governments, with the exception of Jordan, informed the commission "that they were not prepared to enter into general peace negotiations with Israel until the refugee question had been settled, at least in principle," and that "the acceptance by Israel of the right of the refugees, as expressed in paragraph 11 of the resolution 194 (III), to return to their homes, must be regarded as the condition *sine qua non* for the discussion of other questions." The commission found that "Israel, on the other hand, was not prepared to accept as a principle the injunctions contained in paragraph 11, and further, was not prepared to negotiate on any point separately, and outside the framework of a general settlement."[12] Only Jordan expressed its readiness to enter into bilateral peace negotiations without insisting on any preconditions.

The commission considered it inadvisable to assist Jordanian-Israeli negotiations for a separate peace. However, it did involve itself in the Jordanian-Israeli negotiations on Jerusalem, with the double objective of assisting the parties to reach an agreement on the division of the city and of ensuring that any agreement was compatible with its mandate to prepare proposals for an international regime for Jerusalem.[13]

In early March, the Arab states were invited to send delegates to a conference in Beirut, there to continue their discussions with the commission. At the conference, which met on March 21, the refugee question became the dominant issue. The commission's efforts struggled to find a formula that would reconcile the Arab condition that Israel must accept the principle of repatriation *prior* to any peace negotiations, with Israel's insistence that the refugee question must be discussed as part of a peace settlement. In this it succeeded. The Arab delegations, except that of Iraq, were persuaded to drop their stipulation of settling the refugee problem before discussing other issues. Egypt, Jordan, Lebanon, and Syria agreed to continue their talks with the commission at a neutral location where the commission could also maintain contacts with Israeli representatives. Accordingly, it was arranged to meet at Lausanne on April 27.

Before, during, and after the Beirut conference, the commission made considerable efforts to persuade Israel to modify its position on the refugees and to proclaim its acceptance of the principle of repatriation as embodied in the General Assembly resolution. These efforts were strongly supported by American diplomacy, and perhaps by other governments as well. Israel countered that as the General Assembly resolution stated that the refugees who wished to return "should live at peace with their neighbours," the question should be discussed in the context of a peace settlement. Moreover, Israel made it clear that because of considerations of security, and of the economic and social problems involved, it would admit only a limited number of refugees.

When the parties assembled at Lausanne at the end of April, armistice agreements had already been concluded with Egypt, Lebanon, and Jordan. At Lausanne, Israel tried to persuade the commission to convene a joint meeting of Arab and Israeli delegations. The Arabs refused to have any official contacts with Israeli representatives. (There were nevertheless some secret informal meetings.)[14] The commission, and the governments represented on it, continued to press Israel to alter its stand on the refugee question, and thus help create an atmosphere that would get the Lausanne talks off to a good start. While waiting for these efforts to bear fruit, the commission tried to open the way to negotiations by another route. It obtained the parties' signature to a protocol that might serve to link the refugee problem with the territorial issues. This protocol stated that the commission, anxious to achieve the objectives of the General Assembly resolution "regarding refugees, the respect for their rights and the preservation of their property, as well as territorial and other questions," has proposed to the parties "that the working document attached hereto be taken as a basis for discussions with the commission." The working document, significantly untitled, was the map of Palestine showing the partition boundaries according to the General Assembly resolution of November 29, 1947. The protocol further stated that the parties understood that their exchanges of views with the commission "will bear upon the territorial adjustments necessary to the above-indicated objectives." Israel attached reservations to its signature of the protocol, stating that Israel fully reserved its position, and that the protocol did not prejudice its right to "express itself freely on the matters at issue." Israel meant to indicate that it regarded that map as only one basis for discussion, and that it was entitled to propose other bases.[15]

The protocol notwithstanding, the talks failed to make progress. In deference to American pressure, Israel permitted the return of a limited number of refugees under a family reunion program. Furthermore, in July it announced that it would accept 100,000 refugees within the context of a general settlement. But these concessions failed to break the deadlock; the Arab delegations continued to insist that Israel accept the principle that the refugees had the right to be repatriated. The parties remained far apart on the territorial question too. The Arab delegations proposed that the November 29, 1947 partition boundaries be revised to their advantage, while Israel proposed that it retain the territories it held by virtue of the armistice agreements, and that the boundaries be revised to Israel's advantage. On only one question was progress accomplished: both sides agreed to establish a mixed committee to discuss arrangements whereby frozen assets in Israel and in the Arab states could be released on a reciprocal basis.

As it became clear that the Lausanne talks were deadlocked, the United States took the initiative and sent to the area an Economic Survey Mission charged with preparing an integrated program for economic development that would facilitate the repatriation, resettlement, and economic and social rehabilitation of the refugees. The Survey Mission, headed by Gordon Clapp (a former chairman of the Tennessee Valley Authority), was established as a subsidiary body of the Conciliation Commission, but in fact worked independently of it. Its interim report, submitted in November, served as the basis for the establishment of the United Nations Relief and Works Agency for Palestine (UNRWA). The new agency was intended to shift the emphasis from relief to work and self-help, reflecting the Survey Mission's sentiment that a solution would not be achieved through large-scale repatriation, but rather through the resettlement of the refugees in Arab countries.

The Conciliation Commission's lack of effectiveness prompted the U.S. and some other governments to explore possibilities for restructuring it. The Soviet Union, which regarded the commission as a tool of the Western powers, wanted to abolish it. Israel too would have preferred its dissolution, because the commission hindered separate and direct negotiations between Israel and each of its neighbors. Israel's preference for this method was strengthened by its experience with Jordan. Bypassing the commission, the two sides seemed to be making progress in negotiations for a peace treaty. On the other hand, Egypt and some of the other Arab states wanted the commission not only to continue, but to take a more active role by presenting proposals of its own. In view of these differences, the General Assembly did not adopt any new resolution concerning the commission, which continued to work under its original mandate and composition.

During 1949, through a subcommittee, the commission prepared a proposal "for a permanent international regime for the Jerusalem area which will provide for the maximum local autonomy for distinctive groups consistent with the special international status of the Jerusalem area." The proposal, submitted to the General Assembly in the fall of 1949, tried to take account of the de facto control of the city by Israel and Jordan by assigning to local officials in each sector considerable administrative responsibilities, under the supervision of a UN commissioner and UN governing bodies. The commission's proposal was strongly criticized at the General Assembly, not only by Israel and the Arab states, but also by France (which was a member of the commission) and other Catholic states, as well as by the Soviet bloc. The outcome of the General Assembly debate was a rebuff to the Conciliation Commission; its proposals were rejected, the matter was taken out of its hands, and the elaboration of new proposals was assigned to the UN Trusteeship Council.

During 1950 and 1951 the commission's diplomatic activities were less intensive, and equally unsuccessful. Early in 1950, in a new attempt to break the deadlock, the commission tried to satisfy both the Arab desire for mediation and the Israeli desire for direct negotiations by proposing to set up mixed committees. The commission was deliberately vague about the composition of the committees, their agendas, and their procedures, in the hope that vagueness would facilitate the adoption of the proposal. But several months of negotiations on this procedural proposal failed to get substantive negotiations started, as the Arab States continued to insist on the precondition that Israel first commit itself to the repatriation of the refugees.

In 1951, acting on an American initiative, the commission invited the parties to a conference in Paris in September. There it tried to get negotiations started by proposing that the parties adopt a declaration of non-aggression. When this failed, it presented the parties with proposals for a general settlement, which met with objections from both sides. A few weeks later, the conference was adjourned.

In its November 1951 progress report to the General Assembly, the commission stated that the "unwillingness of the parties fully to implement the General Assembly resolutions under which the Commission is operating, as well as the changes which have occurred in Palestine during the past three years, have made it impossible for the Commission to carry out its mandate."[16] Consequently, the commission moved its headquarters from Jerusalem to New York and its search for a settlement was in fact suspended. In 1961 the U.S. undertook a new initiative, under the Conciliation Commission's label, in an attempt to settle the Arab refugee problem. But Joseph E. Johnson, a prominent American and president of the Carnegie Endowment for International Peace, who was appointed the commission's Special Representative, failed to obtain the parties' agreement to his proposals for simultaneous resettlement and repatriation measures. Although the commission was never formally dissolved, its activity had in fact been terminated.

The Commission's Qualifications

The sponsors of the Conciliation Commission had hoped to set up an effective agency. The three-state membership was intended to assure that the new mediating body would have greater international support than lonely Bernadotte had enjoyed. Moreover, it was believed that the members of the commission, the U.S., France, and Turkey, would be able to influence Arab and Israeli policies. Their influence was seen as deriving not only from their power and status, but also from their presumed relationships with the adversaries. As summarized in the report to Washington by John Foster Dulles, the acting chairman of the

U.S. delegation to the 1948 General Assembly in Paris, the theory was that the "U.S. was moderately pro-Israel, Turkey moderately pro-Arab, and France generally neutral, slightly pro-Israel."[17] Implicitly, influence was believed to be related to the commission's acceptability to the parties.

Although some thought was given to the question of acceptability, it was not an overriding consideration. Britain disqualified itself from serving on the commission, and the U.S. sought Britain's opinion about whether the Arabs would object to American membership on the commission. The U.S. tried to find a slate agreeable to all the parties, but when this proved to be unfeasible, they settled for a "balanced" commission. Israel objected to both France and Turkey. It did not want France on the commission because of its presumed strong commitment to the internationalization of Jerusalem, and was reluctant to see Turkey participate because of its persistent support of Arab positions at the UN. Moreover, neither France nor Turkey had yet recognized Israel. But Israel's objections were to no avail, and the commission's composition was approved by the General Assembly.[18]

Even more interesting is the sponsors' disregard for the parties' opposition to the very establishment of a Conciliation Commission. The Arab states voted against it in the General Assembly. Israel, not yet a member of the UN, did not participate in the vote, but Israeli criticism of the commission's terms of reference was an indirect expression of its displeasure with the entire approach.[19] As with Bernadotte seven months previously, the new intermediary was in fact imposed upon the parties without their consent.

While Arab reservations toward the commission seemed to fade, Israel's deepened. Israel's attitude was reflected in its decision to have the return of refugees in accordance with the family reunion program handled by the Mixed Armistice Commissions (established as part of the armistice agreement), rather than by the Conciliation Commission, and in its preference for channels other than the commission for contacts with Arab leaders.[20] It is difficult to assess the significance of the mutual irritation that this engendered, but an examination of the record suggests that it might have been of some consequence.

Some authors have considered the membership of governments with important interests in the Middle East to have been a disadvantage. According to this view, the members of the Conciliation Commission acted in their own governments' interests, rather than the UN's.[21] This argument brings to the fore the more general question of intermediaries' motivation. The fact that someone is prepared to invest resources—moral, political, or material—in mediation indicates that he has an interest in doing so. The governments that supported the establishment of the commission, and those that served on it, were no exception. This is not to deny their desire for peace. But they did not pursue peace in the abstract; they pursued a settlement consistent with their interests.

All three believed that their interests required the exclusion of Soviet influence from the Middle East. In addition, each apparently hoped that its participation in the commission would help it to promote its own influence in the Middle East. The U.S. wished to promote the preservation of Western strategic interests by facilitating the transfer of British bases from the Suez Canal area (where they were no longer acceptable to Egypt) to an Arab-held Negev. It also hoped to get credit for giving the Arabs the Negev and for inducing Israel to accept the return of a substantial number of refugees. France, apparently sought at one stage to earn Syria's good will by promoting a proposal to alter the Syrian-Israeli boundary to Syria's advantage. France also entertained the specific objective of securing an especially favored status for French religious and cultural institutions in Palestine. Turkey hoped that membership on the commission would enhance its international prestige and its standing in the West.[22] The pursuit of these interests naturally affected the work of the commission by constraining the willingness of the three governments to exert pressure upon the parties.

Committees can be assumed to be less effective mediators than single actors. Coordination between the members of the committee and adjustment of their divergent attitudes may consume much time and effort, thereby reducing the effectiveness of its mediation. The most important disagreement between the members of the commission was between France and the United States with regard to Jerusalem. They also entertained different preferences concerning an ultimate territorial settlement, and in August 1949 the French representative opposed an American suggestion that the commission present its own proposal to the parties. These did not develop into major issues, but the consultations required in order to reach agreement were occasionally cumbersome. However, during 1949, France and Turkey deferred to the U.S. on the whole, and the effectiveness of the commission was thus not appreciably reduced by its trinational composition.[23]

Attention has also been given to the question of whether the commission's effectiveness was impaired by the personnel assigned to serve on it. The personalities who served on the commission were described in detail by both Azcárate and Forsythe.[24] Mark Ethridge, the first American representative on the commission, was a newspaper publisher from Kentucky. By July he had to return to the United States to take care of his business and was succeeded by Paul A. Porter, a lawyer from Washington. Both were energetic and likeable, but not nearly as impressive as Bunche. France's Claude de Boisanger and Turkey's Hussen Yalcin were neither particularly forceful nor particularly active. In a way this facilitated smooth working relations with the American delegate. None of the principal representatives was especially knowledgeable about the Arab-Israeli dispute, but the experts on the commission's staff compensated for this weakness to some extent, as did the commission's principal secretary, Pablo de Azcárate, the veteran Spanish diplomat who had been concerned with the Arab-Israeli dispute as a UN official since early 1948. If some of the governments' representatives on the commission weakened the commission, then it was not because of any serious shortcomings but because of a lack of special talents that could have facilitated their task.

In one respect, the individuals serving on the commission had an adverse effect on its operation. Mediation requires patience and perseverance. However, both Ethridge and Porter assumed their task on a short-term basis. Consequently, they quickly became impatient with the lack of results, and this affected their work. It may be that Ethridge's impatience rendered him more critical of Israel's policies than he would otherwise have been.[25]

But these deficiencies, if deficiencies they were, and the parties' basic reservations concerning the commission and its members do not suffice to explain the commission's failure.

The Commission's Tactics

Four principal tactical errors are considered as contributing significantly to the commission's failure. First, there was a fateful hiatus before the commission's assumption of its task. The decision to establish the commission was taken on December 11, 1948. But, for various reasons, mainly delays in the appointment of the American representative, the commission's first meeting with the full membership present took place only on February 2, 1949, when Ethridge arrived in Jerusalem.

The procrastination had far-reaching consequences, since events in the Middle East continued to unfold rapidly. As we have seen, on December 22, Israel had launched its offensive against the Egyptian army in the Negev. Following the Egyptian defeat, and the threat of British military intervention, it was Bunche, the Acting Mediator, who obtained Egypt's agreement to enter into armistice negotiations. The General Assembly resolution establishing the commission charged it with taking over the mediator's functions. However, since the commission was not yet ready to assume its task, it was Bunche who convened and chaired the Egyptian-Israeli armistice conference.

The second tactical error followed from the first. By the time the commission was ready to function, the Egyptian-Israeli armistice negotiations were already well advanced. Consequently, at its meeting in Jerusalem on or about February 2, the commission decided not to involve itself in the Egyptian-Israeli armistice talks which Bunche was conducting. After the Egyptian-Israeli talks were concluded, the commission decided not to involve itself in the remaining armistice talks with Jordan, Lebanon, and Syria, and leave their conduct as well to the acting mediator.[26] These decisions meant in fact that the commission postponed its efforts to reach a political settlement until the armistice talks had been concluded. Meanwhile, it concerned itself with seeking a solution to the refugee problem and the Jerusalem question. The tensions that reportedly developed between the commission and Bunche stemmed from the former's impatience with the slow pace of the armistice negotiations, and from the latter's concern that the commission's negotiations on the refugees and Jerusalem might affect the armistice talks.

As a result of the postponement of peace talks, the political negotiations were insulated from military considerations. When the Lausanne conference convened, the parties no longer faced the risk of military confrontation. The pressure on them to make the concessions necessary for a settlement was thus greatly reduced.

It would be unfair to attribute all the responsibility for this decision to the commission. In fact, the distinction between the military and the political settlements had long characterized thinking on how to settle the conflict. Bernadotte had suggested the distinction in his final report, Bunche pursued it, and it was adopted by the Security Council in November. This approach was also supported by American officials, who invested much time and effort in thinking about the appropriate strategy for negotiating a settlement and seem to have overlooked the armistice's possible impact on the political negotiations. Even Secretary of State Acheson, whose approach to international politics usually reflected an appreciation of "realist" considerations of power, expressed the view that if "armistice negotiations continue to produce successful results, new possibilities for settlement through normal processes may open up."[27]

Although the scenario of separating the military from the political settlement has been written for it by others, the commission shares the responsibility. It too believed that the conclusion of the armistice would "facilitate its own task considerably,"[28] and by its decisions it confirmed the separation. Had the commission decided differently, and involved itself in the armistice negotiations, it would have linked the military and political talks, and it is possible that their course would have developed differently.

One consequence was that the commission's concern with the refugee problem, while waiting for Bunche to conclude the armistice negotiations, projected this issue onto center stage. Unwittingly, this strengthened the Arab claim that the refugee problem must be given priority and should be handled separately from the question of the political settlement. This created tensions with Israel, as Israel resented the pressure put on it by the commission and the participating governments to make concessions on the refugee question without linking it to the overall political settlement. Israel was not alone in being critical of the commission's emphasis on the refugee problem. King Abdullah of Jordan, who wished to expedite the territorial negotiations, was reported to have commented critically that Mark Ethridge was interested in no other problem but that of the refugees.[29] The commission's emphasis on the refugee question affected the Lausanne negotiations. It encouraged the Arabs to take a rigid position, while it strengthened the Israeli impression that the commission's approach and conception of its task were detrimental to Israeli interests.

A third tactical error was the commission's predilection for convening general conferences with Arab states, instead of trying to tackle the problems on a bilateral basis between Israel and each of its neighbors. As will be recalled, the commission convened a conference with the Arab states in Beirut in March. Subsequently, at Lausanne, the delegations of Egypt, Jordan, Syria, Lebanon, and others representing Palestinian refugees were present. These conferences placed the Arab states in situations that required them to reach a consensus. The record indicates that they usually formed a consensus based on rigid and uncompromising positions, while conciliatory tendencies were denounced as treasonous. Moreover, the negotiating frameworks thus created hindered discussion of the specific problems existing between Israel and each neighbor, and instead focused on general principles concerning the refugees and territorial arrangements.[30] Partly as a result of the preference for dealing with the Arab states collectively, the commission ignored a Jordanian suggestion that it help bring about a Jordanian-Israeli settlement. Indeed, Jordan, which was interested in a peace settlement, was maneuvered by the commission into closing ranks with the other Arab states that were less eager to conclude peace.[31]

It should be noted that the commission convened its conferences despite advice to the contrary from the Israeli foreign minister, the U.S. ambassador to Israel, and British officials. The Jordanian prime minister also expressed preference for a separate conference, not a general one. The commission's insistence is therefore puzzling. There is no evidence that the reasons for it were political. More likely, it stemmed from logistics: lacking its own means of transportation, shuttling between the Middle East capitals presented many difficulties. Ethridge's desire for haste may also have prompted the tactic of assembling the parties at one place in the hope that this would prove quicker than shuttle diplomacy, and may well have contributed to the commission's disregard of the advice it received. In any event, the responsibility for this tactical error rests with the commission.[32]

There is some merit to the claim that the commission committed a fourth error, by not insisting that the Arabs and Israelis negotiate face to face—even though direct negotiations are no guarantee of success. In fact it is known that Arab and Israeli representatives did meet secretly at Lausanne and elsewhere. Yet, the commission erred because accepting the Arab refusal to meet Israeli representatives under its auspices implicitly condoned Arab intransigence, and encouraged the Arab states to maintain rigid negotiating positions. Acceptance of the Arab view on this point undermined the Conciliation Commission's standing and effectiveness from the Israeli viewpoint. In 1950 the commission sought to rectify this mistake, but its proposal to form mixed commissions under its chairmanship was probably too late. The parties no longer expected much from the commission, and were thus less inclined to cooperate with it than they had been in early 1949.[33]

American Policy

Some authors attribute the commission's failure to insufficient American backing. U.S. pressure on the parties—especially on Israel—was inadequate, and when applied, it was not consistently maintained.[34] Such criticism implies that with more powerful and more consistent American backing, the Arab states or Israel, or both, would have been induced to offer sufficient concessions to reach a settlement.

An examination of American policy indicates that this claim is not valid. In fact, the United States did exert its influence through most of 1949, mostly in an attempt to alter Israeli positions. Thereafter, the commission's activity declined. The United States, like other governments, disappointed at the failure of the commission's efforts, showed only sporadic interest in its activities.

The relationship between the commission and the governments constituting it was somewhat ambiguous. Formally, the three states constituting the commission represented the General Assembly; in reality, the General Assembly at that time tended to accept U.S. leadership. As I mentioned previously, the French and Turkish delegates to the commission tended to defer to the U.S. delegate. Thus, the Conciliation Commission came to serve American policy. It was not the U.S. that backed the commission, but the other way around—the commission became an instrument of U.S. diplomacy.

Let us take a look at U.S. policy. This was defined in the instructions handed to Mark Ethridge, under the signature of Acting Secretary of State Robert Lovett, dated January 19, 1949:

> The Acting Secretary of State to Mr. Mark F. Ethridge
>
> TOP SECRET WASHINGTON, January 19, 1949.
>
> SIR: Before you depart for Palestine to assume your duties as the American representative on the Palestine Conciliation Commission, I am setting forth the following basic positions for your guidance:
>
> A) A final settlement on all questions outstanding between the parties in Palestine should be achieved by negotiation as set forth in the General Assembly resolution of December 11, 1948. You should do everything possible as a member of the Conciliation Commission to assist the parties to reach an agreement by this means. You should consult the Department periodically during the course of these negotiations.
>
> B) If it becomes necessary during the course of the negotiations for you to express the views of this Government, you should bear in mind that American policy is based on the following premises:
>
> 1. No modifications should be made in the boundaries of the State of Israel as established by the General

Assembly resolution of November 29, 1947, without the full consent of the State of Israel.

2. If Israel desires additions to its territory as defined under the November 29 resolution, i.e., areas allotted by the General Assembly to the Arabs such as western Galilee and Jaffa, now under Israeli occupation, Israel should make territorial concessions elsewhere, i.e. the southern Negev. Israel is not entitled to keep both the Negev and western Galilee and Jaffa. If there is no agreement between the parties, the Israelis should relinquish western Galilee and Jaffa and the Arabs should relinquish the Israeli portion of the Negev.

3. If Israel desires to retain western Galilee and Jaffa, the southern border of Israel should not be drawn further south than the thirty-first parallel within the territory allotted to Israel under the resolution of November 29.

4. *Status of Jerusalem*—The resolution of December 11 states that the Jerusalem area should be accorded special and separate treatment from the rest of Palestine and should be placed under effective United Nations control. This could be accomplished by appointing a United Nations Commissioner for Jerusalem and by establishing machinery to enable him to supervise the administration of the area, to guarantee free access to the city and the Holy Places, and to insure adequate protection of the latter. The effective administration of the area of Jerusalem should be left to Arabs and Jews, the delineation of the parts of the area to be administered by each party to be determined by agreement.

It is not unlikely that Israel may call for a land corridor to connect the State of Israel with Jerusalem. Agreement to such a demand would not be in accord with the November 29 resolution, which provided only for freedom of access to Jerusalem; moreover, since such a corridor would bisect the territory which the November 29 resolution allotted to the Arabs, it would create a geographical anomaly. In the event, however, that the creation of such a land corridor appears to be essential to a final settlement, Israel should be prepared to make territorial concessions to the Arabs elsewhere.

5. *The Port of Haifa*—The State of Israel should give assurances of free access for the interested Arab countries to the port of Haifa. The Arab countries in turn should undertake to place no obstacle in the way of oil deliveries by pipeline to the Haifa refinery. The products of the refinery should continue to be distributed on the basis of the historical pattern.

6. *Lydda airport*—The airport of Lydda should be open to international air traffic without restrictions, and the interested Arab countries should be assured of access to its facilities.

7. *Palestinian refugees*—You should be guided by the provisions of the General Assembly resolution of December 11 concerning refugees.

8. *Disposition of Arab Palestine*—US favors incorporation of greater part of Arab Palestine in Transjordan. The remainder might be divided among other Arab states as seems desirable.

C) If negotiations, either directly between the parties or through the Commission, should fail, you will be authorized to join with the other members of the Commission in an effort to persuade the parties to agree upon frontiers between Israel and Arab Palestine as set forth in paragraph (3) above. At the same time, the United States Government will concert with the British Government to attempt to induce the parties to reach agreement on this basis.

Very truly yours, ROBERT A. LOVETT[35]

In the course of February 1949, U.S. policy came to concentrate on the refugee question. Besides the humanitarian motives, two political considerations contributed to this posture. One was tactical. The United States hoped that Israel's acceptance of the principle of repatriation might elicit a more moderate mood on the Arab side. The other was more fundamental. There was a concern that if repatriation were not begun promptly, Jewish immigration into Israel would preempt the lands and housing on which Arab repatriation depended.[36] But by assigning priority to the refugee problem, U.S. policy came to coincide with the Arab viewpoint.

The United States used a variety of means to influence Israeli policy. In addition to reasoning and argumentation, the U.S. also applied pressure in various forms. When Israel's application for UN membership was due to be brought before the General Assembly and Israel requested American support, Secretary of State Dean Acheson told Eban quite clearly that "if Israel would only make some conciliatory gesture or statement along the lines we have suggested, we would then have some basis on which to talk to the other nations in the General Assembly."[37] The threat that the United States might withhold support for Israel's application for UN membership is credited with bringing about Israel's acceptance of the Lausanne protocol. When it became apparent that despite the protocol, Israel's position remained essentially unchanged, President Truman sent a message to Prime Minister Ben-Gurion on May 28, criticizing Israel's policy and concluding with the threat that if Israel continued to reject the basic principles of the UN resolution of December 11, 1948, and "the friendly advice" offered by the United States, then the U.S. government "will regretfully be forced to the conclusion that a revision of its attitude toward Israel has become unavoidable."[38] Although no revision actually occurred, and the tone of diplomatic exchanges reverted to more restrained criticism, pressure on Israel was quietly stepped up. Israeli requests for assistance in sending Israeli personnel to be trained in the United States and bringing American experts to Israel were left unanswered. More drastic was the suspension of allocations from the

$100 million loan that had been extended to Israel by the Export-Import Bank.[39]

These efforts succeeded in achieving a modification of Israel's positions on a number of occasions. One was Israel's acceptance of the Lausanne protocol mentioned above. Israel also made concessions on the refugee question, agreeing to accept a limited number of Arab refugees to reunite families whose members had been separated because of the war, without linking this to the broader problem of a peace settlement. In July, Israel announced its readiness to admit 100,000 Arab refugees, within the framework of a general settlement of the refugee problem. It also agreed to have the refugee problem placed first on the agenda of the Lausanne negotiations.[40] These concessions fell short of what the U.S. government desired, but even these concessions would not have been offered without American pressure.

Israel remained adamant on rejection of American proposals on boundaries and refugees because Israeli leaders believed that these proposals endangered Israel's survival. In Israel's view, the armistice boundaries furnished it with only minimal security. The territorial changes proposed by the U.S., reducing the territory allotted to Israel by the armistice agreements, would have greatly aggravated its strategic vulnerability. Giving up the Negev would have reduced Israel's territory significantly and diminished its ability to admit large numbers of Jewish immigrants and survivors of the Holocaust, which, it should be remembered, was Israel's raison d'être. American proposals for the admission of a large number of Arab refugees were also unacceptable because this threatened to undermine Israel's internal security, and would sow the seeds of civil strife in later years.

The United States was much less concerned with modifying Arab policies. It did not seek explicit Arab acceptance of the existence of the Israeli state; implicit acknowledgment through the Lausanne protocol was deemed sufficient. The U.S. held to the assumption that if Israel accepted the American proposals, the Arab states would "acquiesce" in a settlement. Nevertheless, in the spring, the United States used its influence to obtain the Arab governments' conceding in principle the need to contribute to the solution of the refugee problem by resettling some of the refugees in their territories. Arab acceptance of the Lausanne protocol can also be attributed to American influence, as can Arab cooperation with the Economic Survey Mission later in the summer. The United States also sought unsuccessfully to persuade Egypt to transfer the Gaza Strip to Israel in return for Israel's commitment to resettle the 250,000 refugees there.

In its efforts to influence Arab policies, the U.S. relied on diplomatic persuasion and on Arab expectations of rewards. In contrast to U.S. exchanges with Israel at that time, there were no threats and no deprivation of aid. Hints that the U.S. might provide large-scale economic aid apparently helped to persuade Syria to agree in principle to the resettlement of some of the Arab refugees in its territory. Arab cooperation with the Economic Survey Mission can similarly be attributed to the expectation that its recommendations concerning the refugees might be coupled with proposals for other aid programs too. Hopes that Arab responsiveness to U.S. requests might lead to the weakening of American sympathies for Israel may also have influenced Arab policies.[41]

Although on some issues Arab policies were modified as a result of American influence, the overall effect of U.S. involvement was to hinder the Arab states from accepting a settlement based on the status quo. The Arab governments were aware of American and British views on the terms of a settlement: they favored the transfer of the Negev, or parts of it, to Arab control, and Israel's admission of a substantial number of Arab refugees. Thus there was no incentive for the Arabs to change their position on these issues. On the contrary, knowing what the American policy was, they expected the United States to bring about a change in Israel's position. The result was that

American policy actually served to encourage the Arabs to stand fast and not compromise. Arab officials were encouraged to remain firm not merely by conclusions drawn from official U.S. proposals, but also by U.S. assurances that efforts were being made to induce Israel to change its position. On one occasion, when Israel's admission to the UN was due to come to a vote, Ethridge told the Arab delegates at Lausanne, on the basis of information from Washington, that the United States would not support Israel's application unless Israel changed its policy. Ethridge was clearly embarrassed when the United States sponsored Israel's admission in return for promises that he and the Arabs considered insufficient.[42] The important point is that the Arab states were led to expect that the United States would make Israel admit a substantial portion of the refugees, and give up the Negev and perhaps other areas it held. This expectation prevented the Arab governments from softening their stand and accepting less than the U.S. told them that it would obtain for them.

The United States and the Conciliation Commission thus became trapped in a policy contradiction that often bedevils mediators. When the mediator's views are close to the position of one side, or when his proposals are acceptable to one side, that side will stand fast and be unlikely to offer concessions. Mediators frequently face the dilemma of how to prevent their proposals from encouraging the party that is willing to accept them from becoming inflexible. In theory, more drastic U.S. pressure might have yielded greater concessions. After all, one of the advantages of U.S. participation in the Conciliation Commission was its presumed ability, as a great power, to exert the influence necessary to make the adversaries change their policies.

Significantly, the U.S. did not resort to one form of pressure that is believed to be potent when exercised by mediators: it refrained from appealing to public opinion, and blaming Israel before that court for hindering progress to peace. Such a policy was apparently considered and rejected. When Ethridge became impatient at the lack of progress in the negotiations and expressed his desire to resign, the State Department drafted a telegram to him on April 20, saying that if the Israelis "as you predict, decide to stall at Lausanne, we would then be disposed to utilize your desire for relief to derive maximum diplomatic advantage."[43] There is no evidence that the telegram was ever sent to Ethridge, but the possibility was considered. American reluctance to go public is reflected also in the cautious handling of the president's threatening note of May 28, 1949. When Israel leaked to the press that it was being subject to pressure, the United States promptly persuaded it to avoid public debate.[44]

U.S. reluctance to appeal to public opinion or to apply more drastic pressures on Israel can be attributed to the administration's domestic political concerns. Although 1949 was not an election year, the common explanation that the administration was inhibited from such a course by the concern that it would arouse strong domestic opposition seems plausible. The reluctance to apply more drastic pressure and risk a public debate on such a policy, must have been strengthened by doubts about the validity of the theory that Israeli concessions on refugees and boundaries would bring about Arab acquiescence in its existence. Secretary of State Dean Acheson expressed such doubts shortly after he assumed office, and similar doubts about the feasibility of an imposed settlement were reportedly entertained by Under Secretary Robert Lovett.[45]

Drastic pressure on the Arab states to make them alter their policies was unthinkable. It would have been contrary to a principal objective of American policy toward the Arab states at that time, namely to win their friendship and to gain their political-strategic cooperation against the Soviet Union. Pressure could have produced consequences that were exactly the opposite of what the policy of peacemaking was intended to achieve.

Implicit in this dilemma of how much pressure the U.S. could apply to influence the adversaries' policies was the fundamental constraint that limits mediators' freedom of action. Since their status as mediators depends upon their acceptability, there is a limit to the pressures they can exert. Brutal pressure on the Arab states or on Israel might have caused them to withdraw their acceptance of the Conciliation Commission or of U.S. participation in it, transforming the American role from conciliation to intervention. Neither the United States nor the other members of the commission wanted this.

Concluding Comments

Several of the factors that contributed to the Commission's failure have been mentioned above: the tactical errors, the cumbersome working of an international commission, the lack of continuity at the head of the American delegation, and perhaps the absence of special talent among its personnel.

Although important, these factors should not obscure some more fundamental reasons for the commission's failure. The most formidable obstacles to its success were of course the issues themselves. Although the issues had been redefined, with the negotiations now concerned with the questions of refugees and boundaries and no longer with the admissibility of partition and of an Israeli state, in fact both sides perceived the refugees and the boundaries in terms of their effect upon Israel's ability to survive. Thus, they were closely linked to "core values." Furthermore, the Arab governments believed that the political survival of their regimes depended on their avoiding the humiliation of accepting the legitimacy of the status quo.

The commission was unable to fractionate or separate these issues into more manageable problems because the parties maintained the linkage. Israel insisted that the refugee problem could not be resolved separately from the question of peace, the Arabs insisted that Israel's acceptance of the right of repatriation was a precondition for a discussion of peace, and both sides linked both the refugee question and the question of peace to the territorial problem. Another approach for separating the issues and rendering them more manageable—by discussing them on a country-by-country basis—was precluded by the commission's tactics. By holding the negotiations within a general conference framework, the negotiators became entangled in general principles and were unable to address themselves pragmatically to specific bilateral problems that existed between Israel and each of its neighbors.

Another fundamental reason for the commission's failure was that at the time neither side enjoyed a decisive advantage, nor felt stalemated. Rather, both sides considered their position as bearable and expected that it might even improve without having to alter their policies. Israel looked forward to a period of consolidation and development to be made possible by the relative stability of the armistice, the influx of immigrants, and external economic assistance. The Arab states came to expect that the great powers would compensate them for having supported the establishment of Israel. In this sense, since both sides expected that if they stood fast the situation might improve, the circumstances were not propitious for successful mediation.

Finally, the commission's failure can be attributed in large measure to American policies. It was not that American backing of the commission was insufficient; throughout 1949, the U.S. gave the commission strong support, or rather, used it as an instrument of its foreign policy. The shortcoming was in the contradictory objectives that the U.S. sought to pursue. At one and the same time it sought to support Israel's survival, to induce it to relinquish much of its territory (the Negev), and to admit into its midst hundreds of thousands of Arab refugees who resented the establishment of the Israeli state. It sought to persuade the Arab states to make peace with Israel, but also encouraged them to reject the status quo by leading them to believe that the U.S. would help them to obtain better terms for a settlement. It seems that American policy-makers were not sufficiently conscious of the inconsistencies of their conception; it was not a conception that could guide effective mediation.

FIVE

The Anderson Mission

The early and mid-1950s saw several attempts to settle the Arab-Israeli conflict. Negotiations between Israel and Jordan during 1949 and 1950 went as far as a draft peace treaty, but the condemnation of these negotiations by other Arab states and opposition inside Jordan deterred King Abdullah from signing. Even so, Abdullah was assassinated in 1951, paying with his life for his willingness to conclude peace with Israel. In 1952, after the Free Officers' Revolution, and again in January 1955, Israel and Egypt explored through direct contacts possibilities of alleviating tensions. Other attempts involved intermediaries. The UN Conciliation Commission was during this period engaged mainly in matters pertaining to property claims. Other UN efforts, by Secretary-General Dag Hammarskjöld and the UN Truce Supervision Organization, were directed at the observance of the armistice agreements and the cessation of border strife. Mediation was attempted also by Ralph Bunche; President Tito of Yugoslavia; Dom Mintoff of Malta; two British M.P.s, Richard Crossman and Maurice Orbach; Elmore Jackson, the American Quaker leader; and perhaps others. None was successful.

The most persistent among the would-be peacemakers was the government of the United States. One of its two major initiatives was an attempt to conclude an agreement on the development of the Jordan River water resources. It was hoped that such an agreement would reduce the tensions arising from Arab objections to Israel's development plans, and also serve to expand negotiations with the view of resolving other issues in dispute. To this end Eric Johnston was sent to the Middle East in 1953. His negotiations lasted two-and-a-half years, but came to nothing. The second initiative, between December 1955 and March 1956, was the mission of Robert B. Anderson, President Eisenhower's special envoy, to bring about an Egyptian-Israeli agreement. The Anderson mission did not succeed either, but it deserves a thorough discussion because it exemplifies a number of features that have received only scant attention in the literature on mediation. One concerns the mission's motive, which seems to have been stimulated as much by the side effects that it was expected to produce as by the desire to resolve the Egyptian-Israeli conflict. Secondly, the course of its endeavors illustrates a tacit bargaining relationship between the mediator and each of the parties, and how such a relationship could render the mediation unacceptable to one of the parties. The Anderson mission reflected a basic American strategy for dealing with the Arab-Israeli conflict.

Mediation in the Context of American Policy in the Middle East

The principal preoccupation of the Eisenhower administration when it assumed office was the Cold War. Its policy was aimed at improving the non-Communist world's defensive capacity, especially along the extended boundaries of the Soviet-dominated land mass in Europe and Asia. Although there did not seem to be any immediate threat to Western interests in the Middle East, changes were taking place in the region that required the U.S. to reexamine and possibly to reshape its existing policies. One element of change was the continuing decline of British influence. Its acute manifestations in the early 1950s were Iran's challenge to British oil interests, and the growing Egyptian pressure for the termination of Britain's privileged status in Egypt and the evacuation of British troops from Egyptian soil. The decline of British influence was worrisome because it signified the removal of an obstacle to Soviet penetration. Another important change was the estrangement between Israel and the Soviet Union. While this development must have given the U.S. satisfaction and relieved any lingering doubt about Israel's alignment in the global struggle, it also strengthened the fear that the Soviet Union, in shifting its sympathy from Israel to the Arab states, would seek to play upon Arab resentment of American support for Israel.

The escalation of the Arab-Israeli conflict was also disquieting. Frontier strife intensified as Arab attacks across the armistice lines provoked retaliatory raids by Israel. The vagueness of the armistice clauses referring to the status of the demilitarized zones also led to armed clashes. Egypt's ban on the transit of Israeli-bound cargoes through the Suez Canal spurred Israel to assert its right to use this international waterway. Public statements by Arab leaders reaffirming their refusal to accept Israel's existence and calling for its destruction deepened the Arab governments' commitment to this goal and kindled their peoples' hostility. The beginnings of an arms race also contributed to increased tensions. These tensions and the domestic instability they engendered in several Arab states provided ample opportunities for Soviet intervention in Middle East affairs.[1]

American concern led Secretary of State John Foster Dulles to visit the Middle East in May 1953, shortly after the Eisenhower administration assumed office. He was the first American secretary of state ever to visit the area, prompted, Dulles told the nation over radio and television, by the danger that the Middle East might fall under Communist domination as China had fallen.[2]

To counter the danger of Soviet influence, American policy sought to establish a regional defense organization. However, the U.S. felt it was greatly handicapped in the pursuit of friendship with the Arabs by common suspicions that the U.S. sided with Britain in its conflict with Egypt, and that in general the U.S. sympathized with British and French colonialism. The U.S. also supported Israel in its conflict with the Arab states. To allay those suspicions and to change the Arab image of the U.S., American Middle East policy under Dulles laid special emphasis on dissociating itself from Britain and France, and on pursuing an "evenhanded" approach toward the Arab states and Israel.[3]

It also sought to eliminate some specific obstacles hindering the pursuit of the above goals, such as the dispute between Egypt and Britain and the Arab-Israeli conflict. Successive Egyptian governments, both before and after the 1952 revolution, had indicated that Egyptian cooperation with a Western-sponsored regional defense organization was difficult as long as the dispute with England was not resolved. The unresolved Arab-Israeli dispute rendered the participation of both the Arab states and Israel unlikely. In fact, the arming and equipping of the Arab states and the pursuit of a policy that would win Arab friendship was likely to encounter sharp domestic criticism in the United States as long as the Arab-Israeli conflict went on. Consequently, the U.S. offered its assistance to the resolution of both these disputes. The U.S. contributed to the successful conclusion of Anglo-Egyptian negotiations, which culminated in the agreement on the withdrawal of British forces from Egypt in October 1954, and thereafter it turned its attention to mediation between Egypt and Israel.

This marked a departure from the pattern of previous American actions seeking to promote an Arab-Israeli settlement. Whereas in 1948 the U.S. was content to exert its influence behind the scenes through the UN mediator, and in 1949 it acted under the cover of its membership in the UN Conciliation Commission, in the mid-1950s the U.S. assumed a direct role acting under its own flag. This change in the manner of American involvement can in large measure be accounted for by its increased concern over developments in the Middle East. But the deep concern was accompanied by a certain air of optimism that the U.S. was indeed capable of bringing about an improvement in Arab-Israeli relations—an optimism nourished by American successes in helping to resolve the Anglo-Iranian dispute, the Anglo-Egyptian dispute, and even the Italian-Yugoslav dispute over Trieste.[4]

Dulles believed in a gradualist method for promoting an Arab-Israeli settlement. In his report on the trip, he stated that the U.S. would use its influence "to promote a step-by-step reduction of tension in the area and the conclusion of ultimate peace."[5] The principal components of the conflict were in Dulles's view the issues of Jerusalem, borders, refugees, development of water resources, and frontier strife. He hoped that progress could be made on each issue as opportunities permitted.

During 1953 and 1954 American initiatives were confined to the reduction of border strife and to a major effort to promote an agreement for the development and distribution of the Jordan River waters.[6] But sometime toward the end of 1954 the conception changed, and efforts began to be directed toward a more comprehensive settlement. In October 1954, Francis H. Russell, who at that time served as chargé d'affaires at the American Embassy in Tel Aviv, was appointed special assistant to Secretary Dulles to work on plans to improve Arab-Israeli relations. Russell, collaborating with British officials, prepared comprehensive and detailed proposals.[7] Informal soundings of Arab governments and Israel suggested that at least some of the parties would resent great-power mediation, and moreover, that both Egypt and Israel objected to significant elements in the American plan. In particular, the idea of linking Egypt to Jordan by a narrow corridor under Arab sovereignty while leaving the Negev within Israel, received an unfavorable reaction in Egypt. Action on the proposals was delayed, the U.S. and Britain apparently being apprehensive that attempts to implement them might provoke a sharp Egyptian reaction, which would hinder British efforts to rally Arab support for the Baghdad Pact.[8]

The Dulles Speech

An initiative was nevertheless taken toward the end of August 1955. On August 26, in an address arranged on short notice to the Council on Foreign Relations in New York, Secretary of State Dulles outlined, in very general terms, American proposals for a settlement. Why, after months of hesitation, did he take the plunge? Until the classified documents of the period are made public, explanations can only be tentative. I believe that Dulles's speech was prompted by the information which was reaching Washington and other capitals about the progress of Egyptian-Soviet arms negotiations. The formal announcement of the Egyptian-Czech arms agreement was made on September 27, but rumors began to reach Western governments as early as June, when Nasser reportedly told the American ambassador that in view of the unsatisfactory American response to Egyptian arms requests, Egypt was negotiating with the Soviet Union.[9]

It is plausible that the decision on the timing and form of the initiative to improve Arab-Israeli relations was influenced by the information about Egyptian-Soviet negotiations, and that the U.S. concluded that it would be preferable to launch the initiative promptly than to delay it further. If it were delayed Egypt might in the meantime conclude an arms agreement with the Soviet bloc, rendering the circumstances for launching an American peace initiative highly unpropitious. Probably, it was also expected that a public statement by the secretary of state would serve as an indication of the seriousness of the American intent to meet some of the Arab demands, especially on territorial matters. It was hoped to make Nasser pause before he went too far in establishing a new relationship with the Soviet Union.

To serve as a "starter," the proposals had to contain

elements that would appear attractive to both sides without including anything that might antagonize either of them strongly enough to reject the initiative. Dulles addressed himself to three principal problems "that conspicuously required to be solved":[10] the plight of the Arab refugees, mutual fears, and the lack of permanent boundaries. He recognized that there were additional problems too, and mentioned Jerusalem, but, significantly, refrained from making any proposals about its status. Dulles expressed his belief that it was necessary to take "further steps toward stability" because of the danger that, unless the situation improved, it would get worse. The U.S., "as a friend of both Israelis and Arabs, has given the situation deep and anxious thought and has come to certain conclusions, the expression of which may help men of good will within the area to fresh and constructive efforts."

On the refugee problem Dulles said that a solution should be found "through resettlement and—to such an extent as may be feasible—repatriation." This phrasing adhered to the accepted formula of resettlement and repatriation, but avoided the controversial questions of whether the refugees had the "right" to return, and whether they should be given free choice, which the Arabs demanded and Israel rejected. An inducement to movement toward a solution was the offer that the U.S. would participate in an international loan to enable Israel to pay compensation to the refugees and would contribute to the realization of development projects that would facilitate resettlement.

The second problem, that of mutual fears, Dulles proposed to solve by guarantees. However, he made guarantees contingent upon the solution of related problems, specifically borders. If these were resolved, he said that President Eisenhower "would recommend that the United States join in formal treaty engagements to prevent or thwart any effort by either side to alter by force the boundaries." He hoped that other countries would be willing to join in such a guarantee and that it would be sponsored by the UN. In fact Israel had already raised the question of guarantees with the U.S., but the U.S. had refused to commit itself and the discussions left a bitter aftertaste in Israel.[11] Dulles's offer was quite different from what Israel had requested; it was a guarantee to be extended to *both* Israel and the Arabs. Moreover, it was conditional upon prior agreement on the borders, and both Israel and the Arab states knew that in the American view such an agreement required that Israel make some territorial concessions to the Arabs.

This was the most difficult problem. Dulles said that the 1949 armistice lines "were not designed to be permanent frontiers." He admitted that the drawing of permanent boundaries would be difficult because "each of two conflicting claims may seem to have merit," and because "even territory which is barren has acquired sentimental significance." To resolve the problem, unspecified "adjustments" were needed, and "the United States would be willing to help in the search for a solution if the parties to the dispute should desire."

The issue was of course the Negev. As we had seen in previous chapters, the U.S. and Britain, for their own strategic interests, wanted between 1947 and 1949 to have it transferred to Egyptian or Jordanian rule. The justification offered then was that in the 1948 war Israel had occupied Western Galilee and Jaffa, which the 1947 Partition Plan had allotted to the Arab state, and if Israel wished to keep those territories it ought to compensate the Arabs by relinquishing most of the Negev. The U.S. later abandoned the position that Israel should give up most of the Negev. But in view of Egypt's persistence in claiming this land, on the grounds that it required territorial contiguity with the Arab states to the east, the U.S. devised a new and original solution. Israel would cede two small triangles north of Eilat, "one to Egypt with its base on the Egypt-Israel frontier, the other to Jordan with its base on the Jordan-Israel frontier. These two triangles were to meet at their corner points, and there a road from Egypt to Jordan, under Arab sovereignty would pass over (or under) the road from Beersheba to Eilat which would remain under Israeli sovereignty."[12] This plan was unacceptable to both Israel and Egypt. Israel objected to any cession of territory, and offered instead to provide free, unhampered communication between Egypt and Jordan. Egypt demanded that the entire southern Negev be ceded to it.[13] By coming out publicly, even if ambiguously, in favor of border "adjustments," Dulles probably hoped that he could engage Egyptian interest without provoking a rejection of his proposals.

All this did not amount to an explicit offer of American mediation, but it came close to it. Dulles offered not only American participation in guarantees and in the financing of refugee compensation and resettlement, but also American "help in the search for a solution" of the boundary problem. Dulles's proposal signaled a departure from the previous cautious approach of tackling separate and relatively less difficult issues such as border pacification and water resources development. But it also stopped short of proposing peace; he only spoke of easing tensions, achieving greater stability, and enabling better lives for the peoples of the region. Probably the U.S. did not believe that the Arab states were ready to recognize Israel formally and explicitly accept peaceful relations with it.

Israeli Perspectives

Three predominant problems occupied Israeli attention in the early 1950s: the integration of hundreds of thousands of immigrants, the economy, and security. Peace with the Arab states was not considered feasible in the short run. Arab terms for peace—the acknowledgment of the refugees' right to return and allowing a substantial number to do so, along with the cession of territories to the neighboring states—appeared to Israel to confirm its interpretation of Arab policy as aimed at destroying Israel, not living in peace with it. Jordan's failure to conclude the peace treaty that had been drafted, the intensification of nationalist and anti-Israeli propaganda in the Arab world, and the growing number of incidents along the borders, led Israeli leaders to conclude that the time was not propitious for peace efforts. This view was shared by Ben-Gurion and Sharett, two rival leaders who often differed on policy and indeed held different views on how peace would *ultimately* come. Ben-Gurion believed that the Arabs would make peace when they finally became convinced that they could not destroy Israel. He consequently advocated demonstrations of strength. Sharett held the view that the problem was mainly one of psychological adjustment on the part of the Arabs, and that peace would come after they had time to overcome the humiliation that Israel's establishment represented for them. Yet the two leaders agreed in their pessimistic assessment of the short-term prospects for peace.[14]

Although pessimistic, Israeli leaders were nevertheless interested in establishing contacts, both direct and indirect, with Arab governments. Besides the general desire to be informed about Arab attitudes, attempts to make contact were prompted from time to time by specific events and requirements, such as the hope of obtaining lenient treatment for Israeli prisoners or of reducing border tensions. On several occasions attempts to establish contact were prompted by reports that Egyptian leaders spoke to Western diplomats and visitors in moderate terms, indicating their desire to reduce tensions. Israelis were constantly on the alert to verify and test such signals, both because of a basically idealistic disposition which led them to believe that change in Arab attitudes was possible, and because of the diplomatic requirement of keeping third parties convinced that the absence of peace was not Israel's fault.

The U.S., with which Israel maintained extensive links in many spheres, occupied a prominent place in Israeli thinking about security and peace. In the mid-1950s Israeli views on American involvement in the attempts to reduce tension with the Arab states were influenced by the awareness that the U.S. favored the cession of a corridor through the Negev to the Arabs and the admission by Israel of a large number of Arab refugees. Moreover, Israel was under the impression that the U.S. was on the verge of proposing that parts of the Sea of Galilee should also be transferred to Arab sovereignty.[15] Israel therefore exercised a certain caution in its dealings with the U.S. on the peace question. Indeed, in the consultations preceding Dulles's 1953 visit to Israel, Prime Minister Ben-Gurion said that in the forthcoming talks, Israel should not place too much emphasis on the question of peace lest it provoke American proposals for major Israeli concessions.[16] Yet Israel's caution in discussing with the U.S. the question of how to make progress toward a settlement did not diminish the American persistence in raising its proposals whenever an opportunity presented itself. When Israel requested an American guarantee in the spring of 1955, it was told that before a guarantee could be extended, agreement on the questions of boundaries, refugees, water, and perhaps other issues as well, had to be reached. Dulles told Abba Eban, the Israeli ambassador to Washington at that time, that the U.S. was preparing proposals on these questions, that not all of them would be to Israel's liking, but that in essence the American proposals would be to Israel's benefit.[17]

It is interesting to note that despite its apprehensions, Israel nevertheless accepted, and on occasion even requested, American mediation. It seems that Israel's attitude was determined mainly by tactical diplomatic considerations. When Israel believed that direct negotiations without intermediaries were possible, it accepted American mediation only grudgingly. Sharett recorded two such occasions: an Israeli attempt to renew negotiations with Jordan in November 1953, and a direct Israeli approach to Egypt in April 1954.[18] On other occasions it welcomed American mediation. An offer by Kermit Roosevelt of the CIA, in January 1955, to arrange a meeting between President Nasser and an Israeli representative, was accepted by the Israeli side, and preparations began to send to Cairo Yigael Yadin, the former chief of staff. Yet, before arrangements for a meeting were completed, two members of an Israeli intelligence and sabotage network were hanged in Cairo, and the atmosphere created by the executions caused these attempts to be discontinued. But at the end of March 1955, and again in June, Israel took the initiative, asking the CIA to renew its efforts for a meeting. Nothing came of either initiative. Israel was informed that Nasser was suspicious of Israel's motives, and moreover, that arrangements were complicated because the State Department was planning to propose a meeting and the CIA was no longer allowed to act on its own.[19]

Israel's favorable attitude to American mediation on these occasions was prompted by immediate practical concerns. In January 1955, the purpose was to save the lives of the agents who were condemned to death in Cairo. In March, the hope was to obtain an improvement in the conditions under which the surviving members of the Israeli network were imprisoned in Egypt, and also to obtain the release of the *Bat Galim* and its crew. (The *Bat Galim* was an Israeli vessel seized in the Suez Canal; its crew was arrested.) The June 1955 Israeli initiative seems to have been prompted by Egyptian claims that they desired to reduce tensions with Israel. According to Sharett, Israel wanted the U.S. to present the proposal for a meeting as if the initiative came from the American side, so as to save embarrassment to Israel in the event of Egyptian rejection, another tactical consideration that rendered American mediation not merely acceptable, but desirable.

Yet Israel's attitude to the initiative contained in Dulles's speech was suspicious, if not negative. Previous American mediation efforts were limited to attempts to arrange meetings between Egyptian and Israeli representatives and discussions of the agenda at the proposed meetings, without going into issues of substance. But Dulles's speech signified a departure: a public statement of American views, ambiguously phrased but nevertheless quite transparent, and an offer to mediate, presumably in order to conclude an agreement conforming generally to the terms advocated.

Moshe Sharett, who was prime minister and foreign minister, was informed by the American ambassador, Edward Lawson, about the speech two days before it was delivered. A revealing passage in Sharett's diary records that Lawson's visit left him "agitated and fearful." He was seized by a feeling similar to one he had had on the eve of the publication of the British White Paper in 1939, which imposed restrictions upon Jewish immigration and settlement in Palestine. In his conversation with Lawson, Sharett warned the U.S. that the planned speech would encourage Arab intransigence and cause irreparable damage.[20] But after the speech was delivered, Israel's public reaction was relatively moderate and cautious. Israel requested further clarifications. In an interview with United Press, Sharett's tone was critical. He declared that Israel would not make any unilateral territorial concessions; it was prepared, however, to consider mutual minor boundary adjustments. He concluded by saying that Israel had always been interested in exploring any possibility of progress toward the settlement of the conflict, and would study Dulles's speech in this spirit.[21] In private, the reactions were much more negative. Israel apparently decided to soften its public reaction in compliance with an American request to that effect, and perhaps also to wait and see how Egypt's negotiations for Soviet arms would affect the fate of the American initiative.

The Egyptian Perspective

When the Free Officers seized power in Egypt in July 1952, the conflict with Israel was not a matter of urgent concern. More pressing issues were the stabilization of the regime, domestic reforms, and the conflict with Britain over the presence of British troops in the Canal zone and over the future of the Sudan. Yet, as time passed, the conflict with

Israel acquired increasing importance. Raids into Israel intensified, and brought in their wake Israeli retaliation. The ban on the passage of Israeli cargoes through the Suez Canal was enforced, and subsequently extended to the Straits of Tiran as well. The propaganda campaign against Israel was also intensified. Why and how this happened is a subject that deserves a separate study. Here it suffices to say that the escalation of the conflict came about in part because the Egyptian government believed that its claim to leadership of the Arab world would meet with wider support if Egypt were seen to be in the forefront of the struggle against Israel. But to an extent thc escalation was fed by the Egyptian ambition to annex the Negev.[22]

The escalation was from time to time accompanied by Egyptian statements that Egypt was prepared to seek a settlement. It is difficult to assess the sincerity of these statements. In private, American officials regarded them with occasional skepticism. Dulles noted after his meeting with General Muhammed Naguib, the nominal head of Egypt's revolutionary regime in May 1953, that "Naguib feels moving forward on arrangements with Israel not too difficult once he solves his problem with the British. How much of this is window dressing for our present support?"[23] But as a matter of practical diplomacy they tended to accept Egyptian conciliatory statements at face value, and the U.S. based its policy on the assumption that the Egyptians were sincere. Israel held the opposite view, that those Egyptian statements that called for the destruction of Israel expressed Egypt's real objectives, and that conciliatory remarks made to foreign diplomats and journalists (but not reported in Egypt itself) were propaganda. It is also possible that the two kinds of statements reflected Nasser's own wish to keep open options for both peace and war.

All that can be said with confidence is that Egypt was aware that conciliatory statements about the Arab-Israeli conflict would have a favorable effect on its relations with the U.S. Good relations with the U.S. were valued because

Egypt was interested in economic aid, arms, and American diplomatic support in its negotiations with Britain. Egyptian statements that it wished to settle the conflict with Israel were inspired by the requirements of Egyptian-American relations. Although Egypt regarded American policy as basically pro-Israeli, it nevertheless accepted and sometimes even encouraged American mediation to mitigate American disappointment at Egypt's refusal to cooperate in the establishment of a regional defense organization and to help obtain arms from the U.S.

These were Egypt's concerns and motives when Dulles delivered his speech advocating an Arab-Israeli settlement. Egypt was at that time seriously engaged in the negotiations for the purchase of Soviet weapons. An angry American reaction to the conclusion of the deal was undoubtedly expected. In this context, an indication of readiness to consider the American proposals could serve to moderate American reactions to the arms deal. But Egypt's initial reaction was reserved, Egyptian officials saying that the proposals required further study. It may be that they were disappointed that Dulles's statement did not go far enough to meet Egyptian goals. In any event, Egypt reiterated its view that a corridor through the Negev linking Egypt and Jordan would not suffice, and reaffirmed its demand for the cession of at least the southern Negev to Egypt.[24]

The Anderson Mission

Dulles's attempt to get negotiations started was soon overtaken by events. On September 27, Nasser made public the conclusion of the arms agreement with Czechoslovakia. In the immediate aftermath of this announcement, the efforts to initiate the Arab-Israeli negotiations were suspended.

In Israel, worries that the arms deal might enable Egypt to acquire a significant military advantage over Israel led to a modification of Israel's diplomatic goals. For the preceding six months Israel's principal objective in its relations with the U.S. was to obtain an American guarantee. After the arms deal had become a fact, priority was given to the acquisition of American arms to balance the weapons that Egypt was to receive from Czechoslovakia. In an attempt to obtain Western military aid and to dissuade the Soviet Union from assisting Nasser further, Moshe Sharett (at that time still prime minister and foreign minister) made a dramatic trip to Paris and Geneva to meet the foreign ministers of the great powers. Sharett received some secret assurances from French officials, but his meetings with Dulles, Macmillan, and Molotov were disappointing.[25]

The announcement of the arms deal triggered a policy debate in the U.S. as well. The basic question was how to react to a move that enabled the Soviet Union to "leap" over the Northern Tier of defense, and that might lead to an increase of Soviet influence in Egypt and perhaps other countries. The initial American impulse, to apply pressure on Egypt and hope to reverse Egypt's drift toward the Soviet Union, was soon reconsidered. Perhaps it was thought that pressure might become counterproductive, because Egypt responded by informing the U.S. that it had received a Soviet offer to finance the Aswan Dam.[26] The strategy finally chosen, in agreement with Britain, was one of attempting to influence Egyptian policy through incentives. It was hoped that by continuing support for Nasser's regime, Soviet penetration could be contained. Perhaps the arms agreement would be an isolated episode, not followed by further agreements with the Soviet bloc. The offer to finance the Aswan Dam, announced on December 17, 1955, was the main incentive offered to Nasser. This strategy also required that measures to which Egypt might object be avoided as much as possible. Thus, American formal adherence to the Baghdad Pact was deferred, and Israel's request for American arms was kept in abeyance.[27]

The renewal of the diplomatic efforts to reduce Arab-

Israeli tensions was another element in this strategy. The escalation of frontier fighting between Egypt and Israel and echoes of the debate in Israel about the advisability of launching a preventive war that reached American and British ears, sparked the resumption of diplomatic efforts.

There was some difference of opinion between the U.S. and Britain on whether the concession to the Egyptian viewpoint contained in Dulles's reference to the need for "adjustments" of the 1949 armistice lines was sufficient, or whether a more explicit incentive should be offered to Nasser. On November 9, 1955, British prime minister Anthony Eden attempted to launch an initiative that reflected his predilection for more explicit incentives to Egypt. In a speech at the Guildhall he said that "the acute dangers of the situation" required that a new attempt at a settlement of the Arab-Israeli conflict be made. He proposed that a compromise be reached between the Arab position of adhering to the boundaries proposed by the UN 1947 partition plan and the Israeli position of standing firm on the 1949 armistice agreement lines. Finally, Eden offered his government's and his personal "service" in this cause. Egypt accepted Eden's mediation offer, and in general, the tone of its reaction was more favorable than its response to Dulles's August speech. It may be that Egypt indeed considered Eden's offer more attractive, since he called for a compromise between the 1947 and 1949 lines in contrast to Dulles, who advocated merely an adjustment of the 1949 armistice lines. Most probably, Egypt's favorable response was also aimed at encouraging British hopes that it might be called upon to mediate, and thus induce it to moderate its drive for expanding the Baghdad Pact, which Egypt regarded as a serious threat to its claim to the leadership of the Arab world. Israel's response, on the other hand, was one of unqualified rejection of Eden's proposals, because of the explicit call for Israeli territorial concessions. But the bitterness and vehemence of Israel's reaction stemmed also from a deep distrust of British policy, which Israel believed to have favored the Arabs in

1948-1949, as well as a distrust of Eden personally, whom Jewish diplomats in the 1930s and 1940s considered unfriendly to Zionism.[28]

In December, after Eden's initiative had failed, the U.S. launched an initiative of its own, which was more cautious and less committing than either Dulles's or Eden's attempts. The U.S. proposed to send an emissary to conduct secret talks with the leaders of Egypt and Israel with the view of exploring the possibilities for a settlement of their conflict. Both Egypt and Israel accepted the American initiative out of tactical considerations. Nasser wanted to make a gesture that would mollify American anger at the arms agreement and encourage the United States to continue supporting his regime. Moreover, Dulles's and Eden's speeches carried indications that the U.S. and Britain might support some of his demands. For these same reasons, Israel did not view the American initiative with optimism. Indeed, Sharett's initial reaction was one of apprehension that the American response to Israel's request for arms would now hinge on the fortunes of this mediation attempt.[29] But a summary rejection of the American initiative would have damaged American-Israeli relations and rendered American agreement to supply Israel with weapons even less likely.

The negotiations were conducted through Robert Anderson, who had previously served as deputy secretary of defense and subsequently served as secretary of the treasury, but did not hold office at the time. Between December 1955 and March 1956 Anderson visited Egypt and Israel several times and held talks with Nasser, Ben-Gurion, and other Israeli officials. The negotiations were kept secret, and the arrangements were made by the CIA rather than through the normal diplomatic channels.

It is difficult to establish at this stage, before governmental archives have been opened, what precisely were Anderson's terms of reference. Sharett and other Israeli officials understood that Anderson's task was to arrange a meeting between President Nasser and an Israeli leader, and that he was not meant to mediate on matters of substance.[30] On the other hand, Miles Copeland, who as a CIA representative in Egypt was involved in the negotiations, claims that Israel had agreed to talk with Anderson on matters of substance but subsequently changed its mind. According to him, the negotiations, code named GAMMA, were to be held in three stages. First, separate American teams were to have talks with Nasser and Ben-Gurion. Kermit Roosevelt, who headed CIA operations in the Middle East and who, according to Copeland, had "masterminded" the negotiations, and Copeland were to talk with Nasser, while two other Americans were to talk with Ben-Gurion. Their task was to prepare a "basic negotiating position." At the second stage, Anderson "would fly back and forth between Cairo and Tel Aviv . . . to narrow differences to an irreducible minimum." At the third stage, "Nasser and Ben-Gurion would meet secretly on a private yacht in the Mediterranean to try to close the gap."[31] In any event, when Anderson informed Ben-Gurion that Nasser, in fear of his life, had reneged on his previous acceptance of a meeting with an Israeli representative (Copeland's third stage), Ben-Gurion refused to continue discussing with Anderson matters of substance.

Yet, in fact, Israel as well as Egypt did talk with Anderson on substantive matters. On the basis of Ben-Gurion's notes on those discussions, which is the most detailed version published thus far, it seems that the talks did not consist merely of the mediator explaining to each side the adversary's position. The U.S. and each side also explained their attitudes toward each other's interests. This was not an exchange of information, but rather triangular tacit bargaining between Egypt and Israel, the U.S. and Egypt, and the U.S. and Israel. The issues between Egypt and Israel were boundaries, refugees, the blockade, the boycott, and the question of an Egyptian-Israeli meeting. Between the U.S. and Egypt the questions were Egypt's stance in the East-West conflict, the Baghdad Pact, Egyptian-Israeli relations, and Egypt's attitude toward the

Johnston water negotiations and the internationalization of Jerusalem (the last two issues to which American prestige had been committed). Anderson's evasive reply to a question of Ben-Gurion's suggests that American-Israeli relations was another issue in the American-Egyptian talks. Between the U.S. and Israel, the questions were Egyptian-Israeli relations, Israel's request for American arms, and Israel's policies on the Jordan water issue and Jerusalem.[32]

The most difficult issues dividing Egypt and Israel were the territorial and refugee questions. These reflected in fact two contrasting approaches to peace. Israel believed that peace should be established on the basis of the political and territorial status quo. Egypt's position was that the boundaries would have to be revised in Arab favor, and that Israel would have to accept in principle the return of the Arab refugees.

In Anderson's discussions on the territorial issue, Nasser took the view that a settlement should be based on the 1947 partition plan borders. In addition, Nasser demanded that the borders be altered so as to create territorial contiguity between Egypt and Jordan; a mere corridor (as advocated by the U.S.), would not suffice. Israel insisted on the boundaries established by the 1949 armistice. It was prepared to consider *mutual* minor border adjustments that would help resolve local problems such as villagers' access to land or water. But Israel did not accept Egypt's demand for territorial contiguity, nor the American ideas about a corridor. According to Israel a corridor was unnecessary, since under conditions of peace, communications between Egypt and Arab states to the east could be established through Israeli territory; Israel would serve as a bridge rather than a barrier between them. Anderson told the Israeli leaders that he called on Nasser to show "flexibility" on this issue, but that Nasser's attitude remained unchanged.

A wide gap separated the parties on the refugee question as well. Nasser insisted that Israel accept the principle of repatriation and of the refugees' free choice whether to return to Israel or to settle elsewhere. Israel disclaimed responsibility for the flight of the refugees, and regarded the demand for their return as a design to destroy its state through the introduction of a sizeable population that was hostile to its very existence. Nevertheless, on this issue Anderson saw some signs of flexibility. He told Nasser of his impression that Israel was prepared to allow for a measure of free choice within a family reunion framework, and he reported to the Israeli leaders that Nasser mentioned Syria and Iraq as possible sites for the resettlement of refugees who did not return to Israel.

The question of the Arab boycott and free navigation through the Suez Canal and the Straits of Tiran did not appear to present serious obstacles. Anderson reported to the Israeli leaders that Nasser told him that the boycott and the blockade would be removed when peace came.

On the question of the Jordan water development scheme Nasser was cooperative. The negotiations that Eric Johnston had been conducting for two years had bogged down, as the Arab states withheld their approval for his proposals. In response to Anderson's request for Nasser's help, the Egyptian president blamed the problem on the instability in Syria and promised to try to obtain Arab acceptance of the proposals. When Anderson expressed the hope that Israel would not proceed to implement its own water development scheme unilaterally as long as the Johnston negotiations were still going on, Ben-Gurion replied that Israel may refrain from doing so "for the sake of the U.S. and for the sake of peace," but that the issue was linked to Israel's request for arms.

There were also some puzzling discussions on the question of Jerusalem. Anderson raised the issue in both Cairo and Jerusalem. Nasser responded that the issue was mainly between Israel and Jordan, and departed from the formal Arab League position by saying that the division of the city was preferable to its internationalization. In response to Sharett's query Anderson acknowledged that the problem did not worry Nasser, but that he (Anderson) raised it because he thought that agreement may be possible on international supervision of the holy places.

Besides these discussions of the perennial issues in the conflict, an attempt was also made to pacify the boundary along which fighting was constantly taking place. This was important for its own sake as well as for the creation of a more favorable atmosphere for the peace negotiations. Anderson proposed that both sides make unilateral promises to President Eisenhower that they would observe the cease-fire and that they would punish those responsible for violations. However, Nasser was unwilling to mention in his letter anything about the punishment of those responsible, and it seems that nothing came of this idea.

Egypt's attitudes toward the West and the Soviet Union were another topic that Anderson discussed with Nasser. Anderson related to the Israeli leaders that Nasser criticized the Baghdad Pact as a British instrument directed against Arab independence. Anderson called to Nasser's attention the fate of the countries that fell into the Soviet sphere of influence. He told him that Egypt's resources would not suffice for both a major rearmament program and development, and that what Egypt needed was peace and development. To Anderson's suggestion that Egypt cease its propaganda against the West, Nasser responded favorably but said that this cannot be done immediately and abruptly, only gradually.

A central issue in the discussions was the proposed Egyptian-Israeli meeting. In principle a high-level meeting had been agreed upon at the time when Anderson's shuttle began. However, Nasser gradually retreated. When Anderson visited Cairo in mid-January, before coming to Israel, Nasser expressed his concern lest news of the meeting become public, and emphasized the need for absolute secrecy. He was unable to discuss specific arrangements, but Anderson was still hopeful, in his talks with Israeli leaders on January 23 to 25, that a meeting could be arranged; if not at the summit, then perhaps at a lower level. When Anderson returned to Cairo at the end of January, he quickly became doubtful whether any meeting could be arranged. Nasser spoke to him about his fears that Israel may use the meeting to deceive him. But his clinching argument was that opposition to peace with Israel in the Arab world was so violent that he risked being assassinated, as King Abdullah of Jordan had been, if his contacts with Israel became known. He said he needed several weeks to consider the question. Diplomatic contacts in the subsequent weeks confirmed that Nasser had completely retreated from his previous position and that even a meeting at a subordinate level could not take place.

Israel's argument in these discussions was that a meeting was necessary because no intermediary could explain Israel's positions on substantive issues as convincingly as Israeli representatives themselves. Israel also expressed the view that such a meeting could produce an agreement on the problem of communications between Egypt and the Arab states to the east. Finally, Israel claimed that direct contacts would help to dispel the distrust presently prevailing between the parties, and that this was essential if tension was to be reduced. Parallel to Nasser's gradual going back on his agreement to meet an Israeli leader, Israel made gradual concessions. If Nasser distrusted Ben-Gurion, it was ready to send Sharett; if Nasser was not prepared to meet at a neutral place, Sharett would go to Cairo; if a top-level meeting was unacceptable to Egypt at this time, Israel would agree to a meeting at a lower level. On January 31, when after another visit to Cairo Anderson expressed doubts whether a meeting could take place, Israel shifted its position about the urgency and importance of a meeting. On this occasion, Ben-Gurion suggested a gradual approach to Anderson. The most urgent measure according to Ben-Gurion was to prevent a war by providing Israel with deterrent weapons. Next, measures should be taken to stabilize the cease-fire. At the third stage, lower level contacts with Egypt should take place in an attempt to resolve minor issues. Only at the last stage, perhaps within a year, should the top-level meeting be scheduled to resolve the major issues in conflict.

The question of armaments was foremost in the minds of the Israeli leaders, and was a central issue in the discussions with Anderson. Ben-Gurion distinguished between two functions that the U.S. could perform: prevent war, and help make peace. To prevent war, it was urgent that Israel receive American weapons to deter Egypt from attacking Israel. Israeli leaders were convinced that when Egypt built up its strength with the newly acquired Soviet weapons, Nasser would attack. Several times in the talks with Anderson Ben-Gurion hinted at the possibility of a preventive war, saying that unless Israel received weapons soon, it would be compelled to take measures to protect itself.

In Israel's thinking, the American initiative and the Anderson negotiations became intimately linked with the delay in responding to Israel's request for weapons to balance the arms Egypt was receiving from the Soviet bloc. At one time, in late November or early December 1955, Israeli officials were under the impression that the U.S. would respond favorably. But after Israel launched a retaliatory raid against Syria on December 11, the U.S. decided that a reply to the arms request would have to be delayed. Then came the Anderson mission. Although American officials did not link the delay to the negotiations, Israel believed that the U.S. would not reply favorably as long as the negotiations continued, for fear that a positive reply would anger Egypt and have a detrimental effect on the talks. Israel also suspected that Nasser's willingness to enter into the negotiations was mainly to gain time to receive and absorb the Soviet weapons, while at the same time placing the U.S. in a position that would prevent it from acceding to Israel's request. Nasser's conduct in the negotiations and his delay in responding to Anderson's suggestions about a meeting confirmed Israel's suspicion that he was using the negotiations for this purpose.

When Anderson put to the Israeli leaders the question whether, in view of Egypt's refusal to meet with them, Israel would agree to American mediation, Israel had two weighty reasons to refuse. In the first place, given the American position on the questions of boundaries and refugees, Israel could not expect such a mediation to lead to a satisfactory outcome. Secondly, it would mean a further delay in the American reply to Israel's request for weapons. As Ben-Gurion told Anderson on March 9: "you will be able to continue the mediation if you first remove the danger of war. . . . If you give us arms within a few weeks—then you will be able to continue your efforts to improve the situation. . . ."[33]

Why Did He Fail?

As usual, it is a combination of causes rather than a single cause that explains the failure of this American initiative. Before examining the reasons that contributed to the failure, let us eliminate those that did not. In considering the identity of the mediator—the United States—it would seem that several of its attributes could have helped it to succeed, and probably did not contribute to its failure. The very acceptance of American mediation, however limited and temporary on Israel's part, can be attributed to the status, prestige, and power of the United States, and the desire of both parties to avoid antagonizing a great power.

As we move from the level of the state to the constituent actors involved, it is interesting to observe that the CIA probably helped to win cooperation, since both Egypt and Israel felt at that time that their interests met with greater understanding with the CIA than with the State Department.[34] Anderson's personal standing appears to have been helpful. He had served as secretary of the navy (1953-1954) and deputy secretary of defense (1954-1956). Because of his formal status as President Eisenhower's special emissary and his reputation of being closely associated with top administration officials, he was believed by both Egyptians and Israelis to be influential. Both sides took the negotiations with him most seriously and did not find it easy to refuse his suggestions.

The goal of his mission was so flexible that it could not have contributed to the failure. It was relatively modest, aiming to reduce only Egyptian-Israeli tensions, not to settle the entire Arab-Israeli conflict. It was not to conclude a peace treaty, but to try to reach an agreement on any of the issues in conflict, or at least on the procedural question of how to conduct negotiations. It cannot be claimed that the mission failed because the goal was overambitious.

The negotiations failed because of the combined effect of three factors: unpropitious timing, the unacceptability of mediation by Israel, and the decline of the mediator's motivation.

The American initiative was launched at a moment when one side believed that its bargaining position was strong and improving, and the other that its was temporarily weak. These assessments led each side, albeit for different reasons, to assume a rigid negotiating stance.

Nasser believed his bargaining power vis-à-vis Israel was improved by the acquisition of Soviet weapons, while the West continued in its willingness to provide Egypt with economic assistance. Indeed, he probably expected that with the passage of time Egypt's military strength and bargaining power would improve even further. Thus, there was nothing in the situation to induce him to be flexible or conciliatory toward Israel, but to the contrary, he could safely adhere to his position and perhaps even escalate his demands. Nasser's flexibility toward the U.S. at the end of 1955 was only temporary, until he felt assured that no dire punishments would be inflicted upon Egypt for the purchase of Soviet weapons. By January 1956 his attitude toward the U.S. and toward Western interests in general began to harden.

Israel was rigid because it believed its bargaining power to be weak. Israeli leaders were convinced that Nasser was dedicated to the goal of destroying Israel. They were concerned that with the help of Soviet weapons, Egypt would improve its overall military capability. Israel also felt abandoned by its friends. All major powers, with the exception of France, were engaged in courting Egyptian friendship and were prepared to pay for it by going some way toward accepting Egyptian demands on territorial and refugee issues. Under these circumstances, Israel accorded priority to strengthening its military power and preferred to postpone negotiations until this had been achieved.

Both Israeli and Egyptian attitudes toward American mediation were not determined by their images of American basic attitudes toward them, but rather by their expectations of the side effects and outcomes of such mediation. Although Egypt regarded the U.S. as basically pro-Israeli, and along with most Arabs blamed Israel's establishment and survival mainly on the U.S., it nevertheless accepted, and perhaps even encouraged American mediation. The Egyptian attitude was motivated by the desire to appear cooperative so as to mollify American anger at the acceptance of Soviet weapons. In addition, as we have seen, Egypt had reason to expect the additional tactical gain of delaying or even precluding altogether the supply of American weapons to Israel. It does not seem probable that Egypt (or anyone else) expected that the negotiations would lead to peace. But if they led to any sort of agreement, then—in view of the American position on the substantive issues in conflict—its terms would be more favorable to Egypt than any Egypt could expect to obtain on its own, without American help.

The same considerations in reverse rendered American mediation unacceptable to Israel. If the negotiations led to any agreement, its terms would be less favorable to Israel than direct negotiations because of the American intervention. Israel's most urgent concern was the acquisition of weapons. Israeli leaders were gradually losing hope that the U.S. would respond favorably to Israel's appeal for American arms, but they were certain that as long as the U.S. was involved as a mediator, a positive reply was out of the question. When confronted in December by the American claim that Nasser was prepared to negotiate for a settlement and even prepared to meet an Israeli leader, and challenged with the question of whether Israel was as interested in peace as Egypt, Israel had no choice but to accept American mediation.[35] But it was a reluctant acceptance, which was withdrawn as soon as Nasser's retractions and evasions permitted the mediation to be terminated without Israel's being blamed.

Finally, the failure of the mediation effort can also be attributed to the decline of American motivation. The American initiative was part of a comprehensive effort to limit Soviet influence and test Nasser's claim that he wanted to preserve American friendship. Peace, however desirable, was not a goal on its own merits. Once the U.S. despaired of Nasser because he proved to be uncooperative in the Aswan Dam negotiations, Egypt's new military relationship with the Soviet Union continued to expand, and Egyptian propaganda continued to attack the West and undermine its position everywhere in the Arab world, the motivation to continue the efforts for an Egyptian-Israeli agreement declined.[36] As it became clear that the mediation could not serve the goal of containing or limiting Soviet penetration, the American willingness to exert itself in the search for peace faded away. In other words, in this case the mediation attempting to reach an Egyptian-Israeli agreement was in part an instrument used in the pursuit of another and more important goal. Once the U.S. concluded that the positive incentives offered to Egypt—the aid for constructing the Aswan Dam and qualified American support for Egypt in the negotiations with Israel—failed to produce the results hoped for, both incentives were withdrawn. America embarked on a different approach to influence Nasser and the mediation attempt was dropped along the way.

SIX

The Jarring Mission

The Sinai War in 1956 did not stimulate any major attempts to settle differences, but only to tackle the immediate crisis produced by the war. Once the crisis was defused, the Arab-Israeli conflict remained relatively quiescent until the mid-sixties. Motivation for new peace initiatives was low, and few attempts were made.

The 1967 war changed this atmosphere. In the wake of the war, numerous attempts were launched to resolve the Arab-Israeli conflict. These efforts were undertaken in a very different setting from the early 1950s. The societies involved, the conflict itself, and the international environment had all undergone important changes. A few observations about those that affected mediation attempts need to be made.

In the decade between the Sinai War and the Six-Day War, Israel enjoyed a period of consolidation. Immigrants were absorbed into the fabric of society and social and economic development made immense progress. In the international arena Israel's relations with other states improved and intensified. Its ties with the U.S., Western Europe, and Latin America were supplemented by new relationships forged with many Asian and African states. Only its relations with the Soviet bloc suffered a decline. Except for the Arab states and a few of their friends, no one questioned Israel's right to exist, nor did anyone challenge Israel's territorial integrity within the boundaries established by the 1949 armistice agreements.

The Arab world was in disarray, and had been for years preceding the Six-Day War. Nasser's ambition for leadership of the Arab world and the awakening of the masses to the call of nationalism were probably among the chief causes of this disarray. A prominent and recurrent issue in inter-Arab quarrels was the competition for leadership in the struggle against Israel. This competition was one of the factors leading to the crisis that culminated in the Six-Day War.

Until the mid-1950s Western influence predominated throughout the Middle East. The Anderson mission coincided with the establishment of the first Soviet foothold in the region. But even Egypt, where this foothold was established, was not yet closely associated with the Soviet Union. The Soviets, although usually supporting the Arabs, still maintained correct, albeit somewhat strained diplomatic relations with Israel. By 1967, this situation had changed. The Soviet Union held predominant influence in Egypt, Syria, and Iraq, and had become identified with the Arab struggle against Israel. This identification became even more complete following the Six-Day War, when the Soviets and their East European allies (except Rumania) broke diplomatic relations with Israel. The Soviets did not share the basic Arab aim of destroying Israel, but for all practical purposes they had become the mainstay of the Arab struggle against Israel.

This brought about a structural change in the Arab-Israeli conflict. Until the mid-1950s the conflict was played on Western turf. Although American and British policies were swayed by their fear that the Soviets would exploit Arab resentments over Israel and other issues to establish their influence, the Arab-Israeli conflict was insulated from direct intervention by the Soviet bloc. By 1967, the conflict had become intertwined with the East-West struggle; the Soviet-American and the Arab-Israeli conflicts had become closely interdependent. Changes in the Arab-Israeli conflict altered the Soviet-American political and strategic balance in the region, carrying with them global ramifications. Conversely, changes in Soviet-American relations carried in their wake changes in the Arab-Israeli conflict. Neither escalation nor deescalation could take place in the Arab-Israeli conflict without the U.S. and the Soviet Union regarding the process as relevant to their mutual relations and vital interests.

*

The first major peacemaking effort following the Six-Day War was launched with the appointment, in November 1967, of Dr. Gunnar V. Jarring, a senior Swedish diplomat, as special representative of the UN secretary-general, in accordance with Security Council Resolution 242. Between 1967 and 1972, Jarring held several rounds of talks with Arab and Israeli officials. His negotiations got nowhere. Nevertheless they raise several interesting questions.

First, why was he appointed, and what were the expectations of the members of the Security Council and the parties to the conflict concerning his mission? After all, the UN had failed in past efforts to resolve the Arab-Israeli conflict. At the time of Jarring's appointment, its prestige had reached a nadir when the withdrawal of the UN Emergency Force from its positions in Sinai in May 1967 had aggravated Arab-Israeli tensions and removed an obstacle to the outbreak of war. Under the circumstances, it should have been clear to everyone that the chances for the success of UN peacemaking were very small indeed. Second, in view of the past friction between Israel (and to a lesser extent also the Arab states) and UN peacemaking and peacekeeping missions, how was the Jarring mission made acceptable to them? Third, notwithstanding Jarring's ultimate failure, the parties made some concessions in the course of the negotiations. How were these concessions brought about? Fourth, what effect did the various interventions of the great powers, ostensibly made in support of the Jarring mission, have upon the negotiations and upon the fortunes of the mission? Finally, there is also the need to explain Jarring's ultimate failure. There are simple explanations, which are probably correct but insufficient. One can say that Jarring failed because he acted on behalf of the UN, which was devoid of influence. But we know that Bunche, in collaboration with the U.S., succeeded. Why didn't Jarring, who worked in collaboration with the U.S., the Soviet Union, Britain, and France, succeed likewise? The obvious answer is because the parties refused to make the necessary concessions. But this only begs the question whether there was anything that Jarring and his supporters could have done and did not do, to induce the parties to make sufficient concessions to enable the settlement of the conflict.

Jarring's Appointment and the Parties' Reactions

The Jarring mission originated in a standard procedure of the international community and the UN Secretariat, which responded to the conflict in the Middle East by sending someone to the area to try to ameliorate the situation. Security Council Resolution 242 that requested the UN secretary-general to send a special representative to the Middle East had two aims: to provide the UN emissary, whose appointment had already been decided upon beforehand, with terms of reference, and to reach some international consensus on principles that would help to moderate the conflict and guide it toward a settlement.

As soon as the Six-Day War ended, on June 11, Israel, the Arab states, and other interested powers all turned their attention to the future. But their positions were far apart, both on the substance and the procedure. Many Israelis believed that the situation created by the outcome of the war was propitious for peace. They had long believed that peace would come when the Arabs realized that they were incapable of destroying Israel. Israel's victory seemed to provide sufficient proof of that. Moreover, the territories Israel occupied were useful both as bargaining assets and instruments of pressure that could serve to persuade the Arabs to make peace. The hopes were, however, marred by fears of a repetition of 1956: that international pressure might be exerted to restore the situation that existed before the war, and thus encourage the Arab states in the belief that peace with Israel was not necessary. The conclusion of peace required, of course, negotiations. Viewing the interventions of mediators in past negotiations as responsible in large measure for their failure, Israel insisted this time that the negotiations be carried out directly between Israeli and Arab representatives, without the interposition of third parties. (Its insistence on direct negotiations notwithstanding, Israel did transmit, in June 1967, its proposals for peace to Egypt and to Syria through the good offices of the U.S.)[1]

The U.S., like Israel, believed that an opportunity for a stable and durable peace had been created by the war. President Lyndon Johnson expressed this view in a speech on June 19, in which he outlined the five principles that ought to shape peace: recognized right of national life, justice for the refugees, innocent maritime passage, limitation of the arms race, and political independence and territorial integrity for all. In the American view, peace was to be achieved through negotiations between the Arab states and Israel. But, unlike Israel, the U.S. also envisaged the need for "appropriate third party assistance" in the process.[2]

To the Arab states, peace with Israel required a total restructuring and reordering of their national goals. To make peace under the circumstances they found themselves in the summer of 1967 was tantamount to surrender. This was difficult psychologically, dangerous from a domestic political standpoint, and unnecessary thanks to massive Soviet assistance which began to flow to Egypt and Syria in the aftermath of their defeat. The Arab states aimed at restoring the situation that existed before the war, both to strengthen the regimes' standing domestically and to improve their ability to continue their struggle against Israel. The Soviet Union, fearing to lose its important footholds in Egypt and in Syria, supported this Arab policy. The Arab states and the Soviet Union therefore demanded an unconditional withdrawal of Israeli forces to the lines established in the armistice agreements of 1949. Since the withdrawal was to be unconditional, it did not require any negotiations, nor any procedures or channels for conducting them.[3]

Following the failure of the Soviet Union and the Arab states in the summer of 1967 to bring about a UN resolution calling for Israel's withdrawal and the inability of the UN to adopt any resolution at all (except for a call on Israel not to alter the status of Jerusalem), a diplomatic deadlock ensued.[4] The only idea on which agreement appeared possible was that a UN envoy be sent to the Middle East. The principal proponent of this idea was the UN Secretary-General U Thant, who probably felt bold enough to advocate it because he knew that it enjoyed some support. In his introduction to the annual report to the General Assembly published on September 19, U Thant stated that direct Arab-Israeli negotiations were not possible, but that "one helpful step that could be taken immediately would be" to authorize the secretary-general to designate "a special representative to the Middle East. Such an appointee could serve as a much needed channel of communication, as a reporter and interpreter of events and views for the Secretary-General and as both a sifter and a harmonizer of ideas in the area."[5]

For the mission to have any positive effect, it was necessary that it be acceptable to the Arab states and Israel as well as to the principal powers. Israel opposed mediation and insisted on direct negotiations. This position stemmed mainly from the fear that the interests of the great powers were likely to result in the mediator favoring the Arab side. It was fed by the memory of previous occasions of third-party involvement in Arab-Israeli negotiations that maneuvered Israel into uncomfortable diplomatic positions. In early September Israel modified its stand somewhat; its Cabinet instructed the delegation to the forthcoming General Assembly to oppose third-party efforts that did not lead to direct negotiations. The implication was, of course, that Israel might accept an intermediary provided his task was to bring about direct negotiations. Prime Minister Eshkol was quoted as saying that "the UN could do a great service if it served as a matchmaker, to bring the two sides together, but if they appoint a mediator they will have accomplished nothing."[6]

Arab acceptance of a UN special representative was also difficult to obtain. In view of the Arab states' initial position calling for Israel's unconditional withdrawal, there was no need for negotiations nor for any special representative to conduct them. By September it became evident that the positions of Egypt and Jordan (but not Syria) had become more flexible. It may be that what induced them to modify their stand was the fear that continued diplomatic deadlock might enable Israel to strengthen its grip upon the occupied territories. In any event, hoping that this step would set Israel's withdrawal in motion, Egypt and Jordan were now prepared to hold discussions with a UN representative.[7]

As the idea of sending a special representative to the Middle East was gaining ground, U Thant took the initiative of recruiting a candidate for the job. He asked for the Swedish government's agreement to the nomination of Dr. Gunnar Jarring as early as October 17, and received it on the 24th, a full month before the Security Council formally requested him through Resolution 242 to appoint a representative. Jarring seemed well qualified for the post. Sweden was not identified with either of the parties in the conflict and maintained neutrality in the East-West contest as well. Jarring's personal experience was considerable and relevant to the assignment: he had held several diplomatic posts in the Middle East, he had served as UN intermediary between India and Pakistan, and had headed the Swedish mission at the UN and subsequently in Washington. At the time of his nomination he was Swedish ambassador to Moscow. His experience gave him an insight into the workings of the UN and of the governments of the two superpowers, and acquainted him with some of the officials with whom he would have to deal. According to Thant, the Arab states, Israel, and the four great powers (the U.S., Britain, France, and the Soviet Union)—all welcomed Jarring's candidacy, some even with enthusiasm.[8]

By the end of October there was agreement on the principle of sending a special representative, as well as on the person who would hold the post. Only at this stage did serious negotiations begin on what the representative's assignment should be. This was crucial, since the acceptance of the principle was tentative and conditional upon the terms of reference. Israel's initial position was that the Security Council should limit itself to appointing the special representative, without attempting to define his terms of reference. Egypt, on the other hand, insisted that the Security Council resolution appointing him contain specific directives.[9] Egypt, though for different reasons than Israel, did not want the UN envoy to serve as a mediator. Rather, according to Egypt, he ought to be instructed to bring about and oversee Israel's withdrawal.

In the weeks that followed, intensive negotiations were conducted about the Security Council resolution. The most controversial issues were the questions of withdrawal and of the special representative's functions. The Arab states and the Soviet Union demanded that Israel be requested to withdraw from *all* the territories it occupied in the Six-Day War, and that this be explicitly stated in the resolution. Israel, on the other hand, maintained that the location of the boundaries should be determined by negotiations with its neighbors. The wording that was finally agreed upon was ambiguous. It called for Israel's withdrawal "from territories," rather than "all the territories" as the Soviets and Arabs had wished. The controversy about the special representative's functions was also resolved by ambiguous wording: he was instructed "to establish and maintain contacts with the States concerned in order to promote agreement and assist efforts to achieve a peaceful and accepted settlement in accordance with the provisions and principles in this resolution."[10] This phrasing did not instruct him to oversee the implementation of Israel's withdrawal, as the Arabs desired. Nor did it confine his duties to "matchmaking," as Israel wished. But Israel could find satisfaction in the explicit instruction "to promote agreement," which was tantamount to negotiation, although the latter term was not used.

The resolution's ambiguity enabled it to gain the acceptance of the great powers, and the reluctant assent of Israel, Egypt, and Jordan. It also allowed the resolution to remain relevant for many years. Interestingly, at the time of its adoption, some commentators believed that because of its ambiguities the resolution would have little practical effect. *The Economist* commented that the only effect of the resolution would be the sending of Jarring to the Middle East, and reported that Lord Caradon, the author of the resolution, maintained that this in itself might do immense good.[11] Subsequent developments were to show how mistaken they were; Jarring's mission did little good. But the resolution, intended to serve as Jarring's terms of reference, has outlived his mission, and has continued to provide the guidelines for Arab-Israeli negotiations ever since.

The First Phase, 1967-1969

Besides the large and fundamental problems, Jarring addressed himself to two more limited issues—the exchange of war prisoners and the release of ships stranded in the Suez Canal. The problem of the prisoners was pressing because of the human suffering it involved. The release of the ships was seen as a step toward the clearance and reopening of the the canal. That was an urgent goal for Britain as well as a large number of other states, the economies of which were seriously hurt by the canal closure. (Indeed, this was an important motive behind Britain's diplomatic activism for Resolution 242.)[12] The prospects of making progress on these limited issues appeared far better than on the larger problems dividing the Arabs and Israelis. It was expected that even a small success at the very outset of the mission would help build up confidence in Jarring and would contribute to the creation of a more favorable atmosphere for the negotiations. Yet the outcome was more modest than hoped for. Jarring was credited with contributing to the prisoner exchange, but the efforts to release the ships trapped in the canal bogged down. Judging by subsequent developments, the exchange of prisoners had no perceptible effect on the negotiations that followed.[13]

The negotiations were held with Israel, Egypt, and Jordan; Syria refused to accept Resolution 242 and the Jarring mission. They were in fact negotiations about negotiations. The initial position of Egypt and Jordan was that Israel's withdrawal from all the territories must precede any discussions about the implementation of the other principles listed in Resolution 242. They claimed that Jarring's first and most urgent task was to arrange for Israel's withdrawal. Israel, on the other hand, regarded the withdrawal as one of the subjects requiring negotiation. It was Jarring's task to arrange direct negotiations, and it was only in direct negotiations with the Arab states that Israel was prepared to discuss matters of substance.[14]

The contradictory views on whether negotiations should precede or follow withdrawal stemmed from each side's desire to "negotiate from strength." From the standpoint of Egypt and Jordan, most of the principles of Resolution 242 were concessions that they were expected to make. Negotiating about the implementation of these principles while the Israeli army was in possession of territories that they regarded as their own would have placed them at a disadvantage. They preferred to postpone the discussion on the concessions they were required to make until after the Israeli army withdrew, at which time they could perhaps avoid making them at all. The Israelis also believed that as long as their forces were stationed in the territories, they were negotiating from strength and could expect a favorable outcome from the negotiations. If negotiations were postponed until after their forces were withdrawn, there was a risk that the situation would revert to what it had been for the preceding nineteen years, and that an opportunity for concluding peace would have been lost.

Both sides also regarded the question whether there were to be direct negotiations as highly important. Israel feared that indirect talks would lead to mediation, and in such a triangular negotiating situation its bargaining advantage would be reduced, as its past experience indicated. For Egypt and Jordan, engaging in direct negotiations was tantamount to recognizing Israel. They viewed Israel's insistence on direct negotiations as an attempt to obtain recognition prior to withdrawal or to any negotiations.

Concern about the domestic political consequences that might follow if they altered their negotiating stances contributed to both sides' rigidity. Israel's coalition Cabinet could fall apart if the government made concessions, since the Gahal faction was strongly opposed to a withdrawal from the territories and to any procedural moves that might lead to it. Egypt and Jordan had been criticized for accepting Resolution 242 by Syria, Iraq, Algeria, and the Palestine Liberation Organization (PLO). Any further concession on their part would expose them to sharper attack, which could lead to domestic unrest.

Despite the good reasons both sides had for adhering to their initial positions, they nevertheless offered some concessions and changed their stance somewhat in the course of the negotiations. The concessions they offered can be regarded as mere tactical maneuvering; nevertheless, these changes should be noted and the reasons for them explained.

Israel's position changed on the questions of the acceptance of Resolution 242 and the form of negotiations. The initial attitude to the resolution was one of neither acceptance nor rejection. During the early months of 1968 several reformulations of qualified acceptance were made, until an unqualified statement of acceptance was delivered by Ambassador Yosef Tekoah in the Security Council on May 1, 1968. This statement almost led to a Cabinet crisis. Yet Tekoah's acceptance was not rescinded and the coalition did not break up.[15] Concerning the Jarring negotiations, Israel's position changed from refusal to accept any intermediary (before September 1967), to the acceptance of a UN representative who would act as a "matchmaker" bringing the parties together for the purpose of direct negotiations, to the acceptance of the pattern of the Rhodes armistice talks (negotiations under the chairmanship of the UN representative), to, finally, the acceptance of separate talks with Jarring on the "understanding" that they would lead to direct contacts between the parties. The most significant modification in Israel's stance occurred in October 1968, when for the first time Israel agreed to discuss with Jarring issues of substance, rather than confining contacts with him to procedural matters.[16]

The Egyptian and Jordanian positions also underwent some modification. Their initial view, that there was nothing to discuss until Israeli forces had been withdrawn, was modified in early 1968 to an acceptance of indirect talks even before withdrawal, on condition that Israel declare its readiness to implement Resolution 242. They were prepared to see the resolution implemented as a "package deal," implying some simultaneity, rather than insisting on prior withdrawal. Their attitude toward the Jarring mission remained, however, essentially unchanged. Although accepting the principle of indirect talks, they did not leave much for discussion. They were not prepared to consider the conclusion of a formal peace with Israel. They continued to interpret Resolution 242 as requiring Israel's withdrawal from *all* territories, and Jarring's mission as one of setting only the mode and timetable for implementation. At this stage Egypt and Jordan were not yet willing to concede to Jarring the role of mediator.[17]

The softening of the parties' positions can be attributed to the work of Jarring and the great powers. The mediator's most effective tactic to induce the parties to offer concessions was the threat that he would quit and return to Moscow. There were rumors to this effect toward the end of January. Subsequently, the question arose whether his mission would come to an end after his initial six months' leave from the Moscow embassy expired in May, and then again when the end of the second six-month period approached in the fall.[18] The impression one gets is that in January and in the spring, the possibility that the mission might be terminated contributed to the decisions of all three parties to offer tactical concessions. If so, their probable reason was the desire to avoid any blame for the termination of the mission, rather than the expectation of positive gains from its continuation. When the November deadline approached, Israel was more eager to extend the life of the mission than the Arab side. By then it appeared that if Jarring's mission came to an end, the diplomatic effort would be assumed directly by the great powers. Israel feared that they might exert upon it severe pressure, and it was probably the same consideration in reverse that made Egypt and Jordan favor great power intervention. In consequence, Israel significantly modified its stand in October. Foreign Minister Eban outlined for the first time Israel's peace proposals in a speech at the UN General Assembly on October 9, and subsequently handed Jarring two memoranda dealing with substantive issues, rather than only procedural ones as hitherto. The Arab states for their part were quick to reject Israel's peace plan. Apparently to underline the failure of Jarring's efforts, and to prod the great powers to intervene, the Egyptian and Jordanian representatives broke off the talks they were holding in New York and departed for home in early November.[19]

Jarring's compromise formulae to break deadlocks were less effective. Hoping that the Arabs could be persuaded to enter into discussions prior to Israel's troop withdrawal if they were assured that the withdrawal would eventually take place, Jarring proposed that the parties provide him with a commitment that "they would implement Security Council resolution 242 (1967)."[20] He apparently believed that this wording was sufficiently ambiguous to allow each party to subscribe to it, without appearing to make a major concession. But in fact Jarring's wording impinged in a significant way upon the Israeli position that the task ahead was to promote *agreement*, and was closer to the Arab viewpoint that the resolution simply required *implementation*. Consequently, in February 1968 Egypt and Jordan gave Jarring the proposed assurance while Israel responded that it would cooperate in the efforts to promote an agreement, basing itself on the wording of the resolution itself. It is also noteworthy that at this early stage in his mission, Israel did not protest Jarring's proposing a formula, although it amounted to an interpretation of the resolution. As we shall see, a subsequent and more detailed proposal by Jarring in February 1971 was rejected by Israel, which claimed that he had exceeded his authority.

Another failure was an attempted compromise based on a precedent. To circumvent the deadlock between Israel's insistence on direct talks and the Arab rejection of them, Jarring proposed to issue an invitation to the parties to meet with him "for conferences" in Nicosia. It was possible to persuade Israel to accept the invitation by claiming that this would lead to the procedure followed by Ralph Bunche at Rhodes in 1949, an event that evoked favorable memories in Israel. But because Israel refused to commit itself about implementation and because the Rhodes talks had come to be regarded by the Arabs in an unfavorable light, Egypt and Jordan rejected the proposal.[21]

Whatever the hopes were at the time when Jarring's mission was launched, it is unlikely that he, or anyone else, believed that his standing as the secretary-general's special representative and the resources of the United Nations would suffice to enable him to fulfil his mission. It was probably taken for granted that Jarring would need some assistance from the great powers. In 1967 and 1968 such assistance was provided behind the scenes, separately by the U.S. and the Soviet Union, with little or no coordination between them. In 1969, an attempt was made to concert great power intervention. In addition, with the advent of the Nixon administration, the U.S. intensified its independent efforts with each of the parties.

Both the U.S. and the Soviet Union used their influence to obtain the acceptance by Israel, Egypt, and Jordan of Resolution 242, and subsequently to persuade them to modify their stance. The U.S. was active in the course of 1968. Early in the year it asked Israel to relax its insistence on direct talks and to agree to indirect talks through Jarring. In the summer, George Ball, who was at that time ambassador to the UN, visited Israel and Jordan and sought to persuade both governments to be more flexible. In September and October the U.S. tried to persuade Israel to engage in substantive talks with Jarring, instead of confining itself to procedural discussions. Diplomatic argumentation and reasoning were sometimes accompanied by incentives. One kind of incentive was assurance of American diplomatic support. Thus, as part of the efforts to induce Israel to accept Resolution 242, the U.S. informed Israel that in the American view the resolution called for the establishment of new borders, different from the lines existing prior to the 1967 war. Jordan's acceptance of the resolution was sought by means of a promise that under its terms the U.S. would work for the return of the West Bank to Jordan with minor boundary rectifications only. In November 1968, Secretary of State Dean

Rusk reportedly informed Egypt that the U.S. might support a full Israeli withdrawal from Sinai if Egypt agreed to conclude a formal peace treaty. A common incentive, and form of pressure as well, was the supply or withholding of arms. President Johnson reportedly assured Prime Minister Levi Eshkol in January 1968 during Eshkol's visit to the U.S. that the U.S. would sell Phantom aircraft to Israel. This may have been meant as an incentive for Israel to cooperate with Jarring. A formal decision was however delayed through most of 1968; it was finally announced by President Johnson on October 9. Although widely regarded as related to the presidential election campaign, it was also linked to Abba Eban's speech at the UN General Assembly one day earlier, in which he announced Israel's readiness to engage in substantive discussions with Jarring. Eban himself hints at a connection between Israel's concession and the presidential decision by noting that the president published his decision one day after the UN speech. To a lesser extent, the supply of weapons was used as an incentive to Jordan as well.[22] Although little has been published about Soviet intervention, there are indications of some Soviet diplomatic activity. Reports that Egypt might agree to the return of UN forces to Sinai and allow Israeli cargoes to transit the Suez Canal were linked in the press to talks conducted by Soviet leaders with President Nasser and with Jarring, and to the Soviet interest in the reopening of the canal.[23]

The nature of the support that the great powers gave Jarring changed in 1969, as an effort was made for concerted joint action. The idea that a settlement of the Arab-Israeli conflict ought to be worked out between the four principal powers—the U.S., the Soviet Union, Britain and France—was not new. It was advocated by France and Britain already in 1967. France and Britain renewed the suggestion toward the end of 1968, as the Jarring talks failed to make progress, and as it appeared that the U.S. and the Soviet Union might discuss the problem. By January 1969, it became generally understood, mainly due to

American insistence, that such talks, should they take place, would be aimed at supporting the Jarring mission. U Thant, presumably expressing Jarring's views as well, strongly favored such a move. American assent was given in early February, shortly after the Nixon administration assumed office. At a news conference on February 6 the president announced an American initiative that would encompass continued support for the Jarring mission, bilateral talks with the Soviet Union, four-power talks, and discussions with Israel and the Arab states.[24]

The initiatives for the two-power and four-power talks have a number of explanations, some stemming directly from the Arab-Israeli conflict and others from the wider concerns of the powers. It was obvious that the Jarring mission was stalemated. In the region itself the cease-fire along the Suez Canal was repeatedly violated and seemed to be breaking down. This raised the prospect that hostilities in the region might spread and escalate, and with it rose the danger of the superpowers being drawn into a confrontation. The image of a Middle East powder keg seems to have been much on President Richard Nixon's mind, and to have influenced his attitude.

In addition, each of the powers was motivated by concerns unrelated to the Middle East. France under Charles de Gaulle wanted the talks in order to promote its standing as a great power that participates alongside the superpowers in shaping the destinies of the world. In the United States, the new administration under President Nixon assumed responsibility with zeal and energy, seeking to pursue a more active diplomacy world-wide and to amend some of the situations that, they believed, the Johnson administration had neglected. One was the Middle East; another was the relations with France. Acceding to De Gaulle's request for four-power talks on the Middle East was one way of mollifying him and mending relations with France. The Nixon administration also wanted to make a new start with the Soviet Union. President Nixon and Kissinger (at that time the president's adviser on national security), wished to do this by opening a dialogue on a wide range of issues on which American and Soviet interests met, and often collided—and high on the list, alongside Vietnam and arms control, was the Middle East. According to Nixon's and Kissinger's conception of negotiations, these ought not to be treated as discrete issues, but should all be linked to an overall policy toward the Soviet Union. Among the Soviet motivations in desiring negotiations on the Arab-Israeli conflict, obtaining recognition of its legitimate interest and involvement in Middle East affairs was probably highly important.[25] Thus the powers were interested in the side effects of their talks as much, if not more, as in the successful conclusion of their negotiations.

At first the powers did not see their talks as aimed at supporting the Jarring mission. This came as an afterthought to lend legitimacy to their intervention. At the start, the Soviet Union and France were prepared to bypass Jarring. But, largely because of Israeli fears of an imposed settlement and its strong opposition to both the two-power and four-power talks, the U.S. considered it essential that the talks be explicitly linked to Resolution 242 and the Jarring mission. This conception accorded with the attitude of U Thant, and presumably of Jarring himself, who hoped that energetic support by the great powers would help the mission to make progress. The conception that the U.S. formulated was that the talks were aimed at arriving at "an agreed interpretation" of Resolution 242 "for UN Special Representative Jarring to use as guidelines to restart his talks with Arab states and Israel."[26] The proposed procedure was described by U Thant as follows: "It was originally agreed that any plan initiated by the U.S. or the U.S.S.R. must first get the endorsement of both, and then be presented to Britain and France. After all four powers agreed to it, the plan would be transmitted to me for transmission to Mr. Jarring for negotiation with Israel and the Arab states."[27] To alleviate Israeli fears, the U.S. repeatedly emphasized that there was no intention to impose a settlement. But, in the words of Secretary of State William Rogers, "if the world community should agree on a certain general formula for the settlement of the Middle East, then I think the governments in that area would want to think long and hard before they turned it down."[28]

Israeli apprehensions arose mainly from the likely shape of the agreement that the powers might reach. The Soviet Union was wholly committed to supporting the Arab states, while the U.S. did not identify with Israel to the same extent. Thus any compromise reached was expected to be much closer to the Arab viewpoint than to Israel's. Israel was unable to prevent the talks. But to underline its opposition and determination not to accept an imposed settlement, Israel let it be known that it "would not receive Mr. Jarring if he was sent to Israel to negotiate an agreement reached by the Big Four."[29]

Egyptian and Jordanian reactions to the great power intervention were more favorable. According to Heikal, Egyptian Foreign Minister Mahmoud Riad was concerned that they might interfere with the Jarring talks. But he was overruled by President Nasser who argued that "Jarring isn't going to solve anything. If he does appear to have produced a solution, this would only be because something had been arranged behind the scenes between the two super-powers."[30] He probably estimated that what might be arranged by the superpowers would be more favorable to Egypt than either the status quo or the concession of actually negotiating with Israel. To lend credence to the view that the situation was explosive and to encourage the powers in their attempt to reach an agreement, Egypt launched the War of Attrition in the spring of 1969 as the two-power and four-power talks got on their way.

Preparations for the great power talks were accompanied by a new spurt of activity by Jarring. Following Israel's concession to enter into substantive talks, Jarring departed on November 27 for the Middle East, but after his talks there concluded that the attitudes of the parties had not changed. In February 1969, after consulting the UN representatives of the four powers, he decided "that the best contribution which he could make to breaking the existing deadlock was to make a further tour of the Middle East in which he would formally submit to the parties a series of questions designed to elicit their attitude towards Security Council resolution 242 (1967)."[31] However, the formal questions merely elicited a recommitment by the parties to previously stated positions.

Three days after receiving the last reply to his questionnaire (Israel's reply on April 2), Jarring returned to Moscow. U Thant's report says that he returned to Moscow because he concluded "that there was no further move which he could usefully make at that stage."[32] There was no reason for Jarring to believe that a formal questionnaire would elicit concessions from the parties. It is therefore conceivable that he expected the parties to reiterate their previous positions, thus giving him an excuse for suspending his mission. Jarring probably concluded, as did the parties themselves, that he ought to await the outcome of the great power negotiations. He may also have hoped that his return to Moscow would serve to prod the powers to reach an agreement. Whatever Jarring's expectations about the duration of the suspension of his mission, it remained in fact suspended for sixteen months, until August 1970.

The Second Phase, 1970 1971

The Jarring mission was renewed in August 1970, not as a result of great power agreement, but because of a unilateral American initiative. The initiative, and the American mediation which led to its acceptance, will be discussed in detail in Chapter 7 below. Here only those aspects of the initiative directly relevant to the Jarring mission are examined.

The American move, known as the Rogers Initiative (as

distinguished from the Rogers Plan), brought an end to the War of Attrition. Both Israel and Egypt accepted the terms of an American-sponsored ninety-day cease-fire. They also agreed to send representatives to hold discussions under Jarring's auspices. The wording of the American proposal for the resumption of the Jarring mission to which Egypt, Jordan, and Israel gave their assent (albeit with qualifications and reservations) made a few innovations. It provided Jarring with wider authority than he had exercised between 1967 and 1969 to recommend the time, place, and procedure of the discussions. And more significantly, for the first time since the passage of Resolution 242, Israel agreed to use the word "withdrawal" in a formal document. The use of this term brought about a Cabinet crisis in Israel and resulted in the resignation of the Gahal ministers, led by Menahem Begin, from the government coalition.[33]

The setting of the talks held with Jarring at the end of 1970 and early 1971 was different in several important respects from the setting of his mission in 1967-1969. They were held after the great power talks, pursued intermittently through most of 1969, had ended in failure. During the first phase of the Jarring mission, the possibility of effective great power intervention appeared real. It tended to induce rigidity on the Arab side, since they hoped that a compromise agreement between the great powers would enable them to obtain better terms than they could get by negotiating through Jarring with Israel. The possibility of great power intervention may also have been a safety net for Jarring; if his efforts prove to be to no avail, then the great powers might agree on an interpretation of his terms of reference and still rescue his mission. In 1970-1971 such hopes no longer existed.

A highly important new element in the situation was the Rogers Plan. This was an American draft formula for an Israeli-Egyptian settlement, submitted to the Soviet Union on October 28, 1969, at a time when the State Department believed that the U.S. and the Soviet Union were very close to an agreement. According to the American proposal, the Egyptian-Israeli border was to be established at the former international border between Egypt and Palestine. This was the line held by Israel before the Six-Day War, except for the Gaza Strip, the future disposition of which remained open. The U.S. adopted a similar view with respect to a Jordanian-Israeli settlement in a document circulated in mid-December, which stated that the border should "approximate" the armistice line. In return for the Israeli withdrawals, Egypt and Jordan were to conclude peace with Israel. The Rogers Plan was intended to be the hard sought American-Soviet agreement, which the two were to present to the four, the four to the secretary-general, the secretary-general to Jarring, and Jarring to the parties. However, the plan failed. It was unacceptable to Egypt, and was consequently rejected by the Soviet Union. Egypt was not prepared to conclude a peace agreement, and objected to the plan's leaving the future of the Gaza Strip and arrangements to guarantee free navigation through the Straits of Tiran for negotiation between the parties in Rhodes-type talks. Israel too rejected the Rogers Plan. In Israel's view, the plan tended to prejudge, if not predetermine, the boundary issue. Only Jordan was reportedly discreetly satisfied with the American proposals.[34] Yet, although the Rogers Plan failed to win Soviet, Arab, or Israeli acceptance, it became a point of reference in subsequent diplomatic exchanges.

The coming into power of new leaders in both Israel and Egypt also affected the course of the renewed negotiations. Golda Meir, who assumed the premiership in Israel in March 1969 after Levi Eshkol's death, was by temperament less flexible than Eshkol had been. Anwar Sadat, who became president of Egypt after Nasser's death in September 1970, was more inclined to attempt diplomatic maneuvering than his predecessor, whose main preoccupation since the Six-Day War was to restore Egypt's military credibility.

After the American-sponsored cease-fire came into effect, Jarring managed to hold only one meeting with the parties before the talks were suspended. In response to Egypt's violation of the cease-fire-standstill agreement by moving its anti-aircraft missiles into the canal area, Israel withdrew from the talks and announced that it would not return as long as the agreement was not observed and the original situation restored. Because the U.S. had sponsored the cease-fire, the issue became the subject of American-Israeli negotiations. It was in part a crisis of confidence, since the U.S., which had assumed the responsibility of supervising the observance of the cease-fire-standstill was slow in acknowledging that massive violations were indeed taking place. In part, it was an urgent military problem. Because there was no certainty that the cease-fire would be extended beyond the ninety days set for it, the U.S. and Israel engaged in negotiations on arms supplies, which would help compensate for the Egyptian buildup and restore Israel's relative advantage. But in part, the American-Israeli negotiations about Israel's return to the talks revolved around Jarring's terms of reference, and Israel's suspicion that the U.S. might seek to introduce the Rogers Plan to serve as the basis for the Jarring negotiations. Such suspicions contributed to Israel's reluctance to accept the American initiative in the first place. Therefore, in addition to assurances of military aid, Israel also requested that the U.S. abandon the Rogers Plan. The American response on this point fell short of what Israel desired, as the U.S. stated that it would not attempt to impose its views, but reserved the right to express them. Another Israeli request, for American support at the UN, was prompted by a General Assembly resolution that could be interpreted as aimed at altering Jarring's terms of reference. This difficulty was in part disposed of by a letter from Jarring stating that he was proceeding on the basis that there was no change in his mandate, as defined by Security Council Resolution 242. But the U.S. refused to promise to use its veto at the Security Council should a resolution that Israel regarded as detrimental to its interests be introduced there. Nevertheless, in view of the American assurances on arms supplies and Israel's unwillingness to be held responsible for the renewal of the war if Egypt refused to extend the cease-fire on the grounds that the Jarring talks had not been resumed, the Israeli Cabinet decided on December 28, 1970, to return to the Jarring talks.[35]

The talks with Jarring were resumed on January 5. Shortly thereafter, on February 4, Sadat delivered a speech proposing an interim agreement for Israeli withdrawal from the canal and announcing Egyptian readiness to extend the cease-fire for another thirty days. However, for reasons that are still obscure, Jarring was not to be swayed from his course, and did not pause to explore Sadat's proposal. Four days after Sadat's speech, on February 8, he launched a new initiative requesting Egypt and Israel to make parallel and simultaneous commitments. From Israel he asked for a commitment "to withdraw its forces from occupied United Arab Republic territory to the former international boundary between Egypt and the British mandate of Palestine." From Egypt he asked for a commitment "to enter into a peace agreement with Israel" and to make explicit therein the undertakings arising from Resolution 242.[36]

Jarring was not the sole author of this initiative. According to William Quandt, the U.S. had decided in the fall of 1970 to encourage Jarring to take a more active role, and "to try to establish the principle that Israel would withdraw from the occupied territories in return for Arab commitments to peace." In January, after Jarring's initial contacts seemed to point to a deadlock, "the United States began to urge Jarring to take a more aggressive approach, abandoning his role as message carrier and putting forward ideas of his own."[37] Then the Jarring mission came to serve as an instrument of American diplomacy.

The Egyptian reply to Jarring expressed readiness to enter into a peace agreement with Israel as Jarring had requested. This marked a significant change in Egyptian policy, for hitherto it had only agreed to specify its obligations under Resolution 242 in a document to be addressed to the Security Council. This readiness to conclude a peace agreement was conditional upon Israel committing itself to withdraw not only from Sinai but also from the Gaza Strip (which Jarring had not requested). A wide gap between the Egyptian and Israeli positions remained, but it had definitely been narrowed.[38]

The change in Egyptian policy cannot be attributed to Jarring, but to American inducements and assurances that the U.S. favored Israel's withdrawal from all of Sinai.[39] American efforts to elicit Egypt's cooperation began while Nasser was still alive and were renewed following Sadat's ascension to power. They now bore fruit because Sadat did not feel strongly committed to Nasser's positions, and was less resentful of the U.S. than his predecessor. Moreover, as was to become subsequently apparent, Sadat was more flexible diplomatically than Nasser had been.

Jarring's initiative met with strong objections from Israel. Israel contended that Jarring overstepped his mandate, since his request for commitments actually expressed substantive suggestions on his part. Israel was determined not to permit the transformation of Jarring's mission into mediation. Besides the aversion to mediation Israel wished to retain some portions of Sinai, and Jarring's initiative, which strengthened Egypt's hand while weakening Israel's bargaining power, made that goal even more difficult to attain. Israel apparently considered the possibility of not sending a substantive reply to Jarring. However, such a posture was ruled out in the face of strong American pressure to respond positively. News of Jarring's initiative and the relatively conciliatory Egyptian reply appeared in the press, and received further publicity through a television interview with Assistant Secretary of State Joseph Sisco, who backed Jarring's initiative and praised the Egyptian reply. The contrast between the publicity given to these diplomatic moves and Jarring's highly discreet diplomacy in the past suggests that this time a deliberate effort was made to mobilize public opinion in support of Jarring's initiative, exerting further pressure on Israel.

The American pressures and the Egyptian reply probably contributed to the softening of Israel's reaction, but did not change its essence. Israel's note, dated February 26, opened by saying that it "views favorably the expression by the UAR of its readiness to enter into a peace agreement with Israel and reiterates that it is prepared for meaningful negotiations on all subjects." As for the boundaries, the note said that Israel would withdraw to "the secure, recognized and agreed boundaries to be established in the peace agreement." It added that "Israel will not withdraw to the pre-June 5, 1967 lines." Israel's refusal to withdraw to the former international boundary, as Jarring had requested, stemmed from its territorial aspirations in Sinai and its desire to frustrate any move that might help to establish the Rogers Plan as the formula for a settlement. Israel's reply was directed at the U.S. as much as at Jarring and Egypt.[40]

Shortly thereafter Israel reminded Jarring that it was expecting Egypt's reply to the February 26 invitation for talks. But Egypt did not consider Israel's note as an adequate reply to Jarring's initiative. An impasse developed. According to U Thant, Jarring now became "convinced that the negotiations under his auspices between Israel and the U.A.R. would continue to be deadlocked until Israel agreed to formulate a new position on borders." Consequently he returned on March 25 to his post as Sweden's ambassador to Moscow.[41]

The Jarring mission in practice came to an end. Several subsequent attempts to revive it came to nothing. Two diplomatic initiatives in the course of 1971 were ostensibly aimed at facilitating the resumption of the Jarring talks: an American attempt to promote an interim agreement for the reopening of the Suez Canal and a mission of inquiry on behalf of the Organization of African Unity. These are discussed in Chapters 7 and 8 respectively. While these efforts were being pursued, Jarring regarded them as "an additional reason for him not to take personal initiatives." He did try to resume his mission in response to a UN General Assembly resolution adopted in December 1971 and revisited the Middle East for talks with Israeli and Arab leaders. But Israel regarded the resolution as another attempt to alter Jarring's terms of reference, and requested an assurance from him that he considered himself bound only by Resolution 242 and not by the new General Assembly resolution, nor by his memorandum of February 8, 1971. Jarring, however, did not provide the requested assurance.[42] The disagreement over the terms of his mandate widened, and the resumption of his mission became unacceptable to Israel.

An Evaluation

An evaluation of the Jarring mission needs to take cognizance not only of his failure to fulfil his assignment, which is obvious, but also of the effects and consequences of his mission: what difference did his mission make?

The failure can be attributed first of all to the incompatibility of the parties' positions and the firmness with which they held them. The weakness of the UN, lacking resources and influence to provide effective backing for its representative, can also be blamed for the failure. But we can explore this matter further by asking whether Jarring utilized his own resources well, whether he applied appropriate tactics, and whether he knew how to mobilize and harness the help of the great powers.

The title of special representative reflected the absence of agreement about the role Jarring would be authorized to play: matchmaker, the most that Israel was then willing to concede; or overseer of Israel's withdrawal as the Arabs desired; or provider of good offices and mediation, as U Thant and perhaps some of the powers wished him to do. The reluctant and qualified acceptance of the mission by the parties caused Jarring to behave with great circumspection during the first phase of his mission. He had to be on his guard constantly lest his actions offend one of the parties, and lest the acceptance of his mission be withdrawn. Characteristic of his diffidence were the protracted negotiations on whether and how he might invite the parties to meet with him in Nicosia or New York. After several attempts to draft an invitation met with Arab objections, he and U Thant finally decided not to issue a formal invitation for talks because "it was felt that a forced acceptance obtained by such an invitation would not be helpful."[43] There was only one conspicuous instance of his acting without receiving the prior approval of the parties, and that was his request for assurances from the parties that they would "implement" Resolution 242.

It is impossible to establish at this time what led him to abandon his caution in the second phase of his mission and to launch the initiative contained in his letter of February 8. American prodding may have led him to believe that he would succeed. It is also possible that he felt that there was nothing to lose, and if the commitments he requested were not provided, at least it would be clear why he gave up. Jarring probably felt hamstrung. But his inability to win wider authority and unqualified acceptance was not the source of his difficulties. It was the symptom, reflecting the distribution of power between himself and his sponsors on the one hand, and the parties on the other hand. It indicated the limitations he and his supporters encountered in trying to influence and modify the parties' positions.

The mission's failure can also be blamed on the ambiguity of his terms of reference. An intermediary can turn ambiguous terms of reference to his advantage, for they afford him with an opportunity to interpret them as circumstances require. But in this case the parties, together at first and later Israel alone, denied Jarring the authority to interpret the terms of reference, and he lacked the ability to overcome their resistance. Resolution 242 defined a highly ambitious goal. It aimed at not less than "the establishment of a just and lasting peace in the Middle

East." Such an objective could not be achieved in one step, or in a single grand package. In the absence of a gradualist conception, the two limited goals Jarring set for himself when he began his mission—the exchange of the prisoners of war and the release of the ships stranded in the canal—could not be utilized to influence the atmosphere and change the parties' disposition toward negotiations under Jarring's auspices. The attempt to release the ships got stranded itself and was soon abandoned. Soviet suggestions in 1968 for a limited Israeli withdrawal to allow clearance and opening of the canal, which pointed to another gradualist approach to a settlement, were not pursued, probably because of American reservations. The U.S.S.R. may have wanted to facilitate the shipment of aid to North Vietnam, a wish Americans would seek to thwart. The priority accorded by Jarring (and the powers) to the Egyptian, over the Jordanian, negotiations was sensible. Although Jordan had fewer inhibitions about negotiating with Israel than Egypt, the problem of the West Bank was much more difficult to resolve than the problem of Sinai. However, an Egyptian-Israeli settlement was still too big for a single step, and beyond Jarring's capability under the circumstances that prevailed in 1971.

Another tactic available to intermediaries, the mobilizing of public opinion in support of their efforts of persuasion, was only rarely used by Jarring, if at all. The media campaign in support of the February 1971 initiative probably emanated from the State Department, and not from Jarring. Part of the reason for Jarring's scant use of public opinion can be found in his personality and professional habits. He was highly discreet, and preferred quiet diplomacy to the flamboyance of the media and of public diplomacy. It is difficult to say what other effects Jarring's personality had on the outcome of his mission. He has been praised for his intelligence, rationality, discretion, and professionalism as a diplomat. These qualities must have helped him in the negotiations, but did not suffice to make a difference. On the negative side, he seems to have lacked sufficient imagination and creativity to overcome some of the obstacles he encountered. Neither did he strike observers as possessing an outgoing warmth and charm such as often helps politicians or salesmen to persuade people to accept their ideas. But had he been perfect, it is still not likely that Jarring's personality could have compensated for the basic structural weaknesses with which his mission was handicapped.[44]

A basic handicap was that Jarring represented the UN, an organization with little influence, no resources or power of its own, and declining prestige. But like many other activities carried on in behalf of the organization, Jarring's mission too could draw upon the help of member states. Indeed, he was assisted by the U.S. and to some extent by the Soviet Union and other states, each acting unilaterally. During 1969, as we have seen, an intensive effort was made to arrive at an agreement between the powers in order to enable them to coordinate their influence upon the parties. However, these negotiations failed because of the complexity of the interests that motivated the superpowers. On the one hand, they sought a settlement of the Arab-Israeli conflict. On the other, because the conflict became polarized, they became identified with their clients. A concession by one's client was seen as a gain for the opposing superpower. In these circumstances, the separate American and Soviet efforts to encourage the parties to show greater flexibility in the negotiations were undermined by the military and economic assistance provided to them, which enabled them to hold fast to their basic positions.

Thus the failure of the Jarring mission cannot be blamed merely on the weakness of the UN or the inadequacy of his tactics. The most important single reason for his failure stemmed from the structure of the conflict, which had come to overlap in part the East-West struggle. Notwithstanding the assistance that the superpowers extended the Jarring mission, the net effect of their manifold activities was that they hindered the mission more than helped it. Their intervention also served to distract the parties from Jarring and draw their attention to the policies of the superpowers themselves, as the only important international actors capable of affecting their destinies.

In spite of its failure, the Jarring mission did make a difference. Although it could not bring about a settlement, it did produce some side effects that had a bearing on the evolution of the conflict and upon the efforts to reach a settlement. At the end of 1967 and through 1968 it served as a substitute for other policies, whether more violent or more conciliatory. It probably helped the Soviet Union to fend off Nasser's requests for more direct Soviet military assistance for the purpose of forcing an Israeli withdrawal. It also provided Egypt and Jordan with a diplomatic alternative to negotiations with Israel. An important function that the Jarring mission performed was as a screen for the American moves to mend relations with Egypt, and the subsequent American attempt to establish some of the elements of the Rogers Plan as the framework for a settlement. Finally, the 1971 Jarring initiative enabled Egypt to make a major concession—accepting the principle of a peace treaty without much loss of face. The concession appeared as a response to an explicit request of the UN envoy, rather than a concession to Israel or a reaction to an American initiative. It is not to disparage the Jarring mission to conclude that it made a difference less by being a dynamic actor on its own than by its being used by the superpowers as an instrument of their own policies.

SEVEN

The Rogers Initiative and the Interim Agreement Talks

In early summer of 1970 the U.S. became the principal intermediary between Egypt and Israel. From 1970 to 1972 it engaged in two major mediation efforts. The first, known as the Rogers Initiative, succeeded in bringing about a cease-fire in the War of Attrition which Egypt had launched against Israel, and an agreement by both parties to resume the Jarring talks. Although these talks ran into difficulties as soon as they started, the Rogers Initiative in itself may be called successful. The second endeavor aimed at an interim agreement for disengagement along the Suez Canal. This attempt failed. At first sight these outcomes are puzzling, because the Rogers Initiative, which succeeded, was met at first by doubts and suspicions, whereas the interim agreement, which failed, was a goal that both sides desired and specifically requested the U.S. to help accomplish.

Even more interesting than the results of these two rounds of negotiations is the very fact that the U.S. became the principal intermediary. At that time, Egypt regarded the U.S. as its archenemy, closely aligned with Israel. Egypt and the U.S. had not maintained diplomatic relations since 1967, when Egypt (falsely) accused the U.S. of participating in the Six-Day War on Israel's side. Yet Egypt's attitude to America and its view of the U.S. as aligned with Israel did not prevent its acceptance of the U.S. as an intermediary. In this chapter I shall attempt to answer both questions: how the U.S., despite its partiality, again became an intermediary in the conflict, and why one of the diplomatic initiatives it promoted succeeded while the other failed.

The Rogers Initiative

On June 19, 1970, the U.S. proposed that Egypt, Jordan, and Israel accept a cease-fire for a period of three months, and resume the discussions under Jarring's auspices. The U.S. also suggested that the parties inform Jarring through identically worded letters of their readiness to do so. This American proposal was in a sense a compromise formula: its wording sought to bridge the known positions of the adversaries on the cease-fire and the resumption of the Jarring talks. But this intervention, which became known as the Rogers Initiative, differed from the procedures usually followed by intermediaries. The U.S. did not receive the parties' prior assent to its initiative, nor did it consult with them about the formula it was preparing. The desirability of a cease-fire along the Egyptian-Israeli front had been discussed intermittently for several months, but this particular proposal was prepared by the U.S. under some secrecy and sprung upon the parties as a surprise. They were presented with a text, and urged to sign on the dotted line.

The United States hoped that reducing Egyptian-Israeli conflict would weaken Soviet influence and strengthen the American position in Egypt and other Arab states. The specific form of this initiative and its timing were inspired by the failures of recent diplomatic endeavors and the worsening circumstances in the region in the spring of 1970. According to Quandt, several lessons were drawn from the failure of the great power talks and the Rogers Plan. One was that the attempt to accomplish a comprehensive settlement was overambitious. The number of parties and other interested actors who had to be satisfied, and the number of issues that had to be resolved rendered this objective too complex and too difficult. Future American initiatives were to be aimed at more limited goals, which presumably would be less difficult to accomplish. The diplomatic efforts should not be given that much publicity. Another conclusion drawn from the failures of 1969 was that the U.S. should make a greater effort to negotiate with Egypt directly, rather than through the Soviet Union and various Arab intermediaries.[1]

The policy reassessment took place against the background of growing Soviet involvement in the escalating war along the Suez Canal. The fighting that Egypt had initiated in early 1969 was meant to bring about Israel's "attrition" and soften its negotiating stance. It was also intended to stimulate the great powers to intervene and exert pressure for an Israeli withdrawal. When Israel's losses began to mount, it threw the air force into action, first along the canal, and later also in bombing raids against targets in the Egyptian interior, including the vicinity of Cairo. Israel hoped that the bombing of the Egyptian heartland would force Nasser to accept the restoration of the cease-fire, and perhaps even undermine his regime and bring about his replacement. But Nasser refused to concede defeat, and turned to the Soviet Union for aid. In the early months of 1970, the Soviet Union installed anti-aircraft missile defenses in Egypt, manned by Soviet crews. In April, Soviet pilots began flying patrols over Egypt. The Soviet activity was interpreted by the U.S. as a double challenge, both military and political: the expansion of Soviet military presence in Egypt could threaten NATO's southern defenses in the Mediterranean, and a Soviet-Egyptian military success could be interpreted by the pro-Western Arab states, and by other observers as well, as signifying the diminishing ability of the U.S. to help its friends.

In view of this challenge, the long-standing Israeli application to purchase an additional number of Phantom aircraft and other armaments met with understanding in the White House. However, the State Department objected to the sale, fearing that it might undercut efforts to improve relations with Egypt. For a while the State Department view prevailed, and on March 23, Secretary of State William Rogers was able to announce that Israel's request for additional Phantom aircraft would be held in abeyance. In April, Assistant Secretary of State Joseph Sisco went to Cairo in an attempt to open a direct dialogue with Egypt. In response, President Nasser appealed to President Nixon, by letter and in his May Day speech, not to provide the military assistance that would enable Israel to attain military superiority. But as Soviet military involvement increased, it was decided in the White House that arms sales to Israel would have to be resumed. At the same time, to prevent this decision from undermining the attempts to improve relations with Egypt, President Nixon approved a proposal prepared in the State Department that the arms supplies to Israel be accompanied by a new diplomatic initiative.[2]

The Rogers Initiative was announced by the secretary of state at a news conference on June 25, as a call on the parties "to stop shooting and start talking." The State Department probably had several objectives. One was to stop further escalation on the front with its attendant risk of a superpower confrontation. A cease-fire would also diminish the urgency of large-scale arms supplies to Israel which, in the view of the State Department, hindered American efforts to improve relations with Egypt. And it could place the U.S. in the position of the "honest broker" to which it aspired. Kissinger's emphasis was different. In an off-the-record briefing on June 26 he explained that the U.S. was "trying to get a settlement in such a way that the moderate regimes are strengthened, and not the radical regimes." He startled the assembled journalists by adding: "We are trying to expel the Soviet military presence, not so much the advisers, but the combat pilots and the combat personnel, before they become so firmly established."[3]

Although the initiative had far-reaching aspirations, the specific task of encouraging the parties "to stop shooting and start talking" was a limited one. It was far less ambitious than the Rogers Plan of 1969. This time the U.S. refrained from addressing substantive issues, and instead confined itself to a procedural proposal. But even this unambitious procedural proposal was first rejected by both Egypt and Israel and encountered many obstacles before it was finally adopted.

The Egyptian Response

The initial Egyptian reaction to the American proposal was negative. The proposal reached Nasser when he was visiting Libya, and in response he delivered a militant speech there attacking the U.S. for its assistance to Israel. The Egyptian media, presumably reflecting official opinion, were critical of the proposal. Anwar Sadat (at that time vice-president of the Republic) explicitly recommended that it be rejected in a speech to a committee of the Arab Socialist Union, the regime's political party. This negative public reaction notwithstanding, Egypt did not formally reject the American initiative. Instead, it sought further clarifications, and it is presumably for this purpose that Foreign Minister Mahmoud Riad conferred with Sisco on June 26. A few days later, on June 29, Nasser departed for Moscow for a lengthy visit, in the course of which he underwent medical treatment and held talks with the Soviet leadership.[4]

Upon Nasser's return Egypt informed the U.S. of its acceptance of the procedures contained in the American proposal, and on July 23, in a speech on the anniversary of the Free Officers revolution, Nasser publicly announced Egypt's acceptance. A few days later Jordan, which had hesitated because of the Palestinian threat to the regime, also accepted the American proposal.

The American proposal was very close to the Egyptian position on two important points: the limited duration of the cease-fire, and the link between the cease-fire and the resumption of the Jarring talks. But on two other issues, no less important, the proposal was not consistent with

Egyptian desires. It did not call on Israel to commit itself to withdraw from the territories occupied in the 1967 war, upon which Egypt had been insisting. Secondly, the proposal suggested that Egypt (along with the other parties) announce its willingness to send representatives to discussions according to procedures, and at times and places as Jarring might recommend. This conflicted with Egyptian policy that had hitherto reserved for itself the right to accept or reject the procedures suggested by Jarring. Therefore, Egypt's acceptance of the proposal cannot be explained by how close the proposal was to Egyptian positions.

Egypt's acceptance reflected a tactical response to the immediate situation. It was clear to Egypt, as to others, that without a cease-fire there was a serious risk that the war might escalate further. During his Moscow visit Nasser had sought a Soviet commitment for additional aid and military backing in such an eventuality. However, the Soviets did not provide the assurances that Nasser requested. (Whether the Soviet attitude was a response to American appeals is a moot point.) If the war continued, there was a strong likelihood that the U.S. would increase its military aid to Israel. Moreover, the prospect of the curtailment of American assistance to Israel, which had opened in the course of the previous months, would disappear. Another explanation, which also attributed the Egyptian acceptance to short-term tactical considerations, was offered by Heikal, who claims that Nasser saw in the cease-fire an opportunity to complete the installation of anti-aircraft missiles.[5]

A different interpretation, which need not preclude the influence of these tactical considerations, places the main emphasis on a strategic shift in Egyptian policy. Nasser's contacts with the U.S. during the spring and his appeals to Nixon in May suggest that he was prepared to explore the possibility of mending relations with the U.S. His acceptance of the Rogers Initiative can therefore be attributed in some measure to his interest in improving relations with the U.S., so as to be in a position to influence the U.S. to reduce its support for Israel.

The Israeli Response

The American proposal was submitted by Ambassador Walworth Barbour to Prime Minister Golda Meir on June 19. Some of the Israeli participants in the conversation subsequently reported that the atmosphere was tense and that they felt very bitter. The prime minister reportedly told the ambassador then and there that the proposal was unacceptable. Israel's rejection was formally confirmed by a unanimous decision of the Cabinet on June 21. Forty days later, on July 31, the Cabinet reversed itself and resolved to accept the American proposal.

Israel's initial rejection can in part be explained as an emotional reaction. The American initiative caught the Israeli leaders by surprise. The prime minister (and perhaps other officials) felt hurt because the American failure to consult Israel before launching the initiative deviated from the close and confidential relationship that existed between the two countries. That the U.S. had sprung a previous surprise on Israel a few months before, when Golda Meir was not told during her visit to Washington in early October 1969 that the U.S. was preparing proposals (the Rogers Plan) for submission to the Soviet Union and Egypt, only compounded her anger.

The rejection was also influenced by political and military considerations. The American conduct during the preceding months suggested that the U.S. was curtailing its arms deliveries to Israel in the expectation that this would help to improve American-Egyptian relations. When Prime Minister Meir asked the American ambassador how the initiative would affect arms deliveries, his response—that a cease-fire would reduce Israel's need for arms—aggravated Israel's fears. Some Israelis were probably reminded of the trauma of 1955-1956, when Israel felt gravely threatened, but was unable to obtain American arms because the U.S. sought to win Egyptian friendship by withholding arms from Israel. Israeli leaders also felt let down by the terms proposed for the cease-fire. The question of reinstating the cease-fire had been discussed intermittently by American and Israeli officials during the previous few months, and in these discussions Israel insisted upon the restoration of an unconditional and unlimited cease-fire, in accordance with the Security Council resolution that ended the 1967 war. But the Rogers Initiative, by proposing a cease-fire for three months and the concurrent resumption of the Jarring talks, implicitly accepted the Egyptian thesis that the cease-fire was conditional upon the progress of the negotiations. Israelis also suspected that when the negotiations opened, the U.S. would exert pressure on Israel to accept the 1969 Rogers Plan, and thus place them in a situation of having to either accept the plan or be held responsible for the resumption of the war after the three months cease-fire expired. This appalling prospect appeared even grimmer in view of the probability that Egypt would take advantage of the cease-fire to complete the installation of anti-aircraft missiles, and thus make the renewed war much more costly to Israel. Finally, an immediate rejection of the American initiative seemed to offer a tactical advantage. Israeli officials hoped that an immediate rejection would prevent the U.S. from committing itself too firmly to its proposals, especially since no public announcement about the American initiative had yet been made. An appeal to President Nixon at this early stage might abort the initiative before it was too late.[6]

The subsequent reversal of the Israeli position was facilitated by the fact that a formal rejection of the initiative was not delivered to the American government. In presenting the American proposal Ambassador Barbour told Prime Minister Meir that there was no need for Israel to respond promptly. The U.S. further urged Israel not to be the first to reject the American initiative, but to await the Arab reply. When the formal Israeli reply flatly rejecting the American proposals reached Ambassador Yitzhak Rabin for transmittal to the White House, he advised that it be reconsidered. Following a debate in the Cabinet, the message to the president was softened and the explicit rejection of the American proposal was not included.[7]

Israel's position was reversed because of three major considerations. During the night of June 29 the Egyptians succeeded in advancing their missile defenses close to the canal. These began taking a toll on the Israeli air force. Israeli officials had realized for some time that if Egypt and the Soviet Union succeeded in erecting an effective anti-aircraft defense, Israel would be forced either to escalate the war further by moving its ground forces across the canal to destroy the missiles, or to concede a setback and withdraw from the canal. After two Phantom aircraft were lost on June 29, it became obvious that the choice could not be delayed much longer. The option to escalate entailed a high risk of a confrontation with the Soviet missile crews and pilots. The escalation was also highly problematic because it required an assured supply of arms. Yet the U.S. was unlikely to provide the military assistance needed for such an escalation, launched in contradiction to American efforts to arrange a cease-fire.

Another consideration for the reversal was a diplomatic one. After Egypt announced its acceptance of the American initiative on July 23, Israel's opposition became untenable. It would have been extremely difficult to justify to American public opinion, and international opinion in general. Criticism of Israeli policy as being too inflexible, which began to be heard in Israel itself, further undermined the government's confidence in its ability to defend a rejection of the cease-fire and to sustain a policy of escalation. Finally, Israel could not ignore the appeals of President Nixon to accept the initiative—appeals that were accompanied by incentives. In addition to two strongly worded public expressions of support for Israel on July 1 and 20, the president sent detailed assurances to Israel on July 24, following the Egyptian acceptance. These assurances referred to issues that Israel had raised in its discussions with the U.S., and implicitly also to some Egyptian statements that accompanied its acceptance of the initiative. The president promised that:

(1) The U.S. would continue to furnish Israel with economic and military aid (this was intended to allay Israeli fears that the improvement in American-Egyptian relations was tied to a curtailment of American military assistance to Israel);
(2) Israel would not be required to withdraw its forces from the occupied territories until a satisfactory peace treaty had been concluded (this was addressed to the Israeli concern that the U.S. would press for Israel's acceptance of the Rogers Plan, and was also meant as an assurance that the U.S. did not share the Egyptian viewpoint that a timetable for Israel's withdrawal should be adopted, and that Jarring should receive directives from the four great powers);
(3) Israel would not be required to accept a solution of the refugee problem that might alter the Jewish character of the state (this was intended to lay to rest Israel's concern, aroused by a certain phrasing of this issue in the Rogers Plan as well as in the Egyptian statement accompanying the acceptance of the American proposal).[8]

Nixon's letter was regarded as very satisfactory by Israeli officials. Nevertheless, because of some ambiguities found in it, and in the hope of averting the withdrawal of the Gahal ministers from the government coalition, Prime Minister Meir requested more explicit assurances about specific arms requests, and on two diplomatic issues: that the Rogers Plan no longer represented American policy, and that the U.S. would prevent, by the use of its veto if necessary, the adoption of any anti-Israeli resolution that might be introduced in the Security Council concerning the terms or procedures for a settlement. Nixon's reply contained an explicit assurance only about the arms.

Nevertheless, after a prolonged and painful debate, the

Cabinet resolved on July 31 to reply affirmatively to the American proposal, but rephrased its answer somewhat. The Cabinet decision was made by a majority vote, following which the Gahal ministers, led by Menahem Begin, resigned from the government.[9]

The Success Explained

The acceptance of the American proposals can be attributed to the circumstances in which the parties found themselves: the stalemate in the War of Attrition and the risks of escalation. But the circumstances by themselves could not produce the cease-fire. The mediator's contribution to arranging the cease-fire was crucial. First, American diplomacy must be credited with making itself acceptable to Egypt. To be sure, the U.S. was in a favorable position to do so. The massive aid America was giving to Israel created a situation in which Nasser came to view the curtailment of such aid as an important objective. The failure of the War of Attrition to bring about diplomatic pressure for Israel's withdrawal, and disappointment at the reluctance of the Soviet Union to provide the amount of military backing Egypt requested, induced Nasser to listen to the American claim that the U.S. was better able to bring about an Israeli withdrawal than the Soviet Union. Yet Nasser and his associates had become accustomed to regard the U.S. as basically hostile to Egypt, so the credit for persuading Egypt to consider cooperation with the U.S., and for enabling him to do so without too much loss of face and without provoking Soviet retribution, belongs to American diplomacy. The Rogers Plan, although rejected by Egypt at the time when it was proposed, undoubtedly contributed to Egypt's willingness to reconsider its policy toward the U.S. Adroit timing of the new initiative, at the very moment when both sides realized that they had come to a stalemate and that the policies that they were pursuing could not be maintained much longer, must also be credited to American diplomacy. The same applies to the actual proposal—the compromise formula—which, although unsatisfactory to both sides, was nevertheless so structured that they felt it would be more advantageous to accept it than to reject it.

Some of the tactics employed should also be noted. The secrecy in which the proposals were prepared saved the American diplomats considerable trouble and avoided the risk of complications that consultations often produce. The surprise provoked an angry reaction by Israel, which believed that it was entitled to better treatment from its friend and ally. This almost caused the initiative to fail at the very outset. But as Israel's ultimate acceptance proves, the risk was well taken. Another noteworthy tactic was the disregard of the qualifications both Egypt and Israel attached to their acceptances. This is reminiscent of the "Trollope Ploy," the tactic President John F. Kennedy employed during the Cuban missile crisis of 1962, when he disregarded one of Khrushchev's messages, which was negative in tone, and addressed himself only to the positive aspects of Khrushchev's communication. The application of this tactic caused a minor crisis in the exchanges with Israel. But again, the expectation that the parties would not withdraw their acceptance at this late stage because of disagreement about details was proved correct.[10]

One tactic could have landed the whole project in disaster. On the arms issue, the U.S. aroused contradictory expectations in Egypt and in Israel. For several months prior to its initiative, the U.S. let Egypt understand that the U.S. wished to play the role of an "honest broker" and that if Egypt enabled the U.S. to play this role the U.S. would feel obliged to reduce its military supplies to Israel. On the other hand, Israel was informed that the supplies would continue, but without publicity. Subsequently, in an effort to secure Israel's acceptance of the proposals, the U.S. repeatedly promised that arms deliveries, including Phantom aircraft, would continue.[11] These contradictory messages did not escape notice in either Egypt or Israel, and probably undermined American credibility to some extent. The U.S. was saved the embarrassment and the possibility of the collapse of the initiative by Egypt's violation of the ninety-day cease-fire-standstill.

The Interim Agreement

In contrast to the Rogers Initiative, the interim agreement negotiations were undertaken as a result of separate Israeli and Egyptian moves, and the U.S. became involved as an intermediary at the express request of the parties themselves.

The originator of the interim agreement concept was Moshe Dayan, at that time Israel's minister of defense. In September 1970 Dayan began exploring informally the idea of stabilizing the cease-fire through a disengagement of forces. The Israeli army would withdraw a short distance from the Suez Canal, and the evacuated area, together with a zone on the west bank of the canal, would be demilitarized. Added stability would be provided by the restoration of Egyptian civilian activity along the canal (most of the civilian population had been evacuated from this war-ravaged area), and the reopening of the canal to navigation. An agreement along these general lines was to be negotiated through the U.S. rather than through Jarring. The preference for the U.S. stemmed in this case not only from Israel's distrust of the UN and its representatives, but also from the expectation that if the U.S. helped in negotiating the agreement, it would incur a commitment to see it observed.

The immediate stimulus to Dayan's initiative was the situation along the canal. The emplacement by Egypt and the Soviet Union of anti-aircraft missiles in the canal area in violation of the standstill agreement increased the likelihood that Soviet personnel might become involved in the fighting if the war were resumed. The ominous risks of a confrontation with the Soviet Union weighed heavily with Dayan, and he hoped that a disengagement of forces along the canal might help to reduce these risks. This led him to the concept of an interim agreement, whereby Egypt would gain a partial Israeli withdrawal and Israel would gain a stable cease-fire. A probable additional motivation was the hope that an interim agreement would create a new situation under which the American inclination to promote the Rogers Plan would diminish.

Dayan's ideas received a mixed reaction in the Israeli Cabinet. The critics, including Prime Minister Meir, regarded the interim agreement as a departure from the policy Israel had consistently pursued since the 1967 war, that Israel would no longer accept a provisional arrangement as in 1949, but would insist on a full and permanent settlement through a peace treaty. They also feared that this would undercut Nixon's promise in his letter of July 24 that Israel would not be required to withdraw its forces until a peace treaty had been concluded.[12]

The interim agreement idea was explored informally with American officials between September and December, but at this stage it was unacceptable to the U.S. The Defense Department, because of global strategic considerations, advised against the opening of the Suez Canal. Secondly, the U.S. believed that the interim agreement would be unacceptable to Egypt, and American officials were reluctant to undertake a diplomatic effort that was likely to fail. Thirdly, the U.S. remained committed to the Rogers Plan, and suspected, probably with good reason, that Israel wanted to delay the resumption of the Jarring talks and forestall movement toward the implementation of the Rogers Plan. Even worse, American endorsement of the interim agreement might have fed Arab suspicions that American assurances of favoring almost total Israeli withdrawal were not to be credited.[13]

Discussion of a disengagement and the reopening of the Suez Canal was renewed in January 1971, following Egyptian inquiries indicating an interest in the idea. It received impetus following President Sadat's public launching of the proposal in a speech to the Egyptian National Assembly on February 4, and in an interview published in *News-*

week on February 22. The Egyptian ideas differed in several important respects from those put forward by Israel. Egypt wanted Israel to withdraw to the Mitla and Giddi passes in Sinai, or, as stated in the *Newsweek* interview, even further, "to a line behind El Arish." Egyptian forces were to cross to the east bank of the canal. The cease-fire was not to be indefinite, as Israel suggested, but for a limited period of three to six months, which would give Jarring sufficient time to work out the arrangements for the implementation of Resolution 242 and for a complete Israeli withdrawal. The interim agreement Egypt had in mind was to be only the first stage of a total Israeli withdrawal.[14]

Again, as in the case of the 1970 initiative, Egyptian policy can be attributed to both tactical needs and long-term strategic objectives. The second three-month period of the cease-fire, which had begun in August, was about to expire. Egypt was not capable of waging a successful war, and Sadat looked for a way out. On February 4 he announced a thirty-day extension of the cease-fire, but was still under pressure to renew the war. He doubted whether any visible progress could be expected from the Jarring talks in so short a time, and therefore adapted Dayan's idea to Egyptian needs and interests, and proclaimed it as his own initiative. The least that could be gained from this proposal was that the negotiations concerning it would exude a more positive atmosphere than the Jarring talks, and thus justify a further extension of the cease fire. Moreover, a positive outcome of the negotiations, with an agreement acceptable to Egypt, could not be ruled out. Such an outcome would carry substantive advantages to the still unstable Sadat presidency. It would enable Sadat to take credit for starting the process of Israeli withdrawal and for returning the inhabitants to the Suez Canal area, thus eliminating the social and economic burden that this internal refugee problem caused. Furthermore, Egypt would earn income from the traffic in the reopened waterway.[15]

Egypt's preference for discussing the interim agreement with the U.S. rather than with Jarring is of special significance. This ought to be attributed primarily to Sadat's desire to improve Egyptian relations with the U.S., and to encourage America to assume a more "even-handed" posture in the conflict. In view of the recent American interest in playing the role of an "honest broker," there was a strong likelihood that the U.S. would agree to serve as intermediary in these negotiations as well. If it did, it would have to move some distance from Israel and place itself closer to a middle position in the Arab-Israeli conflict. This goal of Sadat's was a further development of the first hesitant steps in this direction taken by Nasser in the spring and summer of 1970. It was echoed by Heikal in the pages of *Al Ahram*, where he advocated the "neutralization" of the U.S. in the Arab-Israeli conflict.[16] In addition, American mediation could serve to prod the Soviet Union to respond more generously to Egyptian arms requests. Furthermore, since the reopening of the canal impinged on American strategic interests, it was better that Egypt deal directly with the U.S. on this matter than with Jarring. Indeed, Sadat sent a message to President Nixon assuring him that this was an independent Egyptian initiative, not intended to serve Soviet interests. Negotiations with Israel were also likely to be more efficient if conducted through the U.S. than through Jarring, whom Israel trusted less than it did the U.S.

Israel's public reaction to Sadat's initiative was contained in Prime Minister Meir's speech to the Knesset on February 9. She said that Israel viewed with favor the reopening of the canal, but that the proposal which Sadat made in his February 4 speech left many crucial questions unanswered. Her speech reflected a critical attitude, but she left the door open for further clarifications.[17]

At this stage the U.S. had still not become converted to the interim agreement concept. The U.S. informed Israel of Egypt's interest and discussed the matter with both Israeli and Egyptian officials through January and February 1971. In fact, the U.S. acted as an intermediary, although at this stage it performed this role somewhat passively. The State Department and Jarring were in the midst of the major diplomatic move of presenting the parties with Jarring's memorandum, and trying to persuade them to provide the commitments that Jarring had requested. At the end of February, after Israel refused to make these commitments, attention turned to Sadat's trip to Moscow (March 1 and 2) and to efforts to extend the cease-fire, which was due to expire on March 7. On March 5 Sadat informed Nixon that the cease-fire would be extended de facto, without any formal commitment to maintain it. In his message Sadat reportedly also appealed to Nixon "to launch an initiative to bring about an interim agreement along the lines of his February 4 speech."[18] Sadat's appeal set American diplomacy into motion. Sisco may have been expecting such a development, because he was ready with an American proposal. On the following day, March 6, he unveiled American ideas for an interim agreement and presented them to Ambassador Rabin for his comments. From then on the U.S. was actively involved in mediation. Still, perhaps to protect itself in the event of failure, to avoid the impression that American mediation was now replacing the Jarring mission, and to meet Israeli objections to mediation (as distinguished from good offices), the State Department spokesman understated the American role. He said: "We are not assuming the role of a middleman. . . . The United States has good relations with both countries. They confide in us and we talk separately with the two of them. We think this is a proper function for the United States. . . . We find ourselves very often extending good offices for what we hope is good reason. So our office is available but we are not assuming the role of Ambassador Jarring."[19]

Several considerations brought about the change in the American attitude toward the interim agreement idea. One was the collapse of the Jarring initiative. This produced the danger that the wheels of diplomacy would soon grind to a halt unless a new impetus was provided. The interim agreement idea could serve such a function and help the diplomatic mill to continue moving. The continuation of the diplomatic process was deemed important not only because of the need to continue striving toward a solution, but also because it could help Sadat justify the extension of the cease-fire. The second major consideration was that the talks about an interim agreement appeared to be a suitable vehicle for the continuation of the dialogue with Egypt, and possibly for an improvement of relations. In fact, after Sadat had repeatedly requested the U.S. to explore this idea, refraining from doing so would have appeared a rebuff, and might have set back the movement toward improvement of relations into which so much effort had already been invested. Finally, it may be that American officials believed, at least initially in March, that the talks held some chance for success. Although Kissinger concluded as early as April that the talks were unlikely to lead to an agreement,[20] in the State Department hope lingered on somewhat longer. In any event, these considerations outweighed the strategic disadvantage of the reopening of the Suez Canal and speeding Soviet supplies to North Vietnam. The U.S. revised its attitude and agreed to serve as an intermediary in these negotiations.

The Negotiations

The negotiations about an interim agreement lasted for almost one year. A brief review of their course will help clarify the reasons for their failure. Briefly, the major obstacles were the differences between the Egyptian and Israeli concepts of an interim agreement, and the incompatible premises of the parties regarding the American role in the negotiations.

When on March 6 Sisco presented the American ideas for an interim agreement to Rabin, Israeli diplomacy was again caught by surprise. Although Sisco said that these ideas had not yet been presented to Egypt, and that the

U.S. wished first to consult Israel on whether they could be formulated as a proposal, they caused concern in Israel. First, the American ideas resembled in fact a draft proposal, raising the question of the American role: would the U.S. provide only good offices, or would it seek to mediate? Secondly, several of its terms were close enough to the Egyptian concept of the interim agreement to alarm Israeli officials. The U.S. accepted the Egyptian view that the interim agreement ought to be linked to the overall settlement, and that the cease-fire would be reviewed after one year in the light of the progress of the negotiations in realizing Resolution 242. Furthermore, the U.S. proposed that Israel withdraw to a distance of about twenty-five miles behind the east bank (considerably more than Israel offered). It did not exclude Egyptian military deployments east of the canal, thus leaving the question open, and did not mention any disengagement or thinning out of forces.[21]

It took Israel five weeks to respond to the American proposal. The delay was caused by disagreements in the Israeli Cabinet. The opponents' main argument was that an Israeli withdrawal from the canal would undercut the principle that no withdrawal should take place before a peace treaty had been concluded—a principle to which the U.S. had committed itself in Nixon's letter of July 24, 1970. The Cabinet decided on March 22 to accept in principle the interim agreement approach, but differences about the terms continued to delay the Israeli response. Officials were divided on whether or not to insist that the agreement proclaim the state of belligerence between Egypt and Israel terminated, on the extent of Israel's withdrawal, and on the specific commitments and guarantees that should be sought from the U.S. On only one issue did there seem to be unanimity—that the interim agreement should not formally be linked to the comprehensive settlement. In Israel's view the acceptance of the link implied the acceptance of the Egyptian interpretation of Resolution 242. The main points in Israel's counterproposal, submitted to the U.S. on April 19, were: (1) An end to the state of belligerence, and a cease-fire of unlimited duration. (2) Israel would withdraw from the vicinity of the canal to a line to be agreed upon between Egypt and Israel. But Israeli maintenance crews were to remain in the fortifications along the Bar-Lev line. (3) The new line to be established would not be the final one; the final line would be established by the peace agreement. (4) There would be a thinning-out of Egyptian forces west of the canal. (5) The Egyptian army would not cross east of the canal; only Egyptian civilians would be permitted there. (6) The canal would be reopened for the use of all nations, including Israel. Israel wished to receive American backing in the negotiations with Egypt, and therefore asked for American reactions to these proposals and requested that for the time being they not be transmitted to Egypt. In addition to the proposals for an Egyptian-Israeli agreement, Israel also asked for a reaffirmation by the U.S. of the assurances in Nixon's letter of July 24, for an American-Israeli understanding on guarantees in the event of Egyptian or Soviet violation of the agreement, and for American participation in the supervisory arrangements.[22]

Nixon reaffirmed the assurances, but the U.S. refused to endorse the Israeli proposals or to become identified with them. In the meantime, differences developed within the American administration about the interim agreement negotiations, with Kissinger expressing doubts about their prospects and the State Department taking a more optimistic attitude.[23] Whether reflecting an optimistic assessment about the prospects for an agreement or merely a conviction that the momentum of negotiations ought to be maintained, Rogers and Sisco left on a visit to Egypt and Israel in May.

During the Cairo talks, as related by Sadat, the U.S. sought reassurance that its mediation would be rewarded by substantive gains for American interests, while Egypt tried to gauge American willingness to use its influence to bring about an Israeli withdrawal. According to Sadat,

Rogers was at first circumspect in raising the question of the Soviet presence in Egypt. But after Sadat asked him why he had not asked about it, the connection between Israel's withdrawal, the Soviet presence, and Egyptian-American relations was discussed very explicitly. To Roger's inquiry whether Egypt would agree that after the first phase of Israel's withdrawal from Sinai the Soviet forces would leave Egypt (which was in Israel's interest no less than in America's), Sadat replied that the Soviet SAM crews would leave, and moreover, that Egypt would restore full diplomatic relations with the U.S. But despite his professed eagerness to send the Soviet units home, Sadat indicated that Egypt would continue to provide facilities for the Soviet navy. In the bilateral sphere, besides the question of diplomatic relations, it was also agreed to open negotiations on the rescheduling of payments on the $140 million Egyptian debt to the U.S.[24]

The discussion of Egyptian-Israeli relations touched on the questions of a comprehensive settlement and the interim agreement. The Egyptian side was incredulous at the American claim that they were unable to force Israel to commit itself to withdraw as Jarring had requested in his memorandum (and as Rogers had suggested in his 1969 plan). The Egyptians complained about the continuation of the American supply of arms to Israel, and Foreign Minister Riad suggested that the U.S. impose an arms embargo on Israel. Detailed discussions also took place about the possible terms for an interim agreement. Egypt continued to insist that the interim agreement must be linked to the overall settlement. The interim agreement was to be merely the first of two stages for a full Israeli withdrawal from Sinai and the Gaza Strip. The cease-fire was to be extended for six months only, during which time Jarring was to negotiate a comprehensive settlement. Although proposing that in the first stage Israel withdraw to the line drawn between El Arish (on the Mediterranean), and Ras Muhammed (on the Red Sea), Egypt was nevertheless willing to accept Israel's withdrawal to the east of the Mitla and Giddi passes, with the passes coming under Egyptian control. Egypt also insisted that its troops be allowed to cross into Sinai.[25]

The overall impression that Rogers carried away with him was one of Egyptian flexibility. It could not have derived from the Egyptian attitudes on the interim agreement. More likely, it was caused by Sadat's reiteration of his acceptance in principle of a peace treaty and his attitudes on the questions of the Soviet presence in Egypt and Egyptian-American relations.

The talks in Israel started badly because of the personal antipathy that Golda Meir felt toward Rogers. She held against him the plan that bore his name and the policies advocated by the State Department, both of which appeared to attach little importance to Israeli interests. She could not bear Rogers's praise for Sadat's moderation and flexibility and the discussion, instead of improving mutual understanding, soon deteriorated into an acrimonious exchange of reproaches. When it became evident that the Israeli prime minister and the American secretary of state could not jointly explore the issues confronting them without being carried away by their emotions, Dayan proposed that he conduct the discussions with Sisco.[26]

Their discussion covered three main subjects, which again were interrelated: American military and economic aid, the terms for an interim agreement, and American guarantees. The U.S. held out the carrot by promising to consider Israeli requests for aid. On the interim agreement, Dayan raised Sisco's hopes that Israel's terms might be modified. Dayan told Sisco that he saw two possible approaches to an interim agreement. If the cease-fire was temporary and Egypt's position was that it reserved the right to resume the war, then it was unreasonable to expect Israel to withdraw more than a few miles from the canal. Under these terms, Israel wished to retain the ability "to shoot its way" back to the canal as soon as war was resumed. The other approach was for the parties to renounce the recourse to war and to end the state of belligerence. Dayan emphasized that it was his *personal* view that given such a renunciation, Israel could withdraw a distance of twenty-five to thirty miles, to a line west of the passes, with the passes remaining in Israeli hands. When the American turn came to spell out what the U.S. would do if Egypt or the Soviet Union violated the terms of the interim agreement, the American officials were unable to provide any firm specific guarantees and offered only general and ambiguous promises.[27]

Encouraged by his talk with Dayan, Sisco returned to Cairo on May 9. He informed the Egyptian officials about the Israeli positions—both the formal one and Dayan's personal one. Sisco's interpretation of Israeli attitudes apparently attributed greater weight to Dayan's view than the actual alignments in the Israeli Cabinet warranted. He held out the prospect that Israel might accept Egyptian troops on the east side of the canal. Sisco also reported that Israel flatly refused the Egyptian demand that the interim agreement be formally linked to a comprehensive settlement and that it commit Israel to withdraw to the pre-1967 lines. To circumvent this problem, Sisco suggested that Egypt accept as satisfactory an American declaration about the Egyptian-Israeli border along the lines of the 1969 Rogers Plan. However, Sadat regarded this insufficient. Instead, he proposed that the declaration be issued by the Security Council or by the four great powers, apparently believing that this might carry enough weight to induce the U.S. to use the necessary pressure to force Israel to comply.[28]

The follow-up to Sisco's visit to Cairo was the Bergus affair, an event that rekindled both Egyptian and Israeli doubts about America's good faith and credibility as an intermediary. On May 20, Donald Bergus, the senior American representative in Cairo, received from Foreign Minister Riad the Egyptian reactions to the ideas proposed by Sisco. Reportedly because he thought the tone was too negative, Bergus redrafted the Egyptian reply and on May 23 handed his version to the Egyptian Foreign Ministry as his *personal* suggestion for how Egypt might respond more positively. On June 4, Sadat presented to Bergus formal Egyptian proposals. These bore a close resemblance to the text that Bergus had given to the Egyptian officials. The Egyptians claimed that they understood Bergus's paper to be an American proposal, which for diplomatic reasons the U.S. sought to present as if it had emanated from Egypt. They did not credit Bergus's statement that it was only his *personal* suggestion for how President Sadat might improve the draft of the letter he had prepared for President Nixon. When the U.S. failed to respond to what the Egyptians believed was their acceptance of an American proposal, they were thoroughly irritated and suspicious of American diplomacy. The story and the contents of Bergus's paper, which was very close to the Egyptian position, were leaked to the press. Now it was Israel's turn to become indignant, suspecting that the U.S. was encouraging Egypt to submit proposals that the U.S. knew were unacceptable to Israel.[29]

Rogers's and Sisco's visit took place at a highly inopportune moment. The struggle for power between Sadat and his rivals, which had been going on since Sadat's accession to the presidency, came to a head in early May as a group led by Ali Sabri, a former head of the Arab Socialist Union (the only legal, government-sponsored political party), and a few other former associates of Nasser, known for their pro-Soviet sympathies, openly challenged Sadat's authority. On May 2 Sadat dismissed Sabri from all the posts he held. Rogers's visit on May 4 seemed to confirm the view of this group and of the Soviet Union that Sadat was reorienting Egypt's policy toward the U.S. The growing threat from his rivals not only distracted Sadat from the negotiations with Rogers, but also prevented him from making any concessions that he might perhaps otherwise have been prepared to make. On May 13 Sabri and his associates were arrested. This move naturally increased Soviet apprehensions about their standing in Egypt.[30] In an attempt to tie Sadat's hands and perhaps also to offer him some incentives, Soviet President Podgorny came to Egypt on May 25, and two days later Egypt and the Soviet Union concluded a Treaty of Friendship and Cooperation. Besides tightening the political bonds, Podgorny's visit also produced new Soviet promises for accelerated shipment of additional arms.[31]

The treaty was interpreted by the U.S. as signifying an increase in Soviet influence in Egypt. Reports of expanded Soviet military presence tended to confirm this interpretation, which led to doubts about the value of continuing American mediation. Activity regarding an interim settlement slowed down while the new situation was assessed. In an attempt to find out whether the treaty produced any changes in Egyptian policy, Michael Sterner, head of the Egyptian desk in the State Department, was sent to Cairo on July 6. According to Sadat, who was impatient at the lack of progress in the negotiations, Sterner brought him a promise that American mediation would be renewed and even intensified, subject to satisfactory answers to a few questions. The first question was whether the new treaty with the Soviet Union led to any changes in the Egyptian position or restricted Egyptian freedom in negotiating with the U.S. about a Middle East settlement. Sadat replied that it did not. Sterner also asked whether Egypt would keep its promise to restore diplomatic relations with the U.S. after the first phase of Israel's withdrawal. Sadat answered that it would, "perhaps even before that phase is actually completed." A third question was whether he "still intended to send Soviet personnel home at the end of phase one." This question also received an affirmative reply. Sadat also assured Sterner that he still stood by his February 1971 initiative. Sterner reportedly told Sadat that the U.S. would now "cease to play the part of the mailman," and instead would take a more active role in the negotiations.[32]

Sadat's assurances invigorated the State Department to resume mediation, but the White House continued to have doubts. The State Department wanted Israel to make the concessions necessary for bridging the gap between the Egyptian and Israeli positions, and recommended that the U.S. exert pressure on Israel to that end. Kissinger suspected the Soviets and was skeptical about Egypt. He suggested that the U.S. request the removal of Soviet personnel before Israel's withdrawal from the canal. He also thought that American pressure for Israeli concessions would be a tactical mistake, since it might be interpreted as reflecting an American retreat in the face of a rejuvenated Soviet-Egyptian alliance. By way of compromise between these two viewpoints Sisco was sent to Israel in an attempt to get Israeli concessions, but was told that the White House would not support the application of pressures to obtain them.[33]

Sisco brought to Israel detailed proposals requiring Israeli concessions on several important points. One was a request that Israel accept a link between the interim agreement and the final settlement. Secondly, the U.S. suggested that Israel withdraw beyond the Mitla Pass, a distance of over twenty-five miles from the canal. Thirdly, it should permit a token Egyptian force to cross the canal. Between the Egyptian and the Israeli troops there was to be a buffer zone occupied by UN forces. The cease-fire was to be extended to two or three years.

These proposals were considered so close to the Egyptian positions that they stimulated even further the suspicions that the Bergus affair had only recently aroused in Israel. When Israeli officials inquired whether the U.S. would offer guarantees for the observance of the agreement, Sisco's response was disappointing: the U.S. would be prepared to offer guarantees only for a comprehensive settlement, and not for an interim agreement. While this American position may have been prompted in part by the concern that guarantees for the observance of an interim agreement might make Israel too comfortable in its occupation of the provisional line, it appeared to Israel as a design to press it to accept the Rogers Plan. It seemed to signify that the U.S. would not erect any obstacles to

Egypt resuming the war when the cease-fire expired if within this period Israel failed to accept the Rogers Plan for a comprehensive settlement. Furthermore, the failure of the U.S. to approve Israel's request for additional Phantom planes meant that the U.S. was exerting pressure on Israel to accept the American proposals for an interim agreement, to be followed by the implementation of the Rogers Plan. In the light of its assessment of U.S. policy, not only did Israel reject Sisco's proposals, but publicly warned the U.S. that it was overstepping its role, implying that Israel might withdraw its acceptance of the U.S. as an intermediary.[34]

As the summer went by without Israel making concessions, Sadat became impatient. The lack of progress in the negotiations placed him in some difficulty. He had stated that 1971 would be "the year of decision," but now time was running out without much happening. Sadat claimed to be disillusioned at the failure of the U.S. to influence Israel to make concessions. He had relied on American statements such as that "the U.S. was the only power that could get anywhere with Israel" and Sisco's parting words in May urging Sadat to "have confidence" in the U.S.[35] According to Sadat he was further promised in July that Nixon would personally intervene in the negotiations. Sadat gave vent to his disappointment in a speech on September 16, in which he criticized the U.S. for failing to fulfil its promise to declare publicly its own position on the issues in conflict, and cease playing a mere mailman. He further accused the U.S. of deception. As if to underline Sadat's disappointment, it was announced a few days after his speech that he would soon pay a visit to the Soviet Union.[36]

The stalemate in the negotiations, the Egyptian professions of disillusionment, and the news that Sadat was planning to pay another visit to Moscow stimulated the State Department to renew its efforts to reach an interim agreement. In pursuit of these efforts Rogers proposed in his address to the UN General Assembly on October 4 six points that could serve as a basis for a settlement. At the same time, the State Department suggested that the negotiations be continued through "proximity talks," with both sides' representatives present in the same hotel, and Sisco moving between them.[37]

Egypt accepted in principle this procedure, but wanted the U.S. to take an active part in the negotiations, which was a euphemism for saying that it expected the U.S. to obtain concessions from Israel. The U.S. refused to commit itself, and described Sisco's proposed role in the negotiations as a "catalyst." When Sadat pressed for a more explicit definition, he was informed that Sisco "would not be a passive mailman but an active one."[38]

Israel, on the other hand, withheld acceptance of the proximity talks. To Israeli officials, the situation posed a dilemma. The U.S. had accepted in principle, though not in the specific details, the Egyptian positions on the key questions of the linkage between the interim and final settlements, the provisional nature of the cease-fire, and the introduction of Egyptian troops into Sinai. By accepting active American mediation, Israel would expose itself to strong American pressure to make concessions and accept Egyptian terms that the U.S. now endorsed. If Israel made the concessions, and these led to an agreement, its terms would be unfavorable to Israel. If Israel refused the mediation, then relations with the U.S. would probably be adversely affected. In the hope of minimizing the damage to its interests, Israel sought to reach a prior agreement with the U.S. on the terms of the interim agreement and on the restriction of the American role to one of "good offices."[39]

The negotiations about Israel's acceptance of the proximity talks lasted from October to January. They were accompanied by discussions on two additional subjects. One was a Soviet proposal that another attempt be made for an agreement between the superpowers, on which the U.S. consulted Israel. The second was an Israeli request for military aid, the approval of which had been withheld by the U.S. for many months. In December, during Golda Meir's visit to the U.S., agreements in principle were reached on Israel's arms requests and on its participation in the proximity talks. According to Rabin, Israel made the concession of accepting that Egyptian "uniformed personnel" could be stationed on the east bank of the canal. To avoid any misunderstanding, Kissinger jokingly inquired whether it was clear that these would not be "the uniforms of New York hotel doormen."[40] Israel further agreed to withdraw to a line west of the passes, with the passes remaining under Israeli control. The cease-fire was to last eighteen to twenty-four months at least. The U.S. for its part assured Israel that the linkage between the interim and final settlements would not be interpreted as committing Israel to accept the Rogers Plan. Furthermore, the U.S. promised not to undertake initiatives without consulting Israel first, and satisfied Israel that its bargaining position would not be undercut by American proposals. The ironing out of the details of these agreements took a few more weeks, and they were finally approved by the Israeli Cabinet on February 2.[41]

In the meantime, however, these agreements caused Sadat to lose interest in the proximity talks. Egypt explained that the change in its attitude was brought about by the American decision to resume the delivery of Phantom planes and other weapons to Israel. The decision indeed signified the failure of Egyptian efforts to bring about the curtailment of military supplies to Israel. Furthermore, under the new ground rules for the proximity talks agreed upon between the U.S. and Israel, the opportunities for Egypt to drive a wedge between the U.S. and Israel were greatly narrowed. Consequently, Egyptian acceptance of America as an intermediary was withdrawn. Sadat confirmed the change in Egyptian policy in an interview with Arnaud de Borchgrave of *Newsweek*, who asked him whether the interim settlement idea was dead. Sadat replied: "Under Jarring, and if linked to a final solution, the idea is alive. . . . An American solution is clearly unacceptable to us."[42] Symptomatic of this new turn in Egyptian policy were Sadat's two visits to the Soviet Union in February and April 1972. Although the dialogue between the U.S. and Egypt continued, and although the concept of an interim agreement was occasionally mentioned in the months that followed, the negotiations were in fact terminated, and this American mediation attempt ended in failure.

A Comparison and Search for Explanations

On the face of it, the 1971-1972 negotiations for an interim settlement stood a better chance to succeed than the 1970 Rogers Initiative. In 1970, one side (Israel) did not favor the goals that the initiative set out to attain (a cease-fire and talks under Jarring's auspices), and both had reservations about accepting the U.S. as an intermediary. In the interim agreement negotiations both sides appeared to be interested in the same limited goal—an interim agreement between two states only and not a comprehensive settlement of the Arab-Israeli conflict—both sides invited the U.S. to serve as an intermediary, and the U.S. was eager and strongly motivated to do so. Yet it was the 1970 initiative that succeeded and the 1971-1972 that failed.

In explanation of the discrepancy, a good case can be made that the appearance of favorable conditions was deceptive. First, an important difference must be noted between the goal pursued in 1970 and the one of 1971-1972. The first goal was strictly procedural: a cease-fire and negotiations under Jarring's auspices. On the other hand, the 1971-1972 interim agreement idea contained some substantive elements: a withdrawal of Israeli forces, a line of demarcation to be established, the assertion of Egyptian sovereignty in the area evacuated by Israel, military disengagement and international supervision, and finally Israel's right to use the Straits of Tiran and the Suez Canal. These issues could not be totally separated from questions of right and wrong; they implied precedents for future arrangements, and consequently were much more complex to resolve than the essentially procedural issues of the 1970 initiative.

Secondly, Egypt's fear that the proposed interim agreement would confirm the maxim that "nothing is as permanent as the provisional" generated a dynamic that constantly pressed for the extension of the scope of the negotiations from the relatively limited one of the interim agreement to the terms of the final and full Egyptian-Israeli settlement. The Egyptian insistence that the interim agreement and Israel's withdrawal from the canal be regarded as the first step toward the full settlement and complete Israeli withdrawal, repeatedly caused the negotiations to spill over into the wide ocean of the comprehensive settlement of the Arab-Israeli conflict. This extended beyond the question of the final boundary between Egypt and Israel, for Egypt linked Israel's use of the reopened Suez Canal to the settlement of the Palestinian problem. Moreover, America's acceptability to Egypt as a mediator was largely predicated on the reaffirmation of the American commitment to the 1969 Rogers Plan for a comprehensive settlement. The impact of the negotiations on Egyptian-Soviet, Egyptian-American, and Israeli-American relations, as well as their relation to American supply of military assistance to Israel, also contributed to the extension of the scope of the issues discussed. All in all, it was impossible to insulate the interim agreement goal from much wider issues of utmost importance. Thus, although the goal of the 1971 mediation was ostensibly limited, in fact it was not.

The parties' apparent acceptance of American mediation is also misleading. Both Egypt's and Israel's acceptances were conditional, and their respective conditions were incompatible. Both parties wanted a prior understanding with the U.S. about their negotiating position, an understanding which implied American endorsement. It was not impartiality which they sought from the intermediary, but a de facto coalition with the U.S. against the third party. The U.S. gave each side to understand that it would welcome a prior understanding. The American negotiators probably wished to take advantage of the parties' desire for an American endorsement of their negotiating stance as a means to exact concessions from them. America's strategy was a mistake, because it produced an affirmation of the bargaining relationship between the intermediary and each of the parties, and, in the process, the conditional nature of America's acceptability as an intermediary was emphasized. Israel requested in April that its conditions not be conveyed to Egypt by the U.S., because they had not received American endorsement. Israel's reluctance to modify its position, and later to attend the proximity talks, was provoked by the American acceptance of several of the key Egyptian conditions and by the suspicion that the U.S. intended to take advantage of its mediatory role to promote the Rogers Plan. Israel finally accepted the proximity talks only after a memorandum of understanding on both substantive and procedural issues was concluded with the U.S., and after the U.S. promised it would not engage in active mediation. But this situation was unacceptable to Egypt, since the U.S. was now precluded from playing the role of the active mediator in support of Egyptian terms. At this point Egypt's acceptance of the U.S. as intermediary was withdrawn.

Other circumstances that rendered the negotiations difficult arose from the domestic situation in both Egypt and Israel. It was easier to negotiate with Egypt in the summer of 1970 because then Nasser was firmly in control. In 1971, Sadat was still inexperienced and unsure of himself. His authority had not yet been unreservedly accepted, and it sometimes appeared to the American negotiators that the line of Foreign Minister Riad diverged somewhat from the policy that President Sadat wished to follow.[43] The tendency of Israel's diplomacy to speak with two voices was even more pronounced. In 1970, Israel's acceptance of the American initiative was hindered by the threat of the Gahal ministers' withdrawal from the government coalition, but in those negotiations Israel spoke with a single voice. In 1971, both American and Egyptian negotiators appear to have been misled by the various viewpoints publicly expressed by Israeli negotiators. They certainly knew that only those positions formally approved by the Cabinet expressed official Israeli policy. But Dayan's view that Israel could withdraw to the passes and Rabin's opinion that Israel should not insist on a formal Egyptian commitment to nonbelligerence may have encouraged both American and Egyptian officials to believe that Israel might change its formal stance, and that Egypt need not make concessions.[44]

Another complicating feature was the duality of American policy. In the 1970 negotiations on the Rogers Initiative a high degree of coordination was achieved between the White House and the State Department, with the president providing close and effective backing to the American negotiators. Through much of the 1971 negotiations the White House was only intermittently involved and presidential backing for the negotiators was only sporadic. This situation was created in part by the mutual antipathy between Kissinger and Rogers. The absence of candor that characterized the relations between the White House and the State Department is illustrated by the White House remaining ignorant of the Bergus affair until the controversy reached the press.[45] The lack of enthusiasm displayed by the White House for the interim agreement talks stemmed from Kissinger's doubts as to whether Sadat's limited freedom of action and Israel's limited flexibility would provide sufficient room for American diplomatic maneuver. It can also be explained by Nixon's and Kissinger's preoccupations with Vietnam, relations with the Soviet Union, and the opening to China. These differences between the attitudes of the White House and the State Department detracted from the effectiveness of American diplomacy.

As we saw, the 1970 Rogers Initiative was launched at a particularly propitious moment. In contrast, circumstances were not particularly favorable during the interim agreement talks. True, it was clear to the parties that a failure to conclude an interim agreement would bring in the long run increased pressures for either the resumption of war or for a more vigorous attempt at a comprehensive settlement. Sadat was embarrassed by his pronouncement that 1971 would be "the year of decision," but he apparently did not expect serious repercussions if he failed to meet this deadline. The parties did not face any immediate dilemmas and there was no urgent need to alter their positions.

Yet, the timing was not merely indifferent, but disadvantageous. The negotiations took place during the first year of Sadat's presidency, at a time when his authority was still being challenged. Rogers's and Sisco's visits to Cairo took place at a particularly unfortunate moment when the struggle between Sadat and the Ali Sabri group reached its climax. Sadat's domestic weakness, the fear of provoking the Soviet Union, and the desire not to antagonize Syria and Libya, Egypt's partners in a newly proposed federation, tended to induce rigidity in Egypt's negotiating positions rather than flexibility. If Sadat's original proposal in February for an interim agreement created the impression that Egypt might adopt a more flexible attitude on the issues in dispute, this impression was soon dispelled. This is not to argue that the U.S. could have declined to assume an intermediary's role or that its performance should have been more passive. Such an attitude would have undercut the efforts to improve relations with Egypt and to weaken Egypt's dependence on the Soviet Union. All I wish to say is that the timing was unpropitious.

A tactic that greatly helped to secure the parties' agreement in 1970 was unavailable in 1971. The Rogers Initiative was presented as a purely American move. It was not the product of negotiations with the parties. The parties were asked to accept a genuinely American proposal, and whatever concessions they had to make were being granted to the U.S. and not to the adversary in the conflict. In contrast, all the suggestions made by the U.S. in 1971 carried obvious marks of originating with the parties themselves. The parties were asked to make concessions to each other, which they found difficult to do.

Some of the tactics employed by the U.S. seem to have been counterproductive. The incentives it offered to one side were disincentives to the other. Egypt had been initially persuaded to entrust the U.S. with an intermediary role by the offer of two incentives: the Rogers Plan, which called for Israel's withdrawal to the international border, and hints (perhaps even more than hints) that if negotiations got under way, arms shipments to Israel would be reduced. Both increased Israel's reluctance to accept the U.S. in the role of the intermediary. Israel made its assent to American involvement contingent upon assurances that the U.S. would not seek to implement the Rogers Plan. The recurring suspicions that the U.S. was attempting to use the negotiations to promote the Rogers Plan repeatedly caused the slowing down of the negotiations until new assurances were provided by the White House that this was not the case. It is for the same reason that Israel wished to restrict the American role to one of good offices, and objected to the U.S. playing the role of a mediator entitled to present its own proposals to the parties. The procrastination in replying to Israel's requests for arms assistance, which was intended to serve as an incentive to Egypt, was probably meant also as a way of pressuring Israel to grant concessions. Instead, it induced greater rigidity and greater reluctance to engage in negotiations under these circumstances. This reaction by Israel was motivated in part by the view that one should not make concessions under pressure. Israel was unwilling to assist in the creation of a new pattern of relations between the U.S., Egypt, and Israel, whereby Arab friendship would be contingent upon the reduction of American aid to Israel. The delays in arms approvals did not imply that once Israel made the concessions the U.S. requested, its arms applications would be granted. On the contrary, they implied that after Israel made the concessions, the resumed supplies would be on a reduced scale for the sake of preserving Egyptian good will.

Another reason for Israel's rigidity was that the concessions carried some military risks. In the 1970 negotiations on the Rogers Initiative the U.S. told Israel that aid would continue to be provided at a level enabling Israel to continue to maintain its military superiority. But in the interim agreement negotiations Israel was called upon to take risks without America's offering any insurance or protection. Besides asking for weapons, Israel also inquired whether the U.S. would be prepared to supervise the observance of the agreement, but found out that the U.S. was not prepared to assume any such role. Thus, one of the important contributions that intermediaries can make for the sake of promoting an agreement—the provision of insurance in order to help the parties to manage the risks which the agreement entails—was on this occasion unavailable.

It was only after insurance was provided to Israel through the conclusion of long-term military assistance agreements in November 1971 and February 1972, after it was reassured that the U.S. would not take advantage of its role to promote the Rogers Plan, and after the U.S. agreed to restrict its role to something less than active mediation, that Israel made concessions on the terms of the proposed agreement and agreed to attend the proximity talks. But through these agreements the U.S. in fact withdrew the incentives that it had previously offered to Egypt in order to stimulate a cooperative attitude on its part. Once Egypt realized that the incentives were withdrawn, it refused to continue the negotiations.

There was another tactic which probably backfired. Facing the usual dilemma of whether to present accurately to each side his adversary's position, the American negotiators chose to embellish it. According to Quandt, to the Egyptians they presented the Israeli proposals "as more forthcoming than they actually were," and "with the Israelis, the Egyptian statements were recast in the best possible light. But instead of succeeding in convincing either party of the other's good intentions, Rogers and Sisco seemed instead to lose credibility."[46] This is not to argue that intermediaries must always be candid with the parties; but it is a reminder that misrepresentation can undercut the intermediary's own efforts.

Personal incompatibilities, if not antipathies, also contributed to the failure of the 1971 negotiations. Both Israeli and Egyptian officials tended to attach some of the blame for the sour taste of American diplomacy to Rogers personally. Golda Meir attributed to him the 1969 proposals that carried his name and developed a dislike toward him, as evidenced by their stormy meeting in May. Sadat seems to have come to suspect that Rogers personally shared the responsibility for what he regarded were attempts to deceive him. After losing confidence in him in the fall of 1971, Sadat ceased to negotiate through him and dealt from then on with Kissinger.[47] It is not these personal relationships that caused the negotiations to fail; moreover, despite Golda Meir's view of Rogers, his 1970 initiative succeeded! Nevertheless the personal relationships hindered effective negotiations.

It would be a mistake to evaluate the Rogers Initiative and the interim agreement talks only in terms of their success or failure to produce an agreement. As we saw, the conclusion of an agreement was only one of several goals that guided the policies of the intermediary and of the two adversaries. The U.S. attained some of its objectives. The interim agreement talks enabled the maintenance of the diplomatic momentum after the Jarring talks had collapsed, when progress toward a final settlement did not seem possible. The maintenance of the momentum helped to diminish pressures for a resumption of the war and provided room for diplomatic maneuver. Despite Sadat's disappointment with the U.S., American mediation did contribute to the process of improving Egyptian-

American relations, and to the estrangement between Egypt and the Soviet Union. The new relationship that developed between the U.S. and Egypt in the course of these negotiations helped to embolden Sadat to expel thousands of Soviet military experts in July 1972. Egypt accomplished through these negotiations somewhat less than it probably hoped it would. The talks enabled Sadat to maintain the cease-fire beyond its expiration date. Egypt's relations with the U.S. improved; but it did not "neutralize" the U.S. role in the conflict. The American-Israeli relationship remained close, and American military aid to Israel did not diminish. If Egypt had hoped that its acceptance of American mediation would help to influence the Soviet Union to grant Egypt all the aid and military equipment that Egypt requested, this hope was not fulfilled. But Egypt probably got more Soviet aid than it would have otherwise. Israel succeeded through the interim agreement talks to reduce the pressures on it to comply with Jarring's request for a commitment to withdraw. Indeed, the interim agreement talks replaced the Jarring mission at the center of the diplomatic stage. But Israel did not obtain a more stable cease-fire that it aimed at when Dayan first proposed an interim agreement.

The goals that the intermediary and the two adversaries did attain appear to have been pursued by them with no less dedication than the goal of an interim agreement. Indeed, they seem to have been important in inspiring the diplomatic effort. Considering the extent to which these goals were accomplished, the interim agreement negotiations were not a total failure after all.

EIGHT

The African Presidents

In the second half of 1971 a committee of African heads of state, set up by the Organization of African Unity (OAU), attempted to mediate between Egypt and Israel. Although their attempt failed, it is of interest because it throws light on the resources available to small states and to a regional international organization and on the bargaining relationships that developed in the mediation process. It also illustrates how the diverse goals of the states involved affected the process and determined the final outcome.

Background: Africa and the Arab-Israeli Conflict

The Arab-Israeli conflict, besides being an important international problem, aroused African interest because Israel and the Arabs competed for the friendship and sympathy of the black African states. One means of furthering the Arab struggle against Israel was the attempt to isolate Israel diplomatically, and to prevent, as much as possible, the recognition of Israel by the newly independent Asian and African states. Israel, on the other hand, sought to consolidate its international standing through the establishment of diplomatic relations and the weaving of a web of political, military, economic, cultural, and social relationships with as many states as circumstances permitted. The Arab policy on this issue initially met with failure; all black African states (with the exception of

Somalia, which chose to join the Arab League) recognized Israel and established relations with it.

The black African states' policy of maintaining and developing relations with Israel attracted much criticism from Egypt and other Arab-African states as inconsistent with Pan-African solidarity. Pressure from the Arabs on this account caused embarrassments and friction on countless occasions, from diplomatic receptions to caucuses seeking to formulate common African policies at international conferences. As a consequence, African states often subscribed to anti-Israeli resolutions passed by various international gatherings while at the same time maintaining friendly, and sometimes even close relations with Israel on the bilateral level. This was especially evident at conferences of nonaligned states, and to a lesser extent at the UN, where the African voting record was mixed.

In contrast to such conferences, the Arab-Israeli conflict had never appeared on the OAU agenda between its establishment in 1963 and 1967. It seems that Egypt considered raising the issue, but refrained from doing so for fear of being publicly rebuffed.[1] This situation changed after the 1967 war, when part of Egypt's territory was occupied by a non-African state. This enabled Egypt, supported by the Arab and radical members of the OAU, to claim that this was a situation to which, under the terms of its charter, the Organization was obliged to respond. As many OAU member nations became persuaded that the Organization could not remain indifferent to Egypt's predicament, the OAU summit conference held in Kinshasa in September 1967, as well as subsequent summit and Council of Ministers conferences of the Organization, adopted resolutions expressing sympathy with Egypt and demanding Israel's withdrawal. The passage of these resolutions aroused controversy, since some states claimed that the resolutions were one-sided, espousing the Egyptian interpretation of the situation and of the modes of settlement prescribed by Resolution 242. On occasion, controversy was aroused not only by the text of the resolution but also by the way it was passed. Egypt, for its part, felt that the OAU did not go far enough in support of Egyptian policies.[2]

One of the main purposes of the OAU was the promotion of African solidarity. Before 1967 it therefore protected itself from the controversies of the Arab-Israeli conflict by excluding the issue from its agenda. After 1967, it was impossible to do so, but, as a result, yet another divisive issue came to disturb OAU gatherings.

The Origin of the Presidents' Mission

When the Arab-Israeli conflict came up at the June 1971 OAU summit at Addis Ababa, intra-African differences produced a somewhat different outcome than hitherto: an action-oriented resolution in support of the Egyptian viewpoint, paradoxically accompanied by the establishment of a committee on which the states favoring the Israeli position were strongly represented.

The initial resolution, introduced at the 1971 summit by President Leopold Senghor of Senegal, was somewhat stronger in its support for the Egyptian position than previous resolutions, but still purely exhortative. Like the 1970 resolution, it was entitled "Resolution on the Continued Aggression Against the UAR," and expressed solidarity with Egypt and called for the "immediate withdrawal of Israeli armed forces from all Arab territories to the lines of 5 June 1967 in implementation of the Security Council Resolution 242. . . ." This phrasing, already used on previous occasions, accepted the Egyptian interpretation of Resolution 242, and, similar to previous resolutions, referred to "all Arab territories," not only those of Egypt, a member of the OAU. The new elements in the 1971 resolution were the expressions of support for Jarring's February initiative, and commendation of Egypt's "positive attitude in its reply on 15 February 1971" to Jarring's initiative. The resolution further deplored "Israel's defiance to that initiative" and called upon it "to make a similar positive reply."[3]

According to Ran Kochan, Senghor asked that the resolution be adopted unanimously without debate, but some delegates contested this procedure.[4] Thus, the Middle East controversy threatened to add fuel to the already highly volatile atmosphere of the conference. The African states had just differed sharply on whether to recognize the new Amin regime in Uganda and over the Ivory Coast's call for a "dialogue" with South Africa. The latter issue led the Ivory Coast to boycott the summit. Concerned that in this atmosphere, a debate on the Middle East might have a disruptive effect, Emperor Haile Selassie, the host of the conference and probably the most prestigious African leader at that time, persuaded the opponents of the resolution to permit its passage without debate. At the very last moment, Zambia's President Kenneth Kaunda proposed an addendum to the resolution that "the current Chairman of the OAU should try to consult some of the elder statesmen of Africa so that they may bring pressure on the Big Powers in order that the Israeli occupation should be terminated."[5] His proposal, its form somewhat altered to make it more acceptable to Israel's friends, was added to the resolution requesting the current chairman "to consult with the Heads of State and Government so that they may use their influence to ensure the full implementation of this resolution."[6]

In the consultations that followed the passage of the resolution, it was decided to form a committee of ten heads of state. The committee, which came to be known as "The Ten Wise Men," consisted of the president of Mauritania (then chairman of the OAU), the emperor of Ethiopia, and the presidents of Cameroun, the Ivory Coast, Kenya, Liberia, Nigeria, Senegal, Tanzania, and Zaire.

This addendum, together with the formation of a committee with this particular membership, reflected the effort to end the conference on a note of compromise. Only one of the states on the committee, Mauritania, identified with Arab policy to the extent of not recognizing Israel as a nation. On the other hand, several of the other members maintained particularly friendly relations with Israel—Ethiopia, the Ivory Coast, Kenya, Liberia, and Zaire. Although not fully in agreement with Israel's interpretation of Resolution 242, they were unwilling to see the OAU become an instrument of Egyptian policy. The heavy representation of Israel's friends on the committee, alongside Mauritania (which denied Israel's right to exist), and Nigeria and Tanzania (which maintained diplomatic relations with Israel but accepted the Egyptian interpretation of Resolution 242), suggests that the committee was intended to reconcile the different viewpoints of OAU members and arrive at a compromise that would minimize controversy within the organization. This would accord with the motives ascribed to Kaunda, namely, composing the disagreements among African states on this issue so as to enable them to form a united front in the struggle against South Africa, Rhodesia, and Portugal, to which he, and some others, wished to assign priority.[7]

The desire to avoid further controversy and to attempt to formulate an agreed African position on the Arab-Israeli conflict is also indicated by the ambiguity of the committee's terms of reference, which left room for different interpretations and for diplomatic maneuver. Egypt, and perhaps other states that sympathized with its viewpoint, regarded the summit resolution as providing sufficient guidance to the committee: it was to use its influence "to ensure the full implementation" of Resolution 242 as interpreted by the OAU, that is, requiring the "immediate withdrawal of Israeli armed forces from all Arab territories to the lines of 5 June 1967."

It is unlikely that Egypt expected the OAU to bring about Israel's withdrawal. But Egypt probably hoped that the resolution, and the committee that it created, could be made to serve Egyptian propaganda by blaming Israel for the deadlock in the Jarring mission. The OAU and its committee would prepare the ground for a strong endorsement of the Egyptian position at the forthcoming session of the UN General Assembly. Yet some states apparently had a different view: according to a press report published as early as June 24 (two months before the committee formally decided to send a mission to the Middle East), some delegates maintained that the committee's function would be mediation.[8]

The question of the committee's terms of reference was resolved only when the committee convened for its first meeting in Kinshasa on August 23, 1971. The Kinshasa meeting was attended by six heads of state: Emperor Haile Selassie of Ethiopia, and Presidents Ahidjo (Cameroun), Ould Daddah (Mauritania), Gowon (Nigeria), Senghor (Senegal), and Mobutu (Zaire). The presidents of Kenya, Liberia, and Tanzania sent representatives. The Ivory Coast, which in June had walked out of the presummit OAU Council of Ministers meeting over disagreements arising out of President Houphouet-Boigny's proposal for a dialogue with South Africa and had then boycotted the summit itself, sent no delegates. The meeting decided to apportion its work between two missions. Ould Daddah was to go to New York to consult with U Thant and Jarring. A subcommittee of four heads of state, consisting of Senghor (as chairman), Ahidjo, Mobutu, and Gowon, would visit Egypt and Israel to obtain information that would enable the Ten to formulate conclusions and recommendations.[9] These decisions contrasted rather sharply with the summit resolution that supported Egypt and criticized Israeli policy. They implied a definition of the committee's terms of reference that ignored the summit resolution, but that was consistent with the attempts at reconciliation that had inspired the establishment of the committee.

If the committee's main purpose was the reconciliation of the different positions maintained by African states on the Arab-Israeli conflict, it was not clear how this was to be achieved. One approach would have been to reach some middle ground about substantive issues in the conflict.

But it was doubtful whether a formula could be devised that would meet the approval of Arab OAU members and Israel's friends alike. Another approach which could have formed the basis for a common African stand would have been to set a procedural goal to which no one could object. This probably explains why Senghor placed the emphasis on the resumption of the Jarring mission.

It may be, as some observers have claimed, that the members of the committee sought to promote additional goals, both collective and individual. It seems reasonable to assume that they desired to enhance the international prestige of the OAU and of the states they represented. Moreover, the heads of state involved were probably not indifferent to the possibility that the success or failure of the committee would affect their personal political standing. This perhaps helps to explain Senghor's strong ambition to succeed where others before him had failed. Yet some of the participants were apparently pessimistic about the committee's prospects, and were concerned that their participation might complicate their relations with the Arab states, or with Israel, or with both. This seems to be the reason why Haile Selassie refused to act as chairman, or even to serve on the subcommittee of Four.[10]

Both Egypt and Israel issued statements welcoming the decision to send the four presidents to the Middle East, but these diplomatic welcoming statements did not express their true sentiments. Egypt, which had been uneasy about the composition of the Committee of Ten, now felt even more concerned. Implicitly, the Kinshasa decision to send the Four on a fact-finding mission placed Egypt on the same level as Israel. Coming after the strongly expressed support of the summit resolution, this was a setback for Egypt. It therefore felt constrained to accept the OAU mission so as to prevent a possible further decline in African support. It aimed at persuading the committee to return to the stand expressed by the June summit, and to reaffirm it in its conclusions. To this end Egypt endeavored to show that Israel was to blame for the diplomatic stalemate and for the suspension of the Jarring mission, and sought to keep attention focused on the parties' respective responses to Jarring's February initiative.[11]

Israel also felt constrained to accept the fact-finding mission, despite its aversion to external interventions in the conflict and to intermediaries (which, incidentally, was brought to the attention of some African leaders in the course of Foreign Minister Eban's visit to seven African states just prior to the summit).[12] However, to refuse to accept the mission would have abandoned the field to Egypt and might have entailed alienating some of the African states that maintained friendly relations with Israel. Israel's goals were essentially the exact opposite of the Egyptian ones. Israel wished the committee to arrive at the conclusion that it was not Israel's fault that the Jarring mission was suspended; rather, the cause was Egypt's (and Jarring's) insistence on prior Israeli commitment of withdrawal to the international border as a precondition to the resumption of the Jarring talks. Beyond that, Israel wished to persuade the committee to accept an interpretation of Resolution 242 closer to its own, and thus bring about a modification of the OAU's formal position.[13]

The parties' acceptance of the mission was thus not motivated by expectations about progress toward a resolution of the Arab-Israeli conflict, but by the desire to safeguard their diplomatic positions in Africa. Rather than seeking the committee's help in negotiating an agreement with each other, the main goal of both Egypt and Israel was to influence the committee's conclusions and its final report. In a sense, their attitudes to the committee resembled the attitudes of competitors to the jury of a popularity contest, rather than an attitude to a mediator.

The Negotiations

The visit of the Four to the Middle East was to all appearances an impressive diplomatic event. It was a mission of four heads of state, "Pilgrims of Peace," accompanied by an entourage of eighty. From the information available it appears that they engaged in exploratory discussions, with the resumption of the Jarring mission as the main subject. Senghor apparently believed that this procedural and rather limited goal was attainable, and could serve as a basis for a report that could be supported by all the Ten. In Israel, the talks also dealt with Israel's view that territory and security were linked, and that the determination of "secure and recognized boundaries" should be the subject of negotiations between Israel and each of its neighbors. The Egyptians, for their part, appear to have raised the question of the committee's terms of reference, and objected to the committee performing a mediatory role or taking any action that might detract from the OAU summit resolution. In the course of the visit Egypt agreed to the committee's request that the UN debate on the Middle East be postponed until after the committee had prepared its report. It was apparently agreed that the committee should be given an opportunity to establish a common African position before the General Assembly debate.[14]

Following the tour of the Four in the Middle East, nine members of the Committee of Ten assembled in Dakar to discuss their findings. Seven heads of state attended the meeting: the emperor of Ethiopia, and the presidents of Cameroun, Liberia, Mauritania, Nigeria, Senegal, and Zaire. Kenya was represented by its vice president, and the Ivory Coast by its foreign minister. Tanzania did not send a representative, reportedly because it was dissatisfied that the committee had deviated from the terms of reference as defined by the summit resolution.

The meeting heard reports from Ould Daddah about his consultations with U Thant in New York, a mission entrusted to him by the committee at its Kinshasa meeting, and from the subcommittee of the Four about their talks in Egypt and Israel. The common theme was the question of the resumption of the Jarring mission. According to Ould Daddah, both U Thant and Jarring were of the view "that only a positive reply from the Israeli government to the memorandum of 8 February would make it possible to resume the mission. . . . This presupposed, therefore, that any contribution by the OAU toward the search for a peaceful settlement of the Middle East crisis through action by the Sub-Committee of Four and the Committee of Ten would amount to the Israeli authorities accepting finally to reply favorably to the Jarring initiative and thus enable the latter to continue mediating between the two parties."[15]

Although the committee agreed that its main effort should be directed at the resumption of the Jarring mission, there were, according to Kochan, three views on how they should proceed. Senghor proposed that the committee recommend that the Jarring mission be resumed without mentioning the precondition of Israel's favorable reply to Jarring's February initiative. Nigeria and Mauritania were of the opinion that the committee should request Israel to respond positively to Jarring. The Ivory Coast and Zaire suggested that the committee phrase its appeal to the parties in more general language, merely requesting them to resume talks on the basis of Resolution 242. After some debate, all nine finally agreed on a compromise formula close to Senghor's initial proposal, calling on Egypt and Israel to resume the discussions under Jarring's auspices, without making any mention of Jarring's February initiative.

The meeting thus achieved unanimity, and all nine members present signed a memorandum summarizing the committee's understanding of the parties' positions, and set forth the committee's proposals to them, as discussed below. The committee also decided that Presidents Senghor and Gowon, along with the foreign ministers of Cameroun and Zaire, would return to Egypt and to Israel to submit the committee's memorandum and to obtain replies. A final report would be prepared on the basis of these replies, and would then be presented to the UN secretary-general and the five permanent members of the Security Council.[16]

The decision to submit the report to U Thant and the great powers probably reflected a realization on the committee's part that they were in fact mediating not only between Egypt and Israel, but also between Israel and Jarring and U Thant. Moreover, since Jarring's February initiative was not merely his own, but was inspired by the U.S. and supported by other powers as well, it was necessary to enlist the support of the great powers if the committee's attempt to circumvent the impasse was to succeed.

On their second visit, the Four stopped first in Cairo and then proceeded to Jerusalem. Their visit to Cairo happened to coincide with some tough talk and ostentatious preparations there for the approaching "decisive" stage of the conflict.[17] These may have been directed more at the U.S. and the forthcoming UN debate on the Middle East than at the visiting African mission, but it probably impressed upon them as well the urgency with which Egypt viewed the situation.

The presentation of the memorandum approved by the Nine at Dakar, which contained specific proposals, produced some interesting ripples. Egypt, seeking to avoid any dilution of the stand taken by the OAU June summit, preferred to refer to the Dakar document as a "questionnaire," thus denying that it contained proposals. For the same reason Israel took the opposite view. However, Israel was not unequivocally pleased that the document contained proposals, since they were mostly of a substantive nature and thus exceeded the procedural task of encouraging the parties to resume the Jarring talks.

An important subject in the discussions was Egypt's continuing insistence that the resumption of the Jarring mission was conditional upon Israel's prior favorable response to Jarring, and Israel's continual refusal to make any such commitment. A point that seems to have been stressed by the Four in Cairo was that Egyptian agreement to the guarantees to Israel's security and navigation proposed by the Dakar memorandum was likely to elicit a more flexible Israeli stance on the question of boundaries. In Israel, the memorandum's summary of how the Four had understood Israel's position on territorial issues caused some discussion. According to Legum, the Israelis were "taken aback" by the statement in the memorandum that "Israel does not intend to annex any territories and that the point at issue, as far as she is concerned, is one of 'secure and recognized boundaries.' " According to Legum, Prime Minister Meir sought to explain that this was not an accurate description of Israeli policy.[18]

The committee's proposals as outlined in its memorandum referred to a wide range of issues, and in the committee's view, reconciled the essentials in the respective positions of the parties. Its main proposal was emphasized by a concluding paragraph that appealed to the president of Egypt and the prime minister of Israel to accept its suggestions "and thereby allow the resumption of the Jarring negotiations."[19] Both parties' replies[20] struck a positive tone of acceptance, but both attached qualifications to their acceptances that left the gap between their respective positions on the most important issues as wide as before.

The committee's first proposal called for the resumption "of indirect negotiations under the auspices of Dr. Jarring and within the terms of Resolution 242, in order to reach a peace agreement." Egypt's acceptance referred to the implementation of Resolution 242 and "the implementation of Ambassador Jarring's initiative of February 8," whereas Israel replied that it "agrees to resume negotiations without prior conditions."

The committee's second point proposed "an interim agreement for the opening of the Suez Canal and the stationing, on the Eastern Bank of the Canal, of United Nations forces between the Egyptian and the Israeli lines." Egypt replied that it would be ready to reopen the canal, subject to the same conditions that it raised in the negotiations through the U.S.: that this would be "in return for the first stage of Israeli withdrawal in conformity" with Sadat's initiative, and "on condition that Israel responds positively to Ambassador Jarring's memorandum of 8 February 1971." Israel replied that it "agrees to work out a Suez Canal agreement, the details of which will be negotiated and agreed," the last phrase reflecting Israel's objections to outside intervention.

The memorandum's third point suggested the "acceptance, by the two parties, that 'secure and recognized boundaries' be determined in the peace agreement." Egypt agreed that the boundaries be embodied in the peace agreement, but added that this be "in accordance with the OAU resolution which provides for the withdrawal of Israeli forces from all Arab territories to the lines of 5 June 1967, and in conformity with the borders specified in the Jarring initiative." Israel's acceptance stated that the boundaries "should be determined by negotiation between the parties," a phrase which again reflected Israel's rejection of third party enunciation of where the boundaries ought to be located.

The committee's fourth point suggested that the parties accept that "solution to security problems be found" in UN guarantees, the creation of demilitarized zones, and the presence of international forces at some strategic points. Both Egypt and Israel accepted such arrangements. But Israel's reply hinted that these alone could not solve its security problems; they could come "in addition to the determination of agreed, secure and recognized boundaries." This phrasing indicated that Israel continued to adhere to the view that its security required boundary revisions.

The committee's fifth proposal was "that the terms of the withdrawal from occupied territories be embodied in the peace agreement." Egypt did not respond to this point at all, presumably because it contradicted its interpretation of Resolution 242 to the effect that the withdrawal must be from all territories and unconditional. Israel's acceptance of this point referred to "agreed" terms that should be embodied in the agreement.

The committee's last proposal, for the stationing of international forces at Sharm-el-Sheikh "in order to guarantee freedom of navigation of all ships through the Straits of Tiran" elicited important qualifications from both sides. Egypt's reply omitted the words "all ships," thus leaving open the question whether the freedom of navigation would apply to Israeli ships. Israel's reply hinted at its claim for the annexation of Sharm-el-Sheikh by saying that "the question of Sharm-el-Sheikh" falls under the paragraph dealing with the determination of secure and recognized borders.

The Report and Its Aftermath

Upon the receipt of the Egyptian and Israeli replies, Senghor drafted the committee's report. It included the Dakar memorandum with the committee's proposals, the Egyptian and Israeli replies, and some concluding observations. By now, Senghor had probably learned to understand the codes embedded in the parties' replies, and was aware of the wide gap that continued to separate the Egyptian and Israeli positions. However, his conclusions smoothed over the differences between Egypt and Israel, and thus also among some of the African states, by emphasizing some general points that could be described as constituting common ground between them.

His report drew on a number of positive elements in the parties' replies: the affirmation of both sides of their desire for peace, their adherence to Resolution 242, their acceptance of the resumption of negotiations through Jarring, and their acceptance in principle of an interim agreement. Senghor accepted Sadat's assurances that Egypt would be willing to conclude a peace treaty if Israel withdrew from all territories. Taking this as his premise, Senghor defined the main difficulty as one of persuading Israel to agree to the implementation of the concept of secure and recognized borders through the establishment of machinery for security guarantees that would not require the annexation of Egyptian territory.

But the main point of the report was the one on which the efforts of the Ten had focused, and on which the UN General Assembly's discussion was also expected to focus: the resumption of the Jarring mission. On this issue Senghor proposed a compromise formula, saying that "it appears possible, in the light of the data obtained by the Sub-Committee, to reinstitute the negotiations under the aegis of Mr. Jarring."[21]

On November 30, Senghor sent the report to Ould Daddah in his capacities as chairman of the committee of the "Ten Wise Men" as well as the current chairman of the OAU. Ould Daddah, in conformity with the decision taken by the committee in Dakar, communicated the substance of the Egyptian and Israeli replies to the five permanent members of the Security Council. After consulting the Four, he also sent a mission to New York. Its tasks were twofold: the delivery of the report to U Thant, and "coordinating, on behalf of the current Chairman, the action of the African Group at the United Nations during the debate on the Middle East."[22] The mission presented the report to U Thant in Jarring's presence on December 1. The content of that conversation has not been published, but it is a reasonable guess that there was discussion of the differences between the African presidents' document and the report about the Jarring mission circulated by U Thant only one day before. In direct contradiction to the African proposal, which called for the resumption of the Jarring mission without mentioning the prior requirement of Israel making the commitment requested by Jarring in February, the secretary-general's report reiterated his view that a favorable Israeli response was a prior condition for the resumption of the mission. U Thant's report said that he continued to hope "that Israel would find it possible before too long to make a response that would enable the search for a peaceful settlement under Ambassador Jarring's auspices to continue." It further said that "Ambassador Jarring has clearly defined the minimum conditions that are required to move the peace talks ahead and, until those conditions are met, it is hard to see what else he can do to further his efforts."[23] U Thant and Jarring thus preempted the committee. By recommitting themselves publicly to their position on the Jarring initiative, they made the acceptance of the committee's proposal much less likely.

"Coordinating . . . the action of the African Group at the United Nations" proved impossible. The African states were divided in their attitudes, and despite the high priority they attached to presenting a common front, they were unable to agree and to vote in unison. The significance of this lay not in the split vote, but rather in the fact that they were divided in their attitude to the recommendations of a committee set up by the OAU, and that half the members of the Committee of Ten withdrew their support from their own report.

The African states found themselves buffeted by conflicting currents. On the one hand was the report of the African presidents, calling for the resumption of the Jarring mission without apportioning blame for the diplomatic stalemate and without requiring that Israel first respond favorably to Jarring. On the other was the report of the secretary-general of the UN, presumably reflecting Jarring's own view, saying that the mission could not be resumed unless Israel responded favorably. Egypt and the other Arab and radical members of the OAU essentially agreed with this stand, but went further in their criticism of Israel. Their views were supported by the great majority of the nonaligned states.

After a debate, the majority of African states decided to support a twenty-one power draft resolution that praised Egypt for its positive reply to Jarring's initiative and called on Israel to respond likewise. In the preamble to the resolution, the General Assembly expressed "its appreciation of the efforts of the Committee of African Heads of State," but made no reference to its proposals.[24] Senegal at first joined with other states in sponsoring this resolution, and it was only after the personal intervention of President Senghor that the Senegalese Foreign Minister Amadou Karim Gaye withdrew Senegal's sponsorship, and proposed an amendment to the twenty-one power draft resolution. This amendment reverted to the line advocated by the African presidents' report. It noted with satisfaction the Egyptian and Israeli replies to the African presidents' proposals and considered the replies "sufficiently positive" to make possible the resumption of the Jarring mission, without mentioning the request for prior Israeli acceptance of Jarring's initiative. The amendment was defeated in the votes taken both within the African Group and in the General Assembly. A proposal by Barbados and Ghana, specifically mentioning the African presidents' proposals and also refraining from mentioning the request for a prior Israeli response, was also defeated. Only four members of the Committee of Ten supported Senegal's proposal in the General Assembly vote—the Ivory Coast, Liberia, Senegal, and Zaire; five others voted against it—Cameroun, Ethiopia, Mauritania, Nigeria, and Tanzania. (Kenya, the tenth member, voted differently on each paragraph of the proposal.)

The disagreements among the African states, as expressed in the discussions in the African Group and in the General Assembly, clearly marked the failure of the Committee of Ten. Not only did it fail in its attempt to have the Jarring mission resumed, but also in its effort to reconcile inter-African differences.[25]

Attempts to change this outcome in the months that followed were to no avail. Senghor remonstrated with Israel for failing to confirm explicitly, as Mrs. Meir had allegedly promised, that Israel did not demand the annexation of Egyptian territory. In an attempt to repair the damage, Israel sent Walter Eytan to Senghor in January 1972 with a message from Meir. But, as Israeli assurance was not forthcoming, Senghor's criticism of Israel continued unabated. In February, Jarring went to Africa to confer with Senghor and Ould Daddah, perhaps to seek ways to reconcile his stand with Senghor's. But this attempt too, proved ineffective.[26]

The final repudiation of the committee's report occurred at the June 1972 OAU summit at Rabat. Paradoxically, it also served as a prelude to a convergence of African policies on the basis of support for Egypt, and for the severance of diplomatic relations with Israel in 1973. The discussion of the Middle East situation, not the most important item on the conference agenda, opened with a report by Ould Daddah in his dual capacity as current chairman of the OAU and chairman of the committee of "Ten Wise Men." He described the OAU effort as a failure, blaming Israel which "strongly rejected any peace settlement and was even more strongly opposed to anything that might lead to the withdrawal of its forces from occupied territories."[27] This statement by Ould Daddah was in clear variance with both the content and spirit of the Dakar Memorandum, as well as Senghor's concluding report. Ould Daddah's report apparently did not satisfy Senghor, who felt the need to give his version of the committee's work. He attributed the committee's failure to three main reasons: Prime Minister Meir's inability to confirm formally and explicitly that Israel did not desire territorial annexations, the split in African ranks at the UN in December 1971, and lack of support from the superpowers. Interestingly, he did not mention the roles of U Thant and of Jarring in the fight against his report.

A committee of twelve foreign ministers—those of the countries represented on the Committee of Ten, joined by Algeria and Morocco—was charged with preparing a draft resolution for adoption by the conference. However, as the committee was unable to reach agreement, the issue was brought to the summit plenary. There, at the suggestion of King Hassan of Morocco, the conference host and OAU chairman for 1972-1973, a draft prepared by the Arab states was adopted by consensus, without a vote. The resolution mentioned in the preamble the efforts exerted by the Committee of Ten and the Egyptian and Israeli replies to its memorandum, and resolved to take note of the chairman's report, to express appreciation of the committee's efforts, to congratulate Egypt for its cooperation with the committee, and to deplore "Israel's negative and obstructive attitude which prevents the resumption of the Jarring mission." The resolution further invited Israel to declare its adherence to the principle of nonannexation of territories by force, and reiterated the stance of previous OAU resolutions calling for Israel's withdrawal. Two new points were support for Egypt's struggle to recover its territorial integrity "by every means," implying support for the use of force, and the call on UN members to refrain from supplying Israel with military aid or moral support.[28] With the passage of this resolution, the OAU peace initiative came to a close.

Some Conclusions

Senghor seems to have hoped that the committee could accomplish its task mainly by serving as a face-saving mechanism. His tactic was to minimize, and in part even to disregard the qualifications that Egypt and Israel attached to their acceptances of the committee's proposals, thus enabling both sides to modify their positions without excessive loss of face. Alternatively, if they did not avail themselves of this opportunity to make concessions and break the diplomatic deadlock, he hoped that they would at least not explicitly reject his recommendations. If they played along, all three could claim some gains, at least in the short run: the mission could be described as successful, and Egypt and Israel could each improve its image by appearing flexible and cooperative.[29] However, this was a miscalculation; both Egypt and Jarring continued to insist that the Jarring mission could be resumed only after Israel responded favorably to the February initiative; and Israel let it be understood that it did not regard guarantees without territorial annexations sufficient to provide it with security.

It turned out that it was not enough to have a face-saving mechanism available. It was necessary to induce the parties to change their stance, by pushing them or luring them into availing themselves of this opportunity. However, lacking resources, the committee was unable to do so. The mediators' ability to pressure the parties or to offer them incentives was very limited. Their main asset was the ability to publicly praise or criticize the parties' conduct. The weight of such pronouncements was somewhat augmented by the fact that it was not a single state that served as intermediary, but a committee of ten, acting on behalf of an international organization with a membership of forty-one states. Both Egypt and Israel were sensitive to OAU public statements on the conflict, to which they attached importance not the least because of its influence on the voting of African states in the UN and other international organizations.

The two parties' interest in the attitudes of the African states explains their acceptance of OAU intervention. Israel hoped that the attitude expressed by the 1971 summit resolution could be modified in its favor, while Egypt, despite being critical of the Ten's interpretation of their mandate, accepted the OAU mission for fear that rejection would weaken its standing among the OAU membership. However, neither Egypt nor Israel expected the OAU to help them reach an agreement or to reduce the conflict between them. To the extent that Egypt and Israel were interested in negotiations toward an agreement, their attention was directed to the American attempt to arrange an interim agreement, which was pursued simultaneously.

Within this context, the fear of disapproval was sufficient to induce Egypt and Israel to accept the OAU mission, but not to alter their positions on issues which they considered important. It did not suffice to induce Israel to change its position on the territorial issue, nor to induce

Egypt to give up its attempt to extract from Israel a prior commitment to withdraw to the international border. In refusing to change its stance, Egypt may have counted on its bargaining power vis-à-vis the other African states. Being a member of the OAU, where many issues come up for discussion and interests intersect, and being able to draw on the support of other African-Arab states, Egypt was better placed than Israel to prevent public OAU criticism of its policies.

The committee apparently made an attempt to enlist the support of the great powers for its efforts. However, it met with indifference, if not with opposition. The U.S. was in the midst of its attempt to mediate an interim agreement for disengagement and the reopening of the Suez Canal and was not interested in supporting a competing diplomatic effort. The Soviet Union had no interest in pressing Egypt to modify its stand on the Jarring initiative. And both, concerned with protecting their own freedom of action, probably did not view with favor the intrusion of additional actors into a conflict in which their own interests were deeply involved.

What has been said thus far is sufficient to explain the failure of the attempt to mediate between Egypt and Israel. Yet the committee's failure was greater. It was also unable to reconcile intra-African differences with respect to the Arab-Israeli conflict. The outcome did not enhance the prestige of the OAU or of any of the presidents who served on the committee. The inability of the committee and its members to attain any of their objectives stemmed in part from the different priorities of its members and the relationships between their different goals. In November, at Dakar, Mauritania and Nigeria, who disagreed with Senghor's formula on the resumption of the Jarring mission, nevertheless signed the committee's memorandum, presumably for the sake of the appearance of unanimity. In December, at the UN, where the committee's recommendation ran into opposition, they withdrew their support and henceforth strove to rally support for the Egyptian stance. Obviously, harmony with Egyptian and Arab policies took precedence for them over maintaining unity within the committee.

The OAU's attempt to mediate between Egypt and Israel was, of course, greatly encumbered by the fact that the mediating body was a committee of ten states. Divisions within the committee were far more complex than their attitudes to the Arab-Israeli conflict. Its work was complicated by the many crosscutting interests and issues that simultaneously occupied the attention of the governments represented on the committee. One such issue was the proposal for a dialogue with South Africa; this was vehemently opposed by many African states, including members of the committee (notably Nigeria), and strained relations between them and the Ivory Coast. Another issue was a dispute between Senegal and Guinea, in which Haile Selassie, Ahidjo, Tolbert, Ould Daddah, and Gowon mediated concurrently with their work on the Committee of Ten on the Middle East. Then there was the issue of the expulsion of thousands of foreign Africans, many of them Nigerians and Senegalese, from Zaire. This issue created some bad feeling between these two states and Zaire—all members of the Committee of Ten. Although there is no information on what transpired at the committee meetings, its work must have been affected by these and other issues. It is difficult to imagine that the committee's effectiveness as a mediating body was not impaired by the conflicts among its members.

The reduction of intra-African differences over the Arab-Israeli conflict depended upon the committee's success in reducing Egyptian-Israeli disagreements. Unable to accomplish the latter, the former was unattainable. Lacking resources and lacking cohesion, the committee failed in both its tasks.

NINE

Kissinger, 1973-1975

Henry Kissinger has been called a miracle-worker. The record of his mediation after the 1973 Yom Kippur war is indeed impressive. Within twenty-three months his mediation led to the conclusion of five agreements: the cease-fire between Egypt and Israel, the agreement to convene the Geneva conference, the disengagement agreements between Egypt and Israel and Syria and Israel in 1974, and after an initial dramatic failure to do so, he brought off a second agreement between Egypt and Israel in 1975. He was admired because he succeeded where others failed: in negotiating agreements that led to a significant abatement of the Arab-Israeli conflict. His achievement has been attributed largely to his skillful diplomacy and more specifically, to his consummate practice of the art of mediation. In the words of a scholarly treatise, "his tactical skills as a negotiator and mediator were unsurpassed. Here his originality, his sense of timing, his intelligence, and even his personality served him especially well."[1] Of course he also drew much criticism, but those who criticize him do not dispute his skill. They claim that his goals were ill-conceived and his skills misapplied. Some, like Stanley Hoffmann and George Ball, questioned the wisdom of his much advertised "step-by-step approach." They claimed that he engrossed himself in tactics to the neglect of strategy, and missed an opportunity to engineer a comprehensive settlement.[2] Others believe that he yielded too easily in the face of the Arab oil embargo, and that the agreements concluded under his auspices seriously compromised Israel's security and ability to survive in the long run.[3] Kissinger's critics do not deny that he played a decisive role in the negotiations. But what his admirers regard as a talent for mediation, his critics view as a skill in manipulation. Whatever the differences, admirers and critics alike agree that Kissinger was the moving spirit in these negotiations.

Several questions arise from studying Kissinger's performance. Did his predilection for a gradualist approach stem from a basic philosophy, or did it result from the exigencies of specific situations, merely another manifestation of the common practice of "muddling through"? Another question is whether Kissinger's diplomacy was really mediation. Since the American involvement was on occasion so forceful and brutal that it resembled coercive intervention, it seems necessary to justify why it should nevertheless be termed mediation. Thirdly, the acceptance of Kissinger by Egypt and Syria needs to be explained. It occurred on the morrow of a war in which the American airlift of military supplies helped Israel to defeat the Arab armies once again. He was accepted although he was not regarded as impartial; not only was he the secretary of state of a power that was a de facto ally of Israel but he was also a Jew, and therefore presumably doubly biased against the Arabs. Fourthly, it would be intriguing to find out what his personal contribution to the success of the negotiations was. Success required that he persuade the parties to modify their positions and make concessions. How did he do this? Did they succumb to his oft-mentioned personal charm? Were they overwhelmed by the logic of his reasoning? Was it Kissinger's inventiveness in producing new ideas that helped circumvent obstacles and formulate compromises that bridged the gaps separating the parties? Or is his personal contribution exaggerated? Should one attribute his success mainly to the fact that he was the secretary of state of a great power, and thus able to marshal its resources to apply pressure and provide incentive that induced the parties to make the required concessions? In the search for answers to these questions we shall examine each round of the negotiations in which he was involved.

Before turning to the negotiations, a brief description of their context is in order. The negotiations followed the October 1973 war launched by Egypt and Syria in an attempt to increase pressures that would bring about Israel's withdrawal from the territories it had occupied since 1967. The war demonstrated again the tendency of the Arab-Israeli conflict to draw in the superpowers and endanger the peace of the world. In addition, the embargo imposed in the course of the war by Arab oil producers on shipments to the U.S. and the Netherlands produced shortages and price increases. Besides its disruptive economic effects, the embargo aroused fear and insecurity in the industrialized nations of the West.

The war also affected American attitudes and policies. After the failure of the 1971-1972 interim agreement talks, American pursuit of an Arab-Israeli settlement had subsided, and American diplomacy had assumed a more passive attitude. The war caused this attitude to change, because it threatened to undercut important elements in American foreign policy. It strengthened opposition to the policy of détente, since Soviet complicity in the preparations for the war and its strong support for Egypt and Syria during the hostilities were interpreted as a violation of the spirit, if not the letter, of Soviet-American understandings, and an indication that the Soviet Union would not abide by the restraints that détente supposedly imposed. The Arab oil embargo caused serious damage to the American economy and demonstrated the vulnerability of America's allies. Furthermore, the Western alliance showed ominous cracks as, overwhelmed by their anxiety, America's allies tended to go their own ways without concerting their policies with those of the U.S. In the Middle East it appeared that Egypt, threatened with defeat, might reinvite Soviet military presence, which only a year before had been drastically curtailed. In these circumstances, the search for an Arab-Israeli settlement assumed a new urgency, propelling the Arab-Israeli conflict to the forefront of American priorities.

From the moment war broke out (on October 6), Kissinger managed the crisis with constant regard to how American conduct might affect postwar efforts to establish greater stability in the Middle East. It was generally recognized that the war had unfrozen the situation and that the prospects for a settlement depended to a considerable extent on how the fighting ended. Kissinger himself publicly explained this at a news conference on October 12. He said that "after hostilities broke out, the United States set itself two principal objectives. One, to end the hostilities as quickly as possible. Secondly, to end the hostilities in such a manner that they would contribute to the maximum extent possible to the promotion of a more permanent, more lasting solution in the Middle East. . . ."[4]

There is considerable evidence to support the theory that what Kissinger meant was that the U.S. should see to it that the war ended inconclusively. In other words, he believed that a stalemate would be propitious for a new diplomatic effort. The delay in the airlift of supplies that Israel requested early in the war, the timing of the ceasefire at the moment when the Egyptian army was on the verge of defeat, and the American pressure on Israel to desist from destroying the Egyptian Third Army trapped on the east bank of the canal, appear to have been aimed at creating a stalemate. That these policies served additional goals, such as safeguarding détente, attempting to avoid an oil embargo, protecting the American positions in the Arab world, and preventing the reestablishment of Soviet influence in Egypt, does not contradict the interpretation that the U.S. sought a stalemate. The evidence of participants in the policy-making process lends support to this interpretation. Nixon does not attribute the stalemate theory to Kissinger, but testifies that he himself adhered to it. In his memoirs he says: "I believed that only a battlefield stalemate would provide the foundation on which fruitful negotiations might begin. Any equilibrium—if only an equilibrium of mutual exhaustion—would make it easier to reach an enforceable settlement."[5]

By October 20, when Kissinger arrived in Moscow in response to the urgent invitation by the Soviet leaders, the military equilibrium seemed to have been upset, as Israel's offensive on the west bank of the canal was gaining momentum and the Egyptian army was nearing defeat. This prompted the Soviet Union and the U.S. to reach an agreement on a cease-fire in the positions the opposing forces occupied at that moment. Besides bargaining about the terms of the cease-fire, Kissinger and Brezhnev also discussed the forthcoming diplomatic effort and the undertakings that the parties would be requested to make in this connection. At first, Egypt and the Soviet Union had insisted that the cease-fire resolution be accompanied by a call for Israel's withdrawal to the 1967 lines, but, as Egypt's military situation rapidly deteriorated, the Soviets and the Arabs agreed that the Security Council should merely call for the implementation of Resolution 242. Furthermore, Kissinger and Brezhnev agreed that the Security Council decide that "immediately and concurrently with the cease-fire, negotiations start between the parties concerned under appropriate auspices aimed at establishing a just and durable peace in the Middle East."[6] The U.S. and the Soviet Union reportedly also agreed in principle on the convening of a peace conference, at which the U.S. and the Soviet Union would serve as cochairmen.

THE CEASE-FIRE AGREEMENT

The cease-fire did not take hold on October 22 as ordered by the Security Council, and the continuing fighting created a situation of acute international crisis. Skillful American diplomacy turned the crisis into a fulcrum that increased American influence and enabled the U.S. subsequently to appropriate the mediator's role for itself alone.

As the fighting continued beyond the deadline set by the Security Council and Israeli forces continued to advance on the west side of the Suez Canal, the Soviet Union initiated a number of diplomatic and military moves that were interpreted by the U.S. as indicating the possibility of Soviet military intervention. The U.S. responded to this by warning the Soviets against any unilateral action and by putting its own forces on alert. By the time the cease-fire finally took hold, on October 24, following two more resolutions by the Security Council and strong American pressure upon Israel to halt its advance, the Egyptian Third Army Corps on the east bank of the canal was cut off from the rest of the Egyptian army.

Although the cease-fire was now in effect, Egypt faced the continued peril that the Third Army might be lost. President Sadat addressed "frequent and urgent appeals" to the U.S. to help the entrapped army.[7] Although the Egyptian appeal to the U.S. was prompted by the immediate danger to the Third Army, it did not signify any new departure of Egyptian policy. Egyptian willingness to enlist American mediation had been indicated before the war, in 1971, 1972, and 1973. Egyptian signals during the war, and especially Sadat's speech of October 16, suggested that the new developments had not foreclosed this possibility. A passage in Sadat's speech is especially revealing. After saying that the American airlift of supplies to Israel would not frighten Egypt, Sadat asked the U.S. where this policy was leading it to "when your entire interests are with us and not with Israel."[8] The Egyptian interest in the U.S. playing a role in the negotiations was reconfirmed on October 22, when upon learning that Kissinger was stopping in Israel on his way home from Moscow, Sadat invited him to stop in Egypt as well. Kissinger excused himself, but it was soon agreed that Kissinger would visit Cairo on November 7, en route to Peking.

Sadat's appeal met with a prompt and favorable American response, with Nixon reportedly assuring Sadat that Israel would not be allowed to destroy the Third Army.[9] From the American viewpoint, it was urgent that the Third Army be relieved, because Egypt might call for Soviet assistance to remove the Israelis or at least to airlift supplies to the encircled Egyptian forces. Such a move would have reestablished Soviet military presence in Egypt and restored Soviet influence there. The alternative of the Third Army's surrender carried the risk that Sadat might fall from power and be replaced by a regime which was less inclined to cooperate with the U.S. Furthermore, in such an event the war would end with an overwhelming Israeli victory. Instead of a stalemate there would be a new and probably less propitious situation for negotiations, in which the American ability to influence the course of diplomacy would be greatly reduced.

Acting in response to Sadat's appeal, and still under the impact of the crisis caused by the threatened Soviet intervention (and the consequent American alert), the U.S. firmly warned Israel not to move against the Third Army. It also requested Israel to permit Egyptian supplies to be transported to the entrapped force. Israel refused at first, believing that Egyptian anxiety about the fate of the besieged force would render it more flexible on a number of issues. The most urgent, from Israel's standpoint, was an exchange of war prisoners. Secondly, Israel hoped that the desire to bring about the relief of the besieged army might induce Egypt to agree to enter into negotiations with Israel for a political settlement. The precedent of 1949, when concern for the fate of the force encircled at Faluja brought Egypt to the armistice talks, suggested such a possibility. Finally, Israel expected that its bargaining position in any negotiations that might take place would be stronger if the Third Army remained sealed in its trap.

In these circumstances the U.S. applied strong pressure on Israel to relent. The pressure consisted reportedly of warnings that the Soviet Union might fly the supplies in. According to Marvin and Bernard Kalb, the U.S. also threatened Israel that it would slow down the airlift of military aid unless Israel allowed the transfer of supplies to the Third Army. Israel succumbed to these pressures and conveyed permission through the U.S. on October 27 for a single Egyptian convoy of supplies to be sent to the besieged force. At the same time and in exchange for the Israeli concession, the U.S. agreed to transmit to Egypt Israel's proposal that military representatives of both sides meet under UN auspices to discuss arrangements for the implementation of the UN cease-fire resolutions. In view of its unfavorable situation, and perhaps also as a gesture to the U.S., Egypt agreed.[10]

By halting the Israeli advance on October 24 and later arranging for supplies to reach the Third Army, the U.S. prevented Israel from winning a clear-cut victory, and created the stalemate that was expected to be propitious for negotiations. It probably also saved Sadat's regime. Sadat's inclination to accept American mediation was not only preserved but strengthened.

The meetings between the Egyptian and Israeli military representatives, Generals Aharon Yariv and Mohamed Abdel Ghany el-Gamasy, were opened at Kilometer 101 on the Cairo-Suez road on October 28. At the first meeting, arrangements were made for the Egyptian supply convoy to pass through Israeli lines. Additional issues relevant to the implementation of the cease-fire were discussed. Israel demanded a prisoner-of-war exchange and the lifting of the blockade that Egypt imposed against Israel at the southern entrance to the Red Sea at Bab el Mandeb. Egypt demanded that Israel withdraw to the lines it held on October 22, and that a corridor for regular supplies for the Third Army and the town of Suez be opened. The two men also took advantage of their meetings to expand the scope of their discussions, and explored informally ideas for a disengagement of forces. However, it soon became clear that it was not at Kilometer 101 that the important negotiations would take place, but rather in Washington.[11]

On October 28 Sadat sent his acting foreign minister, Ismail Fahmy, to Washington to prepare for Kissinger's talks in Cairo. Upon hearing that Fahmy was in Washington and that Kissinger would be visiting Cairo, Prime Minister Golda Meir decided to go to Washington herself, "to try to straighten out the rather strained relationship that had come into being" between Israel and the U.S.[12] Her concern was caused by the American pressure on Israel to go beyond the one convoy of supplies that it had permitted and to allow regular supplies for the Egyptian Third Army. The presence of both Fahmy and Meir in Washington provided an opportunity for intensive negotiations, with Kissinger talking separately with each side.

The proposals brought by Fahmy to Washington covered the immediately urgent questions of the Third Army and the cease-fire, as well as the final settlement. As the first and most urgent step Egypt proposed that Israel withdraw to the lines of October 22, a move that would lift the siege of the Third Army. An exchange of the prisoners of war was to take place only after Israel moved back and the Third Army was relieved. The proposal also outlined the stages for Israel's withdrawal to the international border, the clearance and reopening of the Suez Canal, the end of the state of belligerence between Egypt and Israel, and the convening of a peace conference. It further contained an incentive for the U.S., suggesting the restoration of diplomatic relations between Egypt and the U.S. at an early date.[13]

Egypt may have wished to open discussions covering this wide range of issues, but Kissinger preferred to limit them to the most urgent one—the relief of the Third Army. He reportedly told Fahmy that negotiations for a final settlement would be a protracted process. As for the problem of a return to the lines of October 22, Kissinger believed that negotiations might be difficult and proposed instead that an attempt be made to arrange a disengagement of forces, in which case the lines of October 22 would be irrelevant. In the meantime, the U.S. would try to arrange for regular supplies to the Third Army.[14]

Israel believed that its most important bargaining card was the encirclement of the Third Army. Its proposals to the U.S. gave priority to the exchange of prisoners of war, whose fate aroused great concern in Israel, especially since at this stage Egypt and Syria refused to transmit lists of the prisoners they were holding or to permit the representatives of the Red Cross to visit them. Israel also demanded that the blockade that Egypt imposed against Israel at Bab el Mandeb be lifted. Only then would Israel agree to make arrangements for the shipment of nonmilitary supplies to the Third Army and to the town of Suez.

The two main American requests to Israel were that it agree to the establishment of a corridor under UN control through Israeli lines to assure regular supplies for the Third Army, and that Israel drop its insistence that the prisoners be exchanged before any supply arrangements were put into force. To bring about a change in the Israeli position, the U.S. employed mainly warnings and threats; there was no talk of incentives. Nixon told Golda Meir that in an attempt to move toward a settlement, Israel would have to make concessions. But the main effort to soften the Israeli position was made by Kissinger. He raised the possibility of Soviet intervention on behalf of the Third Army and told the Israelis that the U.S. might even consider flying the supplies in themselves rather than let the Russians do it. Israel was warned that if another resolution requesting Israel's withdrawal to the October 22 lines were introduced in the Security Council, the U.S. would veto it only if a supply corridor for the Third Army had been arranged. Behind this warning there was the threat that the U.S. might support the Egyptian demands for an Israeli withdrawal to the October 22 positions, a possibility that greatly worried Israel. Another line of argument was that Israel ought to help the U.S. to improve its standing in the Arab world and to lift the oil embargo, and that this was in Israel's interest no less than in America's. At the same time Israel was given to understand that the American response to Israel's aid requests would be influenced by their readiness to cooperate with the U.S.

These pressures did bring about a softening of Israel's position. Israel still rejected the establishment of a corridor under UN control, because this would cut off the Israeli forces in the southern sector. But it was agreed to create a regular supply route, to allow supplies to move under UN supervision, and to permit the UN to establish a checkpoint to verify the nonmilitary nature of the supplies, on condition that the contents be examined also by Israel. Moreover, Israel agreed that the prisoner exchange could take place concurrently, and no longer made this a precondition for the supply arrangements.[15]

Kissinger obtained Sadat's acceptance of these terms in a three-hour conversation on November 7. However, the importance of the meeting went far beyond the agreement on the terms of the cease-fire. According to the Kalbs, Kissinger looked back upon this meeting "as one of the 'dramatic breakthroughs' of his diplomacy. 'It brought about . . . a major turn in the foreign policy of Egypt and therefore in the whole orientation of the area.' "[16] By all indications the two men reached an understanding about the principles that were to guide the efforts for a settlement of the conflict. Sadat apparently accepted Kissinger's gradualist approach and ceased to insist on a prior explicit statement by the U.S., or by Israel, that a final settlement required a full Israeli withdrawal to the 1967 line. Furthermore, Sadat accepted Kissinger's proposal to subsume the question of Israel's withdrawal to the October 22 lines within a disengagement agreement. Besides the apparent accord on strategy, they agreed on the terms of the cease-fire and an announcement was made that Egypt and the U.S. would soon resume diplomatic relations.

How can the quick and easily accomplished agreement between Kissinger and Sadat be explained? They apparently established easy rapport, and appeared to like and respect each other personally. But Edward Sheehan is probably right in refusing to attribute the agreement to "their instant romance," reports of which were greatly exaggerated. He describes their encounter as one between "a pair of foxes, exchanging oaths of confidence, each of them intent on manipulating the other for his own purpose."[17] The U.S. wanted to remove Soviet influence and reestablish its own, and more urgently desired Egyptian assistance toward the lifting of the Arab oil embargo. Egypt, for its part, wanted American help in relieving the Third Army, recovering Sinai, and perhaps advancing other Arab claims against Israel. But it was not only the possibility of eventual American help that won Sadat's quick acceptance of the terms of the cease-fire. Egypt had little choice but to accept. Sadat reportedly threatened at first to renew the war with Soviet assistance unless Israel returned to the October 22 lines. However, Kissinger warned him that if Egypt renewed the war, the U.S. would again support Israel. On the other hand, it was clear to Sadat that by agreeing to Kissinger's proposals the Third Army would be saved. Egypt was not asked to abandon any of its basic claims. Nor did Kissinger request that Egypt drop its demand for Israel's return to the October 22 lines, but only to agree to have this Israeli retreat subsumed in a greater one within the framework of a disengagement agreement. Sadat was asked to negotiate with Israel. But he had already given his consent to this when he accepted Security Council Resolution 338, and agreed to send General Gamasy to the Kilometer 101 rendezvous. The only concession Sadat made was to give up the prisoners. He got in return an arrangement for the regular supply of the Third Army, implicitly guaranteed by the U.S. Because of its symbolic value, the reestablishment of diplomatic relations with the U.S. was a significant concession, but in return he obtained an implicit American commitment to help bring about an Israeli withdrawal.

The negotiation of final details of the agreement, during a visit by Joseph Sisco and Harold Saunders to Israel on November 8 and 9, gave rise to some last moment difficulties. Israel maintained that the draft that the U.S. now proposed lacked sufficient detail and precision. Israel wanted the agreement to include an explicit statement that the corridor would be under Israeli, and not UN, control; specific inspection arrangements for the supply convoys; a timetable for the prisoner exchange; and an Egyptian undertaking to lift the blockade at Bab el Mandeb. Kissinger was, however, apprehensive that the inclusion of these explicit details might lead to new complications and perhaps prevent Sadat from accepting the agreement. These difficulties were finally resolved by America's offering assurances to Israel on these matters, as a substitute for the explicit inclusion of the terms in the agreement with Egypt. The American assurances opened the way for the formal signing of what came to be known as the Six-Point Agreement. It was signed by Egyptian and Israeli military representatives at Kilometer 101, in the presence of General Siilasvuo, the commander of the UN Emergency Force, on November 11. An important clause in the agreement, besides arrangements about the cease-fire, the supplies, and the exchange of prisoners, was that "discussions" between the parties would "begin immediately to settle the question of the return to the October 22 positions in the framework of agreement on the disengagement and separation of forces. . . ."[18]

The negotiations leading to the cease-fire agreement took place under conditions of an acute crisis. Only by stretching the definition of mediation can the American role be described as such. The basic principle that the Third Army be allowed regular supplies was not really subject to negotiation. It was imposed by the U.S. on Israel. The issues subject to negotiation and mediation were the arrangements under which the supplies would be delivered and the concessions which Egypt gave in return. Furthermore, the U.S. facilitated the agreement by guaranteeing its implementation and observance.

Signing the agreement did not yet remove the danger of the war being renewed. Its most important outcomes were that it consolidated the stalemate that Kissinger desired, established the limited goal of disengagement as the next objective to be pursued, and reinforced Egypt's readiness to accept American mediation in the forthcoming talks.

The Ground Rules for Geneva

In the course of Kissinger's visit to Moscow in October, he and the Soviet leaders agreed that a conference would be convened in Geneva under joint American-Soviet auspices with the participation of Israel and the Arab states. Although Israel, Egypt, and Syria accepted implicitly the conference when they accepted Resolution 338, the procedures and ground rules for the conference remained to be settled. Little is known about Soviet-American contacts on this matter. In the negotiations for an agreement between Israel and the Arab states about the terms of their participation at the conference, Kissinger again played a major part.

Israel's attitude depended to a considerable extent on how the U.S. viewed the function of the conference. To allay Israel's fears, aroused by the long shadow of the Rogers Plan, the U.S. assured Israel that the conference would only be a ceremonial occasion to establish the framework for negotiations, which would take place within working groups, and that the first item of substantive negotiations would be an Egyptian-Israeli disengagement. The U.S. promised not to present any substantive proposals of its own.[19]

The main issues on which the Arab states and Israel were divided were the timing of the conference, the role of the UN, the issue of Palestinian participation, and Israel's demand that Syria provide a list of the prisoners of war it was holding before the conference met.

Initially, both Egypt and Syria wanted an agreement on disengagement, involving some Israeli withdrawal, to be concluded before the conference. Such an agreement would have helped them to justify their participation in a direct conference with Israel, something they had refused to do since the 1949 armistice talks. However, Israel was on the eve of general elections to the Knesset, and the outgoing government felt it did not have the mandate to conclude an agreement entailing the withdrawal of Israeli forces. Kissinger succeeded in convincing Egypt of the seriousness of the American commitment to arrange for a disengagement immediately after the Israeli elections scheduled for the end of December. Egypt consented that the conference precede disengagement. But Kissinger was unable to convince President Assad. Neither did Assad agree to provide a list of the prisoners that Syria was holding. As Israel had threatened that it would not meet the Syrians unless a list was provided and Red Cross visits permitted, a disruption of the conference was averted by Syria's refusal to attend.[20]

The question of the UN's role in the conference was relatively minor. The Arab states hoped to take advantage of their strong influence in the UN by having that organization play a substantive role in the conference. Israel naturally wished to minimize the UN's role. The matter was resolved by an agreement that UN Secretary-General Waldheim would convene the conference and preside over the opening session, and by American assurances to Israel that the UN would not be allowed any significant role.[21]

The most difficult problem to resolve was the Arab request that a Palestinian delegation participate in the conference. This request reflected the change that had taken place in the Palestinian status since 1967. After 1948, the Arab states had claimed that they represented Palestinian interests. The Palestinians did not participate in any of the negotiations aimed at a settlement of the conflict. But subsequent years saw the growth of Palestinian national consciousness, especially after the 1967 war, and the growing influence of the Palestine Liberation Organization in the Arab world. The PLO began to demand recognition as the sole spokesman for the Palestinians; Egypt and Syria supported its claim and demanded its representation at the conference. Jordan opposed it, still regarding itself as speaking for the Palestinian population of the West Bank under Israeli rule. However, to avoid breaking Arab solidarity Jordan did not raise its objections formally. The main opposition came from Israel, which rejected the PLO's participation on the grounds that it was a terrorist organization. A still deeper reason for Israel's refusal was the expectation that Palestinian participation would give added emphasis to the Arab demand for Israeli withdrawal from the West Bank.

Kissinger's attempts to overcome this difficulty resulted in a compromise, according to which the possibility of Palestinian participation at a later stage of the conference would be left open. To meet Israeli objections to any mention of the Palestinians, the letter of invitation to the conference was to say that the parties have "agreed that the question of other participants from the Middle East area will be discussed during the first stage of the Conference."[22] Interestingly, Kissinger enlisted Soviet assistance in obtaining Egypt's agreement to this wording. By thus engaging the Soviets, Kissinger helped to prevent possible Soviet criticism of Sadat for his making concessions at the Palestinians' expense.

The formula still did not satisfy Israel, which insisted that the letter of invitation also explicitly grant the participants the right to veto the invitation of any additional delegations. To this, Egypt was strongly opposed. In view of the possibility that Israel might not attend the conference unless it could veto the invitation of additional participants, the U.S. combined strong pressure with a promise to support Israel's position, in an attempt to induce Israel to change its stand. In a letter of December 13 President Nixon said that in the American view the invitation of additional delegations would require the agreement of all the initial participants, and he coupled this assurance with a warning that "he would no longer be able to justify support for Israel" if Israel refused to attend the conference. Israel's objections to the letter of invitation were finally overcome by the incorporation of Nixon's promise in a formal and secret Memorandum of Understanding.[23] The American role was thus not limited to mediating an agreement on the terms for convening the conference. Because the only text that was acceptable to the parties was ambiguous, the U.S. also extended a guarantee concerning the interpretation of the letter of invitation, thus reducing the risk that Israel believed it was assuming by accepting the ambiguous wording of the letter.

The conference lasted for two days, December 21-22, 1973, and was an important symbolic event. It was attended by the foreign ministers of Egypt, Jordan, Israel, the U.S., and the Soviet Union, as well as by the secretary-general of the UN. But it did not provide the setting for substantive negotiations. These were held elsewhere, within a different framework.

The First Egyptian-Israeli Disengagement

Without belittling Kissinger's contribution to the conclusion of this agreement, it should be noted that it was Moshe Dayan who first formulated the disengagement concept in 1970-1971, and that the agreement concluded in 1974 resembled in many respects the formula he had proposed then. It is, however, difficult to reconstruct when, how, and who introduced the concept into the 1973-1974 negotiations. There is evidence that it was already discussed simultaneously at the end of October in Washington between Kissinger and Fahmi, and at Kilometer 101 between Yariv and Gamasy.[24]

Both Egypt and Israel had a strong interest in disengagement. The cease-fire had caught their forces intertwined, and both sides were vulnerable to surprise attacks from the other. Egypt continued to be concerned about the Third Army, which although regularly supplied, was still endangered. Israel increasingly felt the pressure, both economic and psychological, that the continued mobilization of the reserves imposed upon it, as well as the toll exacted by Egyptian-initiated military activity (a minor war of attrition) along the canal. In addition, both Egypt and Israel hoped to derive from disengagement some political-strategic advantages. Israel expected that disengagement would reduce Egypt's ability and motivation to start a new war, and also that it would relieve the pressure on Israel to withdraw to the 1967 lines. Sadat was interested in the political benefits to be derived from an Israeli withdrawal, and hoped that disengagement would set in motion a process that would produce further Israeli withdrawals.

Besides the obvious questions of substance, there were also the questions concerning the manner and the framework for conducting the disengagement negotiations. They began at Kilometer 101, between General Gamasy and General Yariv. However, on November 29, Israel caused the talks to be adjourned sine die, reportedly at Kissinger's behest. Dayan too favored the interruption. At that stage only Egypt remained interested in the continuation of the talks at Kilometer 101, and it hoped that the disengagement agreement would be concluded then and there.

Kissinger wanted the disengagement talks transferred from Kilometer 101 to the Geneva Conference. According to Matti Golan, he explained to Israeli leaders that this procedure would give the Geneva talks a goal that had a chance of being attained because it was limited. If the talks at Geneva aimed at full settlement of the conflict, they would soon reach issues in which basic principles were at stake and break down. Quandt claims that Kissinger "feared that if Egypt and Israel reached a disengagement agreement before Geneva, Assad would insist on the same," and that this might lead to an indefinite delay in the convening of the conference. But probably the most important reason was that he wanted the U.S. to be given credit for arranging an Israeli withdrawal, however limited. To quote Quandt, Kissinger wanted "to demonstrate that a United States role was essential for sustained diplomatic progress."[25] He believed that the credit the U.S. received for bringing about an Israeli withdrawal could be used to influence the Arab oil producers to lift their boycott of shipments to the U.S., and to enhance America's standing in the Arab world in general.

Israel's preference for American mediation over direct negotiations with Egypt is more surprising. It ran counter to the long-established doctrine, if not dogma, that real progress toward a settlement of the conflict could be made only through direct contacts between the parties. Now that direct talks had begun and seemed to be quite promising, it was Israel that interrupted them. Dayan's main reason for interrupting the direct talks and for seeking American mediation instead was, in his own words, that "it was essential that the United States be involved in the negotiations so that she would share responsibility for its implementation." In other words, Dayan wanted a mediator because he wanted a guarantor.[26]

It was initially expected that the first order of business of the Geneva Conference, following its ceremonial opening, would be the Egyptian-Israeli disengagement negotiations. But it soon turned out that the parties themselves had a different preference. On January 4, 1974, immediately after the Israeli elections of December 31 that returned to power (with a reduced majority) the governing coalition headed by the Labor Party, Dayan visited Washington for talks with Kissinger. He outlined Israel's disengagement proposals and suggested that Kissinger come to the Middle East to expedite the disengagement talks. After checking with Egypt, which also favored the idea, Kissinger proceeded to the Middle East to conduct the talks there in person. At first, Kissinger thought that he would only help establish some agreed framework, or as he was quoted, "grease the wheels" for the detailed negotiations that would be pursued at Geneva. But following the first day of talks in Cairo on January 12, Sadat asked Kissinger to stay in the region and help complete the agreement. Israel concurred, and this is how Kissinger's shuttle diplomacy was launched. An exclusively American mediation was not merely acceptable; it was urgently sought by both sides.[27]

Israel's interest in expediting an agreement resulted largely from the realization that it could not resume the fighting in order to improve its bargaining position (as Dayan occasionally was tempted to do), and that it needed to relieve the economic and psychological strain that the state of continuous mobilization and alert imposed. Egypt wished to reap the political benefit of an Israeli withdrawal which seemed to be within reach. And both parties, as well as the U.S., were concerned that if the talks were held in Geneva, Soviet participation would complicate the negotiations and delay the rapid conclusion of an agreement.[28]

The negotiations during Kissinger's shuttle rested upon the foundations laid in previous talks. Their main stages were the informal clarifications between Gamasy and Yariv at Kilometer 101, Dayan's talks in Washington on December 7, Kissinger's talks in Cairo and Jerusalem in mid-December, and Dayan's second round of talks in Washington in early January. Now it took five additional days of very intensive talks in Aswan and Jerusalem until announcement of the agreement could be made on January 17. The signing took place on the 18th, at Kilometer 101, when the chiefs of staff of the two armies, Generals Elazar and Gamasy, signed the agreement in the presence of General Siilasvuo, the commander of the UN Emergency Force.

Throughout the negotiations, both Egypt and Israel displayed considerable flexibility, making concessions at a fairly rapid rate. In contrast to the negotiations on the cease-fire agreement and the convening of the Geneva conference, in the disengagement negotiations the U.S. did not exert pressures in order to exact concessions. On the contrary, in November, during the Kilometer 101 talks, "Kissinger felt that the talks were proceeding too rapidly," and in his talks with Dayan in December he reportedly urged Dayan not to move too quickly lest Israel appear weak.[29] The American contribution to the parties' readiness to make concessions consisted mainly in interpreting to each the constraints affecting the other side and suggesting compromise formulae. These were of two kinds. Some were ambiguous wordings that helped the parties to avoid the embarrassment of explicit concessions. Others helped to settle *quantitative* disagreements, such as over the details of the mutual reductions of forces. The U.S. further contributed to the successful outcome by helping the parties to reduce the risks that they feared the concessions might entail. Some of the important Egyptian undertakings were spelled out in letters from President Sadat to President Nixon, so as to avoid the appearance that they were concessions to Israeli demands. Israel, for its part, received on some matters American assurances in place of direct Egyptian commitments.

A summary review of the main issues and of the agreements will exemplify the above observations.[30] Perhaps the most important issue, one that bedevilled the 1971 negotiations, was the geographical configuration of disengagement. On this issue, the general outline of the agreement emerged from the talks at Kilometer 101, where both sides tentatively discussed far-reaching concessions before the talks were suspended on November 29. The initial Israeli idea was that Israel would relinquish its hold on the west side of the canal and that Egypt would withdraw its forces to the east bank of the waterway. Egypt's starting position was that Israel would withdraw as far as the line drawn from El Arish to Ras Muhammed. But both sides must have been aware that these ideas were unrealistic. Yariv raised informally as early as November 22 the possibility of Israel's withdrawing from the west side of the canal, provided that there was a significant thinning out of Egyptian forces on both sides of the waterway. Gamasy, for his part, began speaking of an Israeli withdrawal to a line east of the Mitla and Giddi passes. Thus, by the time that Kissinger assumed control of the negotiations the gap between the parties' positions had been considerably narrowed. He was still left with the task of closing it. And not only did he have to make the effort, but the effort had to be public, so that the U.S. could claim credit and persuade the Arab oil producers to lift the embargo. Kissinger accomplished this during the shuttle, when the depth of the Israeli withdrawal was finally agreed upon. Egypt accepted a line west of the passes, leaving the passes in Israeli hands.

In 1971, one of the principal obstacles to agreement was Egypt's insistence that the separation of forces agreement be of limited duration, and that it be explicitly regarded as the first step toward a full Israeli withdrawal. Now Egypt started the negotiations once more with a demand for a timetable for a full withdrawal. This obstacle was circumvented with the help of an American guarantee, embodied in a document that accompanied the disengagement agreement, that the U.S. would use its influence to bring about the full implementation of Resolution 242. This enabled Sadat to drop his demand for an explicit Israeli commitment to withdraw.

From the outset it was agreed between the parties that their respective armies would be separated by a buffer zone in which UN forces would be stationed. In view of the events leading to the 1967 war, Israel demanded that the agreement explicitly state that the removal of the UN force required the consent of both parties. To this Egypt could not agree because it would have amounted to a restriction of its sovereignty over the buffer zone, and could have been interpreted as a tacit acceptance of the disengagement line as a permanent one. The problem was overcome by an American pledge to Israel that the UN force would not be withdrawn without the consent of both parties.

The reduction of forces along the front was a matter of particular difficulty. At the start of the negotiations, Israel demanded that only a symbolic Egyptian presence be allowed on the east bank of the canal, while Egypt rejected any restrictions on the deployment of its forces. By the time of Kissinger's visit to Cairo in mid-December, Egypt modified its position, accepting the principle of mutual force reductions. Thereafter, the bargaining concerned the levels of forces each side would be allowed to keep within designated zones near the disengagement line. These were quantitative issues and no longer questions of principle, and they were resolved during Kissinger's shuttle by both sides' accepting American compromise proposals. Besides the difficulties concerning the levels of forces, there was also the problem of Sadat's reluctance to have the restrictions listed in the agreement, lest this expose him to criticism for conceding to Israeli demands. This problem was resolved by arranging that the force limitations be specified in a separate exchange of letters between President Nixon, President Sadat, and Prime Minister Meir.

Israel's demand that the disengagement agreement proclaim the end of the state of belligerence between the parties had already caused difficulty during the 1971 negotiations. In addition to an explicit statement to this effect, Israel now requested that Egypt commit itself in the agreement to specific measures that Israel hoped would inhibit Egypt from resuming the war. Israel requested that Egypt undertake to clear the canal and reopen it to navigation, to rebuild the cities along its banks, and to restore normal civilian activity in the area. Furthermore, Israel requested that Egypt permit Israeli cargoes to pass through the canal, which was understood to be an indirect acknowledgment of the end of the state of belligerence. Egypt, however, refused to agree to any statement terminating the state of belligerence as long as Israeli troops had not been completely withdrawn, and rejected the Israeli requests concerning the rehabilitation of the Canal zone as intruding on Egypt's domestic jurisdiction. A compromise was reached according to which Israel dropped its demand for an explicit statement of nonbelligerence. Egypt, for its part, agreed to inform the U.S. of its intention to clear and reopen the canal, to rehabilitate the area, and to permit the passage of Israeli cargoes through the canal. The U.S. agreed to convey to Israel the information it had received. This arrangement too helped Sadat to save face and reduced somewhat his vulnerability to criticism. At the same time, the U.S. implicitly assumed some responsibility for the implementation of limitation of forces and for the restoration of normal civilian activity along the canal.

The American insurance was reinforced by an American undertaking to monitor the observance of the agreement through reconnaissance flights, the results of which were to be made available to both parties. Additional American guarantees were given to Israel. The U.S. assured Israel that it regarded the Bab el Mandeb as an international waterway and would support Israel's right to use it. Furthermore, Israel was promised that the U.S. would continue to provide it with military assistance on a long-term basis.

In these negotiations the mediator was able to induce concessions without resorting to pressures. The incentives that the U.S. offered—economic aid to Egypt, and economic and military aid to Israel—do not appear to have been important causes for the parties' flexibility either. It was rather the pressure of the circumstances in which Egypt and Israel found themselves that made them eager to conclude a disengagement agreement rapidly. The mediator's contribution was, however, essential in suggesting compromises and in arranging the indirect transaction of commitments. This procedure helped to reduce Sadat's vulnerability to criticism from the opponents of the agreement, which a direct commitment to Israel might have entailed. And finally, by providing both parties with implicit and explicit guarantees, the mediator encouraged them to feel protected from some of the risks that they believed that their concessions entailed.

THE SYRIAN DISENGAGEMENT

The disengagement agreement between Israel and Syria, signed on May 31, 1974, was much more difficult to negotiate than the one between Egypt and Israel. The negotiations took much longer—they involved a month-long shuttle between Jerusalem and Damascus (as compared with five days for the Egyptian agreement)—and were accompanied by heavy American pressure on Israel to make concessions.

Part of the difficulty was in the history of Syrian-Israeli relations, which for many years were marked with greater hostility and bitterness than the relations between Israel and its other neighbors. The negotiations were also encumbered by domestic political constraints in both countries. Unlike President Sadat, whose authority enabled him to make decisions alone and disregard the advice of his civilian and military advisors, President Assad was circumscribed by his dependence upon the approval and support of his colleagues. The freedom of action of the Israeli government had also become much more limited than in the previous round of negotiations with Egypt. On April 11, just before Kissinger's shuttle began, Golda Meir resigned from the premiership under the pressure of criticism of her government's responsibility for Israel's unpreparedness at the time of the Egyptian and Syrian attack on October 6. From then on, she headed a caretaker Cabinet, the authority of which was weakened. Moreover, in this context, the pressures of groups demanding the annexation of the Golan further constrained the government's freedom of action.[31]

The touchy nature of the Syrian-American relationship was another complicating element. Unlike Egypt, which since the closing days of Nasser's regime had solicited American diplomatic assistance and which since 1972 had sought to free itself from Soviet influence, Syria remained vehemently anti-American and continued to welcome Soviet protection and to collaborate diplomatically with the

Soviet Union. By early 1974, Syria's Soviet protectors had become irritated at their exclusion from the Egyptian negotiations and highly suspicious of American mediation, which they correctly saw as aimed at undermining their influence in the Arab world. Syria's acceptance of American mediation in these circumstances should be regarded as an achievement for American diplomacy. It was won by the successful conclusion of the Sinai disengagement agreement, which seemed conclusively to prove the validity of the American claim that only the U.S. is able to make Israel relinquish its conquests and withdraw. The advice of the Egyptian and Saudi rulers, urging Assad to accept American mediation, probably contributed to the Syrian decision.[32]

Syria had good reason to be interested in disengagement. The cease-fire found the Israeli forces entrenched some twenty-five miles from Damascus, having recovered the area seized by the Syrians in the first few days of the war, and advanced beyond the 1967 line to occupy additional Syrian territory. The Syrian concern at the military situation was greatly heightened following the Egyptian-Israeli disengagement, which left them to face Israel alone. Furthermore, Syria too wished to be able to claim victory in the war, as Egypt did when it regained a strip of Sinai. Disengagement promised to enable the recovery of the territory Syria lost in 1973, and perhaps also a portion of the Golan lost in 1967.

Israel too was interested in disengagement, but for less pressing reasons. In the Golan the Israeli hold on the newly occupied bulge was secure, and it was the Syrians who felt far more uncomfortable at the military situation than the Israelis. Nevertheless, Israel had to maintain a high degree of military preparedness that burdened its resources. In an effort to induce Israeli flexibility, the Syrians initiated a minor war of attrition. The Israeli society was unlikely to tolerate such warfare for long and if the Syrian harassment were to continue Israel would have to escalate and perhaps launch a major new war. Such a prospect carried many risks, not the least of which was a confrontation with the Soviet Union. Moreover, although the likelihood of Egypt coming to Syria's assistance had diminished, there was no certainty that it would not do so. Thus, among the motives for Israel's interest in disengagement with Syria was also the desire to protect the disengagement agreement with Egypt. Concern for the fate of the Israeli prisoners in Syria was another important consideration, and disengagement appeared to be the only means of obtaining their release. American urging that Israel help to maintain the diplomatic momentum also weighed heavily with Israel and contributed to its readiness to seek disengagement on the Syrian front as well.

The interest of the two parties did not suffice to bring about disengagement. It required a strong motivation on the part of the mediator to pursue the negotiations with such energy and persistence. One urgent concern was that unless the Syrians and Israelis disengaged, a new war might break out and jeopardize not only the Egyptian-Israeli disengagement, but also the newly acquired American influence in Egypt. Another motive, no less urgent, was the desire to move the Arab oil-producing states to lift the embargo. The U.S. had expected that the embargo would end following the conclusion of the Egyptian-Israeli disengagement agreement, but it did not. Despite some angry American messages to Saudi Arabia, which held the key to such a decision, the Arabs demanded that the U.S. "do something for Syria" first. This Arab attitude was highly embarrassing to the Americans. The U.S. could not seem to be yielding to blackmail, and encourage the Arabs to believe that all they had to do to bring about Israeli withdrawals was to pull the lever of the oil embargo. The Arab refusal to end the embargo created the impression that American mediation was brought about solely by the embargo. Apparently, the Saudis were persuaded not to persist in embarrassing the U.S. in this way and an understanding was reached to decouple the issues, at least in public. The embargo was suspended on March 18, following the formal start of the disengagement talks. (Significantly, the suspension was opposed by Syria which believed that the move weakened its bargaining position.) The formal end of the embargo was announced only in June, following the conclusion of the Syrian-Israeli agreement.[33] Finally, the U.S. probably hoped that American mediation would help to improve American-Syrian relations. Judging by Syria's agreement in December to accept an American diplomat to look after American interests there (in the absence of diplomatic relations, which Syria had broken in 1967), and the restoration of full diplomatic relations shortly after the conclusion of the disengagement agreement,[34] there apparently was some understanding that the U.S. would be rewarded for its role. However, the U.S. probably did not expect that Syria would go as far as Egypt went, and that its mediation would lead to the replacement of Soviet influence in Syria by American influence there.

Once the U.S. embarked on the path of mediation, its determination to bring the negotiations to a successful conclusion was spurred by domestic political considerations. With Nixon's position rapidly deteriorating as his misdeeds in the Watergate affair came to light, he was anxious to demonstrate some successes in foreign policy, or at least to avoid the image of failure. Occasional messages from the president served to prod Kissinger to continue even when he was close to despair, or when he thought that it was undignified for the American secretary of state to haggle over minor details as he was required to do.[35]

The first problem that Kissinger encountered was how to get the parties to engage in the talks. Israel would not negotiate with Syria until Syria submitted a list of Israeli prisoners of war and permitted Red Cross visits to them. Syria believed that the prisoners were its strongest bargaining card for inducing Israel to withdraw. Syria therefore made its accession to the Israeli demands on the prisoners conditional on Israel's first proving its willingness to conclude a disengagement agreement. The issue of what step would come first was resolved by the U.S. serving as a trustee for both sides. It was agreed that Kissinger would receive a list of the prisoners from Syria, but transmit it to Israel only in return for a formal Israeli disengagement proposal; he would give the disengagement proposal to Syria in return for Syria's permitting Red Cross visits to the prisoners. Kissinger performed the transaction during visits to Damascus and Jerusalem between February 26 and 28. This cleared the way for the opening of formal negotiations in Washington through separate visits there of Israeli and Syrian representatives.[36]

The main issues in the substantive negotiations were the extent of the Israeli withdrawal, arms limitations, the role of the UN, and the question of the Syrian attitude to terrorist attacks across the cease-fire lines.[37] On the first issue, Syria's position in December was that Israel should withdraw from all the territory taken in the 1967 and 1973 wars. Israel's opening position was that the disengagement should take place entirely within the territory occupied in 1973, while the Golan, occupied in 1967, should remain under Israeli control. The territorial problem was difficult to resolve for a number of reasons. It was essential for Syria to show that the 1973 war produced gains. The precedent set by the Egyptian-Israeli agreement in which Egypt regained some of the territory it lost in 1967 hardened Syria's attitude. However, the Golan was much smaller than Sinai, and relatively small withdrawals had significant military implications. Furthermore, any appreciable Israeli withdrawal west of the 1967 line would have required the dismantling of settlements established in the Golan. According to the compromise finally agreed upon, Israel withdrew a short distance west of the 1967 line. The main Syrian gain, which had important symbolic value, was the city of Kuneitra, which before 1967 served as the administrative center of the Golan. The parties had already accepted the general outlines of this settlement by the middle of May. But bargaining over the details, and especially over three strategically important hills in the vicinity of Kuneitra, took another two weeks of nerve-wracking and bitter argument.

The width of the UN buffer zone, the arms limitation provisions, and the size and role of the UN force were also subject to difficult bargaining. The compromises that the U.S. helped to arrange on these issues were largely of a quantitative nature. A disputed question of principle, whether the UN presence would consist of an interposing force as Israel demanded or of unarmed observers as Syria demanded, was left ambiguous. The ambiguity was reflected in the name given to the UN presence, the United Nations Disengagement Observer Force (UNDOF), in distinction to the Sinai United Nations Emergency Force (UNEF).

On the issue of prevention of terrorist raids, Israel wanted a Syrian commitment identical to the one included in the Egyptian-Israeli disengagement agreement, in which the parties undertook to refrain from "all military or paramilitary actions against each other." However, Syria, because of its support of the Palestinian cause, felt unable to make publicly such an undertaking, although Assad reportedly gave Kissinger a private assurance that Syria would not permit the launching of raids from its territory. The issue was resolved by the U.S. formally notifying Israel of its interpretation of the cease-fire clause according to which "raids by armed groups or individuals" were contrary to the cease-fire. Moreover, the U.S. recognized Israel's right to "prevent such actions by all available means" and promised to support politically Israel's exercise of such right.[38] Finally, the agreement provided for an exchange of war prisoners, an issue that apparently did not cause particular difficulty at this stage.

American mediation played a crucial role in the conclusion of this agreement. Yet without belittling the American contribution, it should be noted that the U.S. was not the sole mediator in this case. On occasion Egypt and Saudi Arabia mediated between the principal mediator—the U.S.—and Syria. For instance, they were instrumental in persuading Syria to try American mediation. In February they helped to arrange the procedural compromise on the prisoners list that allowed the commencement of formal negotiations. Subsequently, during Kissinger's shuttle, they brought pressure to bear on Syria to accept some of Kissinger's compromise proposals. There is also some evidence that Sadat made an important contribution toward arranging the compromise formula on which the territorial delineation was based. If not the inventor, he certainly was one of the earliest proponents of the line just west of Kuneitra, which he advocated in his talks with Kissinger on February 28.[39]

Incentives and pressures alike were used by the mediators in their efforts to modify the parties' positions and influence them to make concessions. At first the U.S. possessed little ability to induce Syrian flexibility. The U.S. employed, of course, the usual incentive of economic aid, and let Syria know that aid would be offered once a disengagement agreement had been concluded. However, it is unlikely that promises of aid had much effect on Syrian behavior. The lever for political pressure to induce specific concessions was gradually fashioned by Kissinger. He started from the basic situation that brought Syria to accept American mediation in the first place. Syria was confronted with two alternatives: it could either permit the U.S. to mediate and obtain an Israeli withdrawal within the framework of disengagement, or pursue a policy of continued confrontation with all its attendant risks. Kissinger used his persuasive skills to heighten Assad's awareness of the risks Syria would face if no agreement were concluded by warning him that Syria might be left to face Israel alone, while Egypt continued to pursue the path of a separate understanding with Israel. At the same time Kissinger took care to stimulate and nurture Syrian hopes that the U.S. could and would bring about an agreement containing important gains to Syria. In late March, after gaining the impression that Israel might be prepared to give up Kuneitra and estimating that the Syrians would regard the recovery of the town as an important political plus, Kissinger let them understand that the U.S. would support Syria's claim to the town.[40] Only after Syria knew that Kuneitra was within reach did Kissinger acquire a means of pressure by threatening to suspend the negotiations and return to Washington unless Syria changed its position. This tactic was employed by Kissinger vis-à-vis Assad at least twice, and with good effect: once on May 18 to persuade him to accept the compromise line Kissinger devised, and another time to make him drop some new demands that he raised on May 27, after the agreement had virtually been concluded.[41]

The U.S. employed a variety of means to get Israel to change its position. Incentives were provided at the opening of the negotiations and at their conclusion. In early April the U.S. approved Israel's request for the supply of tanks (but delayed its reply on planes), and toward the end of the month the president converted $1 billion out of $2.2 billion of aid that Israel had received from a loan to a grant. The timing of these measures on the eve of Kissinger's departure for his Middle East shuttle suggests that the administration hoped that they would make the Israeli leaders receptive to Kissinger's proposals.[42] The planes withheld in April were approved along with other military aid at the end of May, when the negotiations were concluded.

The pressures were employed during the intensive bargaining in the course of Kissinger's shuttle. One form of pressure was Kissinger's description of the international situation with emphasis on Israel's isolation: on the danger that if the negotiations failed the oil embargo might be reimposed, the war might be resumed, Egypt might feel compelled to join Syria in fighting Israel, and this would reduce American influence, enable the Soviets to reestablish their position, and undo the promising beginning of a peace process. Israel was asked to make sacrifices for a common cause, and the disengagement agreement was well worth the price, since the alternative might be catastrophic.[43] Besides such warnings of the consequences of a failure to conclude an agreement, Kissinger also threatened Israel that he would blame their side for the breakdown of the talks. The ability to expose the parties to public disapproval is a classic weapon of intermediaries. Yet the parties often possess a similar ability to damage the intermediary's reputation by accusing him of being unfair. According to Golan, it was Golda Meir who began an exchange of mutual threats, by telling Kissinger that she would report to the full Cabinet "that whenever she claimed that a certain area is of strategic importance to Israel he rejected it, but when the Syrians wanted two more destroyed villages it became important, absolutely essential." Soon Kissinger took the offensive saying that he would "explain to the Foreign Affairs Committee that the negotiations failed because Dayan insisted on installing his barbed wire on the outskirts of El Quneitra. How would Israel look then?"[44] When Kissinger's threat of blaming Israel for failure was amplified by messages from President Nixon calling upon Israel to modify its attitude and warning that the U.S. might have to reexamine the relations between the two countries, it carried great weight, since the Israeli leaders feared that in the contest for the sympathy of the American public, the president, though crippled by Watergate, was likely to be the winner. Whether because they were cowed by Kissinger's and Nixon's threats, or because they were persuaded by Kissinger's reasoning that an agreement was in Israel's interest, the Israeli leaders gave in and accepted Kissinger's compromise proposal on the line of demarcation at Kuneitra.

The parties' decisions to make the concessions necessary for the conclusion of the agreement were again facilitated by the mediator's ability to help to protect them from some of the risks that they believed the disengagement agreement entailed.

In a minor but symbolically important way, Egypt too lent its services and helped Syria to save face. As a means of circumventing Syria's reluctance to acknowledge formally its participation in the Geneva Conference (which provided the formal framework of the disengagement agreement), as long as Palestinian participation had not been agreed upon, it was arranged that the Syrian representative sign the agreement not as part of a Syrian delegation, but as a member of the Egyptian-Israeli working group.[45]

But it was the principal mediator, the U.S., that provided the most important guarantees. These were embodied in separate American pledges to Israel and to Syria respectively and were not included in the disengagement agreement proper. Some of the American assurances to Israel were directly related to the agreement concluded with Syria. Among them were the American interpretations of the limitations of forces arrangements, a pledge that the UN force would not be withdrawn without Israel's consent, U.S. aerial reconnaissance to monitor the observance of the agreement, and spelling out the American attitude in case Syria broke the cease-fire. And, as just mentioned, to overcome the obstacle of Syria's refusal to formally commit itself to prevent terrorist attacks from its territory, the U.S. stated that it recognized Israel's right to defend itself against such raids from across the border "by all available means," and that the U.S. would support politically Israel's exercise of its right of self-defense in such cases. In addition, the U.S. approved standing Israeli applications for additional arms. This can be interpreted either as a reward for Israel's cooperation with the U.S. or as compensation for the strategic positions that Israel relinquished. Finally the promise that the U.S. would put aid to Israel on a long-term basis, instead of an annual basis as hitherto, carried an implicit assurance that the U.S. would not use aid as a means to influence Israeli policy in the future.

Syria too received American guarantees concerning future negotiations. It has been reported that these included assurances that the U.S. did not regard the disengagement line as a final boundary and that the U.S. would work for the full implementation of Resolution 338, together with a promise to help arrange for the Palestinians to join the negotiations.[46]

FAILURE—REASSESSMENT—SUCCESS

Following the Syrian-Israeli agreement, two negotiating attempts ended in failure: one between Jordan and Israel that never got off the ground, and another between Egypt and Israel that crashed dramatically in March 1975. Subsequently, another attempt to conclude an Egyptian-Israeli agreement succeeded in the summer of 1975. In this section I shall examine Kissinger's failure to arrange a Jordanian-Israeli disengagement, and shall try to explain why the March attempt to conclude the Egyptian-Israeli agreement failed, only to succeed five months later.

The two signed disengagement agreements had taken care of the immediate problems created by the war, but it was understood by all concerned that diplomatic efforts toward a settlement would continue. The U.S. wanted the momentum of negotiations maintained mainly because it feared that in the absence of diplomatic progress the Arab states would again resort to pressures. The specter of another Arab-Israeli war or oil embargo were the main stimuli for continued American initiatives.

The possibility of a separation of forces along the Jordanian-Israeli line had already been raised in December 1973. Jordan was at that time persuaded by the U.S. to attend the Geneva Conference on the implicit understanding that it too would benefit from the expected Israeli concessions. After the Syrian disengagement agreement, King Hussein got impatient. His need to show some political success had grown urgent, as the PLO's claim for recognition as the sole legitimate spokesman for the Palestinians was gaining gradual acceptance, and thus undermining Jordan's claim to the West Bank.[47]

Israel's attitude was more complex. Its assessment of

Arab intentions and international circumstances was basically pessimistic. Yitzhak Rabin (who succeeded Golda Meir as premier) and his colleagues were of the opinion that the political consequences of the 1973 war had encouraged the Arabs to believe that the tide had turned in their favor, so that they would seek to take advantage of the Western world's fear of another oil embargo to press for a settlement based on the 1967 boundaries as a step toward Israel's ultimate destruction. Rabin thought that it was necessary for Israel to postpone discussion of a comprehensive settlement until the energy shortage had been alleviated and the West felt less dependent on the good will of the Arab world. Time could be gained through additional partial agreements. Israel preferred another agreement with Egypt to an agreement with Jordan that would have required Israeli concessions in the West Bank. This was bound to raise strong opposition in Israel, both on strategic grounds—the West Bank being adjacent to Israel's population centers—and for ideological reasons. An agreement with Egypt seemed less problematic. Sinai was a vast desert, and Israeli concessions there did not seem to pose as grave a threat to Israel's security as concessions on the West Bank. Moreover, Rabin believed that an agreement with Egypt would at one and the same time reduce pressures for a comprehensive settlement, help the U.S. strengthen its position and reduce Soviet influence, and drive a wedge between Egypt and Syria, thus diminishing the military threat to Israel.[48]

During the summer and fall of 1974 Kissinger held exploratory talks with both Jordan and Israel, but he was unable to narrow the gap that separated them. Jordan wanted Israel to withdraw along the entire length of the Jordan valley to the foothills at its western edge. Israel's proposal called for the restoration of Jordanian civilian administration in some populated areas, but leaving the territory under Israeli military control. Kissinger's attempts to persuade both Israel and Jordan to modify their positions were to no avail. Nor would they agree to a compromise that he proposed for an Israeli withdrawal from the town of Jericho. Jordan continued to insist on its stand because Hussein believed that to ward off the PLO's claims, he would have to prove his ability to obtain a substantial Israeli withdrawal. Israel refused to agree to any withdrawal at all, as Rabin also felt politically vulnerable and pledged to submit any withdrawal to the approval of the electorate. Thus even a general formula that might have served as the basis for negotiations was unavailable. Then, on October 28, the Arab summit meeting in Rabat decided to recognize the PLO as the sole legitimate representative of the Palestinians. Deprived of a mandate to negotiate on the Palestinians' behalf, and in fact denied the right to restore the West Bank to Jordanian rule, King Hussein ceased to pursue disengagement.[49]

The failure to arrange a Jordanian-Israeli disengagement strengthened the American feeling that it was urgent that it prove again that it was both willing and capable of producing further movement toward a settlement. Reports of an improved atmosphere in Egyptian-Soviet relations and arrangements for Brezhnev's visit to Cairo in January 1975 (which was subsequently cancelled), served as a reminder that the situation could not be allowed to stagnate. Since the obstacles to a comprehensive settlement of the Arab-Israeli conflict were obviously formidable, the only alternative that had a chance of succeeding quickly and preserving the momentum of American diplomacy was to try to arrange additional partial agreements.

Sadat of course, continued to be interested in another agreement, which would entail another Israeli withdrawal. Additional visible gains would defuse criticism of his cooperation with the U.S. It was necessary for Sadat to justify his policy by demonstrating that it continued to pay dividends. Moreover, he wanted Israeli forces to be removed farther from the canal, so as to improve Egypt's ability to protect the waterway and the cities that were being rebuilt on its banks.

It was clear from the outset that Egyptian and Israeli views about the terms of the proposed agreement were far apart. Israel wanted a political agreement that would include a formal termination of the state of belligerence and Egyptian commitments to end propaganda and economic warfare against Israel. In return, Israel was prepared to withdraw a distance of twenty to thirty miles, but insisted on retaining control of the Sinai passes and oil fields. Israel wished the agreement to be of long duration and proposed that it remain in force for twelve years. Egypt wanted an agreement that would be essentially military, not political, in character. It rejected Israel's demand for a declaration of nonbelligerence. Egypt considered it essential that Israel withdraw from significant portions of Sinai, relinquishing the passes and returning the Abu Rodeis oil field. From Egypt's standpoint, it was unthinkable that the agreement be of long duration. Egypt continued to aim at a rapid Israeli withdrawal from all of Sinai.[50]

The existence of wide differences between the parties was clear throughout the preliminary talks that Kissinger held during the fall and early winter. Although both sides made some concessions in these talks, the basic incompatibility of the two positions was confirmed in the course of his visits to Egypt and Israel in February 1975. Nevertheless, on March 8 he embarked on another shuttle between Egypt and Israel to close the gap and conclude an agreement. On some issues, the gap was indeed narrowed, but it could not be closed. Sadat was prepared to agree to certain "functional equivalents" of nonbelligerence, such as a statement that the conflict would not be solved by military, but by peaceful means. Israel, however, continued to insist on a formal statement proclaiming the end of the state of belligerence and regarded such a clause as a condition for its withdrawal from the passes.

Since Sadat's conclusion of another agreement with Israel was sure to provoke criticism from Syria and other radical Arab states, Kissinger believed that Sadat could not formally accept the end of the state of belligerence, and that in order to justify his policy Sadat required an Israeli withdrawal from the passes as well as the Abu Rodeis oil field. Therefore, Kissinger pressed Israel to change its position, not Egypt. After another effort to persuade Israel to change its stance failed on March 21-22, Kissinger concluded that he was unable to bring the parties to an agreement, and on March 23, after a moving ceremony at the airport in which his voice was choked by tears and emotion, he departed for Washington.[51]

Upon Kissinger's return to Washington he and President Ford announced the end of the step-by-step tactic and the need for a reassessment of American policy. There were two aspects to the "reassessment." One was the reexamination of possible approaches for the continuation of the diplomatic effort. The other was the application of pressure on Israel to soften its stance.

In reexamining its policy options, the administration was left with only two main alternatives. It could attempt multilateral negotiations aimed at a comprehensive settlement—the Geneva approach. Or, it could revert to the step-by-step approach and resume mediation for the Egyptian-Israeli agreement. The Geneva approach seemed highly unpromising. Besides the difficulties expected over the question of the PLO's participation and of simultaneously negotiating with several Arab delegations, at Geneva the mediator's effectiveness was also bound to be impaired. With the Soviet Union as cochairman, the bargaining structure would change, and American efforts to induce the Arabs to moderate their stands were likely to be countered by Soviet support for a hard line. Considering the important gains achieved by the U.S. acting alone, sharing the mediator's role with the Soviets must have appeared as highly unwise. Since it was known that both Egypt and Israel regarded Geneva with disfavor and preferred to have the U.S. as the only mediator, it is not surprising that the administration decided to return to the step-by-step approach.[52]

Although formally the administration did not assign

blame for the failure of the negotiations, informally Kissinger blamed Israel. Discussion of the possibility of reconvening the Geneva Conference was a means of pressure on Israel. It signalled to Israel that the alternative to American mediation might be a conference at which the demand for Israel's withdrawal to the 1967 lines would have wide support. Delays in the delivery of promised military supplies and in the consideration of the Israeli application for economic and military assistance for the following year, were additional signals to Israel that its refusal to make further concessions in the negotiations might cost it dearly.[53] Israel countered these pressures by mobilizing support in Congress. In May a letter signed by seventy-six senators was sent to President Ford saying that "any Israeli withdrawal must be accompanied by meaningful steps toward peace by its Arab neighbors," and calling upon him to be "responsive to Israel's urgent military and economic needs."[54]

Talks aimed at breaking the deadlock were held throughout the summer, with Ford and Kissinger meeting Sadat and Rabin. Further talks were held at the subordinate level as well. By mid-August the main points of the new agreement had won the consent of all parties. At this stage, when the conclusion of the agreement was no longer in doubt, Kissinger departed on August 20 for another shuttle. Within a few days he settled the remaining details, and on September 1 Egyptian and Israeli officials initialed the new agreement.[55]

The agreement was modelled on the previous one, with a UN buffer zone separating the two parties and limited armament zones drawn on both sides. The issues over which the negotiations had broken down in March were resolved mainly through Israeli concessions, compensated for mainly by American contributions. Israel dropped its insistence for a formal ending of the state of belligerence, and contented itself with some "functional equivalents" instead. The two sides agreed that the conflict between them would be resolved by peaceful means; that they would not resort to the threat or use of force, and that the mandate of the UN Emergency Force would be extended annually. Moreover, this time Egypt agreed to commit itself publicly to permitting the transit of nonmilitary cargoes to or from Israel through the Suez Canal. (As will be recalled, in the January 1974 agreement Egypt agreed to give such a commitment secretly to the U.S., but refused to have it included in the agreement signed with Israel.) The line of withdrawal also reflected Israeli concessions. Israel agreed to withdraw from the passes and the Abu Rodeis oil fields. The main Egyptian concession was its agreement that Israel could continue to operate the electronic early warning station at Umm Hashiba.

The Egyptian-Israeli agreement was supplemented by an Annex, and by separate American-Israeli and American-Egyptian agreements. In the accompanying documents the U.S. assumed numerous commitments: (1) to serve again as a trustee for undertakings by the parties that were not included in the Egyptian-Israeli agreement; (2) to guarantee each side against violations of the agreement; (3) to provide the parties with compensation, and with additional insurance against certain risks that they believed arose from the agreement and their participation in the diplomatic process.

The U.S. served as a trustee for secret undertakings by the parties on at least two issues. One was the duration of the agreement. As will be recalled, Israel wanted the agreement to be of long duration, while Egypt objected to this, wishing to ensure that further Israeli withdrawals would take place soon. It has been reported that Egypt promised to the U.S. to agree to two annual extensions of the mandate of the UN force, thus in fact accepting that the agreement remain in force for three years. The second issue on which secret commitments were deposited with the U.S. concerned additional "functional equivalents" of nonbelligerence. Israel promised not to attack Syria, and Egypt promised not to join the war in Syria's support if Syria attacked Israel. Furthermore, Egypt promised to relax some of the economic boycott measures, and to tone down its propaganda against Israel.[56]

The American commitments as a guarantor of the agreement were embodied in the published documents. The most important was the establishment of an American presence in the buffer zone, in addition to the UN presence. It was agreed that American civilian personnel would verify that the Egyptian and Israeli technicians in their respective early warning stations performed only those operations authorized by the agreement, and that the U.S. would set up and operate additional tactical early warning installations in the buffer zone. Furthermore, American aerial surveillance of the limited arms zones would continue. The U.S. also gave parallel, though separate promises to both Egypt and Israel, to consult with each as to possible remedial action in the event that the other side violated the agreement. Additional guarantees for Israel were contained in the American-Israeli Memorandum of Agreement. The understanding about the three-year duration of the agreement was hedged by an American assurance that in its view, the agreement would remain binding in the event that the UN forces were withdrawn before the agreement has been superseded by another one. The U.S. also pledged itself to veto any Security Council resolution that in its view would affect the agreement adversely.

The third function of American commitments was to protect the parties against some of the risks that resulted from their participation in the diplomatic process. Israel was promised in the Memorandum of Agreement that the U.S. would make "every effort to be fully responsive" to Israel's military, economic, and energy needs, that it would consult Israel periodically about its needs and prepare contingency plans for a military resupply in an emergency. In compensation for Israel's relinquishment of the Abu Rodeis oil fields, the U.S. promised to supply it with oil in the event of Israel's being unable to meet its requirements through normal procedures. To allay some other Israeli security concerns, the U.S. promised to support Israel's right to free passage through the Bab el Mandeb and the Strait of Gibraltar. Even more significant was the American promise to consult with Israel as to what support it could lend it in case Israel was threatened by "a world power." Finally, Israel received assurances about American policy with respect to future diplomatic moves. To allay Israel's concern that it would be requested to divest itself from additional territory in Sinai without adequate political returns, the U.S. agreed with Israel "that the next agreement with Egypt should be a final peace agreement." Similarly, Israel was assured that the U.S. shared the view that "under existing political circumstances" negotiations with Jordan would also be directed toward an overall peace. An additional American-Israeli Memorandum of Agreement contained American assurances with respect to the possible reconvening of the Geneva Conference. It reiterated commitments made by the U.S. on December 20, 1973 in the negotiations over Israel's participation in the conference, and stated that the U.S. would not recognize or negotiate with the PLO as long as it did not recognize Israel's right to exist and did not accept Resolutions 242 and 338. The U.S. also promised to veto any Security Council initiative changing Resolutions 242 or 338 "in ways which are incompatible with their original purpose." While the commitments to Israel were numerous and far-reaching, Egypt received only three additional promises in the Memorandum of Assurances concluded with it. The U.S. promised technical assistance for an Egyptian early warning station in Sinai; it reaffirmed its offer of economic aid to Egypt, and it assured Egypt that it "intend[ed] to make a serious effort to help bring about further negotiations between Syria and Israel."

Why could not the same agreement have been concluded in March, and why did the negotiations fail at that time? Some of the explanations offered are insufficient, because they attribute the March failure to circumstances that also prevailed in August and September when the negotiations succeeded, or because they attribute the successful negotiations in the summer to factors that were also present in the winter, when they failed. Explanations of the March failure that place emphasis on the political weakness of the Israeli government appear highly plausible. According to this explanation, Rabin's political inexperience and the weakness of his government prevented him from making concessions. His government was torn by the rivalries between its three leading personalities: Prime Minister Yitzhak Rabin, Foreign Minister Yigal Allon, and Defense Minister Shimon Peres. The rivalry among these three men, who represented Israel in the negotiations, hindered flexibility and accommodation. Yet, whatever the contribution of Israel's domestic political situation to the failure of the negotiations, this alone was not the obstacle to a successful outcome. After all, the same team, handicapped by the same shortcomings, brought the subsequent round of talks to a successful conclusion.

There is a similar difficulty with the argument that the negotiations failed because they took place at a time when American prestige, and Kissinger's personal standing as a statesman, were at a low ebb. At the very moment when Kissinger was negotiating in the Middle East, the peace treaty that he had concluded in Vietnam was being violated, as the North Vietnamese forces invaded the South and conquered it while the U.S. stood passively by. Consequently, America's credibility as an ally was seriously undermined, which made it difficult for Kissinger to persuade Israel to make concessions and put its trust in American guarantees. This is plausible, except that American prestige had not been restored by the summer. On the contrary, doubts about America's credibility grew as the U.S. suffered a setback in Angola, where the Soviet-backed MPLA was gaining the upper hand in its struggle against American-backed forces. Thus, although declining confidence in the U.S. may have influenced the negotiations in March, it could not have been an important reason for their failure.

A case can be made for attributing the March failure to tactical errors. Israel's diplomacy seems to have been particularly maladroit. Rabin's interview in *Haaretz* on December 3, 1974, in which he discussed Israel's desire to drive a wedge between Egypt and Syria, probably served to stiffen Sadat's behavior. In the same interview, Rabin also expressed the opinion that Israel's demand for a proclamation of nonbelligerence was unrealistic. The statement aroused the expectation both in Cairo and in Washington that Israel would not insist on that particular demand. But to Kissinger's surprise, and probably Sadat's as well, Israel did. In early February, an interview with Rabin by John Lindsay was broadcast by ABC, in which Rabin announced even prior to the shuttle negotiations that "in exchange for an Egyptian commitment not to go to war . . . the Egyptians could get even the passes and the oil fields."[57] The Egyptians, if not the Americans, interpreted the statement as expressing Israel's opening position for the bargaining that was to take place during the shuttle. The rules of the game required that further concessions be made during that final round, and Egypt behaved accordingly, making a few concessions and expecting further Israeli concessions above the ones announced in February. But when Israel did not budge, the Egyptians, and perhaps Kissinger too, felt deceived. Not only were Rabin's interviews misinterpreted by the Egyptians, they probably also confused Kissinger, diminishing his ability to serve as a channel of communications explaining Israel's true position to Egypt.

A tactical error by the U.S. may have contributed to the March failure. As on previous occasions, this time too a tough message from the president was sent to Israel at the moment when negotiations reached a crucial stage. But contrary to the usual pattern, this time it apparently served to harden, not soften, the Israeli stand. Past governments and stronger leaders than Rabin, such as Ben-

Gurion and Golda Meir, justified their concessions as being necessitated by threatening notes from American presidents. However, this time the political weakness of the government was such that Rabin feared that if he gave in, the excuse of American pressure would not save his government. Kissinger, at whose suggestion the presidential message was sent, erred by failing to foresee that under the prevailing political circumstances such a message might backfire.[58]

It is probable that poor diplomacy and tactical errors contributed to the failure of the March negotiations. But this explanation could be regarded as decisive only if we assume that the same people practiced a much superior diplomacy in the summer.

Kissinger reportedly claimed that one of the reasons for the failure of the March negotiations was that he was misled by Israel. Allon's suggestion in January that Kissinger come to the Middle East to conduct intensive negotiations indicated to him that Israel would make the necessary concessions, namely forego the claim for nonbelligerence and agree to withdraw from the passes.[59] If indeed he interpreted Allon's suggestion in this way, then his political talents seem to have failed him, for his mistaking of Allon reflects an error in timing and in the assessment of the overall circumstances within which the negotiations were taking place.

A satisfactory explanation of the contrasting outcomes of the negotiations must take account of the different circumstances under which they were held. The March negotiations were conducted under conditions of relative quiescence. The situation in which the parties found themselves was not such as to press them to make concessions. The alternative to a successful conclusion of the negotiations, however worrisome, did not entail any immediate danger. Negotiations were renewed during the summer in a crisis atmosphere. This change was brought about by the dramatization of the March failure, and the fear of the consequences that were expected to follow from it. It was the failure of the March negotiations, and Kissinger's reaction to it, that created new conditions, leading the parties to see the necessity for making a greater effort and to granting greater concessions than they had been willing to do in March. Kissinger felt that the U.S. and he personally could not afford to appear in Arab eyes as incapable of persuading Israel. Sadat felt an even greater need than before to prove that his reliance upon the U.S. was bearing fruit. The Israeli leaders, under the pressure of reassessment and the lure of the incentives that the U.S. offered, felt that they had to make the concessions required of them. The crisis was here for all to see, and concessions made under these circumstances did not jeopardize the Rabin government's ability to remain in power.

Perhaps the impact of the March failure and the concern that it could lead to a weakening of America's position in the Arab world caused the U.S. to exert itself during the summer negotiations much more than in the previous round. In contrast to March, the U.S. now offered an array of incentives to the parties. To Israel the U.S. was ready to provide large-scale economic and military aid, advanced weapons, a guarantee in the form of an American presence in Sinai, and assurances about future American policy. Egypt too received incentives in the course of the summer negotiations. President Ford reportedly told Sadat during their meeting in Salzburg in June that the U.S. would work for a settlement based on the old international border (the Rogers Plan). He also promised Egypt large-scale economic aid, and held out the prospect for military aid as well.[60]

In conclusion, it was the crisis that was precipitated by the March failure that enabled the new round of negotiations to succeed. Israel felt under greater pressure to make concessions; Egypt was more flexible; and the U.S. responded to the need to make deeper commitments for the sake of an agreement.

An Assessment

Having examined the negotiations conducted under Kissinger's aegis, let me return to the questions posed at the beginning of this chapter: (1) What effect did the step-by-step approach have on the negotiations, and what was Kissinger's part in shaping it? (2) Was Kissinger a mediator? (3) How did Kissinger obtain the parties' acceptance of his role? (4) What was Kissinger's personal contribution to the success of the negotiations?

Kissinger described the step-by-step approach as one that separated "the Middle East problem into individual and therefore manageable segments." The policy was "to segment the issues into individual elements, to negotiate each element separately, and therefore to permit each party to adjust itself domestically and internationally to a process of gradual approach toward peace."[61] This approach required that the U.S. refrain from committing itself about the shape of the ultimate settlement. Although both the Arab states and Israel were aware that American ideas had not changed and that the U.S. continued to believe that a final Egyptian-Israeli settlement would require Israel's withdrawal to the proximity of the old international border, the issue was removed from the agenda. In this, Kissinger's policy contrasted with the one pursued while Rogers was secretary of state.

Kissinger's policy set limited goals. Although difficulties were encountered in the pursuit of each limited goal, each exacted from the parties smaller concessions and adjustments than a full and comprehensive settlement would have done. Furthermore, the step-by-step approach enabled Kissinger and the parties to avoid issues pertaining to "core values," or to most vital interests, such as Arab recognition of Israel, the status of the Palestinians, or Israel's final boundaries. While the critics of the gradualist approach claim that a comprehensive settlement was feasible, the fact remains that partial settlements were easier, and therefore more likely to be accomplished, than a comprehensive settlement.

There remains the question of how Kissinger came to adopt the step-by-step approach. Was it developed beforehand as a guiding concept of the negotiations, or was it merely a series of pragmatic adaptations to immediate situations? The distinction between the gradualist and the comprehensive approaches to international problems had attracted Kissinger's scholarly attention many years before he became secretary of state, in the context of his studies of styles of leadership. He described it first as a philosophical distinction between the Statesman's approach and the Revolutionary Leader's approach, and subsequently as one between the Statesman's and the Prophet's. The Prophet "objects to gradualism as an unnecessary concession to circumstance. He will risk everything because his vision is the primary significant reality to him." The Statesman, on the other hand, is more of a pessimist.

> His view of human nature is wary; he is conscious of many great hopes which have failed. . . . He is, therefore, inclined to erect hedges against the possibility that even the most brilliant idea might prove abortive. . . . He will try to avoid certain experiments, not because he would object to the results if they succeeded, but because he would feel responsible for the consequences if they failed. . . . To the statesman, gradualism is the essence of stability.[62]

The analogy is imperfect because the advocates of a comprehensive settlement were to be found not only in the Communist, Arab, and Third World states (where Kissinger would expect them), but also in Europe and the U.S., and even in the East Coast foreign policy establishment. However, Kissinger identified with the Statesman. His views on how the Arab-Israeli conflict ought to be approached reflect his theoretical model of the Statesman's approach to world order. He sympathized not only with the Statesman's philosophical perspective, but also with his pessimism. Kissinger did not believe that a "solution" to the Arab-Israeli conflict that was satisfactory to all concerned could be found. Therefore he sought to attain only relative stability, and did not try to "solve" the conflict.

Kissinger's predilection for gradualism was reinforced by the flow of events. These propelled the U.S. to meet urgent needs that could not wait for the uncertain outcome of negotiations for a comprehensive settlement. At first, it was urgent to relieve the Egyptian Third Army and reduce the risk of a resumption of the war. This was accomplished through the cease-fire and first Egyptian-Israeli disengagement agreement. Next, it was necessary to protect Sadat from criticism by Syria and other radical Arab states and encourage the Arab oil producers to lift the embargo. A disengagement agreement between Israel and Syria was a much more effective and speedy means to achieve this than a comprehensive settlement. Then it was necessary to strengthen King Hussein's position; hence the attempt to arrange for a disengagement between Israel and Jordan. When this failed, it was urgent to keep up the momentum and to counter the trend toward the restoration of the Egyptian-Soviet link. The failure of the attempt to conclude another Egyptian-Israeli agreement in March, made the need to restore Arab confidence in the U.S. doubly urgent; thus again circumstances did not permit taking the risk of searching for a comprehensive settlement. Whether the step-by-step approach is attributable to Kissinger's personal proclivity or to the pressure of circumstances, Kissinger should be credited with defining for each negotiating round goals that were feasible and attainable.

Another question that Kissinger's negotiations raise is: was he a mediator? Or was the nature of the American involvement such that some other term should be used to describe it? American involvement on behalf of the Egyptian Third Army and the Cease-Fire Agreement resembled coercive intervention rather than mediation. The very strong pressure applied by the U.S. on Israel on several occasions in the course of these negotiations tends to strengthen doubts whether the U.S. in fact engaged in mediation.

Although some American actions went beyond the bounds of normal mediation, the American role can still best be described by that term. First, the professed purpose of the American intervention was to help the parties conclude agreements. Secondly, the U.S. (and Kissinger) performed the normal functions of mediators. Kissinger helped the parties to communicate, interpreted for each his adversary's position, sought to persuade them by way of reasoning to change their positions, formulated compromise proposals and presented them to the parties, helped the parties to save face when making concessions, and provided guarantees that facilitated the conclusion of agreements. Thirdly, Kissinger was a mediator because both parties welcomed his intervention and cooperated with it. His intervention was resented on only one occasion—when he acted to save the Egyptian Third Army, disregarding Israel's bitter objections. On other occasions American mediation was in fact solicited by both parties.

The definition of Kissinger's role is also relevant for explaining his acceptability to the parties. Although Egypt had accepted American mediation in the recent past (1970-1971), and even appeared to have solicited Kissinger's personal involvement shortly before the 1973 war, the nature of the American role nevertheless caused some concern. Egyptians perceived Kissinger to be doubly biased. The U.S. was regarded as Israel's patron and had again demonstrated its commitment to Israel by supplying military aid to that country during the war that had just ended. In addition, Kissinger himself was Jewish and therefore assumed to be sympathetic to Israel. Egypt had probably been concerned on previous occasions that the American approach to the Arab-Israeli conflict might favor Israel, but this time the concern was acute, and Kissinger was asked to clarify his role. The clarification was requested in the course of a conversation between Kissinger and Mohamed Hassanein Heikal, who was at that time a close confidant of Sadat and editor of *Al Ahram*, on November 7, 1973, during Kissinger's first visit to Cairo. According to Heikal's account he queried Kissinger:

> If your role is not the role of the "other party," the "role of the negotiator," what exactly is your role? Is it the role of the "mediator"? Again, I do not think so—indeed I am sure not. The role of mediator requires neutrality between the two parties—or at least that the two parties should feel that this neutrality exists or could exist. We do not feel this. Your bias towards Israel needs no proof. The latest indication of it is the air and sea bridge which is bringing arms and ammunition from the United States to Israel. So you are not and cannot be neutral; you cannot be a mediator. Then if you are not a negotiator because you are not a direct party, and if you are not a mediator because you are not neutral—what exactly is your role?

Kissinger assured Heikal that the U.S. was not a party to the conflict, but he granted that it is not a mediator either. He defined his status as representing:

> the role of the "concern" of the United States for a grave crisis which is taking place in an area that is sensitive as far as we are concerned, an area in which we have strategic, political and economic interests—and security interests—and we want to protect these interests.

After explaining American interests and goals, Kissinger added:

> I agree with you that I am not a "party," nor a mediator. And perhaps you will agree with me that what I represent is American "concern" with the Middle East crisis, a concern that is trying to perform its role to protect its interests without conflicting with the interests of others.[63]

The conversation reflects Egyptian worries at that time. However, what made Kissinger acceptable to Egypt was not his definition of his role as representing American "concern," but rather Egyptian needs and expectations. In October 1973, in the immediate aftermath of the war, two courses of action were open to Egypt. It could renew the war and rely for this purpose on the Soviet Union. But the prospects of such a course were not promising, because in a war the U.S. could be expected to help Israel so as to prevent Israel's defeat at the hands of an Arab-Soviet combination. The alternative was to seek a political solution, in which case American assistance would be necessary. The question was whether Egypt could expect such assistance.

As in 1970-1971, in 1973 Egypt recognized that although the U.S. was not impartial, Egypt could nevertheless gain from American mediation. This expectation may have stemmed in part from the Egyptian assessment of the American interest in regaining influence in the Arab world and in ending the Arab oil embargo. In other words, the Egyptian expectation stemmed from the view that American policy would be guided not by American sympathies and sentiments, but by the logic of the bargaining situation. But no less important in encouraging Egypt to expect that it could gain from American mediation were the signals sent by Kissinger. In the immediate aftermath of the war he dramatically demonstrated America's willingness and capacity to help Egypt by forcing Israel to permit supplies to the Third Army. In his conversation with Heikal on November 7, Kissinger reportedly told him: "The Soviet Union can give you arms, but the United States can give you a just solution which will give you back your territories."[64] No wonder Sadat decided to try American mediation, despite the fact that the U.S. was not impartial.

Israel's acceptance of American mediation was not determined by its images of American attitudes either. It was not the view that the U.S. favored Israel or that Kissinger was Jewish, that made Israel accept American mediation. Kissinger's Jewishness may even have aroused some fear that he might lean over backward in order to demonstrate that his policy was not influenced by his inherent pro-Israeli sentiments. Moreover, Israel was apprehensive because it expected that, given the political and economic situation in which the U.S. found itself, the U.S. wished to mediate because it saw an opportunity of buying influence, inducing the Arabs to lift the oil embargo, and paying for it with Israeli concessions.

To win Israel's acceptance and allay Israel's fears, the U.S. sought to reassure Israel not only about America's underlying friendship and its commitment to Israel's survival, but also about the specific issues on the agenda. Kissinger therefore made it clear from the outset that the U.S. would refrain from taking a position on the final settlement. What would be discussed were the immediate problems created by the war, and the outcome of these negotiations would not be predetermined by the Rogers Plan. These assurances alone did not suffice. More weighty was the lack of acceptable alternatives for Israel. Israel could not refuse American mediation, because it could not dismiss the possibility that if in the wake of such a refusal the war were renewed, American support might not be as forthcoming as it was in October. Other alternatives were an American-Soviet understanding for imposing a settlement or a multilateral conference where the Soviet Union would take part, at which the U.S. would compete with the Soviets for Arab good will. Thus Israel's acceptance was not determined by its images of general American attitudes and biases, but rather by the concrete situation in which Israel found itself and the consequences that might ensue if mediation was refused.

The fourth question concerns Kissinger's personal contribution to the overall success of the negotiations. Kissinger, the "miracle worker," was the most lavishly praised of all the mediators in the Arab-Israeli conflict. The praise bestowed upon him could not but provoke the question whether, and if so in what way, he personally contributed to the success of the negotiations. Or should their successful outcome be attributed to the American prestige and resources that backed him up?

Much of what has been said in Kissinger's praise pertains to his intellectual qualities and skills—his vast knowledge, ability to generate new ideas and formulate compromises, capacity for logical reasoning, and tactical skills. One of his intellectual contributions, the step-by-step approach, has already been discussed. As for other important ideas raised in the course of the negotiations, some, but not all, were contributed by Kissinger or his staff; others, no less important, were contributed by the parties themselves. As we had seen, the concept of disengagement, which was central to three of the agreements concluded, was Dayan's contribution. The compromise formula on which the Syrian disengagement was based, allowing Syria the symbolically important gain of Kuneitra and drawing the line just west of that town, seems to have been Sadat's. The idea of creating an American presence in Sinai and entrusting the operation of early warning installations to American personnel, which was crucial for breaking the deadlock over the second Egyptian-Israeli agreement, came from Sadat and from Peres.[65] But other important ideas have been attributed to Kissinger or his staff. The proposal to circumvent the problem of Israel's withdrawal to the October 22 lines by subsuming it in a disengagement of forces was apparently Kissinger's.[66] So was the suggestion to circumvent Israel's demand for a formal proclamation of nonbelligerence through the device of "functional equivalents" of nonbelligerence.[67] Various other compromise proposals, such as the one resolving the controversy about the hills overlooking Kuneitra; the one drawing the line of Israel's withdrawal in the Sinai passes so that Egypt could claim that Israel withdrew, while meeting Israel's military concerns by enabling it to retain positions overlooking the passes; and proposals for the status and composition of the UN force in the Golan, came from the American side. (The last has been attributed to Sisco.)[68] What can be said about Kissinger's role in generating new ideas is that although he did not invent all the important ones, he knew which of the many proposed by the parties and his staff were useful, and could contribute to the construction of agreements.

To persuade the parties to make concessions through reasoning and argumentation is an important function of mediators. Kissinger has been much praised for his skill at this. His ability to construct logical arguments certainly served him well. A technique that he reportedly used to much effect was to point out and emphasize to each side the constraints that circumscribed the adversary's freedom of action, and that set limits to the concessions that can be expected from him.[69] Another technique was to impress upon the parties those aspects of the environment and the situation that required that they modify their policies. He also tended to paint for them "worst case" scenarios of what might follow if they failed to heed his advice. In pleading for concessions he often displayed a talent that years before he had recognized in Metternich, who, according to Kissinger, possessed "the art of defining a moral framework which made concessions appear, not as surrenders, but as sacrifices to a common cause."[70] On other occasions Kissinger requested concessions as a personal favor to himself. It is of course impossible to tell what effect Kissinger's persuasiveness had on the parties. For almost every concession it can be claimed that it was made because all the alternatives looked worse or because the party had no choice but to concede. In any event, the least that Kissinger contributed was to sharpen the parties' awareness of the constraints imposed by the situation and the environment, and of the dire consequences that might follow if they failed to make the required concessions. In these endeavors, his breadth of knowledge and ability to master details served him well.

Kissinger's tactical skills have also attracted much attention. He usually displayed a fine sense of timing, which enabled him to apply pressures and to present compromise proposals at the most propitious moment. Presidential interventions in the negotiations were normally made at Kissinger's request, and except for Ford's message to Rabin in March 1975, they usually achieved their purpose. Kissinger's threats in the course of the Syrian negotiations that he would return to Washington were also well-timed. His skill in manipulating the media, and through them creating a supportive environment for his mediation, has also been noted. Somewhat exaggerated attention has been paid to his liking for gossip and telling each side demeaning stories about the other. Whatever impression this might have made in the beginning, before the parties realized that they were not the exclusive beneficiaries of such talk, it is unlikely that it had much effect in causing the parties to modify their positions and make concessions.

Some of Kissinger's personality traits, as distinct from his intellectual talents, need to be mentioned as assets. One is his personal charm, which has gained wide recognition. This quality helped him to establish a quick and easy rapport with his interlocutors, and thus facilitated the negotiations. But it is unlikely that it was important in inducing the parties to change their policies and make concessions. Personal qualities that seem to have made much difference were Kissinger's strong will, personal ambition, and aversion to failure. These encouraged him to try, and to persevere, and thus to overcome difficult moments when many another mediator would have given up in despair.

However impressive Kissinger's tactical skills, persuasive powers, and intellectual prowess, their impact upon the parties' positions should not be overemphasized. Much more important for bringing about concessions were the resources that Kissinger was able to wield. His arguments moved governments not because of their logic, but because he was the American secretary of state. It was the weight of American pressure and the lure of U.S. incentives that produced the decisive impact.

No less important was the American ability to serve as a guarantor of the agreements concluded. Again, American resources as a superpower played an important role, as in the case of providing aerial surveillance and early warning installations in Sinai. Had Kissinger come as a private person, or been the emissary of an international organization or a medium power, without the vast resources of the U.S. to back him up, he would not have been able to bring the parties to change their positions and make the concessions required for the conclusion of the agreements.

The only possible exception to this evaluation is the first Egyptian-Israeli disengagement agreement. As will be recalled, both sides found themselves in a situation where they needed either to resume the fighting or to disengage. This is why the talks at Kilometer 101 produced rapid modifications in the parties' positions, and why in the subsequent talks both sides made rapid concessions without American pressures or incentives being brought to bear. This agreement could perhaps have been concluded even with the help of a less talented diplomat who did not possess the vast resources of the U.S. to back him up.

Finally, at least as important as Kissinger's inventiveness and persuasive skills and nearly as important as America's resources were his analytical talents, his leadership, and his managerial ability. Kissinger's role as a leader was important because the presidents under whom he served were handicapped: Nixon was preoccupied with Watergate and Ford was inexperienced. Thus Kissinger was both the leader of the American diplomatic effort and its manager. His analytical talents enabled him to comprehend the complex system within which American foreign policy operated and to take account of its many parts. He was the one who conducted the negotiations in person, directed the supporting activities of the bureaucracies in Washington, and orchestrated public opinion. While negotiating with the Arabs and Israelis he also kept up his efforts vis-à-vis the Soviets and Europeans and successfully fended off their attempts to intervene. He was at one and the same time the composer of the music and the conductor of the orchestra. His talents enabled him to discern what was possible, to define the goals, to devise the tactics for pursuing them, and to direct and manage the versatile diplomacy required to attain them.

Kissinger was a successful mediator not only because he brought about the conclusion of five agreements, but also because his mediation produced some of the political consequences at which his efforts were ultimately aimed. The elimination of Soviet influence in Egypt and the establishment of American dominance there was one. But more important in a historical perspective, the Egyptian-Israeli agreements that he helped to negotiate initiated the evolutionary process that led to the conclusion of the Egyptian-Israeli peace treaty in 1979.

TEN

Carter, 1977-1979: The Camp David Accords and the Egyptian-Israeli Peace Treaty

American mediation under President Carter helped to conclude three major agreements between Egypt and Israel: in September 1978, at Camp David, they worked out "The Framework of Peace in the Middle East" and "The Framework for the Conclusion of a Peace Treaty between Egypt and Israel," and in March 1979, in Washington, Prime Minister Begin and President Sadat signed a peace treaty between their two states. These were momentous events, the import of which has not been diminished by Sadat's assassination. Even if relations between Egypt and Israel revert to hostility, these agreements will remain historical landmarks because it was the first time after many decades of conflict, and thirty years after Israel's establishment, that an Arab state made peace with Israel. The two sides also agreed on a framework for a comprehensive peace which they recommended to the Palestinian population of the West Bank and Gaza and to Israel's other neighbors. Why did this attempt succeed in bringing about a peace agreement when all previous ones had failed? There were of course, numerous historical developments that helped bring about these agreements, but my concern here is to assess the mediator's contribution.

I have claimed in previous chapters that one of the reasons for the failures of Bernadotte, the Conciliation Commission, and Jarring was that the goal was overambitious. They tried to settle the Arab-Israeli conflict, a task that required them to bring the parties to make concessions on issues that they regarded as "core values." How did the 1977-1979 settlement overcome this major obstacle? This mediation differed from previous attempts in that Egypt and Israel maintained direct communication in addition to the contacts they had through the mediator; moreover, the president of the U.S. was personally and intensively involved in the negotiations, much more than any previous president. Do these, or perhaps other unique features of this mediation, help to explain its unique achievement?

The Initial Concessions

In 1977 both Egypt and Israel made major concessions. Israel decided to offer Egypt the restoration of Egyptian sovereignty over all of Sinai within the context of a peace treaty, thus abandoning its claims to Sharm-el-Sheikh and other large areas in Sinai. Egypt decided to recognize Israel even before a peace treaty, and before Israel formally committed itself to withdraw from Sinai; President Sadat expressed this recognition in his highly dramatic visit to Jerusalem on November 19 to 21, 1977.

These concessions were not the product of mediation, although several intermediaries provided good offices and channels of communication. The U.S., as mediator, contributed to the concessions only indirectly, by embarking upon a new approach to the settlement of the conflict, which neither Egypt nor Israel deemed desirable. Their concessions were aimed in part at thwarting the mediator's new initiative; however, dissatisfaction with American policy was only one of the factors that prompted them to reconsider their policies. Other important factors were domestic—economic, social, and political. A thorough analysis of how Egypt's and Israel's policy changes came about would lead us far outside the scope of this study. Therefore, I shall confine my discussion here to the mediator's indirect contribution. Its significance lies not only in the substance of the concessions that it stimulated, but also in the structure of the situation that developed: the two adversaries formed a tacit coalition aimed at forcing the mediator to change his policy.

The new American approach to the peace efforts was the attempt to reconvene the Geneva Conference for the purpose of pursuing a comprehensive settlement. This policy replaced Kissinger's step-by-step approach and his preference for a U.S. monopoly on mediation. The new approach was broached by the new Carter administration, which accorded high priority to the settlement of the Arab-Israeli conflict. The policy indicated a change in U.S. motives. Kissinger had aimed at replacing Soviet influence in Egypt and lessening the likelihood of another oil embargo. His efforts to reduce the danger of another Egyptian-Israeli war served both these objectives. By 1977 the danger of another Egyptian-Israeli war had receded, and American influence was established in Egypt. Not feeling impelled by a concrete immediate threat to American interests, the Carter administration could aim at the larger objective of remedying a situation that, if left unattended, might develop into a sudden crisis. It aimed also at fostering Saudi goodwill, in the expectation that such good will would express itself in Saudi help in preventing steep increases in OPEC oil prices.

A settlement of the conflict had therefore to meet at least three conditions: assuring Israel's survival, enhancing stability, and winning the good will of certain Arab actors. The administration's views about the shape of the settlement were expressed by Carter as early as March 1977, when he said that Israel would have to withdraw to the 1967 lines and that a "homeland" for the Palestinians would have to be established in the West Bank and Gaza. Furthermore, Carter believed that such a settlement would have to be full peace, with normal neighborly relations between Israel and the Arab states. To achieve this, and to assure that the settlement be a stable one it was necessary to obtain Soviet cooperation and to buttress the settlement with great power guarantees. The administration believed that these objectives could best be attained by reviving the Geneva framework and convening a conference with the participation of Israel, Egypt, Jordan, Syria, the PLO, the Soviet Union, and the U.S.[1]

The American initiative coincided with the accession of a new government in Israel led by Menahem Begin, following the Likud victory in the general elections of May 1977. Begin appointed Dayan as his foreign minister, and together they charted a new course for Israel's foreign policy to meet the challenge of the American approach. Several aspects of the new American policy were particularly objectionable to Israel. One was the apparent American readiness to enable the Palestinians to establish their own entity or state in the West Bank and Gaza. Begin's government, much more than any previous Israeli government, was committed to the retention of the West Bank under Israeli control for ideological reasons, not merely because of security considerations. Second, Israel objected to the American intention to invite the PLO to the negotiations. Israel refused to negotiate with the PLO not only because it was a terrorist organization, but also because accepting PLO participation in the negotiations would have implied the acceptance of a Palestinian entity in the West Bank. Third, Israel was highly suspicious of the Soviet Union, and had misgivings about the American efforts to bring the Soviets into the peace negotiations. Finally, Israel feared that the resumption of the Geneva Conference would leave it isolated, as both superpowers vied for the sympathy of the Arab states.[2]

Because of its ideological commitment to the West Bank, the new Israeli government had a clear conception of priorities. Previous Israeli governments had refrained from offering concessions for fear of criticism from Begin. The new government had no one to fear on its right; it embodied the right wing and possessed impeccable ultranationalist credentials. This enabled Begin and Dayan to make concessions to Egypt in Sinai, in the hope that this would help assuage demands for concessions on the West Bank.

Through a variety of channels, including the U.S., Morocco, and Rumania, the Israeli prime minister renewed past Israeli proposals for a meeting between Egyptian and Israeli leaders. These overtures led to a secret meeting between Dayan and the Egyptian Deputy Prime Minister Hassan al Tuhami in Morocco on September 16, 1977. Besides the question of a meeting between Begin and Sadat, the parties explored in their talks a wide range of subjects, including Israel's withdrawal, guarantees and security arrangements, the Palestinian problem, and possible frameworks for negotiating a comprehensive settlement. Although Dayan did not make an explicit commitment, Tuhami apparently came away with the impression that Israel would be prepared to accept the restoration of Egyptian sovereignty over Sinai.[3]

Sadat had sent Tuhami to meet Dayan because he too had misgivings about the new American approach. Sadat's misgivings did not concern the terms that the U.S. advocated, but rather the process—the diplomatic route on which the U.S. proposed to embark. He had grave doubts as to the possibility of reconvening the Geneva Conference and reconciling the interests of all participants. The inability of the U.S. and Israel to reach agreement on PLO participation at Geneva confirmed those doubts and increased his fear that the Geneva route might postpone indefinitely the attainment of Egyptian goals in Sinai.

Thus, the mediator's policies contributed to Sadat's search for alternatives and to his decision to go to Jerusalem. Because of Sadat's distrust of the Soviet Union, the secret American-Soviet talks that led to the joint American-Soviet statement on the Middle East on October 1, 1977 increased his dissatisfaction with American policy. Sadat claims in his autobiography that a private handwritten letter from Carter "indirectly" suggested to him "an entirely new course of action." He "realized that we were about to be caught up in a terrible vicious circle."[4] By October, Sadat faced two alternatives. Either risk being caught up in this "terrible vicious circle," or explore further the possibility of a settlement through direct contacts with Israel. Sadat could have pursued his talks with Israel in secret; his decision to visit Jerusalem, and thus proclaim Egypt's recognition of Israel, was prompted by his desire to create a psychological atmosphere in which these talks would yield rapid gains for Egypt, and possibly by a desire to short-circuit American efforts to reconvene the Geneva Conference and force the U.S. to focus its diplomatic energy on the new possibilities opened up through his visit.

The Emergence of an Agenda

Sadat's visit to Jerusalem marked a turning point in the Arab-Israeli conflict. In the twenty-nine years since Israel's establishment, no Arab state had recognized Israel. Now Egypt, the most powerful and most populous state among them, reversed this policy most dramatically by the sudden gesture of its president's visit to Jerusalem and address to the Knesset proclaiming "we welcome you among us with full security and safety," and "we accept to live with you in permanent peace based on justice."[5] Because of the symbolic and dramatic way in which recognition was expressed, the policy reversal had an immense impact both in Egypt and Israel. Sadat explained that he intended his visit to break the "psychological barrier" that had prevented progress toward peace. His visit indeed produced a "psychological breakthrough," but, as we shall see, some central issues to the conflict remained to be negotiated.

The visit had far-reaching repercussions and consequences. It changed the nature of the Egyptian-Israeli relationship, the mode of negotiations, and affected the role of the mediator. It transformed inter-Arab relations, creating a rift between Egypt and Saudi Arabia, which henceforth assumed a posture of reserve toward Egyptian policies. Furthermore, it greatly intensified the mutual hostility between Egypt and the radical states, most notably Syria, Lybia, and Iraq.

Sadat's surprising gesture left Israel and the U.S. somewhat perplexed about Egyptian intentions, and especially about whether Egypt was prepared to conclude a separate peace with Israel without insisting upon the solution of the Palestinian problem and Israeli withdrawal from the West Bank, Gaza, and the Golan. In his Knesset speech on November 20, Sadat was very firm in reiterating Egyptian insistence upon Israeli withdrawal from all territories occupied in 1967, "including Arab Jerusalem," and added that "there can be no peace without the Palestinians."[6] Nevertheless, there was much debate in Israel as to his real intentions. One school of thought claimed that the fact that Sadat took the initiative to recognize Israel and visit Jerusalem, although he was cognizant of the Begin government's determination to retain control of the West Bank and Gaza, signified that he was prepared to settle for less. This school believed that Sadat was prepared to conclude a separate peace and that all he would require to do so, besides the recovery of Sinai, was a mere "fig leaf" reference to the remaining issues which would cover him against charges that he had betrayed the cause of his Arab brothers. Others argued that Sadat meant what he said, and that he would not conclude a separate peace unless Israel committed itself to withdraw from all Arab territories and recognized the Palestinians' right to establish their own state.[7]

The U.S. was also puzzled by Sadat's initiative. The role it played at this stage, immediately following Sadat's visit, was not merely that of an intermediary seeking to ascertain Egypt's intentions and convey this information to Israel. Simultaneously it also played the roles of the concerned patron, counseling Egypt as to where its interests ought to lie; and the interested third party, seeking to protect its own self-interests. The dominant American reaction was one of concern that Sadat's move might isolate him. He was jeopardizing his political future. His initiative encumbered American policy with the delicate task of supporting Sadat and helping him fend off his critics, while at the same time keeping on friendly terms with Saudi Arabia and Jordan, both of which took a sour view of his policy. These considerations led the U.S. to counsel Sadat to refrain from making a separate peace, and to urge Israel to offer publicly a significant concession that would help Sadat justify his initiative.[8]

The question of whether at that time Sadat intended to conclude a separate peace cannot be answered unequivocally. Perhaps Sadat himself wished to keep both options open. But in the negotiations that took place over the coming months, Egypt, Israel, and the U.S. came to accept that an Egyptian-Israeli peace treaty would have to be accompanied by some agreement on the Palestinian issue and on the future of the West Bank and Gaza. The question of *how much* of an agreement on these issues would be necessary—whether a vague declaration of principles would do, or whether detailed and explicit terms had to be agreed upon—became the subject of bargaining and negotiations.

The agenda for the negotiations thus crystallized around three main issues. One was the bilateral Egyptian-Israel issue—the time schedules of Israel's withdrawal from Sinai, security and arms limitation arrangements, the fate of the Israeli settlements in Sinai, and the pace of the normalization of Egyptian-Israeli relations. The second was the Palestinian question and the future of the West Bank and Gaza. The third was the form and degree of the link between the first two issues. Would the settlement of the bilateral issues in a peace treaty stand on its own, be conditional upon the settlement of the Palestinian problem, or would it perhaps be linked to the Palestinian problem only in a vague and imprecise manner?

The Negotiations

Negotiations began almost immediately after Sadat's visit. As is evident from the Chronology, these were very intensive and prolonged. They continued uninterrupted for sixteen months and led to the conclusion of the Camp David accords in September 1978 and the Egyptian-Israeli peace treaty in March 1979. It would be difficult to analyze them in detail. For our purposes it will suffice to review the evolution of the parties' goals, the changes in the mediator's role, and how the issues in dispute were settled.

Four phases in the negotiations can be distinguished. The *first phase*, lasting from Sadat's visit to the breakup of the meetings of the Political Committee in Jerusalem on January 18, was characterized by a lack of clarity about the concrete goals of the negotiations and the procedures for conducting them.

Israel's response to Sadat's initiative was designed more to meet known American expectations than uncertain Egyptian ones. Even before submitting his proposals to the Israeli Cabinet or to Sadat, Begin took his proposals to Carter. He suggested a framework for negotiating a peace treaty with Egypt that addressed itself not merely to the bilateral Egyptian-Israeli relationship, but also to the Palestinian problem and the future of the West Bank and Gaza. It offered Israeli recognition of Egyptian sovereignty over Sinai and troop withdrawal to the international border. It also suggested that the *inhabitants* of Judea and Samaria (the West Bank) and of the Gaza Strip be accorded *administrative* autonomy.[9]

Encouraged by the American reaction, Begin presented the Israeli proposals to Sadat at a meeting in Ismailiya on December 25, 1977. The Egyptian response was cool. Egypt refused to enter into a discussion about the detailed Israeli proposal, and suggested instead that the two parties issue a much shorter and more general declaration of principles. The Egyptian draft of the declaration called for the estab-

Chronology of the 1977-1979 Negotiations

1977	November 19-21	Sadat's visit to Jerusalem
	December 2-3	Second meeting between Dayan and Tuhami in Morocco
	December 9	Vance begins tour of Middle Eastern capitals—Cairo, Jerusalem, Amman, Beirut, Damascus, Riad
	December 14	Cairo conference opens
	December 16-17	Begin and Carter confer in Washington
	December 20-21	Weizman in Egypt
	December 25-26	Sadat-Begin meeting in Ismailiya
1978	January 1-4	Carter's meetings with King Hussein (in Tehran), King Khaled and Crown Prince Fahd, and Sadat in Aswan
	January 11-13	Egyptian-Israeli Military Committee meetings in Cairo; Weizman in Egypt
	January 16	Vance in Jerusalem
	January 17-18	Political Committee Meetings in Jerusalem
	January 20	Vance in Cairo
	January 21-February 1	Atherton shuttles
	January 31-February 1	Military Committee meetings in Cairo
	February 3	Sadat arrives in Washington for talks with Carter
	February 16	Dayan holds talks with Carter and Vance
	February 21	Atherton begins another shuttle
	March 20-22	Begin holds talks with Carter
	March 30-31	Weizman meets Sadat
	April 21-25	Atherton shuttles
	April 26	Dayan meets Vance in Washington
	May 1-2	Begin in Washington
	June 30-July 3	Mondale in Jerusalem and in Alexandria
	July 9	Sadat meets Peres in Austria
	July 13	Sadat meets Weizman in Austria
	July 18-19	Leeds Castle conference (Egyptian, Israeli, U.S. foreign ministers)
	July 27	Israeli military mission returns from Egypt
	July 28	Atherton begins another shuttle
	August 5-8	Vance visits Israel and Egypt
	September 6-17	Camp David conference
	September 17	Agreements signed

Chronology—continued

1978	September 20-22	Vance in Jordan and in Saudi Arabia
	September 30	Atherton begins another shuttle
	October 12	Blair House talks begin
	October 21	Saunders in Jerusalem
	November 2	Begin, on private visit, confers with Carter in New York
	November 13	Begin confers with Vance in New York
	December 10-11	Vance in Cairo and Jerusalem
	December 23-24	Dayan, Khalil, and Vance meet in Brussels
1979	January 16-28	Atherton shuttles
	February 21-25	Dayan, Khalil, and Vance confer at Camp David
	March 1-5	Begin in Washington for talks with Carter
	March 8-10	Carter in Cairo
	March 10-12	Carter in Jerusalem
	March 12	Carter meets Sadat at Cairo airport
	March 24-25	Final talks in the U.S. between Sadat and American officials, between Begin and American officials, and between Begin and Sadat
	March 26	Peace treaty signed.

lishment of peace based on Israeli withdrawal from Sinai, the Golan, the West Bank, and Gaza in accordance with Resolution 242, and a just settlement of the Palestinian problem on the basis of the Palestinians' right to self-determination. Sadat reportedly explained the purpose of the declaration of principles by saying: "I don't want to discuss issues which do not concern us. . . . I want our declaration of principles to contain an explicit statement about the termination of the occupation of Arab lands and the solution of all aspects of the Palestinian problem. Any side involved in the conflict . . . can negotiate later on with Israel about security problems."[10]

The Egyptian text was unacceptable to Israel, as it negated the Begin government's aim of keeping the West

Bank and Gaza under Israeli control. Having failed to adopt a joint declaration of principles, Begin and Sadat agreed to set up two ministerial committees to continue the talks. A Military Committee was to discuss the problems of Sinai, while a Political Committee was to seek agreement on a declaration of principles. The Military Committee duly began its work in Cairo on January 11, 1978. The Political Committee convened in Jerusalem on January 17. However, continued harsh criticism of Sadat's policy by other Arab states, Israel's construction of new settlements in Sinai (after it had agreed in principle to the restoration of Egyptian sovereignty there), and Israeli disregard of Egyptian sensitivities, led Egypt to terminate the work of the Political Committee as soon as it convened.[11]

The uncertainty about Egyptian intentions in the negotiations was accompanied by uncertainty about the channels and procedures. Another meeting between Dayan and Tuhami in Morocco in December, Israeli Defense Minister Weizman's meetings with the Egyptian Minister of War General Gamasy and with Sadat, and the subsequent meeting between Begin and Sadat at Ismailiya all signified the parties' desire to conduct talks bilaterally. But parallel to these bilateral talks, additional frameworks were established. On November 26, 1977, a mere week after Sadat's visit to Jerusalem, Egypt invited all parties involved in the conflict, including the PLO as well as the U.S., the Soviet Union, and the UN, to a conference in Cairo for the purpose of preparing the Geneva Conference. Only the U.S., Israel, and the UN accepted the invitation. As no progress was made at the bilateral level, the Cairo conference produced no accomplishments.[12]

The priority they accorded to bilateral negotiations notwithstanding, both sides probably expected that the U.S. would mediate when difficulties were encountered. Begin was the first to enlist American help when he went to Washington to seek American endorsement for the proposals he was planning to present to Sadat at Ismailiya. It is important, however, to note that he did not seek American mediation, only diplomatic support of his efforts at Ismailiya. It was only after Egypt and Israel failed to reach agreement on a declaration of principles at Ismailiya that the U.S. was called upon to participate in the work of the Political Committee on problems that were not of exclusively bilateral Egyptian-Israeli interest. Significantly, the U.S. was not invited to participate in the work of the Military Committee, which was charged with discussing the arrangements for Israel's withdrawal from Sinai. Only after these bilateral talks reached a deadlock (at the end of January), did the U.S. formally become involved in the Sinai negotiations as well.

Throughout this period the U.S. also engaged in a major effort to mitigate Saudi and Jordanian criticism of Sadat's initiative and to persuade Jordan to join in the talks. This was probably the main theme of the talks Secretary of State Vance and Carter had with Arab rulers during their visits to Middle Eastern capitals in December and January. In those efforts, the U.S. in fact became an intermediary between Egypt on the one hand and Saudi Arabia and Jordan on the other.[13]

The *second phase* of the talks, from the breakdown of the Political Committee meeting in January until the invitation to the tripartite summit at Camp David in August, was marked by intensive American efforts to break the deadlock, and continuous discussion of the role that the U.S. ought to play in the negotiations.

Egypt refused to reconstitute the Political Committee, and instead sought to increase pressure on Israel by altering the nature of the American involvement. Realizing that American views were closer to Egypt's position than Israel's and believing that the role of mediator restrained the U.S. from pressing Israel more strongly to accept these views, Sadat urged the U.S. to become an arbiter and to submit its own plan. Israel, for the same reason, preferred the U.S. to act as mediator. The U.S., for its part, pledged itself to continue to mediate in the conflict, and to work intensively for a settlement.[14]

At first, the discussions held through U.S. diplomats

aimed at seeking agreement on a declaration of principles. When this failed they turned to an attempt to solve concrete issues. This attempt also failed as Egypt reverted to its pre-1977 position: provisionally, until the Palestinians could determine their own future, the West Bank should be restored to Jordanian rule and the Gaza Strip to Egyptian administration. Since this was unacceptable to Israel, a new deadlock developed.

American mediation was carried on mainly through separate meetings with both sides. Both Sadat and Begin visited Washington, as did senior members of their Cabinets, for talks with Carter and Vance. In between, Assistant Secretary of State Alfred Atherton shuttled between Cairo and Jerusalem, with side trips to Amman and Riad. Only one tripartite meeting was held, between Vance, Dayan, and Egyptian Foreign Minister Kamel, at Leeds Castle in England in July.[15]

However, the parties continued to maintain direct bilateral links as well. These were facilitated by the personal rapport formed between Weizman and Sadat. Meeting in Egypt on March 30 and 31 and in Austria on July 13, Weizman and Sadat engaged in substantive talks, but failed to break the deadlock. Another channel for continued bilateral contact was the Israeli military mission, which stayed in Cairo throughout this period until requested to leave at the end of July. In July Sadat also conferred with Israel's Labor Party leader, Shimon Peres.[16]

The negotiations gave rise to disagreements between the U.S. and both parties. The main disagreements with Egypt were about the role that Egypt desired the U.S. to play and the Egyptian proposal for a settlement, which the U.S. did not regard as a suitable basis for negotiations. The disagreements with Israel concerned Begin's interpretation of Resolution 242 as not necessarily applicable to the West Bank and Israel's policy of establishing Jewish settlements there. Perhaps because America was concerned about protecting Sadat from his Arab critics, and felt for this reason that Israel must make visible and far-reaching concessions, American-Israeli disagreements occasionally became very bitter.

There was even debate in Israel as to whether the main negotiations should take place through the U.S. or bilaterally. Weizman's apprehensions that the U.S. would side with Egypt led him to prefer direct negotiations, limiting American participation to a minimum. His contacts with Sadat and with Egyptian officials apparently encouraged Weizman to believe that "agreement could be reached more quickly with Boutros Ghali than with Alfred Atherton."[17] Dayan, on the other hand, preferred continued U.S. involvement. He was probably motivated not so much by the considerations of the effectiveness of the negotiating process as by the political need to protect Israel's relations with the U.S., and to commit the U.S. to guarantee and actively support any agreement concluded.

The *third phase* in the negotiations was the Camp David conference. The deadlock that had developed threatened to bring the negotiations to a halt. The U.S. viewed such a prospect with alarm, because the suspension of the negotiations would be a setback for Sadat and for the entire peace process. Tensions between Egypt and Israel might be renewed, and the danger of war—and the accompanying peril of another oil embargo—might reappear. A deadline also lurked ahead, as the last of the extensions of the term of the UN force in Sinai, to which Egypt had committed itself under the 1975 agreement, was about to expire. These dangers prompted Carter to try to break the deadlock through a new initiative, and he invited Begin and Sadat to meet with him at Camp David for what was to become high-pressure mediation at the summit.

Although it was probably unthinkable that the invitation be declined, the terms of the meeting and the ground rules of the conference required delicate negotiation. Sadat had not abandoned his request that the U.S. become an arbiter in the conflict, or that it at least present its own plan, which he apparently expected would be closer to the Egyptian position than to Israel's and would vindicate his initiative. Israel continued to object to the U.S. assuming any such role. The U.S. itself probably preferred to keep its engagement at the level of mediation, and not deepen it further.

The formula agreed upon between Egypt and the U.S. was that the U.S. would become "a full partner" in the negotiations. It is significant that only the U.S. and Egypt used this wording; Israel did not, and apparently withheld its acceptance of any change in the American role.[18] To avoid controversy, the meaning and implications of this term were left ambiguous, with each side free to interpret it as it desired. Begin's reaction, as published in an interview in *Newsweek*, was:

> I don't know what it means to be a full partner. If it means that the American delegation takes interest in the talks and sometimes even brings a concrete proposal or formulation, that is one story. But I do not expect the U.S. to propose a so-called peace plan, because that would be unhelpful. . . . My personal advice would be for the United States to fulfill the very useful function of honest broker, and bring the two parties together for face-to-face negotiations.[19]

Mediation at the summit was no innovation. In recent history it was successfully used by the Soviet Union in its mediation between India and Pakistan at Tashkent in January 1966. Nevertheless, the Camp David summit had some unique features. The delegations were to be secluded there in an informal atmosphere, insulated from the mass media and from domestic political pressures. The intention was that they remain there until they reached agreement.

In this instance the meetings of the three principal leaders were not conducive to success. After two meetings between Begin and Sadat at the beginning of the conference had produced tensions and increased disagreements, procedures were arranged so as to avoid further confrontations between the two. Instead, Carter, Vance, and Carter's National Security Assistant Zbigniew Brzezinski met with Begin and Sadat separately. It was at these separate meetings between the U.S. and each party that the most important negotiations took place and the most significant concessions were made. However, trilateral meetings continued to take place at the technical level, and on one occasion Carter spent a whole day negotiating and drafting with the legal experts of both sides. In addition, there were also some bilateral meetings between Egyptian and Israeli representatives without the presence of American delegates. Weizman met Sadat several times, Dayan met him once, and there were meetings between other members of the two delegations.

The conference lasted twelve days. Only after repeated crises, and after a deadline for the conclusion of the conference had finally been set, was agreement finally reached. It consisted of two documents. One was entitled "The Framework of Peace in the Middle East" and the other, "The Framework for the Conclusion of a Peace Treaty between Egypt and Israel." These were signed ceremoniously at the White House on September 17, and became the basis for the negotiations that followed.[20]

The *fourth and final phase* of the negotiations,[21] from the conclusion of the Camp David accords in September to the signing of the peace treaty in March, produced some unexpected difficulties. In the framework for a peace treaty between Egypt and Israel the two parties undertook "to negotiate in good faith with a goal of concluding within three months of the signing of this framework a peace treaty between them." It was believed that these negotiations would not be difficult since matters of principle had been settled at Camp David; all that remained was to translate the guidelines of the framework concluded there into operative details and embody them in a treaty.

Negotiations began at Blair House in Washington on October 11. Egypt was represented by its Minister of Defense Kamal Hassan Ali and the Acting Foreign Minister Boutros Ghali, and Israel by Dayan and Weizman. This site was chosen in order to facilitate the intervention of the secretary of state and the president in the event that difficulties developed. Their intervention was indeed helpful, and by early November a draft peace treaty had been formulated. Difficulties developed, however, when the draft failed to receive the approval of the Israeli Cabinet and of the Egyptian president. Both sides requested amendments and made new demands in an effort to improve the results they had obtained at Camp David.

These obstacles to an agreement stemmed mainly from the pressures to which the Egyptian and Israeli leaders were subjected. The framework for comprehensive peace, which was intended to show that Sadat was not abandoning the common Arab cause, but was achieving something for the Palestinians and Israel's other neighbors as well, not only failed to appease criticism of Sadat's policy in the Arab world but actually increased it. Jordan did not join the negotiations as it was invited to do by this document, but maintained and even intensified its opposition to the peace process; Saudi Arabia's quiet dissatisfaction now became louder; Egypt was also criticized and threatened with sanctions by a special summit meeting of the Arab League convened in Baghdad in November. There was some grumbling in Egypt, even within the Cabinet, as evidenced by the resignation of Foreign Minister Muhammad Ibrahim Kamel. These reactions placed Sadat under greater pressure to show that his policy was yielding real gains not only for Egypt, but for the Palestinians and the Arab cause in general; hence the attempt to improve the results obtained at Camp David. The Israeli Cabinet also came under political attack because of the concessions Israel made at Camp David. The upheaval in Iran contributed new difficulties. The rise of extreme Islamic fundamentalism as a political movement added to the pressures with which Sadat had to reckon. It also aroused anxiety in Israel, because Iran had been Israel's main source of oil, but after the Shah's overthrow, Iranian oil deliveries stopped. This prompted Israel to demand assurances of continued access to the Sinai oil wells, which under the peace treaty it was about to transfer to Egypt.

The efforts to overcome the new obstacles were conducted through the U.S. and not directly between the parties. As in the spring of 1978, these negotiations caused much friction between Israel and the U.S. The American attitude was again much influenced by anxiety for Sadat's political standing and the need to prevent his isolation in the Arab world. It may also have been influenced by the American need to meet Egyptian expectations, reportedly stimulated by the U.S., that it would "deliver" Saudi support for the Camp David accords.[22] Furthermore, the U.S. was caught between the risk of losing face if the negotiations failed and the concern that if they succeeded, they would not win good will for the U.S. in the Arab world unless the agreement went much further in satisfying Arab demands. Consequently, American requests for concessions were directed much more frequently at Israel than at Egypt, and much effort was invested by the U.S. in persuading Arab opinion that the Camp David accord was a framework within which additional Arab parties, and not only Egypt, could expect to advance their interests. The American conduct nourished Israeli suspicions and played into the hands of Begin's political critics, inducing greater rigidity in the Israeli positions. Thus, Israel's announcement on October 26 that it was going to expand existing West Bank settlements was apparently provoked by Assistant Secretary of State Harold Saunders's contacts with West Bank politicians and by the American responses to Jordan's queries about U.S. policy, which Israel regarded as detrimental to its interests.[23] Subsequently, after the failure of Vance's talks with Egyptian Prime Minister Khalil and Dayan in February, Carter invited Begin to meet him and Khalil in Washington, and Begin refused. The pretext was that he and Khalil were not of equal rank, but the real reason was the suspicion of American-Egyptian collusion and the desire to avoid being placed under extreme pressure for concessions. After a few days Begin relented. Ostensibly, he changed his mind because of the change in the format of the talks to a meeting between him and Carter without Khalil, but the real reason was strong American pressure. Reportedly, the U.S. threatened to withdraw from the negotiations and place the onus for the failure of the peace process on Israel's unwillingness to negotiate.[24]

Once again, the final breakthrough occurred as a result of a dramatic and forceful intervention by President Carter. His talks with Begin in Washington in March yielded important Israeli concessions. Thereafter, Carter visited Cairo and Jerusalem and obtained further concessions from both sides. These paved the way to the settlement of the last details, and to the formal signature of the peace treaty at an impressive ceremony at the White House on March 26.

The Effects of Direct Channels Upon the Mediation Process

The 1977-1979 negotiations differed from all previous Arab-Israeli negotiations in that they were conducted through two parallel channels of communication. In addition to the communications and negotiations through the U.S., there were numerous direct Egyptian-Israeli contacts. Cabinet ministers and other government officials met each other, for much of the time an Israeli military mission was stationed in Cairo, and Israeli journalists reported and interpreted from Cairo Egyptian views and attitudes.

The existence of these channels, and the frequent friction between the U.S. and Israel, led Weizman to question the advisability of continued resort to American mediation. Yet, despite such doubts, which were probably shared by other Israeli officials, the American role was not challenged. The termination of American mediation seemed unattainable first and foremost because Egypt sought to strengthen the American role. Furthermore, both sides assigned greater importance to preserving and improving their relations with the U.S. than to the settlement of the conflict. To disregard American interests and exclude the U.S. from the negotiations would have been counterproductive to this aim. Finally, both sides were aware that they could not settle their conflict without American guarantees that the agreement they reached would be honored. Although the American role was not challenged, it was nevertheless affected by the direct bilateral contacts maintained between Egypt and Israel. These contacts facilitated the mediation in some respects and impaired its effectiveness in others.

The direct Egyptian-Israeli contacts produced mixed results on the personal level. Sadat's meetings with Begin at Ismailiya and with Begin and Dayan at Camp David reportedly did not come off well. But in other respects the direct contacts helped the two parties arrive at a better understanding of each other's positions and the constraints to which they were subjected. They thus contributed to the gradual readjustment of attitudes and positions. Dayan's conversation with Khalil in Brussels on December 23, 1978 is an example; while waiting for Vance, Dayan and Khalil met alone, and reportedly this conversation served to reassure Dayan of Egypt's continued keen interest in an agreement.[25] Furthermore, the talks that Weizman held with Sadat and with General Gamasy and the talks between the Israeli military mission headed by General Abraham Tamir and their Egyptian counterparts, examined many of the details concerning Israel's withdrawal and security arrangements in Sinai and thus prepared the ground for a rapid agreement on many of these points at the Blair House conference.[26] Sadat's tentative agreement, in his talk with Weizman on March 30, to Israel's continued military presence in the West Bank under the autonomy regime may be considered in the same light.[27] Although Sadat withdrew his consent the following day, this and other tentative concessions by both sides provided the parties with a better understanding of the possibilities, and paved the way to the eventual conclusion of the Camp David accords and the peace treaty.

Yet, in other respects the existence of parallel channels of communications and negotiations tended to impair the effectiveness of mediation and in some ways hindered the conclusion of the agreements. The multiple channels of communication sometimes yielded inconsistent information. The parties received somewhat different impressions about their adversary's terms. For example, Begin and Dayan were baffled when told in Washington by Carter that Sadat wanted Egyptian troops to be stationed east of the Sinai passes, since this contradicted what Sadat had told them in Jerusalem in November.[28] Another example was the position Sadat took in his talks with Weizman in March and July 1978. Although unacceptable to Israel, it held out some hope for more flexible Egyptian attitudes. While Sadat told Weizman that he wanted the talks to continue, he told the Americans that there was nothing to talk about until Israel changed its position. Whether this was a deliberate tactic or a case of misunderstanding is irrelevant; the important point is that the multiple channels sometimes caused confusion. Another problem was that the mediator sometimes felt that his information about the direct Egyptian-Israeli contacts was inadequate.[29] Although both sides kept the U.S. routinely informed of their talks, bilateral Egyptian-Israeli talks without American presence probably impaired the mediator's effectiveness.

There is nothing unusual about negotiations suffering through inconsistent information and misunderstandings. But this was a novel feature in the history of mediation in the Arab-Israeli conflict. In previous endeavors, the mediator was much more in control of communications and of the transmittal of positions and proposals. Mediators never exercised a monopoly over communications, for there were always multiple channels, but the mediators were the authoritative channel and in effective control of the negotiations. However, in the negotiations that took place after Sadat's visit to Jerusalem, the mediator lost control. Although the existence of direct contacts between the parties was in some respects beneficial for the negotiating process, these benefits were offset by the reduction in the effectiveness of the mediator.

Much of this was remedied at Camp David, where circumstances enabled the U.S. to regain control of the negotiating process. To be sure, there were direct contacts at Camp David too, but the U.S. determined the agenda and the procedures and steered the negotiations. It was the repository of drafts and the authorized agency for combining them and presenting formal compromise proposals. Such reassertion of the mediator's control was a necessary condition for the successful conclusion of the conference.

Issues and Solutions[30]

In order to assess the mediator's contributions to the conclusion of the agreements, we must first briefly review the issues and the solutions found for them, and identify those that aroused most controversy. As already noted, some of the most important concessions were made by both sides even before the negotiations started and did not require the mediator's direct involvement. Israel let it be known that it was prepared to recognize Egyptian sovereignty over Sinai. Egypt recognized Israel, and let it be known that it accepted the view that peace meant normal neighborly relations. Egypt also agreed in principle to the establishment of security arrangements in Sinai.

The resolution of numerous other issues required relatively little help from the mediator. Among these were many of the questions concerning Israel's withdrawal from Sinai, such as schedules and timetables, limited forces zones, the role of UN forces and the principle that they would be withdrawn only by mutual agreement, the wording of a renewed Egyptian commitment to respect Israel's navigation rights, the establishment of a commission to examine mutual financial claims, and the construction of a highway between Jordan and Sinai with guaranteed free passage by Egypt and Jordan.

There were, however, a number of issues pertaining to Egyptian-Israeli relations that provoked sharp controversy, and required the mediator's intensive involvement. The most difficult question concerned the Israeli settlements in Sinai. Because of the symbolic meaning that settlements had acquired in Israeli politics, and the fear that their removal might be regarded a precedent applicable to the West Bank and the Golan as well, Israel sought to persuade Egypt to agree that they remain in place under Egyptian sovereignty. For the same reasons in reverse, Egypt insisted that they be removed. The U.S. made it clear that it supported Egypt on this issue, and helped persuade Israel that Sadat would not make peace unless the settlements were removed. On the other hand, the U.S. tried to persuade Egypt to agree to Israel's request to retain control of some of the air bases in Sinai for a limited period after its withdrawal. Again, the symbolic importance of this was such that Egypt insisted upon their removal. Israel's agreement to this was facilitated by a U.S. promise to aid in the construction of new air bases in the Negev.

In the negotiations on the peace treaty following the Camp David accords, controversy developed over Israel's demand that it be clearly stated that obligations under the peace treaty take precedence over any previous obligations undertaken by the parties. Israel's insistence on such a clause stemmed from the concern that Egypt might claim that it was committed by inter-Arab agreements to maintain various discriminatory anti-Israeli practices; or that Egypt might claim that the peace treaty notwithstanding, Egypt was under a legal obligation to come to the assistance of a sister Arab state engaged in a war against Israel. The U.S. helped to overcome this obstacle by supplying ambiguous wording for this article (no. VI) and by providing Egypt with a legal interpretation of it according to which Egypt could claim that the article did not contradict Egypt's pan-Arab commitments.

Intensive American mediation was also required to resolve disagreements over new claims raised by both sides after a draft for a peace treaty had been completed by the negotiations at the Blair House conference and submitted to their governments for approval. Egypt now demanded the right to establish a liaison office in Gaza, and requested that Israel advance the date of its withdrawal from El Arish. Furthermore, Egypt claimed that it was not required to send a resident ambassador upon the opening of diplomatic relations, one month after the first stage of Israel's withdrawal had been completed, and that this could be delayed until Israel had fully withdrawn from Sinai in the second stage. Israel, in its turn, demanded an Egyptian commitment to supply it with oil from the oil fields Israel had developed in Sinai. Carter personally helped to resolve these issues by persuading Egypt to withdraw its request for a liaison office in Gaza, and Israel to withdraw its request for an Egyptian commitment on oil sales. The oil supply issue was settled by Sadat subsequently giving Begin his word that Egypt would supply the oil, but without making this a formal part of the peace treaty. The U.S. also helped to assure Israel about its oil supplies by renewing and extending its own promise to supply Israel, should Israel be unable to obtain oil from other sources. (As will be recalled, America made such a commitment to Israel in 1975.) Carter also arranged a package agreement whereby Egypt would send its resident ambassador to Israel after the first stage of Israel's withdrawal in return for Israel's turning over El Arish to Egypt earlier than had previously been agreed.

The most difficult issues were those pertaining to the Palestinian problem. The two fundamental questions on which the parties were divided were the ultimate disposition of the West Bank and Gaza and the claim for Palestinian self-determination. Egypt demanded that Israel recognize the Palestinians' right to a state and to self-determination, and that it commit itself to withdraw from all territories occupied in 1967, according to the Arab interpretation of Resolution 242. Israel rejected the establishment of a Palestinian state, on the grounds that such a state would by reason of geography and national ideology constitute a mortal danger to Israel. Furthermore, Israel viewed the acknowledgment of the right of self-determination as synonymous to the acceptance of Palestinian statehood. Israel's proposal, as presented in December 1977, was to grant the *inhabitants* of the West Bank and Gaza administrative autonomy. It further suggested that in view of conflicting claims for sovereignty over these areas the question of sovereignty be left open.

The U.S. helped to overcome these disagreements by supporting a formula deferring the resolution of the controversy, and providing the inhabitants of the West Bank and Gaza with autonomy for a transitional period of five years, after which the final status of those areas would be determined. This was a formula for an interim agreement on procedures, necessitated by the parties' inability to make concessions on "core values." Yet it was impossible to avoid substantive issues entirely, because the transitional arrangements were expected to affect the ultimate outcome. Israel wished to shape the autonomy regime in a manner that would enable Israeli presence and control to continue after the transitional period, while Egypt wished to prevent this. The compromises that the U.S. proposed reflected the fact that the American concept of autonomy was much closer to Egypt's than to Israel's. Strong American pressure was often required to induce Israel to yield.

Thus, the compromise on the question of self-determination was based on the wording used by Carter at Aswan on January 4, 1978. It was agreed to enable the Palestinians "to participate in the determination of their own future" by the election of the self-governing authority for the transitional period, by their participation in all the negotiations (on the establishment of the autonomy regime and "the final status of the West Bank and Gaza"), and by submitting the agreement on the final status of the West Bank and Gaza "to a vote by the elected representatives of the inhabitants." The compromise between Egypt's demand that Israel withdraw from the West Bank and Gaza upon the commencement of the transitional period and Israel's insistence upon continued control took the form of an agreement for the withdrawal of the Israeli administration and of some of the Israeli armed forces, and the "redeployment of the remaining Israeli forces into specified security locations."

Not only the operative arrangements but also the wording of many of the clauses were subject to much wrangling because they were believed to give one side or the other a handle on its ultimate goal. For example, while Israel insisted on using the phrase "administrative council," Egypt pushed for the phrases "full autonomy" and "self-governing authority," thus opening the way for investing this authority with legislative powers as well. The wording was subject to debate also because over the years certain phrases had become code words. For example, acknowledgment of the Palestinians' "right to self-determination" was believed to be equivalent to an acknowledgment of their right to statehood, and "all aspects of the Palestinian problem" was interpreted as referring to the 1948 refugees. Such semantic disagreements were overcome by using the preferred phrases of both sides, which augmented the ambiguity of the agreements.

No agreement was reached on the issue of the establishment of new settlements in the territories occupied in 1967. Egypt wanted the establishment of new settlements halted and so did the U.S., which regarded them as illegal. Israel, on the other hand, insisted on the right of Jews to settle and live in all parts of Palestine. At the close of the Camp David conference a compromise was believed to have been agreed upon, according to which Israel would refrain from establishing new settlements while the negotiations were in progress. This understanding was to have been embodied in an exchange of letters appended to the Camp David accords. However, the letters were not exchanged because of a disagreement about the interpretation of the ambiguous oral understanding: Begin claimed that it referred to the negotiations for a peace treaty with Egypt (initially intended to last for three months), while Carter claimed that it referred to the negotiations concerning the autonomy arrangements, which were to extend over a much longer period.

Jerusalem was another issue on which no agreement was reached. Egypt wanted the arrangements regarding the West Bank to apply to the part of Jerusalem that between 1948 and 1967 was under Jordanian rule, and declared that "Arab Jerusalem should be under Arab sovereignty." This was unacceptable to Israel, which had annexed the Arab part of Jerusalem in 1967 and maintained that the city should remain undivided under Israeli sovereignty. Because of the strong attachment of the parties to these positions no agreement was possible, and the issue was left out of the Camp David accords. Instead, it was decided that both sides, as well as the U.S., would state their position on this subject in letters to be appended to the accords.

The issue of a separate peace had ostensibly been resolved by the agreement entitled "The Framework of Peace in the Middle East" which was concluded at Camp David at the same time as "The Framework for the Conclusion of a Peace Treaty between Egypt and Israel." Yet the issue continued to cause concern to Egypt and the U.S. until the signature of the peace treaty in March. In view of the sharp criticism of Egyptian policy by other Arab states, it became important to Egypt and to the U.S. to demonstrate that the peace treaty was merely a step toward a comprehensive settlement, and to establish an explicit link between the Egyptian-Israeli peace treaty, the framework for a comprehensive settlement, and the forthcoming negotiations on the autonomy for the West Bank and Gaza. Egypt therefore proposed that the connection be embodied in the peace treaty. While Israel agreed with the desirability of a comprehensive settlement and stood by its commitments to enter into negotiations about the autonomy arrangements, it insisted upon keeping the two issues separate and rejected any explicit linkage that might render the observance of the terms of the peace treaty conditional upon the settlement of other issues. This disagreement delayed progress on the peace treaty negotiations for many weeks, until a compromise was agreed whereby the link would be mentioned only in a general way in the preamble to the peace treaty, while the details about the forthcoming autonomy negotiations were relegated to an exchange of letters appended to the treaty. The wording of the letters was also the subject of difficult negotiations and strong pressures by the mediator, until a compromise was reached to establish a target date for the conclusion of the negotiations, rather than a more demanding timetable for the elections as Egypt had initially demanded.

As is evident from the foregoing, several issues of principle perceived by the parties in ideological terms remained unresolved and were deferred for future negotiations. The negotiations for setting up Palestinian autonomy were postponed until after the conclusion of the peace treaty, and the determination of the eventual status of the West Bank and Gaza was postponed until the end of the interim five-year autonomous regime. The question of Jerusalem, another highly emotional issue on which the parties were sharply divided, was postponed indefinitely.

The compromises by which other issues of principle were disposed of were vague, and enabled each side to interpret the agreement as being consistent with its viewpoint. "The Framework of Peace in the Middle East" is replete with ambiguities, and the guidelines established by this document for the autonomy negotiations left key questions, such as the composition and the powers of the "self-governing authority (administrative council)," for future negotiations.

Contentious issues that were not perceived in ideological terms, such as schedules and timetables for Israel's withdrawal, arms limitations and security arrangements, and the pace of normalization, were resolved by packaging concessions and counterconcessions. In these cases, compromise took the form of barter on concrete values rather than agreement on ambiguous wording that in fact left the issues open.

Significantly, two issues perceived by Israel as affecting important security interests could not be resolved by an Egyptian-Israeli agreement but required an American-Israeli agreement. It was the American promises to construct new air bases in the Negev and to provide Israel with its oil requirements that enabled Israel to withdraw from the Sinai air bases and oil wells, rather than Egyptian promises of peace and of continued supply of oil.

Inducing Concessions

Devising appropriate solutions for the different kinds of issues was not enough; the mediator also had to bring the parties to change their policies, to make concessions, and to accept the compromises it proposed. Although some of the tactics employed by the mediator to this end led to complications, especially in the period after Camp David, American pressures and incentives played a crucial role in bringing the parties to agreement. The pressures brought to bear upon the parties were both direct and indirect.

The U.S. generated indirect pressure by creating circumstances that forced the parties to yield and modify their positions. The indirect pressures were created through the dramatization of the mediating process, first with the Camp David conference and subsequently, in March 1979, with Carter's visits to Cairo and Jerusalem. Mediation at the summit carried the usual advantages and disadvantages of summit diplomacy. Carter, who convened the conference, and by virtue of his role as mediator, took the greatest political risk. But the prestige of Sadat and Begin were also at stake. By its very conspicuousness, and because the prestige of all three leaders had become committed, failure would have been dramatic. It would have hurt all three politically; worse, it would have increased tensions in the Middle East. Thus, the circumstances of the conference itself created strong pressures on Egypt and on Israel to make concessions, and greatly intensified the American motivation to assure success. A similar situation was created by Carter's decision to go in person to Cairo and Jerusalem in March 1979 to bring the deadlocked negotiations to a successful conclusion. Again, the prestige of the president became committed; failure would have been highly publicized, with severely damaging consequences to all three participants.

American mediation prior to 1977 also involved the president of the U.S. on occasion but the participation of previous presidents was much less intensive and dramatic. With Carter, the president himself became personally involved in the negotiations, and his involvement was accompanied by much publicity. His strong commitment from the first weeks of his administration to finding a solution to the Arab-Israeli conflict changed the nature of the Egyptian-Israeli negotiations. It added much weight to American mediation, as the advice of a U.S. president dedicated to this task could not lightly be set aside. Whatever considerations of national interest may have prompted Carter to take an active role, his commitment should in part be attributed to his personality. It seems likely that his deep religious feelings as well as an optimism about a president's ability to shape the course of international affairs, yet untamed by experience, contributed to his decision to become closely involved in the negotiations.

Since the most painful concessions made by Begin and by Sadat were made after private conversations with Carter, it seems that Carter applied direct and highly effective pressures during such private talks. In contrast to the detailed accounts leaked about other aspects of the negotiations, very little is known about these talks. However, from the little that has been published[31] about Carter's talks with Begin on September 10 and 16, 1978 at Camp

David, and on March 3, 1979 at Washington, following which Begin made the most difficult concessions, it appears that Carter applied both warnings and threats.

He claimed that the outcome of the negotiations depended upon Israel. More than once, the particular negotiations were described as the "last chance" for peace, because if no progress were achieved, then the opponents of the peace process (Sadat's political enemies, radical Arab states, the Soviet Union) would probably gain the upper hand. Thus, the responsibility resting upon Israel and upon Begin personally was immense: he held the key not only for the success or failure of a particular round of negotiations, but for the course of history. Such warnings, reminiscent of Kissinger's lectures to the Israeli Cabinet, were accompanied by threats. If the negotiations failed, a rift would develop between the U.S. and Israel; Carter would no longer regard Israel as interested in peace; he would have to explain to Congress and the American public Israel's responsibility; it would be difficult for him to ask congressional approval for aid, and the U.S. would not be able to extend Israel political support.

It seems that Carter used the threat of accusing Israel in front of Congress and of public opinion more frequently than his predecessors did. Begin often countered by threatening that he too would go to the American public. Some such skirmishing even took place before television cameras, with Carter saying that "absolutely insignificant differences" were holding up peace and Begin replying that the vital interests and the fate of his nation were at stake.[32] Another Israeli means of counterpressure was to question whether the U.S. was playing the role of an impartial intermediary. The matter was raised by a Knesset resolution on December 19, 1978 that described the American attitude as "one-sided." Begin made further reference to this in an ABC television interview in March 1979.[33]

The questioning of the mediator's impartiality illustrates again the constraints that the role imposes. Begin raised the question because he thought that public opinion expected the mediator to be impartial, and that it might react critically if Carter were shown to deviate from this norm. Sadat apparently shared this view of mediation; this is why he wished the U.S. to redefine its role and be a "full partner." Yet, it is not only the mediator whose conduct is constrained. Once Israel had accepted American mediation, it could not easily withdraw its acceptance. Begin's refusal to come to Washington in February 1979 implied that Israel might suspend its acceptance of American mediation unless the U.S. ceased supporting Egyptian demands. But the U.S. had an effective response: indicating that *it* might suspend its mediation effort. It is unclear which side would have been hurt more had these threats been implemented.

Another form of pressure, used at Camp David by all participants but most effectively by Carter, was the setting of a deadline for the conclusion of the talks. At first, no time limit was set for the conclusion of the conference. This placed some pressure on the parties to strive for an agreement, for whoever rose first to leave before an agreement had been reached would have carried the onus of causing the peace efforts to fail. (As may be recalled Bunche claimed to have used the same tactic successfully at Rhodes.) But this also encouraged each side to hold fast and wait for the other to lose his patience. Either because they got impatient or for tactical reasons, Dayan and Weizman indicated after about a week that they had had enough and were ready to leave. Subsequently, Sadat too let it be known that he was prepared to leave even without an agreement. Since all three of them were temperamental, highly unpredictable, and quite capable of suddenly departing, the American delegation decided to change its tactics and set a definite deadline for the conclusion of the conference. It was announced that the president would be reporting to Congress on Monday September 18. This had a double effect. It pressed the parties to make a final effort and reminded them of the need to assure, even at great cost, that if the conference failed the blame would not fall on them. The powerful pressure of deadlines was also in evidence on March 12, when preparations for Carter's departure from Jerusalem helped to soften Israel and to speed up its concessions.[34]

As in previous mediation rounds, incentives were also offered to the parties. Egypt was given to understand that following the conclusion of peace it could expect massive economic aid, comparable in scope (and it was hoped in effect) to that of the Marshall Plan. A large-scale military aid program was also promised. The link between aid and the successful conclusion of the negotiations was not merely tacit. Visiting Egypt in February 1979, Secretary of Defense Harold Brown publicly declared that no substantial supply of arms would be possible until the peace treaty was signed. Israel also expected large-scale aid, both in the continuation of regular programs and in assistance for the construction of airfields and military installations in the Negev to replace those relinquished in Sinai. These expectations materialized upon the conclusion of the peace treaty, with the U.S. pledging very substantial amounts of aid—$2 billion to Egypt and $3 billion to Israel. It is difficult, however, to assess how much expectations of aid affected the parties' conduct in the course of the negotiations.[35]

Specific compensation for concessions that the parties made and American guarantees were more directly related to the successful outcome of the negotiations. Israel's agreement to withdraw from the Etzion and Etam air bases adjacent to the international border in Sinai was facilitated by the U.S. promise of assistance in constructing new air bases in the Negev. Israel's withdrawal from the Alma oil field in Sinai was also made easier by the extension, from five years to fifteen, of the 1975 American commitment to supply Israel with oil in the event that it would not be able to secure its needs.

Egyptian concessions on the Palestinian issue were probably facilitated by the American promise to take an active part in the negotiations about the autonomy arrangements that were to take place after the conclusion of the peace treaty.

The U.S. also guaranteed to both sides the observance of the peace treaty. In identical letters to Begin and Sadat, Carter promised that "subject to the U.S. Constitutional processes" the U.S. would "consult" with the parties in the event of an actual or threatened violation of the peace treaty, and that it would take action "as it may deem appropriate and helpful to achieve compliance with the Treaty." The U.S. also undertook to monitor the implementation of the limitation of forces arrangements, as requested by the parties. In the event of the UN Security Council failing to establish and maintain a UN force in Sinai as agreed by the parties in the peace treaty, the U.S. promised in a letter appended to the treaty, that it would "ensure the establishment and maintenance of an acceptable alternative multinational force."

In addition, supplementary guarantees were provided to Israel in a Memorandum of Agreement signed by Vance and Dayan. The U.S. promised to "provide support it deems appropriate for proper actions taken by Israel" in response to violations of the peace treaty, and to consider the strengthening of its presence in the area in such event. The memorandum also contained assurances about navigation and overflight rights, on American opposition to UN resolutions that may adversely affect the peace treaty, about future economic and military aid, and on the prevention of unauthorized transfer of American weapons for use against Israel.

The Mediator's Contribution

Let us return to the questions posed at the beginning of this chapter. Did unique aspects of the mediation process contribute to the achievement of these agreements? What was the mediator's contribution to the adversaries' making concessions on issues they regarded as "core values"?

As we have seen, some aspects of the mediation process

were indeed different from those encountered before. One was the degree of the president's personal involvement. This contributed to the determination and drive of American policy, and it provided leadership and effective policy coordination. Perhaps most important were the situational pressures generated by the president's involvement and the direct pressures he was able to exert. These appear to have been crucial for bringing the parties to make concessions, and thus bridging the gap between their positions. Assuming that Carter's strong motivation to resolve the Arab-Israeli conflict and his unflinching personal commitment stemmed to a large extent from his personality, it would seem that the personality of the American president and the diplomatic style to which it gave rise had a significant effect on the outcome. Also contributing to the successful outcome were some qualities already encountered in previous mediation efforts—effective staff work and tactical skill.

On the other hand, some unique aspects of this mediation do not appear to have made much difference to the outcome. The somewhat greater attention paid to public opinion and the effects of multiple channels of communication were different, but the unique achievement of these agreements cannot be attributed to them.

Finally, the mediator's contribution should be kept in perspective. Although he did induce the parties to make concessions even on issues that were perceived by the parties in ideological terms or associated with "core values," those concessions did not involve basic policy changes. In most cases, the concession was only a willingness to accept ambiguous phrases as satisfactory or to agree to postpone the consideration of highly contentious problems. The really important concessions—Israel's readiness to withdraw from Sinai and Egypt's readiness to recognize Israel even without an Israeli commitment to withdraw from all territories occupied in 1967 and to give in on the Palestinian problem—were made before the mediation began. They were brought about by other factors, with the mediator making only an indirect contribution to them. The mediator's contribution, however crucial and indispensable, did not bring about basic attitude changes or policy transformations, but only built on them.

ELEVEN

Two Perspectives on Mediation

In conclusion let me offer some observations on mediation from two perspectives—the broad context of international politics and the narrower framework of peacemaking. I do not claim that these observations, derived from the cases examined in this book, are valid for all international mediation, but I suspect that the relevance of many of them extends beyond the cases examined here.

Mediation as Power Politics

Mediators, like brokers, are in it for profit. It is, of course, a profit that can be earned in the pursuit of a praiseworthy cause. Whether they should be called "honest brokers" is another matter; the question of their honesty arises only insofar as the term is applicable to power politics.

In the political context, mediation is a form of intervention in a conflict. It differs from other forms of intervention because it requires the acceptance and cooperation of the adversaries. As a result, it is subject to constraints that do not obtain in other forms of intervention. The chief of these is that mediators may not employ violence. No negative connotation is intended by the use of the term "intervention." Indeed, one can say that mediation, since by definition it precludes violent means, is a relatively benign form of intervention.

Because of its potential effect on the interests of many

states, the Arab-Israeli conflict has drawn numerous and diverse forms of outside intervention. Since 1948 various powers became involved in the conflict by providing political, economic, and military assistance to one party or another, to support that party's ability to pursue the struggle. For the same reason—to protect their interests under the impact of the conflict—these powers also became involved in peacemaking, either directly or through the international organizations to which they belonged.

As we have seen throughout, mediators hoped that the resolution or abatement of the Arab-Israeli conflict would produce beneficial consequences for them. They engaged in mediation not only for the sake of the Arabs and Israelis, but no less for the sake of the benefits that they expected to reap from the resolution or abatement of the Arab-Israeli conflict. Occasionally, it was not only the reduction of the conflict that was expected to promote the mediator's goals, but also the mere assumption of the status of mediator. Sometimes they were motivated by the pursuit of the side effects of mediation no less than by the reduction of the Arab-Israeli conflict.[1]

The self-interested goals pursued by mediators were of several kinds. The international organizations that engaged in mediation, the UN and the OAU, did not serve as instruments only of their members. Their efforts at mediation were in part motivated by the pursuit of the institutional self-interest of the organization itself. The UN's involvement was inspired and necessitated by its Charter, which places upon it the responsibility to assist in the peaceful settlement of international disputes. It was a normative goal that the membership and the Secretariat wished to pursue, and it was also in the interest of the organization to prove its effectiveness and realize its raison d'être. Even a partial success in reducing the Arab-Israeli conflict would serve both these ends. The initiatives and the conduct of successive secretary-generals of the UN—Trygve Lie, Dag Hammarskjöld, U Thant, and Kurt Waldheim—were aimed to a significant extent at the pursuit of these goals. The UN was only partly successful. Bernadotte and Bunche succeeded in reducing the conflict, and Bunche's success, more than any other UN peacemaking effort, rekindled temporarily hopes in the organization's potential as a peacemaker. But the Conciliation Commission and Jarring failed to bring about any abatement in the conflict, and their failures did not win respect for the authority of the UN, nor enhance confidence in its ability to realize the lofty aims of its Charter. The OAU's mediation was prompted by the need to remove a contentious issue dividing the African states and impairing the effective functioning of the Organization. It was also motivated by the wish to pursue one of the basic aims for which the OAU had been established—the defense of the territorial integrity of African states. Again, having failed in its mediation, it failed to advance its institutional self-interest as well.

The U.S., besides seeking to reduce Arab-Israeli conflict, aimed at different times at two additional goals. One was to protect or expand its sphere of influence. In the 1950s, and again after 1974, it sought to reduce the opportunities for Soviet interference and influence in the area. Between 1970 and 1974, the U.S. utilized mediation to pry Egypt away from the Soviet embrace, to reduce Soviet influence and to increase American. In the 1950s mediation failed to reduce opportunities for Soviet interference. In the American-Soviet competition the Soviet Union gained the upper hand because Egypt and Syria believed that Soviet military assistance might increase their freedom of action and enable them to pursue the destruction of Israel, while American mediation could procure limited gains at best. In the 1970s, mediation *was* an effective instrument in the American competition with the Soviet Union, for it helped to detach Egypt from the Soviets. This became possible for two main reasons. One was the change that occurred in Egyptian goals and priorities after the Soviet option was tried and had failed. Egypt's immediate goal became the restoration of the territories it lost in 1967, and it came to assign greater priority to economic and social development than heretofore. The U.S. appeared much better equipped to help Egypt toward these objectives than the Soviet Union. Secondly, American bargaining power had been strengthened. American-Israeli relations were now much closer than they had been in the 1950s, and consequently the Egyptian motivation to "neutralize" the American role in the conflict became much greater.

Since 1973, the U.S. sought to utilize mediation in the pursuit of an additional goal—reducing Arab motivation to interfere with Western oil supplies. To the extent that peace efforts help in preventing Arab-Israeli warfare, they indeed help to prevent oil boycotts. But as Saudi Arabia and the majority of Arab states came to oppose the Camp David process, and because other issues besides the Arab-Israeli conflict may lead producers to use the oil weapon against the West, and furthermore because the West's bargaining position vis-à-vis Arab (and other) oil producers is weak, mediation in the Arab-Israeli conflict may be an ineffective instrument for assuring Western oil supplies.

Not all of the mediators' goals necessarily required success in peacemaking. For example, the U.S. failed to bring about an interim agreement in 1971-1972. Nevertheless, its attempt to do so was instrumental in developing working relations with Egypt and in encouraging Sadat to turn Egypt away from the Soviets and to reorient it toward the U.S. Thus, the power-political goals of the mediators can sometimes be attained through the mere exercise of mediation, even if the mediation fails to reduce the conflict between the principal parties.

If the mediators utilized their role to pursue power-political goals, the parties used the mediators for similar purposes. The Arab states preferred to negotiate through intermediaries in the expectation that this would result in more favorable terms for them than if they negotiated directly with Israel, and both sides looked to the mediator to guarantee whatever agreements were concluded. Moreover, the parties too utilized mediation for the sake of side effects. Mediation helped the parties to gain time and to avoid having to choose between war and concessions. The Arab states used the UN Conciliation Commission in this way; Egypt, Jordan, and Israel used the Jarring talks similarly. Another use made of mediation was as a buffer against other unwelcome interventions in the conflict. The Jarring mission was thus utilized by Israel. Finally, the enlistment of the mediator was used to induce the reduction of that mediator's support for the adversary. This was one of Egypt's main goals with respect to American mediation since 1970, and it was a goal pursued by both sides with respect to the OAU's attempt to mediate.

That mediators are motivated by self-interest, that they pursue additional goals besides the abatement of the conflict which they are mediating, and that in the process the distinction between goals and means becomes blurred, does not denigrate the normative value of the endeavor. Power politics can be pursued by more destructive means than mediation.

Mediation and Peacemaking

A few additional points on the functions of mediators and the requisites for a successful performance of their task suggest themselves at the conclusion of this study. These lend emphasis to two sources of the mediators' influence: the triangular structure created when a mediator intervenes in a conflict, and the mediator's resources.

As already claimed in Chapter 1, it is not necessary for mediators to be perceived as *impartial.* Most, if not all, of the mediators discussed in this book had an underlying sympathy for one side or another, of which the parties were quite aware (Bunche is a possible exception to this). Yet awareness of the mediator's bias did not prevent his acceptance by the less-favored side. On the contrary, it was the prospect of reducing the third party's support for the adversary that increased the attractiveness of this option.

A would-be mediator's *acceptability* depended on the parties' expectations of the consequences of the mediator's intervention, and the relative advantages and disadvantages of acceptance or rejection. These expectations were usually closely related to the tactical considerations of the moment, and not to the mediator's reputation of impartiality. Moreover, such tactical considerations were not limited to the expected terms of the settlement that might be concluded. Like the mediator, the parties too were interested in the side effects of mediation. Their response to mediation offers was determined not only by the expectations about the proposals for a settlement, but by the diplomatic side-effects of the acceptance or rejection of the proposed mediation. Egypt welcomed American mediation not only because it expected to obtain Israeli concessions through the U.S., but also because it wished to drive a wedge between the U.S. and Israel. Israel's rejection of American mediation in 1956 was caused not only by the concern that American proposals would be disadvantageous, but also because such mediation would have foreclosed the possibility of obtaining American arms, and would have strengthened that faction in Washington that advocated that Nasser be appeased and not punished for his acceptance of Soviet arms.

The mediator's ability to induce the parties to make concessions and accept compromise proposals did not derive from his impartiality, but from the material resources at his disposal. These enabled the mediator to exert pressure on the parties. But because the mediator's role depended on the parties' acceptance, his ability to apply pressure on them was limited, lest their acceptance be withdrawn. More important than the pressures were the incentives offered to the parties and the compensation given them for the concessions they made. An incentive to one side may, however, be a disincentive for the other. When this was the nature of the incentives provided, and when its relative importance overshadowed other aspects of the three-sided relationship (as in the case of the Anderson mission and some aspects of the Rogers interim agreement negotiations), the party that saw itself hurt by the incentives that the mediator was offering to its adversary withdrew its acceptance. Incentives were more effective when they enabled both sides to benefit from the mediation. The promotion of an agreement through the granting of incentives to the parties can be likened to enlarging a pie, thus enabling both adversaries to gain sufficiently, so as to make an agreement attractive. If the parties perceive the conflict as a zero-sum situation, the incentives offered by the mediator may alter the payoff structure and transform the situation into a positive sum game in which a compromise, enabling gains to both sides, is possible.

A different form of a contribution to an agreement, perhaps rare, but nevertheless interesting, is the "triangular barter." For such a barter to take place it is not enough that the mediator possess resources that enable him to distribute incentives. It is necessary that each of the three participants be able to provide another with a specific commodity required by him. The transaction is illustrated by the American role in bringing about the 1975 Egyptian-Israeli agreement. Egypt wanted to obtain the return of its territory from Israel, but was incapable of procuring for Israel the commodity that Israel required in exchange—security. The U.S. was able to provide Israel with security, but Israel was incapable of securing for the U.S. in return what it desired—the elimination of Soviet influence in Egypt and the propagation of good will toward the U.S. among the Arab oil producers. It was Egypt that could do that. No two parties could consummate an exchange bilaterally. It was only through a triangular barter that an agreement could be concluded.

The analysis of mediation in the Arab-Israeli conflict suggests that the mediator's function of *reducing the risks* that the adversaries assume by the concessions they make and by the agreement they conclude may be much more extensive and more important than is reflected by the theoretical literature. To be sure, the mediator's ability to perform this function is conditioned by the resources that he commands. On a number of occasions the potential American ability to perform this function influenced heavily the choice of the U.S. as mediator over the other possibilities (like direct bilateral negotiations, the UN, West European states, Rumania). Both the UN and the U.S. undertook to monitor compliance with the agreements they helped to conclude. Furthermore, as we saw, the U.S. committed itself to explicit guarantees of the Egyptian-Israeli agreements. The compensations that the U.S. promised to give in lieu of the assets given up by Israel were very substantial. They probably weighed heavily in Israeli decisions, and enabled it to face military, economic, and political risks entailed by the concessions with greater confidence.

Because the mediator's need for acceptance and consent by the parties limits his ability to exert pressures, the existence of situational pressures is important for inducing the parties to make concessions. Hence the importance of the *timing* and the circumstances of mediation. Two kinds of situational pressures were propitious for successful mediation. One was a combination of a highly uncomfortable situation with a military *stalemate.* When both sides believed that they could not bear a situation much longer and that they could not relieve their predicament by military action, they were relatively more flexible and more responsive to the mediator's proposals for compromises. Such were the circumstances in which Bernadotte persuaded the parties to accept the truces, Bunche to conclude the armistice agreements, Rogers to accept the 1970 cease-fire, and Kissinger to accept the 1973 cease-fire and to conclude the 1974 disengagement agreements.

In periods of quiescence, when situational pressures did not help induce the parties to flexibility, mediation attempts failed. The Conciliation Commission, the Rogers interim agreement negotiations, the OAU, and Kissinger in March 1975 are examples of such failures. Agreements were reached during the periods of military quiescence only when the mediator created a situation of *political crisis.* The U.S. created such crises by committing itself so deeply and dramatically to the success of the negotiations that all participants felt that a failure would produce grave domestic-political difficulties for each and would seriously affect relations between their respective states. Such situations were created by the U.S. in the summer of 1975 in its "reassessment" policy, which led to the second Egyptian-Israeli disengagement agreement, at Camp David in September 1978, and by Carter's visit to the Middle East in March 1979. The expectations created by the U.S. on these occasions seem to have pressed the parties to make concessions, and compensated for the mediator's inability to exert greater direct pressure on them.

In the mediation attempts discussed in this book, the *personality* traits and *skills* of the individuals involved were highly important and seem to have made some difference for the outcome. Not much can be said about the specific qualities that have been suggested by the literature, except that one personal quality that was important in these mediation attempts received inadequate attention. The strong motivation and persistence of the principal mediator seems to have contributed to the success of Kissinger and of Carter. On the other hand, the lack of persistence on the part of the American representatives on the UN Conciliation Commission and of Jarring may have contributed to their failures. It was not enough for the government or the international organization to be highly interested in the success of the mediation. For the mediation to succeed, the individuals engaged in this effort need to persevere in their task.

The *issues* on which agreement is sought, and the goal which the mediator sets himself have an important bearing on his chances to succeed. The mediation attempts discussed in this book lend support to the view that on issues perceived by a party as affecting its "core values" associated with the "national self," concessions would be unlikely and the probability of agreement would be low. The more important the issue in dispute and the more comprehensive the scope of the agreement sought, the more difficult it will be to achieve. Bernadotte and the Conciliation Commission failed when they sought a comprehensive solution to the conflict. On the other hand, some of the attempts to conclude agreements on a limited, narrowly defined issue succeeded: Bernadotte was able to arrange the two truces, Bunche helped conclude separate armistice agreements between Israel and each of its neighbors, Rogers achieved the 1970 cease-fire, and Kissinger was successful with the cease-fire and disengagement agreements. Rogers failed to arrange an interim agreement, and Jarring and the OAU also failed, because their ostensibly limited goals were linked to a formula for a comprehensive settlement.

How can one explain Carter's success? The Egyptian-Israeli peace treaty and the framework agreement for peace in the Middle East concluded at Camp David required major concessions from both sides. Egypt agreed to recognize Israel and to make peace; Israel agreed to return the Sinai peninsula to Egyptian sovereignty and to establish an autonomous regime in the West Bank and Gaza.

Yet these major concessions were not brought about by American mediation. They were the product of internal changes in the two countries that led to the reordering of their national priorities. Only after these transformations took place did mediation succeed in bringing the parties to an agreement. Moreover, the agreement on the autonomy for the West Bank and Gaza was possible because it stopped short of seeking to resolve the issue. It avoided a decision on the future of the West Bank and Gaza. The agreement only outlined procedures that might ultimately determine the future of these areas, and thus in fact postponed the issue for future negotiations.

For all the important contributions mediators made to

the conclusion of Arab-Israeli agreements, there are limits to what they could accomplish, and to what mediators should aspire to accomplish. Mediation was not successful in modifying basic Arab or Israeli attitudes, nor has it *resolved* the Arab-Israeli conflict. The root causes of the conflict are too complex and too deeply embedded in national ideologies. Such conflicts can be *resolved* only as a result of transformations in national values and ideologies, transformations that may come about as a result of gradual evolution, rather than skillful mediation. Nevertheless, by helping to conclude "small" agreements *reducing* the conflict, mediators can contribute to such an evolution, which over the years may lead to mutual accommodation.

Notes

CHAPTER 1, THE COMPLEAT MEDIATOR

1. Kenneth E. Boulding, *Conflict and Defense* (New York: Harper & Row, 1963), pp. 316-17; John W. Burton, "Resolution of Conflict," *International Studies Quarterly* 16 (March 1972): 5-29; Oran R. Young, *The Intermediaries* (Princeton: Princeton University Press, 1967), pp. 32-33, 37-38, 63-64, 69-72. Since the completion of this chapter, Jeffrey Z. Rubin has published a comprehensive and thoughtful discussion of the theory of third-party peacemaking. See his "Introduction" in *Dynamics of Third Party Intervention: Kissinger in the Middle East*, ed. Jeffrey Z. Rubin (New York: Praeger, 1981), pp. 3-43.
2. Young, *Intermediaries*, pp. 42-43; Burton, in "Resolution of Conflict," uses the term "mediation" to describe these functions. See also Adam Curle, *Making Peace* (London: Tavistock Publications, 1971), p. 177.
3. Boulding, *Conflict and Defense*, pp. 316-18; Frank Edmead, "Analysis and Prediction in International Mediation," in *Dispute Settlement Through the United Nations*, ed. K. Venkata Raman (Dobbs Ferry, N.Y.: Oceana Publications, 1977), pp. 247-59; Jerome E. Podell and William M. Knapp, "The Effect of Mediation on the Perceived Firmness of the Opponent," *Journal of Conflict Resolution* 13 (1969): 511-20; Jeffrey Z. Rubin and Bert R. Brown, *The Social Psychology of Bargaining and Negotiation* (New York: The Academic Press, 1975), pp. 47-58; Young, *Intermediaries*, pp. 32-37; Oran R. Young, "Intermediaries: Additional Thoughts on Third Parties," *Journal of Conflict Resolution* 16 (1972): 55-63.
4. For a different approach, using quantitative data to examine the conditions for successful mediation, see Daniel Frei, "Erfolgsbedingungen für Vertmittlungsaktionen in Inter-

nationalen Konflikten," *Politische Vierteljahresschrift* 16 (1975): 447-90.

5. Arthur Lall, *Modern International Negotiation* (New York: Columbia University Press, 1966), pp. 83, 100; F. S. Northedge and M. D. Donelan, *International Disputes* (New York: St. Martin's Press, 1971), p. 304; Marvin C. Ott, "Mediation as a Method of Conflict Resolution: Two Cases," *International Organization* 26 (1972): 597, 616.
6. On "fractionating issues," see Roger Fisher, "Fractionating Conflict," in *International Conflict and Behavioral Science*, ed. Roger Fisher (New York: Basic Books, 1964), pp. 91-109.
7. Cf. Ernst B. Haas, Robert L. Butterworth, and Joseph Nye, *Conflict Management by International Organizations* (Morristown, N.J.: General Learning Press, 1972).
8. Inis L. Claude Jr., *Swords into Plowshares*, 4th ed. (New York: Random House, 1971), p. 239; Elmore Jackson, *Meeting of Minds* (New York: McGraw-Hill, 1952), pp. 27, 137; Boulding, *Conflict and Defense*, p. 325; Vratislav Pechota, "The Quiet Approach: A Study of the Good Offices Exercised by the United Nations Secretary-General in the Cause of Peace," in *Dispute Settlement*, ed. Raman, pp. 606-8.
9. Claude, *Swords into Plowshares*, pp. 238-39.
10. Ott, "Mediation as a Method," p. 616. Among those who share this view are Jackson, *Meeting of Minds*, pp. 27-28, 137-39; George Modelski, "International Settlement of Internal War," in *International Aspects of Civil Strife*, ed. J. N. Rosenau (Princeton: Princeton University Press, 1964), pp. 137, 143; Young, *Intermediaries*, pp. 43-44.
11. Edmead, "Analysis and Prediction," pp. 250-51; Northedge and Donelan, *International Disputes*, pp. 307-8.
12. Edmead, "Analysis and Prediction," pp. 247-49, 261-63.
13. Modelski, "International Settlement," p. 143; Edmead, "Analysis and Prediction," pp. 251-59.
14. Young, *Intermediaries*, pp. 81, 309.
15. Jackson, *Meeting of Minds*, pp. 125, 129.
16. Northedge and Donelan, *International Disputes*, p. 299. For additional views stressing impartiality and neutrality as essential attributes of intermediaries see Curle, *Making Peace*, pp. 239-40; Ott, "Mediation as a Method," p. 599.
17. Young, *Intermediaries*, p. 81.

18. Carl M. Stevens, *Strategy and Collective Bargaining Negotiation* (New York: McGraw-Hill, 1963), p. 131.
19. Young, "Additional Thoughts," p. 57.
20. Robert Jervis, "Hypotheses on Misperception," *World Politics* 20 (1968): 454-79.
21. Northedge and Donelan, *International Disputes*, p. 299. See also Jean-Pierre Cot, *International Conciliation* (London: Europa Publications, 1972), pp. 33-35; K. Venkata Raman, "A Study of the Procedural Concepts of United Nations Intermediary Assistance in the Peaceful Settlement of Disputes," in *Dispute Settlement*, ed. Raman, pp. 376-78.
22. Young, *Intermediaries*, pp. 37, 41; Boulding, *Conflict and Defense*, p. 318.
23. Young, "Additional Thoughts," pp. 59-60.
24. For a comprehensive treatment see Theodore Caplow, *Two Against One* (Englewood Cliffs, N.J.: Prentice-Hall, 1968).
25. Podell and Knapp, "The Effect of Mediation," pp. 511-12.
26. Northedge and Donelan, *International Disputes*, pp. 308-9; Thomas A. Kochan and Todd Jick, "The Public Sector Mediation Process," *Journal of Conflict Resolution* 22 (1978): 217.
27. Burton, "Resolution of Conflict," pp. 20-22.
28. Jackson, *Meeting of Minds*, p. 155; Kochan and Jick, "Public Sector Mediation," p. 219; Northedge and Donelan, *International Disputes*, pp. 308-9; Young, *Intermediaries*, pp. 87-88; Young, "Additional Thoughts," p. 56.
29. Carl Stevens, "Mediation and the Role of the Neutral," in *Frontiers of Collective Bargaining*, ed. John T. Dunlop and Neil W. Chamberlain (New York: Harper & Row, 1967), p. 272.
30. Cot, *International Conciliation*, pp. 8-9, 169.
31. A discussion of the relative advantages of private intermediaries as compared to governments or international organizations is not relevant for our purposes. On this, see Cot, *International Conciliation*, pp. 1-2, 332; Maureen R. Berman and Joseph E. Johnson, eds., *Unofficial Diplomats* (New York: Columbia University Press, 1977); C. H. Mike Yarrow, *Quaker Experiences in International Conciliation* (New Haven: Yale University Press, 1978).
32. Edmead, "Analysis and Prediction," pp. 276-78.
33. For a discussion of the advantages and disadvantages of sin-

gle intermediaries and of commissions, see David P. Forsythe, *United Nations Peacemaking: The Conciliation Commission for Palestine* (Baltimore: Johns Hopkins University Press, 1972), pp. 156-59; Jackson, *Meeting of Minds*, 97-98, 128, 146-57.

34. Forsythe, *United Nations Peacemaking*, pp. 160-65; Jackson, *Meeting of Minds*, pp. 128, 146-47.

CHAPTER 2, BERNADOTTE

1. United Nations, General Assembly, *Official Record of the Second Special Session*, Annex to Volumes I and II, pp. 35, 43 (A/C. 1/292), May 4, 1948 and (A/C. 1/299), May 13, 1948. The evolution of the American draft resolution is reflected also in the published U.S. diplomatic documents. See United States, Department of State, *Foreign Relations of the United States, 1948*, vol. V, pt. 2 (Washington: United States Government Printing Office, 1976), pp. 942-44.
2. United Nations, General Assembly, Resolution 186 (S-2), May 14, 1948.
3. Stephen M. Schwebel, *The Secretary-General of the United Nations* (New York: Greenwood Press, 1952), pp. 116, 141; Trygve Lie, *In the Cause of Peace* (New York: Macmillan, 1954), p. 185. Previously, the U.S. had proposed Paul van Zeeland, the Belgian statesman, but van Zeeland declined. See Lie, *In the Cause of Peace*, pp. 181, 185.
4. For Bernadotte's background and political attitudes see Sune O. Persson, *Mediation and Assassination: Count Bernadotte's Mission to Palestine in 1948* (London: Ithaca Press, 1979), pp. 225-35. This is the most detailed and best documented study of Bernadotte's mission to appear to date. See also Ralph Hewins, *Count Folke Bernadotte, His Life and Work* (London: Hutchinson, 1948).
5. For a critical evaluation see H. R. Trevor-Roper, "Kersten, Himmler and Count Bernadotte," *Atlantic Monthly*, February 1953, pp. 43-45.
6. Persson, *Mediation and Assassination*, pp. 229-30, quoting from Folke Bernadotte, *Instead of Arms: Autobiographical Notes* (Stockholm and New York, 1948), p. 225. See also Folke Bernadotte, *To Jerusalem* (London: Hodder and Stoughton, 1951), pp. 1-2.
7. United Nations, Security Council, Resolution 43, April 1,

1948; Res. 46, April 17, 1948; Res. 48, May 22, 1948; Res. 50, May 29, 1948.

8. In 1948, Jordan was still usually referred to as Transjordan. To avoid confusion, the name Jordan is used throughout this study.
9. David Ben-Gurion, *Medinat Israel Hamehudeshet* [The Restored State of Israel], 2 vols. (Tel Aviv: Am Oved, 1969), 1: 155-60.
10. Until 1949, Sharett was known as Shertok. For the sake of consistency, the name Sharett is used throughout.
11. Israel, *Moetset Hamedina Hazmanit* [Proceedings of the Provisional State Council], Vol. 1, 4th meeting, p. 5.
12. Bernadotte, *To Jerusalem*, p. 115; *Foreign Relations of the U.S., 1948*, pp. 1105-6, 1114-15; King Abdullah of Jordan, *My Memoirs Completed*, trans. H. W. Glidden (Washington, D.C.: American Council of Learned Societies, 1954), pp. 23-24.
13. Bernadotte, *To Jerusalem*, p. 72.
14. Bernadotte, *To Jerusalem*, pp. 19, 30-80; Ben-Gurion, *Medinat Israel Hamehudeshet*, 1: 152-54.
15. Bernadotte, *To Jerusalem*, p. 115.
16. Bernadotte, *To Jerusalem*, p. 33.
17. Bernadotte, *To Jerusalem*, pp. 126-31; United Nations Document S/863, reprinted in United Nations, Security Council, *Official Records*, 3rd yr., Supplement for July 1948, pp. 18-21.
18. Lie, *In the Cause of Peace*, p. 188; Pablo de Azcárate, *Mission in Palestine 1948-1952* (Washington: The Middle East Institute, 1966), p. 132.
19. Bernadotte, *To Jerusalem*, p. 110.
20. Bernadotte, *To Jerusalem*, pp. 113-14. On Bernadotte's attitude to the Palestinian Arab leaders, see Persson, *Mediation and Assassination*, pp. 139, 150, 239.
21. Bernadotte, *To Jerusalem*, p. 119.
22. Bernadotte, *To Jerusalem*, pp. 138-39; Persson, *Mediation and Assassination*, pp. 251, 289.
23. *Foreign Relations of the U.S., 1948*, pp. 1192-95. See also pp. 1189-90, 1203-5.
24. Ben-Gurion, *Medinat Israel Hamehudeshet*, 1: 214.
25. Ben-Gurion, *Medinat Israel Hamehudeshet*, 1: 164-65, 214-21.

26. For contemporary views on Bernadotte's connections with the British see James G. McDonald, *My Mission in Israel* (New York: Simon and Schuster, 1951), p. 22; Michael Bar-Zohar, *Ben-Gurion*, 3 vols. (Tel Aviv: Am Oved, 1977), 2: 821; Dov Joseph, *The Faithful City* (New York: Simon and Schuster, 1960), pp. 313-15; Jon Kimche, *Seven Fallen Pillars* (New York: Praeger, 1953), pp. 258-60. On the British perception of their strategic interests see *Foreign Relations of the U.S., 1948*, pp. 1611-12.
27. *Foreign Relations of the U.S., 1948*, pp. 1088-90, 1099-1101, 1122-24, 1132-37, 1143-44, 1161-70, 1171-79, 1180-86.
28. Quoted in Persson, *Mediation and Assassination*, p. 291.
29. Bernadotte, *To Jerusalem*, pp. 12, 94, 118, 131.
30. Bernadotte, *To Jerusalem*, pp. 137-64.
31. United Nations, Security Council, Resolution 54, July 15, 1948.
32. *Foreign Relations of the U.S., 1948*, pp. 1202-3 (Bernadotte's message); 1210, 1228-29 (other messages). See also Persson, *Mediation and Assassination*, p. 159, and John B. Glubb, *A Soldier with the Arabs* (London: Hodder and Stoughton, 1957), p. 150.
33. United Nations, Security Council, *Official Records*, 3rd yr., 333rd meeting (July 13, 1948), pp. 7-8.
34. United Nations, General Assembly, *Progress Report of the United Nations Mediator on Palestine*, Suppl. 11 (A/648), [September 1948], p. 17. The same idea is expressed also on pages 4 and 11.
35. Bernadotte, *To Jerusalem*, pp. 183-84.
36. Bernadotte, *To Jerusalem*, pp. 186-87, 196, 201.
37. Bar-Zohar, *Ben-Gurion*, 2: 818; Ben-Gurion, *Medinat Israel Hamehudeshet*, 1: 248-49. See also *Davar*, July 23, 1948 (editorial)
38. Bernadotte, *To Jerusalem*, pp. 189, 204. For Sharett's statement to Israel's provisional parliament, see *Moetset Hamedina Hazmanit*, Vol. 1, 12th meeting, July 29, 1948, 5-12.
39. Bernadotte, *To Jerusalem*, p. 185.
40. Bernadotte, *To Jerusalem*, p. 196.
41. Bernadotte, *To Jerusalem*, pp. 201-2.
42. Bernadotte, *To Jerusalem*, pp. 192-95; *Foreign Relations of the U.S., 1948*, p. 1265.

43. *Foreign Relations of the U.S., 1948*, p. 1309.
44. *Foreign Relations of the U.S., 1948*, pp. 1295, 1340-41, 1369; Bernadotte, *To Jerusalem*, p. 222.
45. *Davar*, August 15, 16, 17, and 27, 1948; Bernadotte, *To Jerusalem*, p. 221.
46. Bernadotte, *To Jerusalem*, pp. 222, 229-30, 233.
47. Bernadotte, *To Jerusalem*, pp. 232-33.
48. *Progress Report of the UN Mediator*, pp. 17-19.
49. Fred J. Khouri, "United Nations Peace Efforts," in *The Elusive Peace in the Middle East*, ed. Malcolm H. Kerr (Albany: State University of New York Press, 1975), p. 26; David P. Forsythe, *United Nations Peacemaking: The Conciliation Commission for Palestine* (Baltimore: Johns Hopkins University Press, 1972), p. 26. See also Azcárate, *Mission in Palestine*, p. 133.
50. *Foreign Relations of the U.S., 1948*, pp. 1266-71, 1288-91, 1303-6, 1308-10, 1342-45.
51. Ibid., pp. 1355-59, 1365, 1369, 1371-72, 1381-82, 1396.
52. Ibid., pp. 1363, 1373.
53. Ibid., pp. 1398-1400; Persson, *Mediation and Assassination*, pp. 308-10.
54. Bernadotte, *To Jerusalem*, pp. 245-70; Ben-Gurion, *Medinat Israel Hamehudeshet*, 1: 281-85; Persson, *Mediation and Assassination*, pp. 203-9. For an account by a former member of LEHI see Baruch Nadel, *Retsah Bernadotte* [The Murder of Bernadotte] (Tel Aviv: J. Gutman, 1968).
55. *Foreign Relations of the U.S., 1948*, p. 1415; Great Britain, *Parliamentary Debates* (Commons), 5th ser., 456: col. 899 (September 22, 1948).
56. *Moetset Hamedina Hazmanit*, Vol. 1, 20th meeting (September 27, 1948), pp. 4-17.
57. *Foreign Relations of the U.S., 1948*, pp. 1449, 1602; Rony Gabbay, *A Political Study of the Arab-Jewish Conflict* (Geneva: Droz, 1959), pp. 220-37; John Snetsinger, *Truman, The Jewish Vote and the Creation of Israel* (Stanford: Hoover Institution Press, Stanford University, 1974), pp. 124-32; Jacob C. Hurewitz, *The Struggle for Palestine* (New York: Norton, 1950), pp. 321-22. The resolution is known as General Assembly Resolution 194 (III).
58. About Bernadotte's staff, see Persson, *Mediation and Assassination*, pp. 263-69.

59. The quote from Bernadotte on bombing truce violators is in Persson, *Mediation and Assassination*, p. 237. On Bernadotte's ideas on a plebiscite see Bernadotte, *To Jerusalem*, pp. 131-32, 170, and United Nations, Security Council, Official Records, Third Year, 333rd meeting, July 13, 1948. Persson traced the origin of the plebiscite idea to John Reedman, one of Bernadotte's close advisors (*Mediation and Assassination*, pp. 294-95).
60. *Foreign Relations of the U.S., 1948*, p. 1398. His mistaken assessment of Israeli attitudes may have stemmed in part from the conversation he had in Paris with Dr. Nahum Goldman on May 25. Bernadotte probably was not aware that Goldman's views did not reflect mainstream Israeli opinion. See Bernadotte, *To Jerusalem*, pp. 8-12; Persson, *Mediation and Assassination*, pp. 119-21.

CHAPTER 3, RALPH BUNCHE

1. Trygve Lie, *In the Cause of Peace* (New York: Macmillan, 1954), p. 192; James G. McDonald, *My Mission in Israel* (New York: Simon and Schuster, 1951), p. 172; David Ben-Gurion, *Medinat Israel Hamehudeshet* [The Restored State of Israel], 2 vols. (Tel Aviv: Am Oved, 1969), 1: 338; Walter Eytan, *The First Ten Years* (New York: Simon and Schuster, 1958), p. 32.
2. Alec Kirkbride, *From the Wings: Amman Memoirs 1947-1951* (London: Frank Cass, 1976), p. 55. Pablo de Azcárate, *Mission in Palestine 1948-1952* (Washington: The Middle East Institute, 1966), p. 106.
3. For Bunche's statements to the First Committee see United Nations, General Assembly, *Official Records*, 3rd sess., 1948, First Committee, pp. 162-65 (October 15, 1948), and pp. 768-72 (November 25, 1948). For examples on Bunche's diplomatic activity see United States, Department of State, *Foreign Relations of the United States, 1948*, Vol. V, Pt. 2 (Washington: United States Government Printing Office, 1976), pp. 1481, 1484-85, 1549-1625.
4. Ben-Gurion, *Medinat Israel Hamehudeshet*, 1: 296-97.
5. Ralph Bunche, "The Palestine Problem," in *The Near East and the Great Powers*, ed. Richard N. Frye (Cambridge: Harvard University Press, 1951), pp. 116-17.
6. *Foreign Relations of the U.S., 1948*, p. 1512.

7. Jon and David Kimche, *Both Sides of the Hill* (London: Secker and Warburg, 1960), pp. 238-52; Michael Bar-Zohar, *Ben-Gurion*, 3 vols. (Tel Aviv: Am Oved, 1977), 2: 826-30.
8. Ben-Gurion, *Medinat Israel Hamehudeshet*, 1: 297-98; *Foreign Relations of the U.S., 1948*, pp. 1442, 1464.
9. United Nations, Security Council, *Official Records*, 3rd yr., 367th meeting, October 19, 1948, pp. 25-38.
10. Ben-Gurion, *Medinat Israel Hamehudeshet*, 1: 300-301; Bar-Zohar, *Ben-Gurion*, 2: 848-53.
11. United Nations, Security Council, *Official Records*, 3rd yr., 373rd meeting, October 26, 1948, pp. 23-24.
12. United Nations, Security Council, *Official Records*, 3rd yr., *Resolutions and Decisions of the Security Council 1948*, (S/1044), pp. 25-26.
13. United Nations, Security Council, Resolution 61, November 4, 1948.
14. United Nations, General Assembly, Third Session, *Progress Report of the United Nations Mediator on Palestine* (A/648), p. 18.
15. United Nations, Security Council, *Official Records*, 3rd yr., 374th meeting, October 28, 1948, p. 9 and 378th and 379th meetings, November 8 and 9, 1948, pp. 62-64. See also *Foreign Relations of the U.S., 1948*, pp. 1555, 1559, 1574.
16. United Nations, Security Council, Resolution 62, November 16, 1948.
17. Moshe Sharett, *Beshaar Haumot, 1946-1949* [At the Gate of Nations] (Tel Aviv: Am Oved, 1958), pp. 334-35; Ben-Gurion, *Medinat Israel Hamehudeshet*, p. 332. Israel's reply is in *Foreign Relations of the U.S., 1948*, pp. 1614-16.
18. *Foreign Relations of the U.S., 1948*, p. 1616.
19. Sharett, *Beshaar Haumot*, pp. 334-35; Bar-Zohar, *Ben-Gurion*, 2: 858-65; Yigal Allon, *Massach Shel Hol* [A Curtain of Sand] (Tel Aviv: Hakibbutz Hameuchad, 1968), pp. 15, 404; Yerucham Cohen, *Leor Hayom Ubamachshach* [In Daylight and in Darkness] (Tel Aviv: Amikam, 1969), pp. 250-56, 269-74.
20. Azcárate, *Mission in Palestine*, pp. 111-13.
21. Kirkbride, *From the Wings*, pp. 56-69; Yosef Nevo, *Abdullah Vearviei Eretz Israel* [Abdullah and the Arabs of Palestine] (Tel Aviv: Shiloah Institute of Tel Aviv University, 1975), pp. 95-116.

22. Moshe Dayan, *Story of My Life* (Tel Aviv: Steimatzky's, 1976), pp. 108, 104-118; Abdullah al-Tall, *Zikhronot Abdullah al-Tall* [The Memoirs of Abdullah al-Tall] (Tel Aviv: Maarakhot, 1960), pp. 303-26.
23. Ben-Gurion, *Medinat Israel Hamehudeshet*, 1: 312-16; *Foreign Relations of the U.S., 1948*, pp. 1544-45.
24. Nissim Bar-Yaacov, *The Israel-Syrian Armistice: Problems of Implementation 1949-1966* (Jerusalem: The Magnes Press, 1967), pp. 33, 35. United States, Department of State, *Foreign Relations of the United States, 1949*, vol. VI (Washington: United States Government Printing Office, 1977), pp. 799, 809, 851.
25. Eytan, *The First Ten Years*, pp. 32, 30.
26. *Foreign Relations of the U.S., 1949*, pp. 698-700; Yehoshaphat Harkabi, "Heskemei Shvitat Haneshek" [The Armistice Agreements], in *Sefer Hashana Shel Haitonaim 1950* [The Journalists' Yearbook 1950] (Tel Aviv: Agudat Haitonaim, 1950), p. 17.
27. Bunche, "The Palestine Problem," pp. 70-71; cf. *Foreign Relations of the U.S., 1949*, pp. 707-8.
28. United Nations, Security Council, *Official Records*, 4th yr., Special Supplement no. 3, Egyptian-Israel Armistice Agreement. The armistice agreements have been widely reprinted. For a convenient reference see John Norton Moore, *The Arab-Israeli Conflict: Readings and Documents* (Princeton: Princeton University Press, 1977). On this controversy see Harkabi, "Heskemei Shvitat Haneshek," pp. 19-20.
29. Harkabi, "Heskemei Shvitat Haneshek," p. 17; *Foreign Relations of the U.S., 1949*, p. 691 n. 1, pp. 699-702.
30. Abba Eban, *An Autobiography* (Tel Aviv: Steimatzky's, 1977), pp. 137-38; Eytan, *The First Ten Years*, pp. 35-36; Harkabi, "Heskemei Shvitat Haneshek," pp. 17-18; *Foreign Relations of the U.S., 1949*, pp. 707-8, 718-20, 723-24, 755-56.
31. A. A. Ben-Asher, *Yahasei Hutz 1948-1953* [Foreign Relations 1948-1953] (Tel Aviv: Ayanot, 1956), pp. 36-38; *Foreign Relations of the U.S., 1949*, pp. 802, 808, 846-47.
32. Bar-Yaacov, *The Israel-Syrian Armistice*, pp. 37-65.
33. Dayan, *Story of My Life*, pp. 109-16; John B. Glubb, *A Soldier with the Arabs* (London: Hodder and Stoughton, 1957), pp. 227-37; al-Tall, *Zikhronot*, pp. 327-89; *Foreign Relations of*

the U.S., 1949, especially pp. 808, 810, 815-16, 821, 853 ff., 869 ff., 878, 886.

34. References to his personality are made by many of the sources listed above. See especially Dayan, Eban, Eytan, Harkabi, McDonald. There is much biographical information in Alvin Kugelmass, *Ralph S. Bunche: Fighter for Peace* (New York: Julian Messner, 1953). See also Rolf Italiaander, *Drei Friedensmacher* (Kassel: J. G. Oncken Verlag, 1965), pp. 19-63.
35. Lie, *In the Cause of Peace,* pp. 160, 187.
36. Dayan, *Story of My Life,* p. 111; Bar-Yaacov, *The Israel-Syrian Armistice, passim.*
37. On the American involvement in the negotiations see *Foreign Relations of the U.S., 1949,* pp. 689-1233, *passim.*

CHAPTER 4, THE UNITED NATIONS CONCILIATION COMMISSION

1. Fred J. Khouri, "United Nations Peace Efforts," in *The Elusive Peace in the Middle East,* ed. Malcolm H. Kerr (Albany: State University of New York Press, 1975), pp. 26-27, 89; Fred J. Khouri, *The Arab-Israeli Dilemma* (Syracuse: Syracuse University Press, 1968), p. 295.
2. David P. Forsythe, *United Nations Peacemaking: The Conciliation Commission for Palestine* (Baltimore: Johns Hopkins University Press, 1972), p. 36; Nadav Safran, *From War to War* (Indianapolis: Pegasus, 1969), pp. 37-38; Nadav Safran, *The United States and Israel* (Cambridge: Harvard University Press, 1963), pp. 215-17.
3. Safran, *From War to War,* p. 37.
4. Rony Gabbay, *A Political Study of the Arab-Jewish Conflict* (Geneva: Droz, 1959), pp. 270-73. Elsewhere, pp. 316-22, Gabbay claims that an opportunity existed briefly in January-February 1950. At that time, the coming to power in Egypt of the Wafd party (which did not feel committed to past policies with respect to Palestine) and the reconciliation between Egypt and Iraq, made it possible for Egypt to conclude peace. Gabbay attributes much of the blame for missing "the golden opportunity" to Israel, which at that time conducted negotiations with Jordan but displayed indifference toward Egypt. In early February, a new government took power in Iraq, and inter-Arab rivalries flared up

again. Thereafter the opportunity no longer existed. One need not accept Gabbay's view that this brief moment in history actually provided an opportunity, to find his description of the circumstances that created the supposed opportunity interesting.

5. United States, Department of State, *Foreign Relations of the United States, 1949*, vol. VI (Washington: United States Government Printing Office, 1977), p. 750, n. 1 and p. 751, n. 3.
6. There is no unanimity on this. Azcárate, who was secretary of the commission, disputes this interpretation of Arab attitudes. See Pablo de Azcárate, *Mission in Palestine 1948-1952* (Washington: The Middle East Institute, 1966), pp. 118-19.
7. Khouri, "United Nations Peace Efforts," pp. 26-27; Forsythe, *United Nations Peacemaking*, pp. 36, 102.
8. See for example, *Foreign Relations of the U.S., 1949*, pp. 703-5, 747-48, 777, 781, 797, 962n., 965-66, 988-89.
9. Nadav Safran, *Israel: The Embattled Ally* (Cambridge: Harvard University Press, 1978), p. 336. See also Safran, *From War to War*, pp. 37-38; Forsythe, *United Nations Peacemaking*, pp. 101-2; Walter Eytan, *The First Ten Years* (New York: Simon and Schuster, 1958), pp. 31, 51-52.
10. This summary is based mainly on Forsythe, *United Nations Peacemaking*, Azcárate, *Mission in Palestine*, and the commission's progress reports. See United Nations, General Assembly, 4th session Ad Hoc Political Committee, Annex, Vol. II, pp. 1-14, *First Progress Report* (A/819), March 1, 1949, *Second Progress Report* (A/838), April 5, 1949, *Third Progress Report* (A/927), June 13, 1949, *Fourth Progress Report* (A/992), September 22, 1949; United Nations, General Assembly, 5th session Annexes, pp. 9-11, *Fifth Progress Report* (A/1252), December 14, 1949; and United Nations, General Assembly, *General Progress Report and Supplementary Report of the United Nations Conciliation Commission for Palestine*, 5th session, Suppl. 18 (A/1367/Rev. 1). The best and most comprehensive account of the PCC is Forsythe's *United Nations Peacemaking*. Also useful are Azcárate, *Mission in Palestine*, Eytan, *The First Ten Years*, Gabbay, *A Political Study*, and Khouri, "United Nations Peace Efforts."

11. United Nations, General Assembly, Resolution 194 (III), December 11, 1948.
12. *General Progress Report*, p. 2.
13. *Foreign Relations of the U.S., 1949*, pp. 683-84.
14. A glimpse of these secret discussions is provided by the letters of Eliahu Sasson, a senior member of the Israeli delegation at Lausanne to Moshe Sharett, published in *Yediot Aharonot*, February 4, 11, and 18, 1972.
15. *Third Progress Report* (A/927).
16. Forsythe, *United Nations Peacemaking*, p. 93.
17. United States, Department of State, *Foreign Relations of the United States, 1948*, Vol. V, pt. 2 (Washington: United States Government Printing Office, 1976), pp. 1663-64.
18. *Foreign Relations of the U.S., 1948*, pp. 1450, 1597, 1663; *Israel and the United Nations*; Report of a Study Group set up by the Hebrew University of Jerusalem, prepared for the Carnegie Endowment for International Peace (New York: Manhattan Publishing Company, 1956), p. 93; George E. Gruen, "Turkey, Israel and the Palestine Question, 1948-1960: A Study in the Diplomacy of Ambivalence," Ph.D. dissertation, Columbia University, 1970 (reproduced by Xerox University Microfilms, Ann Arbor, Mich.), pp. 78-84.
19. *Israel and the United Nations*, pp. 91-92.
20. *Foreign Relations of the U.S., 1949*, pp. 1206, 1256-57, 1264, 1446, 1483-85, 1508n., 1528.
21. Azcárate, *Mission in Palestine*, pp. 145-46; Earl Berger, *The Covenant and The Sword: Arab-Israeli Relations 1948-56* (London: Routledge and Kegan Paul, 1965), p. 42.
22. American motives for membership on the Conciliation Commission are summarized in *Foreign Relations of the U.S., 1948*, p. 1649. American interests as defined in National Security Council memoranda are reproduced in *Foreign Relations of the U.S., 1949*, pp. 1009, 1339-41, 1430-40. For a discussion of how French interests affected Franco-Israeli relations in 1948-1949, see M. Bar-Zohar, *Suez* (Paris: Fayard, 1964), pp. 33-41. On the French ideas regarding the Syrian-Israeli border, see Sasson in *Yediot Aharonot*, February 11 and 18, 1972. On the effect of Turkish interests on its attitudes to Israel, see Gruen, "Turkey, Israel . . . ," pp. 75-78, 82.
23. Forsythe, *United Nations Peacemaking*, pp. xiii, 102-3; *For-*

eign Relations of the U.S., 1949, pp. 793-94, 819, 904n., 910-11, 913, 920-21, 1286-87, 1299-1301.

24. Azcárate, *Mission in Palestine*, pp. 135 ff.; Forsythe, *United Nations Peacemaking*, pp. 37 ff., 55-56.
25. Azcárate, *Mission in Palestine*, p. 137; *Foreign Relations of the U.S., 1949*, pp. 927-28.
26. Forsythe, *United Nations Peacemaking*, pp. 40, 44; First Progress Report (A/819), p. 1; *Davar*, February 2 and 6, 1949.
27. *Foreign Relations of the U.S., 1949*, p. 771. The telegram, dated February 25, 1949, and addressed to the U.S. ambassador to Egypt, Stanton Griffis, was probably not drafted by Acheson himself. But it went out under his signature and he presumably agreed with the reasoning.
28. *First Progress Report* (A/819), p. 1; *Foreign Relations of the U.S., 1949*, p. 776. Azcárate, *Mission in Palestine*, p. 119, perhaps with the benefit of hindsight, claims that the armistice agreements had *slowed* the advance toward peace.
29. *Foreign Relations of the U.S., 1949*, p. 1078.
30. Forsythe, *United Nations Peacemaking*, pp. 70-71, 102, 168; Safran, *The U.S. and Israel*, p. 216; Eytan, *The First Ten Years*, pp. 31, 51-53.
31. On the Jordanian request see *Foreign Relations of the U.S., 1949*, pp. 744-46; for a justification for the commission's conduct, see Azcárate, *Mission in Palestine*, pp. 142-43.
32. Forsythe, *United Nations Peacemaking*, pp. 42-44; James G. McDonald, *My Mission in Israel* (New York: Simon and Schuster, 1951), p. 178; *Foreign Relations of the U.S., 1949*, pp. 737, 745, 785-86.
33. Eytan, *The First Ten Years*, pp. 63-64; Forsythe, *United Nations Peacemaking*, pp. 168-69; Azcárate, *Mission in Palestine*, pp. 159-60.
34. Azcarate, *Mission in Palestine*, pp. 137-38, 145-46, Forsythe, *United Nations Peacemaking*, pp. 71, 102, 155; Khouri, "United Nations Peace Efforts," p. 38.
35. *Foreign Relations of the U.S., 1949*, pp. 681-83 [footnote in text omitted].
36. Ibid., p. 782.
37. Ibid., p. 945.
38. Ibid., pp. 1072-74; McDonald, *My Mission*, pp. 181-84.
39. *Foreign Relations of the U.S., 1949*, p. 1062, 1110, 1263, 1311-13.

40. There is much interesting information on American pressures and Israeli responses in ibid. See in particular pp. 855, 880, 890-94, 964, 1060-63, 1072-74, 1176-77, 1206, 1235-37, 1249-52, 1261-66, 1281-82, 1311-13, 1328-31.
41. Ibid., pp. 796-98, 959-60, 962-66, 982-83, 1007-8, 1034-35, 1044-45, 1047-48, 1115-17, 1318, 1350-54, 1358-61, 1367-69, 1389-90, 1489.
42. Ibid., pp. 1003, 1028.
43. Ibid., p. 927.
44. Ibid., pp. 1092, 1095.
45. Ibid., p. 771; Dean Acheson, *Present at The Creation* (New York: W. W. Norton, 1969), p. 259.

CHAPTER 5, THE ANDERSON MISSION

1. For a discussion of American concerns and policies in the early 1950s see John C. Campbell, *Defense of the Middle East* (New York: Harper & Brothers, 1960), pp. 3-98.
2. "Report on the Near and Middle East by Secretary of State John Foster Dulles, 1 June 1953," reprinted in *Diplomacy in the Near and Middle East*, ed. J. C. Hurewitz, 2 vols. (Princeton: D. Van Nostrand Co., 1956), 2: 338.
3. Ibid., pp. 341-42.
4. John C. Campbell, "American Efforts for Peace," in *The Elusive Peace in the Middle East*, ed. Malcolm H. Kerr, (Albany: State University of New York Press, 1975), p. 264.
5. "Report on the Near and Middle East," p. 342.
6. Some of the American interventions aiming at the reduction of border strife are reported in Sharett's diary: Moshe Sharett, *Yoman Ishi* [Personal Diary], 8 vols. (Tel Aviv: Ma'ariv, 1978), 1: 199-200; 2: 446, 450, 465 ff. See also Michael Bar-Zohar, *Ben-Gurion*, 3 vols. (Tel Aviv: Am Oved, 1977), 2: 1030. On the Johnston negotiations for an agreement on the Jordan waters development plan see Michael Brecher, *Decisions in Israel's Foreign Policy* (London: Oxford University Press, 1974), pp. 173-224; Kathryn B. Doherty, "Jordan Waters Conflict," *International Conciliation*, no. 553 (New York: Carnegie Endowment for International Peace, May 1965); Yoram Nimrod, *Mei Meriva* [Disputed Waters] (Givat Haviva, Israel: Center for Arabic and Afro-Asian Studies, 1966); Georgiana G. Stevens, *Jordan River Partition* (Stanford: The Hoover Institution, 1965).

7. John R. Beal, *John Foster Dulles: 1888-1959* (New York: Harper & Brothers, 1959), pp. 251-52; Campbell, "American Efforts," pp. 264-65.
8. Harold Macmillan, *Tides of Fortune, 1945-1955* (New York: Harper & Row, 1969), pp. 631-33.
9. Mohamed Heikal, *Nasser: The Cairo Documents* (London: The New English Library, 1972), pp. 58-59 says that Nasser's first warning to Ambassador Byroade was delivered as early as May 22. On the debate in Washington on whether the matter was serious, see Townsend Hoopes, *The Devil and John Foster Dulles* (Boston: Little, Brown, 1973), pp. 325-27.
10. Dulles's speech has been reprinted in a number of places. For a convenient reference see Hurewitz, *Diplomacy in the Near and Middle East*, 2: 395-98.
11. Bar-Zohar, *Ben-Gurion*, 3: 1158-59.
12. This description is taken from Macmillan, *Tides of Fortune*, p. 631, and Sharett, *Yoman Ishi*, 5: 1305.
13. For Nasser's derisive reaction to the American plans see Heikal, *Nasser*, pp. 64-65. See also Macmillan, *Tides of Fortune*, pp. 631-32.
14. Sharett, *Yoman Ishi*, 1: 81. See also Michael Brecher, *The Foreign Policy System of Israel* (New Haven: Yale University Press, 1972), pp. 282-90.
15. Sharett, *Yoman Ishi*, 3: 790, 792.
16. Bar-Zohar, *Ben-Gurion*, 2: 912.
17. Sharett, *Yoman Ishi*, 4: 926, 939, 992, 1050.
18. Ibid., 1: 199-200, 2: 459, 465.
19. Ibid., 3: 675, 677, 716, 856, 866, 899, 4: 1047, 1050, 1056-57.
20. Ibid., 4: 1147.
21. *New York Times*, September 7 and 11, 1955; *Haaretz*, September 11, 1955.
22. Jean Lacouture, *Nasser* (New York: Alfred A. Knopf, 1973), pp. 266-82.
23. Dulles's notes on his visit to the Middle East as recorded under the title "Important Points of Trip," pp. 1-2. These are deposited in a 1953 file on the Middle East, in Box 73 of the Personal Papers of John Foster Dulles, Princeton University Library.

24. *New York Times*, August 28, 1955; Macmillan, *Tides of Fortune*, p. 635.
25. See Sharett's statement to the Knesset on October 18, 1955, in Hurewitz, *Diplomacy in the Near and Middle East*, 2: 405-12. On the policy debate in Israel following the announcement of the arms deal see Sharett, *Yoman Ishi*, 4: 1180, 1185, 1197, 1215. A detailed account of his trip to Paris and Geneva can be found in Sharett, *Yoman Ishi*, 5: 1243-78.
26. *New York Times*, October 11, 14, and 18, 1955.
27. Louis L. Gerson, *John Foster Dulles* (New York: Cooper Square Publications, 1967), pp. 266-72; Macmillan, *Tides of Fortune*, p. 642.
28. Eden's speech and Ben-Gurion's response are reprinted in Royal Institute of International Affairs, *Documents on International Affairs, 1955*, ed. Noble Frankland (London: Oxford University Press, 1958), pp. 382-88. On the Egyptian response see Fred J. Khouri, *The Arab-Israeli Dilemma* (Syracuse University Press, 1968), p. 302; *New York Times*, November 14, 1955. On Anglo-American differences, see *New York Times*, November 19, 22, and 30; December 5, 1955. In his memoirs, Eden subsequently thought that "it was unwise" on his part to raise the border problem after Russian arms had begun to flow to Egypt. See his *Full Circle* (Boston: Houghton Mifflin, 1960), p. 368.
29. Sharett, *Yoman Ishi*, 5: 1306 (December 8, 1955).
30. Ibid., p. 1316.
31. Miles Copeland, "Nasser's Secret Diplomacy with Israel," *The Times* (London), June 24, 1971.
32. Ben-Gurion's diary record of the talks was published in installments in the Tel Aviv newspaper *Maariv*, July 2, 9, 16, and 23, 1971. Short versions were also published by Miles Copeland, "Nasser's Secret Diplomacy"; by Heikal, in *Nasser*, p. 64; in Michael Bar-Zohar's story of Isser Harel and Israel's security services, *Hamemune* (Jerusalem: Weidenfeld and Nicolson, 1971), pp. 125-28; and in Teddy Kollek, *For Jerusalem* (Tel Aviv: Steimatzky's, 1978), pp. 115-16. Scattered references in volume five of Sharett's diary are also of interest. The account that follows is based on Ben-Gurion's version in *Maariv*.
33. *Maariv*, July 16, 1971 (My translation from Hebrew).

34. On the role of the CIA in Egyptian-American relations, see Miles Copeland, *The Game of Nations* (London: Weidenfeld and Nicolson, 1969), and Heikal, *Nasser.* For some indications of its role in Israeli-American relations see Sharett, *Yoman Ishi*, 4: 1056; Kollek, *For Jerusalem*, pp. 97-98; Bar-Zohar, *Hamemune*, pp. 124-29.
35. Bar-Zohar, *Hamemune*, p. 126.
36. Cf. Gerson, *Dulles*, pp. 274-77.

CHAPTER 6, THE JARRING MISSION

1. For a more detailed discussion of Israeli attitudes after the war, see Nadav Safran, *Israel: The Embattled Ally* (Cambridge: Harvard University Press, 1978), pp. 415-17. On Israel's peace offer on the morrow of the war see Abba Eban, *An Autobiography* (Tel Aviv: Steimatzky's, 1977), p. 436.
2. Lyndon B. Johnson, *The Vantage Point* (New York: Holt, Rinehart and Winston, 1971), pp. 303-4; Arthur Lall, *The UN and the Middle East Crisis, 1967*, rev. ed. (New York: Columbia University Press, 1970), pp. 137-39; Bernard Reich, *Quest for Peace: United States-Israel Relations and the Arab-Israeli Conflict* (New Brunswick, N.J.: Transaction Books, 1977), pp. 83-87. Reich's study is particularly valuable for its rich documentation.
3. Lall, *The UN and the Crisis*, pp. 128-31; Safran, *Israel: The Embattled Ally*, pp. 420-22.
4. A detailed account of the diplomacy at the UN in the summer of 1967 can be found in Lall, *The UN and the Crisis*, pp. 107-219.
5. *Introduction to the Annual Report of the Secretary-General on the Work of the Organization, 16 June 1966-15 June 1967*, United Nations, General Assembly, 22nd Session, Supplement No. 1a (A/6701/Add.1), p. 7. For statements advocating the dispatch of a special representative in the course of the summer and fall, see Lall, *The UN and the Crisis*, pp. 134, 136, 223-24, 226, 227.
6. Quoted in Reich, *Quest for Peace*, p. 130, n. 26. For the evolution of the Israeli position see the *New York Times*, August 15 and September 11, 1967.
7. *New York Times*, October 15 and 17, November 24, 1967; U Thant, *View from the UN* (London: David & Charles, 1978), p. 285.

8. Thant, *View from the UN*, pp. 285, 287-88. An interesting account of the Jarring negotiations published after this chapter was written is in Gideon Raphael, *Destination Peace: Three Decades of Israeli Foreign Policy* (New York: Stein & Day, 1981), pp. 186-200, 250-57.
9. It is of interest to mention that Robert Anderson played some part in the negotiations with President Nasser on these questions. In the absence of diplomatic relations he apparently served as one of the channels for American-Egyptian contacts (*New York Times*, November 2 and 3, 1967).
10. United Nations, Security Council, Resolution 242 (November 22, 1967). On the negotiations leading to the adoption of the resolution see Lall, *The UN and the Crisis*, pp. 220-63; Thant, *View from the UN*, pp. 284-94; Eban, *An Autobiography*, pp. 448-53; Gideon Rafael, "UN Resolution 242: a Common Denominator," in *The Israel-Arab Reader*, ed. Walter Laqueur, 3rd ed. (New York: Bantam Books, 1976), pp. 342-59.
11. *The Economist*, November 25, 1967, p. 837.
12. Richard Crossman, *The Diaries of a Cabinet Minister*, 3 vols. (New York: Holt, Rinehart and Winston, 1977), 2: 537 (Entry for October 26, 1967).
13. United Nations, Security Council, Official Records, 23rd yr., Supplements, Document S/8309/Add.1, January 17, 1968; Thant, *A View from the UN*, p. 296.
14. United Nations, Security Council, *Official Records*, 26th yr., Supplements, Document S/10070, January 4, 1971.
15. *New York Times*, May 2, 1968; *Yediot Aharonot*, May 21, 1968.
16. UN Doc. S/10070, January 4, 1971; Eban, *An Autobiography*, pp. 455-56; *New York Times*, October 9 and November 7, 1968. Israel's gradual concessions are traced in detail in Anders Lidén, *Security and Recognition: A Study of Change in Israel's Official Doctrine 1967-1974* (Lund: Studentlitteratur, 1979), pp. 83-98.
17. UN Doc. S/10070.
18. *Yediot Aharonot*, January 26, 1968; *New York Times*, May 2 and October 27, 1968.
19. *New York Times*, October 9, November 7, 8, and 10, 1968.
20. UN Doc. S/10070.
21. Ibid., Eban, *An Autobiography*, pp. 455-56.

22. William B. Quandt, *Decade of Decisions* (Berkeley: University of California Press, 1977), pp. 65-67; John C. Campbell, "American Efforts for Peace," in *The Elusive Peace in the Middle East*, ed. Malcolm H. Kerr (Albany: State University of New York Press, 1975), pp. 286-87; Eban, *An Autobiography*, pp. 457-58; Mohamed Heikal, *The Road to Ramadan* (Glasgow: Fontana/Collins, 1976), p. 51; Henry Kissinger, *White House Years* (Boston: Little, Brown, 1979), p. 345; *New York Times*, February 22, March 6, July 18, 1968; *Maariv*, June 28, 1968.
23. Lawrence L. Whetten, *The Canal War: Four-Power Conflict in the Middle East* (Cambridge: MIT Press, 1974), p. 67; *New York Times*, June 30, July 5, 6, 7, 9, 11, and 13, 1968.
24. Lall, *The UN and the Crisis*, pp. 289, 293; Thant, *View from the UN*, pp. 313-15; Reich, *Quest for Peace*, pp. 90-96, 98-102; *New York Times*, January 1, 2, 3, 4, 5, 8, 13, 16, and 18, 1968.
25. Campbell, "American Efforts," pp. 288-90; Quandt, *Decade of Decisions*, pp. 76-83; Reich, *Quest for Peace*, pp. 97-102; Charles Yost, "Israel and the Arabs," *Atlantic*, January 1969, pp. 80-85; Stanley Hoffmann, "Franco-American Differences Over the Arab Israeli Conflict, 1967-1971," *Public Policy* 19 (Fall 1971): 539-65. For Kissinger's critical view of these efforts, and the differences between him and the State Department, see his *White House Years*, pp. 350-53.
26. Quoted in Reich, *Quest for Peace*, p. 143, n. 107.
27. Thant, *View from the UN*, p. 328.
28. News conference, April 7, 1969, quoted in Reich, *Quest for Peace*, p. 143, n. 108.
29. Thant, *View from the UN*, p. 329.
30. Heikal, *The Road to Ramadan*, pp. 54-55.
31. UN Doc. S/10070. See also S/8309/Add.4, December 3, 1968.
32. UN Doc. S/10070.
33. The American proposal is reproduced in ibid.
34. A number of interesting analyses of the great power talks and the related political-military contests, and of the Rogers Plan have been published. See Kissinger, *White House Years*, pp. 349-79; Campbell, "American Efforts," pp. 288-94; Quandt, *Decade of Decisions*, pp. 83-98; Reich, *Quest for Peace*, pp. 103-25; Safran, *Israel: The Embattled Ally*, pp. 431-41; and Whetten, *The Canal War*, pp. 67-88.

35. UN Doc. S/10070; Quandt, *Decade of Decisions*, pp. 131-33; Reich, *Quest for Peace*, pp. 166-67; Whetten, *The Canal War*, pp. 129-44.
36. UN Doc. S/10070/Add.2, March 5, 1971. The full text of Jarring's *aide-mémoire* to Egypt and Israel is reproduced in John Norton Moore, ed., *The Arab-Israeli Conflict: Readings and Documents*, abr. and rev. ed. (Princeton: Princeton University Press, 1977), pp. 1148-50.
37. Quandt, *Decade of Decisions*, pp. 131, 134. See also Kissinger, *White House Years*, pp. 1277-79.
38. UN Doc. S/10070/Add.2; for the full text of the Egyptian reply see Moore, *The Arab-Israeli Conflict*, pp. 1151-53.
39. On these assurances see Quandt, *Decade of Decisions*, pp. 134-35; Kissinger, *White House Years*, p. 1279.
40. UN Doc. S/10070/Add.2. For the text of Israel's reply see Moore, *The Arab-Israeli Conflict*, pp. 1154-56. On Israel's reaction to Jarring's initiative, and the debate on how to respond to it, see Eban, *An Autobiography*, pp. 472-74; Yitzhak Rabin, *Pinkas Sherut* [Service Notebook], 2 vols. (Tel Aviv: Maariv, 1979), 2: 331-34; Safran, *Israel: The Embattled Ally*, pp. 457-59; *New York Times*, February 13, 16, 17, 18, and 20, 1971; *Maariv*, February 12, 14, 15, 1971.
41. Thant, *View from the UN*, pp. 348-49; United Nations, Security Council, Official Records, 28th yr., Supplements, Document S/10929, May 18, 1973.
42. UN Doc. S/10929.
43. UN Doc. S/10070.
44. For observations on Jarring's personality, see Eban, *An Autobiography*, p. 454; "Discreet Messenger to the Middle East," *Time*, August 17, 1970, p. 18; "Diplomat Gunnar Jarring—The Man in the Middle," *Newsweek*, August 17, 1970, p. 12.

CHAPTER 7, THE ROGERS INITIATIVE AND THE INTERIM AGREEMENT TALKS

1. William B. Quandt, *Decade of Decisions* (Berkeley: University of California Press, 1977), pp. 92-93, 99. An illuminating account of the negotiations discussed in this chapter, published after the manuscript was completed, is in Gideon Raphael, *Destination Peace: Three Decades of Is-*

raeli Foreign Policy (New York: Stein & Day, 1981), pp. 221-30, 258-72.

2. This background of the Rogers Initiative is based on Quandt, *Decade of Decisions*, pp. 94, 97-98; Nadav Safran, *Israel: The Embattled Ally* (Cambridge: Harvard University Press, 1978), pp. 438-41; Lawrence L. Whetten, *The Canal War: Four-Power Conflict in the Middle East* (Cambridge: MIT Press, 1974), pp. 94-95, 98-99; Mohamed Heikal, *The Road to Ramadan* (Glasgow: Fontana/Collins, 1976), pp. 89-90; Anwar el-Sadat, *In Search of Identity* (Glasgow: Fontana/Collins, 1978), p. 238. See also Henry Kissinger, *White House Years* (Boston: Little, Brown, 1979), pp. 558-79.
3. Rogers's statement is reprinted in *United States Foreign Policy, 1969-1970: A Report by the Secretary of State* (Washington: U.S. Government Printing Office, 1971), p. 458. For Kissinger's briefing, see his *White House Years*, pp. 579-80; Marvin Kalb and Bernard Kalb, *Kissinger* (Boston: Little, Brown, 1974), p. 193.
4. Heikal, *The Road to Ramadan*, p. 91; Sadat, *In Search of Identity*, pp. 239-40; *New York Times*, June 26 and 27, 1970; Daniel Dishon, ed., *Middle East Record, 1969-1970* (Jerusalem: Israel Universities Press for the Shiloach Center for Middle Eastern and African Studies, Tel Aviv University, 1977), pp. 66-67.
5. Heikal, *The Road to Ramadan*, p. 91; Sadat, *In Search of Identity*, p. 157; Safran, *Israel: The Embattled Ally*, pp. 444-45; Whetten, *The Canal War*, pp. 103-6; Dishon, *Middle East Record*, pp. 67-70.
6. Michael Brecher, *Decisions in Israel's Foreign Policy* (London: Oxford University Press, 1974), pp. 489-90; Dan Margalit, *Sheder Mehabayit Halavan* [A Message from the White House] (Tel Aviv: Otpaz, 1971), pp. 122-23, 127-29; Safran, *Israel: The Embattled Ally*, pp. 442-43; Kissinger, *White House Years*, pp. 567-69.
7. Margalit, *Sheder Mehabayit Halavan*, pp. 132-37; Yitzhak Rabin, *Pinkas Sherut* [Service Notebook], 2 vols. (Tel Aviv: Maariv, 1979), 1: 293-95.
8. Nixon's letter has not been published. This account is based on Brecher, *Decisions in Israel's Foreign Policy*, p. 493; Quandt, *Decade of Decisions*, p. 102; Safran, *Israel: The Embattled Ally*, p. 446.

9. Brecher, *Decisions in Israel's Foreign Policy*, pp. 495-97; Margalit, *Sheder Mehabayit Halavan*, pp. 156-83; Quandt, *Decade of Decisions*, p. 102; Safran, *Israel: The Embattled Ally*, pp. 446-47.
10. Brecher, *Decisions in Israel's Foreign Policy*, pp. 491-92, n. 6. The text of Israel's reply is reproduced in Meron Medzini, ed., *Israel's Foreign Relations: Selected Documents, 1947-1974*, 2 vols. (Jerusalem: Ministry of Foreign Affairs, 1976), 2: 916-17. See also Margalit, *Sheder Mehabayit Halavan*, pp. 179-82; Rabin, *Pinkas Sherut*, 1: 297-99; Bernard Reich, *Quest for Peace* (New Brunswick, N.J.: Transaction Books, 1977), p. 162. On Kennedy's use of the "Trollope Ploy" see Graham T. Allison, *Essence of Decision* (Boston: Little, Brown, 1971), p. 227.
11. Abba Eban, *An Autobiography* (Tel Aviv: Steimatzky's, 1977), p. 466; Quandt, *Decade of Decisions*, pp. 98-99; Rabin, *Pinkas Sherut*, 1: 287, 290.
12. Eban, *An Autobiography*, p. 472; Yehoshua Raviv, "Nisyonot Mukdamim Lehesder Benayim Bein Israel Lemitsrayim (Bashanim 1971-1972)" [Early Attempts for an Interim Agreement Between Israel and Egypt (in the years 1971-1972)], *Maarachot*, nos. 243-44 (April-May 1975): 2-17 (the author, Brig. Gen., Res. Raviv served at the time of the interim agreement negotiations as military secretary to Dayan); Gad Yaakobi, "Hahesder Shelo Haya" [The Agreement that Was Not], *Yediot Aharonot*, September 9, 16, 23, 1977.
13. Rabin, *Pinkas Sherut*, 2: 326-27; Raviv, "Nisyonot Mukdamim"; Yaakobi, "Hahesder Shelo Haya"; Whetten, *The Canal War*, pp. 167-68.
14. For Sadat's speech see *The New Middle East*, no. 30 (March 1971): 32-35; and *Arab Report and Record*, February 1-14, 1971, pp. 96-97; Arnaud de Borchgrave, "A Talk with Sadat on Peace Terms," *Newsweek*, February 22, 1971, pp. 12-13; Quandt, *Decade of Decisions*, pp. 136-37; Sadat, *In Search of Identity*, p. 263.
15. Some evidence to support this interpretation can be found in Heikal, *The Road to Ramadan*, pp. 115-18 and Sadat, *In Search of Identity*, pp. 249-50, 262-65.
16. Heikal, *The Road to Ramadan*, p. 114; *New York Times*, March 12, 1971.

17. Israel, *Divrei Haknesset* [Parliamentary Debates], Vol. 59, February 9, 1971, p. 1305.
18. Quandt, *Decade of Decisions*, p. 138.
19. Quoted by Whetten, *The Canal War*, p. 193.
20. Quandt, *Decade of Decisions*, p. 140.
21. Rabin, *Pinkas Sherut*, 2: 338-39.
22. Moshe Dayan, *Avnei Derech* [Milestones] (Jerusalem and Tel Aviv: Edanim and Dvir, 1976), pp. 526-27; Eban, *An Autobiography*, pp. 474-75; Quandt, *Decade of Decisions*, pp. 139-40; Raviv, "Nisyonot Mukdamim"; *New York Times*, April 20 and 21, 1971; Rabin, *Pinkas Sherut*, 2: 346-49.
23. Kissinger, *White House Years*, pp. 1281-83; Quandt, *Decade of Decisions*, pp. 139-40; Rabin, *Pinkas Sherut*, 2: 349.
24. See Sadat's interview in *Newsweek*, December 13, 1971, pp. 15-17; *New York Times*, May 7, 1971.
25. *Newsweek*, December 13, 1971, pp. 15-17; Heikal, *The Road to Ramadan*, pp. 131-32.
26. Dayan, *Avnei Derech*, pp. 526-27.
27. Ibid., pp. 527-28; Eban, *An Autobiography*, pp. 475-76; Golda Meir's statement to the Knesset, *Divrei Haknesset*, Vol. 61, June 9, 1971, pp. 2669-70; *New York Times*, May 7, 8, 9, 1971.
28. *Newsweek*, December 13, 1971, pp. 15-17; Quandt, *Decade of Decisions*, p. 141.
29. Heikal, *The Road to Ramadan*, pp. 144-45; *Newsweek*, December 13, 1971; Kissinger, *White House Years*, pp. 1283-84; Quandt, *Decade of Decisions*, pp. 142-43; Reich, *Quest for Peace*, pp. 185, 223-24, n. 127; Whetten, *The Canal War*, pp. 190-91.
30. Heikal, *The Road to Ramadan*, pp. 126-38.
31. Sadat, *In Search of Identity*, pp. 269-70. Heikal claims that the initiative for the treaty came from Sadat in March 1971. See Mohamed Heikal, *The Sphinx and the Commissar* (New York: Harper & Row, 1978), pp. 222, 227-28. On the treaty and its probable connection with the Rogers negotiations, see also Alvin Z. Rubinstein, *Red Star on the Nile* (Princeton: Princeton University Press, 1977), pp. 144-52.
32. There are some differences between the two versions that Sadat gave of his conversation with Sterner. See *Newsweek*, December 13, 1971; and Sadat, *In Search of Identity*, pp. 339-40.

33. Safran, *Israel: The Embattled Ally*, p. 461; Quandt, *Decade of Decisions*, p. 143.
34. *New York Times*, August 9, 1971; Yaakobi, "Hahesder Shelo Haya," *Yediot Aharonot*, September 30, 1977; *Maariv*, August 1, 2, 3, 4, 5, 6, 8, 9, 1971.
35. *Newsweek*, December 13, 1971.
36. Sadat, *In Search of Identity*, pp. 340-41; *New York Times*, September 17, 1971; *Arab Report and Record*, September 16-30, 1971, p. 514.
37. Rogers's address to the UN General Assembly is reprinted in *United States Foreign Policy, 1971* (Washington: U.S. Government Printing Office, 1972), pp. 461-68. On the proposal for "proximity talks," see *New York Times*, October 17, 1971.
38. *Newsweek*, December 13, 1971.
39. Prime Minister Golda Meir's statement to the Knesset, *Divrei Haknesset*, Vol. 62, October 26, 1971, pp. 9-14.
40. Rabin, *Pinkas Sherut*, 2: 367; Kissinger, *White House Years*, pp. 1288-89.
41. Rabin, *Pinkas Sherut*, 2: 353-68; Dov Goldstein's interview with Rabin in *Maariv*, December 1, 1972; Quandt, *Decade of Decisions*, pp. 146-47; *New York Times*, January 21, February 3, 1972.
42. *Newsweek*, March 6, 1972, p. 24.
43. Quandt, *Decade of Decisions*, p. 142; Heikal, *The Road to Ramadan*, pp. 141-42.
44. Dayan, *Avnei Derech*, pp. 527-28; Rabin, *Pinkas Sherut*, 2: 344-49, 354-55.
45. Quandt, *Decade of Decisions*, p. 144.
46. Ibid., p. 141. Both Quandt (ibid., p. 144) and Rabin (*Pinkas Sherut*, 2: 353) report that Kissinger criticized the State Department for employing this tactic.
47. This is implied in Heikal, *The Road to Ramadan*, pp. 153-54. See also Sadat, *In Search of Identity*, pp. 340-41, 347; and Kissinger, *White House Years*, pp. 1292-95.

CHAPTER 8, THE AFRICAN PRESIDENTS

1. For a background on Israel's relations with Africa, see Elliott P. Skinner, "African States and Israel: Uneasy Relations in a World of Crises," *Journal of African Studies* 2 (1975): 1-23.
2. For the resolutions of OAU conferences after 1967 and the

controversies that accompanied them, see *Africa Research Bulletin*, Political, Social and Cultural Series (September 1967): 854, 856, 857; (February 1968): 972; (September 1968): 1174-75; (February 1969): 1315, 1316; (September 1969): 1515, 1517; (March 1970): 1691; (September 1970): 1860-61. See also Jon Woronoff, *Organizing African Unity* (Metuchen, N.J.: The Scarecrow Press, 1970), pp. 616-18.

3. The full text of the resolution is reproduced in Colin Legum, ed., *Africa Contemporary Record, 1971-1972*, Annual Survey and Documents (London: Rex Collings, 1972), pp. C 5-6. The members of the OAU in 1971 were:

Algeria*	Ghana	Nigeria
Botswana	Guinea	Rwanda
Burundi	Ivory Coast	Senegal
Cameroun	Kenya	Sierra Leone
Central African Republic	Lesotho	Somali Republic‡
Chad	Liberia	Sudan*
Congo Democratic Republic	Libya*	Swaziland
Dahomey	Malagasy Republic	Tanzania
Egypt*	Malawi	Togo
Equatorial Guinea	Mali	Tunisia*
Ethiopia	Mauritania†	Uganda
Gabon	Mauritius	Upper Volta
Gambia	Morocco*	Zambia
	Niger	Zaire

* Member of the Arab League
† Joined the Arab League in 1973
‡ Joined the Arab League in 1974

4. Ran Kochan, "An African Peace Mission in the Middle East," *African Affairs* 72 (April 1973): 188. My account of the African initiative has benefited from Kochan's article, as well as from Colin Legum, "Israel's Year in Africa: A Study of Secret Diplomacy," in *Africa Contemporary Record, 1972-1973*, pp. A 123-36; Yassin El-Ayouty, "The OAU and the Arab-Israeli Conflict: A Case of Mediation That Failed," in *The Organization of African Unity After Ten Years*, ed. Yassin El-Ayouty (New York: Praeger Publishers, 1975), pp. 189-212; Susan Aurelia Gitelson, "The OAU Mission and the Middle East Conflict," *International Organization* 27 (1973): 413-19.
5. Quoted in Kochan, "An African Peace Mission," p. 188.
6. Legum, *Africa Contemporary Record, 1971-1972*, p. C 6.

7. Zdenek Červenka, "The Organization of African Unity 1971," in *Africa Contemporary Record, 1971-1972*, p. A 87; Legum, "Israel's Year in Africa," p. A 125.
8. *Maariv*, June 24, 1971.
9. *Africa Research Bulletin* (August 1971): 2187; Kochan, "An African Peace Mission," pp. 189-90; Legum, "Israel's Year in Africa," pp. A 125-26.
10. Kochan, "An African Peace Mission," pp. 193-95; Gitelson, "The OAU Mission and the Middle East Conflict," pp. 415, 419; Mohamed A. El-Khawas, "Africa and the Middle Eastern Crisis," *Issue* 5 (1975): 37. On the difficulty in selecting a chairman for the subcommittee, see Kochan, "An African Peace Mission," p. 190, n. 17.
11. El-Ayouti, "The OAU and the Arab-Israeli Conflict," p. 193; Legum, "Israel's Year in Africa," p. A 125.
12. *Africa Research Bulletin* (June 1971): 2144-55.
13. *Le Monde*, November 2 and 4, 1971; *New York Times*, November 3, 1971.
14. *New York Times*, November 6 and 8, 1971; *Africa Research Bulletin* (November 1971): 2275-76.
15. Quoted by Legum, "Israel's Year in Africa," p. A 126. According to Legum, Mobutu did not attend the Dakar meeting. See also *Africa Research Bulletin* (November 1971): 2276; Kochan, "An African Peace Mission," p. 190, n. 18.
16. Kochan, "An African Peace Mission," p. 190; *Maariv*, November 14, 1971.
17. *New York Times*, November 21 and 22, 1971.
18. Legum, "Israel's Year in Africa," p. A 128. On this round of talks see also *Africa Research Bulletin* (November 1971): 2276-77; *Le Monde*, November 24, 1971; *Maariv*, November 23 and 26, 1971.
19. The committee's proposals were made public by Israel. See United Nations, General Assembly and Security Council, Official Records, Twenty-sixth year, "Letter dated 9 December 1971 from the representative of Israel to the Secretary-General," document A/8566-S/10438. They are reproduced in Legum, "Israel's Year in Africa," p. A 128.
20. For the Israeli reply see A/8566 and S/10438, December 9, 1971; for the Egyptian reply, see United Nations, General Assembly and Security Council, Official Records, Twenty-sixth year, "Letter dated 10 December 1971 from the rep-

resentative of Egypt to the Secretary-General" document A/8576-S/10443. Both are reproduced in Legum, "Israel's Year in Africa," pp. A 128-29.

21. As quoted by the representative of Guinea in the General Assembly debate, December 13, 1971, United Nations, General Assembly, *Official Records* (A/PV. 2016), p. 10. The summary of the report is drawn from Legum, "Israel's Year in Africa," pp. A 129-30.
22. Quoted from Ould Daddah's report by Legum, "Israel's Year in Africa," p. A 130.
23. United Nations, General Assembly and Security Council, *Report of the Secretary-General on the Activities of the Special Representative to the Middle East* (A/8541-S/10403), November 30, 1971. The quotes are from paragraphs 27 and 28.
24. United Nations, General Assembly, Resolution 2799 (XXVI), December 13, 1971.
25. On the discussions in the African Group and in the General Assembly see Legum, "Israel's Year in Africa," pp. A 130-32; El-Ayouty, "The OAU and the Arab-Israeli Conflict," pp. 199-205; Gitelson, "The OAU Mission and the Middle East Conflict," pp. 416-17; and United Nations, General Assembly, *Official Records* (A/PV. 2016).
26. *Africa Research Bulletin* (February 1972): 2392.
27. *Africa Research Bulletin* (June 1972): 2497.
28. Legum, "Israel's Year in Africa," pp. A 132-33; Kochan, "An African Peace Mission," pp. 195-96. The text of the Rabat resolution is reproduced in *Africa Contemporary Record, 1972-1973*, pp. C 23-24. For Senghor's explanation of the committee's failure see also his interview with Tullia Zevi, "Africans, Arabs, Israelis: A Triad of Suffering Peoples," *Africa Report* 17 (July-August 1972): 11-13.
29. Cf. Kochan, "An African Peace Mission," pp. 193-95. Kochan reports (p. 194, n. 26), that after the humiliation at the UN the Senegalese Foreign Ministry claimed that Senghor acted on the supposition that Israel's reply to the committee was in fact an indirect favorable reply to Jarring.

CHAPTER 9, KISSINGER, 1973-1975

1. William B. Quandt, *Decade of Decisions* (Berkeley: University of California Press, 1977), p. 285. As this book was

going to press interesting analyses of Kissinger's mediation from different perspectives were published in *Dynamics of Third Party Mediation: Kissinger in the Middle East*, ed. Jeffrey Z. Rubin (New York: Praeger, 1981). Kissinger's second volume of memoirs, *Years of Upheaval* (Boston: Little, Brown, 1982) was published when this book was already in proof, and I was therefore unfortunately unable to use this important source in analyzing his mediation.

2. Stanley Hoffmann, *Primacy or World Order* (New York: McGraw-Hill, 1978), pp. 73-78; George W. Ball, *Diplomacy for a Crowded World* (London: The Bodley Head, 1976), pp. 137-39.
3. Gil Carl Alroy, *The Kissinger Experience* (New York: Horizon Press, 1975).
4. Quoted by Quandt, *Decade of Decisions*, p. 181.
5. Richard Nixon, *RN: The Memoirs of Richard Nixon* (London: Sidgwick & Jackson, 1978), p. 921. See also Quandt, *Decade of Decisions*, pp. 176-91. Quandt's account is of particular interest since he served at that time on the National Security Council staff. Kissinger denies that "the Nixon Administration deliberately withheld supplies from Israel to make it more tractable in negotiations." See Kissinger, *Years of Upheaval*, p. 496. Furthermore, his account does not mention any desire to create a stalemate.
6. UN Security Council Resolution 338, October 22, 1973.
7. Quandt, *Decade of Decisions*, p. 214.
8. Quoted in Walter Laqueur, ed., *The Israel-Arab Reader*, 3rd ed. (New York: Bantam Books, 1976), p. 469. For details on American-Egyptian communications during the war, see Kissinger, *Years of Upheaval*, pp. 481-82, 499-500, 522-23, 527, and 530-31.
9. Mohamed Heikal, *The Road to Ramadan* (Glasgow: Fontana/Collins, 1975), p. 250; Shlomo Aronson, *Conflict and Bargaining in the Middle East: An Israeli Perspective* (Baltimore: Johns Hopkins University Press, 1978), p. 191.
10. Matti Golan, *The Secret Conversations of Henry Kissinger* (New York: Bantam Books, 1976), pp. 93-94; Marvin Kalb and Bernard Kalb, *Kissinger* (Boston: Little, Brown, 1974), p. 501; Walter Laqueur, *Confrontation* (London: Abacus, 1974), p. 187; Nadav Safran, *Israel: The Embattled Ally* (Cambridge: Harvard University Press, 1978), pp. 507-8.

11. Golan, *The Secret Conversations*, pp. 95-103, 107, 110-11.
12. Golda Meir, *My Life* (Tel Aviv: Steimatzky's, 1975), p. 375.
13. Quandt, *Decade of Decisions*, p. 214.
14. Ibid., pp. 214-15.
15. Golan, *The Secret Conversations*, pp. 105-10; Kalb, *Kissinger*, pp. 503-4; Quandt, *Decade of Decisions*, pp. 214-16; Safran, *Israel: The Embattled Ally*, pp. 508-10.
16. Kalb, *Kissinger*, p. 510. See also Mohamed Heikal, *The Sphinx and the Commissar* (New York: Harper & Row, 1978), p. 263.
17. Edward R. F. Sheehan, *The Arabs, Israelis, and Kissinger* (New York: Reader's Digest Press, 1976), pp. 48-49. See also Quandt, *Decade of Decisions*, p. 217; Safran, *Israel: The Embattled Ally*, pp. 510-11; Kalb, *Kissinger*, pp. 507-10.
18. The text of the agreement is reprinted in John Norton Moore, ed., *The Arab-Israeli Conflict: Readings and Documents*, abr. and rev. ed. (Princeton: Princeton University Press, 1977), p. 1195. On the last stages of the negotiations see Golan, *The Secret Conversations*, pp. 112-15; Kalb, *Kissinger*, pp. 513-14; Quandt, *Decade of Decisions*, p. 217; Safran, *Israel: The Embattled Ally*, p. 511.
19. *Haaretz*, December 17, 1973. A detailed account of Soviet-American contacts concerning the Geneva Conference was published after this book was set in proof. See Kissinger, *Years of Upheaval*, pp. 755-56, 758, 767, 785, 794-95.
20. Quandt, *Decade of Decisions*, pp. 220-23; Safran, *Israel: The Embattled Ally*, pp. 516-17; Sheehan, *The Arabs, Israelis, and Kissinger*, pp. 95-97.
21. Kalb, *Kissinger*, pp. 522-23.
22. The text of the invitation is reproduced in Sheehan, *The Arabs, Israelis, and Kissinger*, p. 238.
23. Golan, *The Secret Conversations*, p. 127; Quandt, *Decade of Decisions*, p. 222; Sheehan, *The Arabs, Israelis, and Kissinger*, p. 108.
24. Golan, *The Secret Conversations*, p. 96; Quandt, *Decade of Decisions*, p. 215.
25. Quandt, *Decade of Decisions*, p. 220. See also Abba Eban, *An Autobiography* (Tel Aviv: Steimatzky's, 1977), p. 541; Golan, *The Secret Conversations*, pp. 120, 124; Kalb, *Kissinger*, p. 518; Sheehan, *The Arabs, Israelis, and Kissinger*, pp. 80-81.

26. Moshe Dayan, *Story of My Life* (Tel Aviv: Steimatzky's, 1976), p. 458. The Hebrew version of Dayan's autobiography is somewhat more detailed on this point. See Moshe Dayan, *Avnei Derech* [Milestones] (Jerusalem and Tel Aviv: Edanim and Dvir, 1976), pp. 675-76, 695-96.
27. Kalb, *Kissinger*, p. 530. See also Kalb, *Kissinger*, pp. 520-21; Sheehan, *The Arabs, Israelis, and Kissinger*, pp. 88, 109; Quandt, *Decade of Decisions*, p. 226.
28. Safran, *Israel: The Embattled Ally*, pp. 521-23.
29. Quandt, *Decade of Decisions*, pp. 220-21.
30. The following is based mainly on Golan, *The Secret Conversations*, pp. 119-20, 150-51, 159-69; Kalb, *Kissinger*, pp. 532-39; Quandt, *Decade of Decisions*, pp. 219-20, 224-28; Safran, *Israel: The Embattled Ally*, pp. 518-19, 522-27; Sheehan, *The Arabs, Israelis, and Kissinger*, pp. 109-11; Dayan, *Avnei Derech*, pp. 692-94, 696-704. For the text of the agreement see Moore, *The Arab-Israeli Conflict*, pp. 1197-98 or Sheehan, *The Arabs, Israelis, and Kissinger*, pp. 239-40.
31. For a detailed discussion see Aronson, *Conflict and Bargaining*, pp. 232-38.
32. Quandt, *Decade of Decisions*, pp. 235-38. On Soviet attitudes to these negotiations see Galia Golan, *Yom Kippur and After: The Soviet Union and the Middle East Crisis* (Cambridge: Cambridge University Press, 1977), pp. 219-32.
33. Quandt, *Decade of Decisions*, pp. 229-31, 234-35. According to Sheehan, *The Arabs, Israelis, and Kissinger*, p. 116, Kissinger promised to undertake the shuttle in return for the lifting of the embargo. See also the *New York Times*, March 20, 1974.
34. *New York Times*, January 5 and June 17, 1974, respectively.
35. Quandt, *Decade of Decisions*, p. 239.
36. Golan, *The Secret Conversations*, pp. 182-83; Quandt, *Decade of Decisions*, pp. 231-32; Safran, *Israel, The Embattled Ally*, p. 528.
37. The following is based mainly on Golan, *The Secret Conversations*, pp. 182-208; Quandt, *Decade of Decisions*, pp. 230-43; Sheehan, *The Arabs, Israelis, and Kissinger*, pp. 114-24. For the text of the agreement see Moore, *The Arab-Israeli Conflict*, pp. 1200-1202 or Sheehan, *The Arabs, Israelis, and Kissinger*, pp. 241-43.

38. The text of the American assurance is reprinted in Sheehan, *The Arabs, Israelis, and Kissinger*, pp. 243-44.
39. Quandt, *Decade of Decisions*, pp. 232-33, 239-41, 243.
40. *New York Times*, March 31, 1974; Quandt, *Decade of Decisions*, pp. 235-36.
41. Quandt, *Decade of Decisions*, p. 242; Sheehan, *The Arabs, Israelis, and Kissinger*, pp. 126-27; Golan, *The Secret Conversations*, p. 207; *New York Times*, May 28 and 31, 1974.
42. Quandt, *Decade of Decisions*, p. 239; Dayan, *Story of My Life*, pp. 473-74.
43. Golan, *The Secret Conversations*, pp. 189-90; Sheehan, *The Arabs, Israelis, and Kissinger*, p. 118.
44. Golan, *The Secret Conversations*, pp. 198 and 200.
45. *New York Times*, June 1, 1974. See also Paragraph D of the agreement.
46. Aronson, *Conflict and Bargaining*, p. 243; Golan, *The Secret Conversations*, p. 208; Quandt, *Decade of Decisions*, p. 244; Safran, *Israel: The Embattled Ally*, p. 531; *New York Times*, May 31 and June 1, 1974. The texts of these assurances have not been published, except for the assurance to Israel about terrorist raids, which is reproduced in Sheehan, *The Arabs, Israelis, and Kissinger*, pp. 243-44.
47. Sheehan, *The Arabs, Israelis, and Kissinger*, pp. 99 ff.; Quandt, *Decade of Decisions*, pp. 229-30.
48. Prime Minister Rabin revealed his thoughts in an interview published in *Haaretz*, December 3, 1974. On Israeli hesitations about an agreement with Jordan see also Aronson, *Conflict and Bargaining*, p. 251; Golan, *The Secret Conversations*, pp. 218-19; Safran, *Israel: The Embattled Ally*, pp. 537-38.
49. Golan, *The Secret Conversations*, pp. 217-23; Quandt, *Decade of Decisions*, pp. 255-57; Sheehan, *The Arabs, Israelis, and Kissinger*, pp. 147-49.
50. Golan, *The Secret Conversations*, pp. 229-31; Quandt, *Decade of Decisions*, pp. 256, 262; Safran, *Israel: The Embattled Ally*, p. 541.
51. On the shuttle and the breakdown of the talks see Golan, *The Secret Conversations*, pp. 234-41; Quandt, *Decade of Decisions*, pp. 264-67; Safran, *Israel: The Embattled Ally*, pp. 541-47; Sheehan, *The Arabs, Israelis, and Kissinger*, pp. 155-63; Aronson, *Conflict and Bargaining*, pp. 276-92; Yitz-

hak Rabin, *Pinkas Sherut* [Service Notebook], 2 vols. (Tel Aviv: Maariv, 1979), 2: 449-59.

52. Quandt, *Decade of Decisions*, pp. 269-70; Safran, *Israel: The Embattled Ally*, pp. 549-50; Sheehan, *The Arabs, Israelis, and Kissinger*, pp. 165-68.
53. Safran, *Israel: The Embattled Ally*, pp. 548-49; Sheehan, *The Arabs, Israelis, and Kissinger*, p. 165; Quandt, *Decade of Decisions*, p. 268.
54. The senators' letter is reprinted in Sheehan, *The Arabs, Israelis, and Kissinger*, p. 175.
55. On this round of negotiations see Aronson, *Conflict and Bargaining*, pp. 293-300; Golan, *The Secret Conversations*, pp. 243-52; Quandt, *Decade of Decisions*, pp. 271-76; Safran, *Israel: The Embattled Ally*, pp. 553-60; Sheehan, *The Arabs, Israelis, and Kissinger*, pp. 176-94; Rabin, *Pinkas Sherut*, 2: 466-92. The agreement and the unclassified accompanying documents are reprinted in Moore, *The Arab-Israeli Conflict*, pp. 1209-12, 1219-23; Sheehan, *The Arabs, Israelis, and Kissinger*, pp. 245-57.
56. Information about the undertakings contained in the classified documents is derived from Yitzhak Navon, "Haashamot Hasrot Shahar" [Groundless Accusations], *Haaretz*, March 5, 1976 (a defense of the agreement by Navon, at that time chairman of the Knesset Foreign Affairs and Security Committee, against criticism by Professor Yuval Ne'eman); Safran, *Israel: The Embattled Ally*, p. 556; Sheehan, *The Arabs, Israelis, and Kissinger*, pp. 190, 194.
57. Quoted in Golan, *The Secret Conversations*, p. 232.
58. For this episode see Golan, *The Secret Conversations*, pp. 237-38; Safran, *Israel: The Embattled Ally*, p. 545; Rabin, *Pinkas Sherut*, 2: 460-61.
59. Golan, *The Secret Conversations*, pp. 241-42.
60. On some of the promises made to Egypt and to Israel in the course of negotiations see Sheehan, *The Arabs, Israelis, and Kissinger*, pp. 176-77; *New York Times*, July 4 and 7, August 29, September 7, 1975.
61. Kissinger's news conference on March 26, 1975, as reproduced in Richard P. Stebbins and Elaine P. Adam, eds., *American Foreign Relations 1975* (New York: New York University Press, 1977), pp. 79-80.
62. Henry A. Kissinger, "Domestic Structure and Foreign Pol-

icy," in *Conditions of World Order*, ed. Stanley Hoffmann (Boston: Houghton Mifflin, 1968), pp. 187-88. For Kissinger's earlier thinking on the subject, see his *A World Restored* (Boston: Houghton Mifflin, 1957), pp. 315-24.

63. Reproduced in Sheehan, *The Arabs, Israelis, and Kissinger*, pp. 52-54.
64. Sheehan, *The Arabs, Israelis, and Kissinger*, p. 58.
65. *New York Times*, September 2, 1975; Rabin, *Pinkas Sherut*, 2: 480-81, 486; Amos Perlmutter, *Politics and the Military in Israel 1967-1977* (London: Frank Cass, 1978), pp. 175-76.
66. William B. Quandt, "Kissinger and the Arab-Israeli Disengagement Negotiations," *Journal of International Affairs* 9 (1975): 41.
67. Rabin, *Pinkas Sherut*, 2: 453.
68. Sheehan, *The Arabs, Israelis, and Kissinger*, p. 168.
69. Quandt, "Kissinger and the Arab-Israeli Disengagement Negotiations," pp. 39-40.
70. Kissinger, *A World Restored*, p. 326.

CHAPTER 10, CARTER, 1977-1979: THE CAMP DAVID ACCORDS AND THE EGYPTIAN-ISRAELI PEACE TREATY

1. On the policy adopted by the Carter administration upon its accession to office see Nadav Safran, *Israel: The Embattled Ally* (Cambridge: Harvard University Press, 1978), pp. 565-69; John C. Campbell, "The Middle East: The Burdens of Empire," *Foreign Affairs* 57 (1979): 614-18. For an early expression of some of the ideas which this policy reflected, see Zbigniew Brzezinski, François Duchêne, and Kiichi Saeki, "Peace in an International Framework," *Foreign Policy* 19 (Summer 1975): 3-17. For a detailed account see Harvey Sicherman, *Broker or Advocate?: The U.S. Role in the Arab-Israeli Dispute 1973-1978* (Philadelphia: Foreign Policy Research Institute, Monograph no. 25, 1978), pp. 18-62.
2. Cf. Shlomo Avineri, "Peacemaking: The Arab-Israeli Conflict," *Foreign Affairs* 57 (Fall 1978): 51-61; Raymond Cohen, "Israel and the Soviet-American Statement of October 1, 1977: The Limits of Patron-Client Influence," *Orbis* 22 (Fall 1978): 613-33.
3. Somewhat different accounts of this meeting have been made public. See Moshe Dayan, *Halanetsah Tochal Herev* [Shall

the Sword Devour Forever] (Jerusalem: Edanim, 1981), pp. 41-49 (An English language version of this book is *Break-through: A Personal Account of the Egypt-Israel Negotiations* [New York: Knopf, 1981]); Eitan Haber, Zeev Schiff, and Ehud Yaari, *The Year of the Dove* (New York: Bantam Books, 1979), pp. 2-13; Yoel Markus, *Camp David: Hapetach Lashalom* [Camp David: The Opening to Peace] (Tel Aviv: Schocken, 1979), pp. 32-40. Tuhami's version appeared in an interview with him in *Al-Siyasa* (Kuwait), January 21-26, 1980. (A Hebrew translation is on file at the Shiloah Center, Tel Aviv University.)

4. Anwar el-Sadat, *In Search of Identity* (Glasgow: Fontana/Collins, 1978), pp. 358-64 (the phrases quoted are from pp. 359 and 360); Shimon Shamir, *Mitsrayim Behanhagat Sadat* [Egypt under Sadat] (Tel Aviv: Dvir, 1978), pp. 226-31.
5. The speech is reprinted in Sadat, *In Search of Identity*, pp. 393-409 (the phrases quoted are from pp. 399 and 400).
6. Sadat, *In Search of Identity*, pp. 403-4.
7. Markus, *Camp David*, pp. 45-46.
8. *New York Times*, November 28 and 29, December 1, 8, 11, 12, 1977.
9. Haber, Schiff, and Yaari, *Year of the Dove*, pp. 105-13, Markus, *Camp David*, pp. 44-50. For the full text of the Israeli proposal, see Israel, *Divrei Haknesset* [Parliamentary Debates], vol. 82, December 28, 1977, pp. 925-26.
10. Haber, Schiff, and Yaari, *Year of the Dove*, p. 125. For detailed accounts of the Ismailiya meeting, see ibid., pp. 114-37; Dayan, *Halanetsah Tochal Herev*, pp. 95-96; and Ezer Weizman, *The Battle for Peace* (New York: Bantam Books, 1981), pp. 121-35.
11. On the work of the Military and Political Committees see Haber, Schiff, and Yaari, *Year of the Dove*, pp. 155-67; Dayan, *Halanetsah Tochal Herev*, pp. 98-101; Weizman, *Battle for Peace*, pp. 136-96.
12. On the Cairo conference and on bilateral meetings during this period see Haber, Schiff, and Yaari, *Year of the Dove*, pp. 84-86, 92-104, 151-54.
13. *New York Times*, December 12, 13, 14, 15, 1977 and January 2, 3, 1978.

14. *New York Times*, February 4, 5, 6, 7, and July 20, 1978; *Haaretz*, February 17 and April 30, 1978.
15. For accounts of Begin's talks in Washington in March 1978, see Dayan, *Halanetsah Tochal Herev*, pp. 107-12, and Haber, Schiff, and Yaari, *Year of the Dove*, pp. 175-87; for a detailed report on the Leeds Castle conference, see Markus, *Camp David*, pp. 69-79, and Dayan, *Halanetsah Tochal Herev*, pp. 119-25.
16. For Weizman's talks with Sadat in March and in July, see Haber, Schiff, and Yaari, *Year of the Dove*, pp. 187-92, 202-6; Markus, *Camp David*, pp. 55-60, 67-68; and Weizman, *Battle for Peace*, pp. 289-302, 313-31.
17. Weizman, *Battle for Peace*, pp. 255, 115-16, 126-27, 252-53; Haber, Schiff, and Yaari, *Year of the Dove*, pp. 187, 206; Markus, *Camp David*, p. 118.
18. *New York Times*, August 9, 10, 15, 1978.
19. *Newsweek*, August 28, 1978.
20. Markus, *Camp David*, pp. 83-185; Haber, Schiff, and Yaari, *Year of the Dove*, pp. 214-78; Weizman, *Battle for Peace*, pp. 340-77; and Dayan, *Halanetsah Tochal Herev*, pp. 132-60, contain very detailed accounts of the Camp David conference.
21. See Markus, *Camp David*, pp. 185-285; Haber, Schiff, and Yaari, *Year of the Dove*, pp. 279-305; Dayan, *Halanetsah Tochal Herev*, pp. 167-228.
22. Hermann Frederick Eilts, "Improve the Framework," *Foreign Policy* 41 (Winter 1980-81): 9.
23. Dayan, *Halanetsah Tochal Herev*, pp. 168-70, 186; Markus, *Camp David*, pp. 200-201; Haber, Schiff, and Yaari, *Year of the Dove*, pp. 282-83.
24. Markus, *Camp David*, pp. 236-44.
25. Ibid., pp. 226-27. Dayan is uncharacteristically reticent about his private meeting with Khalil. See Dayan, *Halanetsah Tochal Herev*, p. 205. On his meeting with Sadat at Camp David, see pp. 159-60; Eilts, "Improve the Framework," p. 5.
26. For details on these talks see Haber, Schiff, and Yaari, *Year of the Dove*, pp. 155-64, 169-72, 285-86; Weizman, *Battle for Peace*, 156-87, 207-12, 289-303, 313-31, 359-62.
27. For a detailed summary of this agreement see Markus, *Camp David*, pp. 58-59; Weizman, *Battle for Peace*, pp. 292-302.

28. Haber, Schiff, and Yaari, *Year of the Dove*, pp. 176-78.
29. Ibid., p. 245; Markus, *Camp David*, pp. 213-15.
30. The description of the Egyptian and Israeli positions in the section that follows is derived from Haber, Schiff, and Yaari, from Markus, from Weizman, and from Dayan. The texts of the Camp David Accords, the Peace Treaty, and the accompanying documents are reproduced in the *New York Times*, March 27, 1979. For the American guarantee of Israel's oil supplies and the American-Israeli Memorandum of Understanding, see the *New York Times*, March 29, 1979.
31. Markus, *Camp David*, pp. 173-74, 250-51.
32. *New York Times*, February 28, 1979; Markus, *Camp David*, pp. 250-51.
33. *New York Times*, December 20, 1978; Haber, Schiff, and Yaari, *Year of the Dove*, pp. 293-94; Markus, *Camp David*, p. 252. Israel, *Divrei Haknesset*, Vol. 86, December 19, 1978, p. 571.
34. Markus, *Camp David*, pp. 152, 161, 167-68, 273.
35. *New York Times*, February 16, 18, and March 20, 21, 26, 1979. Detailed summaries of the 1977-79 negotiations are contained in the annual *Middle East Contemporary Survey*, ed. Colin Legum, Haim Shaked and Daniel Dishon, Vol. 2, 1977-78 (New York & London: Holmes & Meier, 1979), and Vol. 3, 1978-79 (New York & London: Holmes & Meier, 1980).

    Another account of the 1977-79 negotiations, published after the manuscript of this book was completed, is Uzi Benziman, *Rosh Memshala Bematsor* [Prime Minister Under Siege] (Jerusalem: Adam/Devir, 1981). It corroborates the main points of this chapter.

CHAPTER 11, TWO PERSPECTIVES ON MEDIATION

1. On negotiations for "side effects" see Fred Charles Iklé, *How Nations Negotiate* (New York: Praeger, 1964), p. 42.

Index

LIBRARY OF CONGRESS CATALOGING IN PUBLICATION DATA

Touval, Saadia.
The peace brokers.

Includes bibliographical references and index.
1. Jewish-Arab relations—1949- 2. Mediation, International. I. Title.
DS119.7.T667 341.5'2'0956 81-47955
ISBN 0-691-07638-3 AACR2
ISBN 0-691-10138-8 (pbk.)

Saadia Touval is Professor of Political Science at Tel Aviv University. He is the author of *Somali Nationalism* (1963) and *The Boundary Politics of Independent Africa* (1972).